THE ONE YEAR® **MEN OF THE BIBLE**

THE ONE YEAR®
Men of the Bible

365 MEDITATIONS ON THE CHARACTER OF MEN AND THEIR CONNECTION TO THE LIVING GOD

James Stuart Bell

Tyndale House Publishers, Inc., Carol Stream, Illinois

Visit Tyndale online at www.tyndale.com.

TYNDALE, Tyndale's quill logo, *The One Year,* and *One Year* are registered trademarks of Tyndale House Publishers, Inc. The One Year logo is a trademark of Tyndale House Publishers, Inc.

The One Year Men of the Bible: 365 Meditations on the Character of Men and Their Connection to the Living God

Designed by Erik M. Peterson

Edited by Linda Schlafer

Library of Congress Cataloging-in-Publication Data

Bell, James S.
  The one year men of the Bible : 365 meditations on the character of men and their connection to the living God / James Stuart Bell.
    p. cm.
    ISBN 978-1-4143-1607-9 (sc)
1. Men in the Bible—Meditations. 2. Character—Biblical teaching. 3. Devotional calendars. I. Title.
  BS574.5.B45 2008
  242'.5—dc22   2008015336

Printed in the United States of America

23   22   21
10   9   8

To my father, James S. Bell Sr.,
who has a lot in common with the
godly men of the Bible.

Acknowledgments

To Jon Farrar, managing editor of the One Year devotional series, for his vision for this project and his patience in seeing it through.

Introduction

When I look at the night sky and see the work of your fingers—
the moon and the stars you set in place—
what are mere mortals that you should think about them,
human beings that you should care for them?
PSALM 8:3-4

King David, who wrote Psalm 8, sat in wonder as he considered God's awesome, vast creation. He marveled that a God of such surpassing greatness would give even a fleeting thought to the daily life of a man such as himself.

Yet David knew God well enough to understand that he *is* concerned about every aspect of our lives, large and small. He reveled in the love, compassion, provision, and protection that God poured out on him daily.

Have you ever wondered whether God *really* thinks about you personally, and if so, what he thinks? The Bible teaches that God doesn't just think about us as humans in general, but as *individuals.* He cares *deeply* about each of us and works tirelessly—sometimes behind the scenes—to mold, love, correct, and provide for us.

As we'll see in the pages of this devotional, God cares passionately about men. The Bible is filled with stories of both God's interactions with men and their interactions with one another. Some of these stories are about positive examples of godly living, such as Abraham, Gideon, David, Simon Peter, the apostle Paul, and, of course, Jesus. Other stories aren't pleasant because they are about the consequences of men's failures and sins. All these accounts have been recorded in the Bible to inspire, teach, warn, and illustrate how to live—and how *not* to live.

Although the focus of this devotional is on the *men* of the Bible, and the devotions are written primarily from a male perspective, the principles also apply to female readers, though perhaps not in the same ways.

As you read the daily entries in this book, you'll get to know these men in new ways. You will look into their hearts and minds and understand what made them tick. You will see how they responded to God and how God related to them.

God recorded these stories in his written Word because he wants more than anything for us to get to know him at a deeper level. There is no better way to do that than to see how God has interacted with the men whose stories he included in the Bible.

As you read this book, you will find out what pleases God, what grieves and angers him, what caused him to move on behalf of the men of the Bible, and what will invite him to move on your behalf today.

As you spend your daily time with God, take a few minutes to read the stories in this book and the personal applications that follow. Think about the context of each man's life and the role he played in God's plans. Then prayerfully ask yourself, *What has this man's story taught me about my own place in God's plans?*

You may learn more than you expect about God and how he desires to relate to you.

January 1

Trusting Obedience
ABRAHAM

"Take your son, your only son—yes, Isaac, whom you love so much—and go to the land of Moriah. Go and sacrifice him as a burnt offering on one of the mountains, which I will show you." Genesis 22:2

Have you ever faced a situation in which you knew that God was calling you to do something very specific—such as change your job, move to another community, or make a daunting personal sacrifice—but instead of immediately stepping out in obedience, you waited to see what he would do next?

Abraham, the father of the Jewish race, once faced a situation in which delayed obedience must have seemed very tempting. God had given him a command that made little sense from a human perspective: "Take your son, your only son—yes, Isaac, whom you love so much—and go . . . sacrifice him as a burnt offering."

What was Abraham to do?

We don't know what Abraham thought or prayed as he and Isaac made their way to Moriah, and we can only imagine what he felt. It was bad enough to face the loss of a child, but this was the son that God had promised and given to him in such a miraculous way. God had commanded him to sacrifice the boy as if he were just a goat or a sheep. It must have seemed like a horrifying negation of everything that God had promised.

Abraham didn't know that God's shocking instruction to sacrifice Isaac was a test of his willingness to obey all the Lord's commands—even those that appeared to make little sense. Abraham's obedience opened the door to all the blessings God had promised him. In choosing obedience—even with fear and trembling—Abraham took a huge step toward the high calling of God in his life.

The path to divine blessedness in your family, your career, and your ministry is your willingness to obey God's commands whether or not they make sense to you.

What "commands" is God putting on your heart today?

How will you respond?

January 2

It's All about Jesus
JOHN THE BAPTIST

"He must become greater and greater, and I must become less and less."
JOHN 3:30

Race-car driver Dale Earnhardt Jr. caught the attention of NASCAR fans worldwide when he said, "I believe I'm the best driver out there. You have to think that way." Some thought that Earnhardt's comment was cocky and self-aggrandizing; others thought it was the attitude *any* successful driver would need.

Either way, Earnhardt's words echo a perspective shared by many professional athletes who have yet to learn the difference between healthy self-respect and harmful self-worship.

It's hard to imagine such words coming out of John the Baptist's mouth. Even when given the perfect opportunity, he shunned self-advancement. He attracted big crowds through his powerful preaching, but he remained humble. Instead of pointing to himself as *Numero Uno*, he pointed to Jesus and said, "This is the one I was talking about when I said, 'Someone is coming after me who is far greater than I am, for he existed long before me'" (John 1:15).

For John, it was all about Jesus.

John avoided the trap of self-glorification. He knew that he was just God's messenger. When a crowd eagerly sought to know if John was the Messiah, he deferred to Jesus. "Someone is coming soon who is greater than I am—so much greater that I'm not even worthy to be his slave and untie the straps of his sandals" (Luke 3:16).

John's humble stance was not a ploy to build a personal following. It was so real that John encouraged his own disciples to follow Jesus. The day after he baptized Jesus, John pointed two of his disciples to him. "Look," he exclaimed. "There is the Lamb of God!" (John 1:36).

Are you a humble person? When given the chance, do you gladly defer to Jesus and let him shine, or do you feel tempted to share the spotlight? Humility may be scarce today, but it is a jewel in the crown of righteousness.

It's all about Jesus!

January 3

Excuses, Excuses
ADAM

"Who told you that you were naked?" the LORD God asked. "Have you eaten from the tree whose fruit I commanded you not to eat?" The man replied, "It was the woman you gave me who gave me the fruit, and I ate it." Genesis 3:11-12

Following the release of photographs depicting the shocking abuse of Iraqi prisoners of war, former secretary of defense Donald Rumsfeld told the Senate Armed Services Committee, "These events occurred on my watch. As secretary of defense, I am accountable for them. I take full responsibility."

Though Rumsfeld's words did little to quiet his critics, many observers found them refreshing because they demonstrated an uncommon willingness to take responsibility for the deplorable environment he had allowed to develop.

Every failure seems to attract a corresponding excuse. The murderer says, "I'm really not a bad person," or the embezzling CEO insists, "I didn't know," but excuse making is nothing new. It goes as far back as the dawn of human history when Adam began making excuses for his willful disobedience.

When God uncovered Adam's sin, the man offered a "sort of" admission: "Well . . . it was the woman . . . the woman *you* gave me, I might add. She gave me the fruit, and . . . well . . . yeah, I guess I ate it. But I mean, look at her, Lord! I mean c'mon! I'm only human!"

Excuses! Excuses!

Adam led the blame-shifting parade that so many of us have marched in ever since, faulting God and others for our own shortcomings. What would have happened if Adam had owned up to his failure? We'll never know.

The far more relevant question is whether we will own up to ours.

When you sin or err in any way, you need to come clean with God without offering alibis or excuses as Adam did. That's the way to receive God's forgiveness and restoration.

January 4

The High Cost of Envy
CAIN

One day Cain suggested to his brother, "Let's go out into the fields." And while they were in the field, Cain attacked his brother, Abel, and killed him.
GENESIS 4:8

Fans of the NBA's Los Angeles Lakers found their 2002 celebration of yet another championship tempered when the well-publicized friction between superstars Shaquille O'Neal and Kobe Bryant sharply escalated. Despite their three league championships together, the two players simply could not get along.

Each colossal ego wanted to establish the Lakers as "his team," and both men refused to back down. When the dust finally settled, what had looked like a long-term dynasty abruptly fell apart. The team traded away O'Neal, and since then, the Lakers have not come close to recapturing their championship form.

Take a bow, envy and jealousy.

The Bible introduces us to the destructive power of envy in the person of Cain, who murdered his brother Abel. When God accepted Abel's sacrifice and rejected Cain's, the latter flew into a murderous rage.

Cain didn't kill Abel on a whim. He let feelings of envy and jealousy build up until he had devised a scheme for taking the life of his brother, who had done him no wrong. Cain and his entire family paid a heavy price for his envy.

Unfortunately, a little bit of Cain lives in every man. Think about the twinge of anger you feel when someone you believe is less qualified gets promoted ahead of you. What about the surge of jealousy that erupts when you hear a friend praise a business rival? That's envy at work, and it needs to be confronted, rejected, and crucified.

You can overcome envy, jealousy, and the anger and frustration that always follow by learning to be content with what God has given you and where he has placed you.

Combat envy by consciously choosing to rejoice with others. Envy has no room to take root in the soil of genuine joy!

January 5

Standing Out in the Crowd
NOAH

The LORD said, "I will wipe this human race I have created from the face of the earth. Yes, and I will destroy every living thing—all the people, the large animals, the small animals that scurry along the ground, and even the birds of the sky. I am sorry I ever made them." But Noah found favor with the LORD. Genesis 6:7-8

Cynthia Cooper and Sherron Watkins made the term *whistle-blower* a household word a few years ago when they exposed massive financial scandals within WorldCom and Enron. Whistle-blowers make themselves vulnerable to persecution and opposition, particularly from those who have something to hide.

They are nonetheless willing to stand out in a crowd for what they know is right.

Noah stood out that way. His contemporaries had become so corrupt that God expressed great sorrow over having ever made them. Their constant sin so offended God that he decided to destroy the world and every living thing.

Noah was the exception.

Noah's uniquely righteous life set him apart in a world made crooked by sin. No doubt Noah found it tempting to conform to the world around him—as all of us do—but somehow he remained true to God and his righteous standards.

When you build your life on God and live by his standards, you *will* stand out in a crowd. You might feel the sting of ridicule and persecution, but you will be in good company! Like Noah, you will find favor with God and enjoy his blessings.

Forces in this world will always try to conform you to their corrupt images. You will find favor with the Lord by choosing to stand out in the crowd because of your desire to identify with Christ and live by his standards.

January 6

Overcoming Fear
NEHEMIAH

During the twentieth year of King Artaxerxes' reign, I was serving the king his wine. I had never before appeared sad in his presence. So the king asked me, "Why are you looking so sad? You don't look sick to me. You must be deeply troubled." Then I was terrified, but I replied, "Long live the king! How can I not be sad? For the city where my ancestors are buried is in ruins, and the gates have been destroyed by fire." Nehemiah 2:1-3

Following a fateful bombing mission over Japan during World War II, the B-25 of U.S. Army Staff Sergeant Jacob DeShazer crash-landed in China. Enemy soldiers quickly captured and imprisoned him, then tortured him for the remainder of the war. Despite his brutal treatment, DeShazer did what most would find unthinkable. For three decades following the war, he was a Christian missionary in Japan.

Perhaps the greatest enemy of faith is the fear that takes our attention away from God and places it on whatever we perceive as a threat. Jacob DeShazer was able to minister effectively to his former captors because he had the faith to overcome his fears. His faith empowered him to look past his brutal mistreatment to what God had called him to do.

Centuries before, Nehemiah faced a similar challenge. As he served the most powerful king of his time, the Persian ruler Artaxerxes, he had to maintain a sunny disposition at all times so his personal problems would not disturb the king. Failure could result in severe consequences, so when the king asked Nehemiah, "Why are you looking so sad?" this godly man had every reason to be afraid.

Because of his love for God, Nehemiah spoke his heart and revealed his troubles. The king could have punished him, but instead he reacted with mercy and practical assistance as he sent Nehemiah to rebuild the walls of Jerusalem.

In your own life of faith, has God proven trustworthy in all things? When you keep your focus on his goodness and faithfulness, you will find the strength to overcome your fears.

January 7

Semper Fi
TYCHICUS

Tychicus will give you a full report about how I am getting along. He is a beloved brother and faithful helper who serves with me in the Lord's work.
COLOSSIANS 4:7

On the morning of November 15, 2004, a mortally wounded U.S. Marine sergeant named Rafael Peralta completed one final act of heroism as he lay dying near the entrance to a terrorist hideout in Fallujah, Iraq. As Marines from his squad stepped over his bloody body, he reached out and grabbed a live enemy grenade that had landed near him. He tucked it under his torso just moments before it exploded, thus saving the lives of several of his comrades.

Officials later praised Peralta for living up to the Marines' motto, *Semper Fidelis (often shortened to Semper Fi),* which means "always faithful." He spent his last months defending his nation's freedom and his last moments protecting his fellow Marines. Even as he drew his last breath, Rafael Peralta remained faithful.

A man in the Bible named Tychicus was cut from the same cloth. The apostle Paul commended him as a faithful and "beloved brother." Although the name *Tychicus* means "fate," the Lord, not fate, brought Tychicus into Paul's life.

The faithfulness of Tychicus won Paul's confidence so thoroughly that the apostle later considered sending him to Crete, a notoriously difficult mission field (see Titus 1:12-13; 3:12). Only a truly faithful comrade could handle such a tough ministry assignment. Paul's confidence in Tychicus as a faithful coworker never wavered, and even as the apostle neared the time of his martyrdom, he sent Tychicus to Ephesus on a special mission (see 2 Timothy 4:12).

Be honest: Does the term *faithful* describe you? Could you appear on the same list as Rafael Peralta and Tychicus, the "faithful helper"?

You don't have to be a U.S. Marine to live by the motto *Semper Fi.* You can be "always faithful" as a husband, father, friend, or disciple maker. Someone is counting on your faithfulness.

January 8

Righteous in the Midst of Corruption
LOT

God also rescued Lot out of Sodom because he was a righteous man who was sick of the shameful immorality of the wicked people around him. Yes, Lot was a righteous man who was tormented in his soul by the wickedness he saw and heard day after day. 2 Peter 2:7-8

The recent discovery in South Africa of a diamond *twice* the size of the former record holder has stunned the world's diamond community.

The gem had been there all the time, of course, hidden in the dirt, but someone had to dig for it. However harsh their surroundings, diamonds are worth the effort it takes to separate them from the mud and muck.

The Bible calls Lot a "righteous man" although he lived in the wicked city of Sodom. As the only upstanding man to make his home in the midst of such corruption, Lot remained alone in his anguish over the sin he saw day after day. He remained alone in suffering the jeers of people who despised his way of life almost as much as he was grieved by theirs.

Can you imagine how Lot felt? Maybe you can even identify with it.

Perhaps you live in a modern-day Sodom. Maybe your neighbors, friends, and even family would feel right at home in such a moral sewer. Maybe you're the only godly man living in an environment that lacks any hint of morality or righteousness. Perhaps you feel totally alone in your desire to hold on to a godly life.

Though Lot was far from perfect, his love for God made him a gem that shone from the ancient city of Sodom. Like Lot, you can hold on to righteousness, despite ridicule and opposition, and be a man willing to shine for God in the midst of corruption.

God never promised us an easy ride. It's difficult to be righteous in the midst of corruption. If God calls you to live as a diamond amid the dirt of this world, he will also encourage and equip you.

January 9

Good Conduct Yields a Clear Conscience
PAUL

We can say with confidence and a clear conscience that we have lived with a God-given holiness and sincerity in all our dealings. We have depended on God's grace, not on our own human wisdom. That is how we have conducted ourselves before the world, and especially toward you. 2 Corinthians 1:12

Have you ever cringed as you looked at a news report or article exposing some unsavory sin in the life of a well-known Christian? When the criticism and finger-pointing begin, the average believer can only respond by highlighting the obvious problem of focusing on people instead of on God.

You know what a black eye such situations can give the church and the cause of Christ, and you grieve.

The apostle Paul understood the importance of maintaining good conduct within his ministry, whether among fellow believers or before a watching world. For integrity and credibility, he refused to tolerate dishonesty or corruption within his team.

Is it any wonder that he was confident and enjoyed a clear conscience?

Paul set a great example for us in his self-examination, good conduct, confidence, and clear conscience. His life and words were consistent with his personal commitment as a faithful representative of Jesus Christ to a needy, battered world.

Many have pointed out that believers in Christ provide the only reflection of Jesus that the world will ever see. Ask yourself how you can better reflect Jesus Christ in all you say and do.

Are you *confident* in your own walk of faith? Do you have a clear conscience about your personal expression of faith? How do people generally see you, both within and outside of the church? When did you last examine yourself seriously about these things?

January 10

Look Past Your Limitations
MOSES

Moses protested to God, "Who am I to appear before Pharaoh? Who am I to lead the people of Israel out of Egypt?" God answered, "I will be with you."
EXODUS 3:11-12

Think of the last time that you felt you were in over your head. What made you feel ill-equipped, either mentally or spiritually?

Maybe you had a conflict with your wife that refused to work itself out. Perhaps you couldn't understand the behavior of a rebellious child. Do you have a problem at work that you can't get past? Did a falling-out with a friend result in serious relational damage that you don't know how to fix?

Life has a way of overwhelming us at times. The good news for every believer in Christ is that when you feel completely inadequate, God has you right where he wants you.

Moses certainly felt ill-equipped when he heard God's command to return to Egypt: "The cry of the people of Israel has reached me, and I have seen how harshly the Egyptians abuse them. Now go, for I am sending you to Pharaoh. You must lead my people Israel out of Egypt" (Exodus 3:9-10).

Surely Moses felt that twinge we all feel when an overwhelming problem or challenge confronts us. He responded, "Who am I to appear before Pharaoh? Who am I to lead the people of Israel out of Egypt?" (Exodus 3:11).

God never directly answered Moses' question. Instead, God emphasized his own impressive credentials (see Exodus 3:12).

Moses focused on himself when he needed to focus on God. The Lord responded by patiently shifting his chosen deliverer's attention to the God of unlimited power who had expressed his unchanging commitment to accomplish *everything* he had promised.

When you feel you are in over your head, what would happen if you took the focus off of yourself and consciously placed it on God? Certainly you have shortcomings and weaknesses—we all do. God didn't remove Moses' weaknesses when he called him into leadership, but he did promise Moses his presence, and he makes this same promise to you.

Do you think that God will do any less for you than he did for Moses? What does the promise of his presence mean to you? How can you turn your focus from your own shortcomings to the One through whom you can accomplish any task and solve any problem?

January 11

Applied Understanding
THE MEN OF ISSACHAR

All these men understood the signs of the times and knew the best course for Israel to take. 1 Chronicles 12:32

Every four years, candidates of all political persuasions say and do everything they can to convince us that *they* best understand our post-9/11 world and know how to keep our nation safe.

Whom do you picture as a person who understands our times? You probably think of a leader with a firm grasp of our culture, someone who knows what kind of leadership we need in order to deal with the forces currently affecting us.

The Bible tells us that the men of Issachar (one of the original twelve tribes of Israel) not only understood the times in which they lived, but also knew what should be done. That is a rare and valuable gift.

The men of Issachar fought for King David and helped him form effective strategies for defending Israel from all threats. They were the brains of David's military and used their God-given wisdom to decipher what was best for the kingdom.

The men of Issachar had the all-important trait of applied understanding that we all need. They understood what was going on, and more importantly, they had the wisdom to form practical strategies that would meet the needs of the kingdom.

Like Israel during David's reign, we live in perilous times. We need men who understand the times and who know what to do. If you believe in Christ, then *you* can be one of those men. If the Spirit of Christ dwells within you (as he lives in the heart of every genuine believer), you have all the resources you need to be a man of applied understanding. The world has never needed you more.

You don't have to be a political or military leader to be a man of applied understanding. God calls you to understand your own times, and he will give you the wisdom and insight to know what to do, what to say, and what to pray. As a man of God, a husband, a father, a boss, or an employee, you have the opportunity to make a real difference.

January 12

People Are Watching and Listening
THE PHILIPPIAN JAILER

The jailer woke up to see the prison doors wide open. He assumed the prisoners had escaped, so he drew his sword to kill himself. But Paul shouted to him, "Stop! Don't kill yourself! We are all here!"   Acts 16:27-28

Experts on motivational speaking know the importance of making a strong first impression. That is done, they say, by demonstrating the personal benefits of applying your message.

Everyone wants to see a cause-and-effect relationship between what you say and how you live. That is especially true in the spiritual context.

A jailer in the Macedonian city of Philippi got a close look at how real faith in Jesus affected two men. The encounter changed his life for eternity. As this jailer slept on the job, an earthquake shook open all the prison doors and rattled loose the stocks and chains holding all the prisoners, including the apostle Paul and his companion Silas. They were both in jail for preaching about Jesus.

Believing that his prisoners had escaped, the jailer knew he was in *big* trouble! Rather than die painfully at the hands of the Romans, he decided to take his own life. Just then, he heard two of the prisoners imploring him not to harm himself. These were the same voices that he had heard singing praises to their God, although he and his fellow guards had stripped them naked, beaten them nearly senseless, and thrown them in jail the evening before.

The Philippian jailer knew immediately that Paul and Silas had something that he wanted for himself. "Sirs," he said, his voice probably trembling with relief and anticipation, "what must I do to be saved?" (Acts 16:30).

The jailer recognized Paul and Silas—and Jesus, about whom they preached—as the real deal. Before that evening ended, he felt the same joy and peace that Paul and Silas so openly demonstrated in their damp and cold Philippian jail cell.

Is your life a beacon of God's joy and peace? You will present no better witness to Jesus' power to change a man than by living a fully submitted life of obedience and trust in God. People are watching and listening to see if what you say you believe translates into real-life differences.

January 13

Our Weapon of Choice
JESUS CHRIST

The devil came and said to him, "If you are the Son of God, tell these stones to become loaves of bread." But Jesus told him, "No! The Scriptures say, 'People do not live by bread alone, but by every word that comes from the mouth of God.'"
MATTHEW 4:3-4

Military strategists know that knowledge is one of the most devastating weapons a field commander can have. A strong knowledge of the enemy's weapons, strategies, tendencies, strengths, and weaknesses can mean the difference between success and failure on the battlefield.

The devil knows a lot about effective spiritual battle—especially about our weaknesses and faults—and he loves to use his diabolical knowledge to harass us, lie to us, and tempt us. Since he's been doing this for thousands of years, he has developed his skills into a real art form—twisted, evil, and devastatingly effective.

How can we fight the tactics of such a formidable enemy? Jesus Christ, the man who faced the worst temptation the devil had to offer and came out completely unscathed, gives us the perfect example.

Matthew 4:1-11 tells how Jesus left the scene of his baptism and headed straight into the wilderness, where he spent forty days fasting and praying. There he faced some very real temptations from his very real enemy.

Right off the bat, the devil pounced on Jesus' most immediate weakness: hunger. You'd be hungry, too, after fasting for forty days! Satan wanted to derail the divine plan that Jesus had freely chosen to follow, so he offered up this little suggestion: "*If* you're really the Son of God, turn these rocks into bread."

Jesus recognized the devil's tactics. Though Satan had unleashed his weapon of choice, Jesus had one that was far more effective and more devastating: the Word of God. The battle ended before it began because the devil has no counterattack strong enough to overcome the man who uses God's Word as his weapon of choice.

The devil can tempt you, lie to you, and try to deceive you, but when you use the Word of God as your weapon of choice, he can never defeat you.

January 14

Are You Resolute?
DANIEL

When Daniel learned that the law had been signed, he went home and knelt down as usual in his upstairs room, with its windows open toward Jerusalem. He prayed three times a day, just as he had always done, giving thanks to his God.
DANIEL 6:10

During some of the most difficult days of World War II, British prime minister Winston Churchill made one of the toughest decisions of the war. When British intelligence learned that the Germans planned to bomb the city of Coventry, Churchill found himself with a simple yet terrible choice: evacuate the city and save hundreds of lives (but risk tipping off the Germans that the British had broken their communication code), or do nothing and allow hundreds of people to die (but keep the secret safe). Churchill, resolute as always, chose the welfare of his entire nation and allowed the enemy to bomb Coventry.

In a similar way, God calls you to be a resolute man who refuses to compromise the well-being of your family or the dignity of your work or ministry even when you face hard choices.

The Old Testament prophet Daniel knew the importance of remaining resolute in difficult times. His enemies had duped King Darius into creating a law that outlawed all forms of worship except worship of the king. The penalty for breaking the law was death at the jaws of hungry lions. Daniel, too, faced a terrible but simple choice: either worship Darius and live, or continue faithfully praying to God and risk becoming an evening snack for the lions.

Daniel loved God, so he refused to bow in worship before a man. In fact, when Daniel first heard of the new law, he headed directly to his room and bowed before God in fervent prayer. His enemies observed his defiance and had him thrown into the lions' den. God honored Daniel's resolute faithfulness and delivered him from death. Daniel didn't receive so much as a scratch.

What temptations are whispered in your ears that would compromise your faithfulness to God? Name them. Create and execute a plan for remaining resolute in your commitment to God, no matter what.

January 15

Standing against the Consensus
JOSHUA AND CALEB

"Do not rebel against the LORD, and don't be afraid of the people of the land. They are only helpless prey to us! They have no protection, but the LORD is with us! Don't be afraid of them!"   Numbers 14:9

Frank Tracz had been the Kansas State University band leader for fourteen years when someone asked him, "Do you realize that the K-State students at home football games are shouting a vulgarity instead of 'Hey!' when the band plays the popular 'Rock and Roll Part 2'?"

When Tracz heard the report, he was disappointed, and he went into action. Hoping to promote a more positive environment at K-State sporting events, he eliminated the song from his band's playlist. This disappointed many Wildcat fans who hadn't shouted the profanity when the band played the song.

At times, standing for what is good and right means taking an unpopular position. Consider the example of Joshua and Caleb, two of the twelve tribal leaders that Moses sent to Canaan to spy out the Promised Land. This mission took place as the people of Israel readied themselves to claim what God had already said was theirs.

Upon their return, all twelve spies agreed that Canaan was beautiful and that anyone would be delighted to make their home there. Ten of the spies also reported a land crawling with giants who would kill them if they tried to possess what God had given them.

Joshua and Caleb remained ready to go. Filled with faith and courage, they told the frightened people, "We can beat the giants! The Lord has brought us this far, and he's not going to abandon us now. *Let's go!*" Sadly, the people of Israel sided with the other ten spies and thus rebelled against God. They didn't know it, but they had chosen disaster.

Joshua and Caleb stood out as men willing to oppose the consensus. They vocally chose to put their faith in God rather than bow to the opinions of the majority and to "reason." Since they took that stand, they were the only ones of that generation who received what God had promised.

A life of faith isn't always easy or popular. When you keep your eyes on the One who has the desire and ability to keep all his promises, you will emerge victorious over any giants that get in your way.

January 16

Hurry Up and Wait on God
MICAH

As for me, I look to the LORD for help. I wait confidently for God to save me, and my God will certainly hear me.   Micah 7:7

If you've traveled via commercial airlines since 9/11, you have no doubt learned the meaning of the expression "Hurry up and wait." You arrive at the airport two hours prior to takeoff, wait in long lines to check in, wait in longer lines at the security checkpoint, and then wait again at the gate to board your plane.

Most men don't like to wait. We want things to happen *right now,* but patient waiting *always* pays off in the crucial area of waiting on God.

An Old Testament prophet named Micah knew well the importance of waiting confidently on God. He understood that regardless of how bad his current circumstances might be, the Lord would certainly act on his behalf in his own good time.

Waiting on God was like money in the bank for Micah. He didn't just *hope* that God would act; rather, he *expected* God to move on behalf of every man who remained faithful in prayer and carefully followed through on what God had called him to do.

G. Campbell Morgan, a British preacher of the previous generation, rightly said, "Waiting for God is not laziness. Waiting for God is not going to sleep. Waiting for God is not the abandonment of effort. Waiting for God means, first, activity under command; second, readiness for any new command that may come; third, the ability to do nothing until the command is given."

What commands has God given *you*? Are you waiting for him to do his part without running ahead of him or taking a nap? Receiving God's best in every area of your life often means waiting for him to do what he has promised.

Are you in a hurry to wait on God, who always keeps his promises? How will you respond if he keeps you in suspense for a while and acts along timelines you don't particularly like?

January 17

God's Plan for Good
JOSEPH

Judah said to his brothers, "What will we gain by killing our brother? We'd have to cover up the crime. Instead of hurting him, let's sell him to those Ishmaelite traders. After all, he is our brother—our own flesh and blood!" And his brothers agreed.
GENESIS 37:26-27

In the classic Western film *Silverado,* a drifter named Paden counts his blessings after his soon-to-be-friend Emmett rescues him from certain death in the desert. Paden says of the men who robbed him, stripped him, and left him alone to die of dehydration, "At least they didn't kill me. That was right considerate, I thought."

There's something courageous about a character who sees simple survival as a blessing, especially in the face of undeserved abuse. Many believers see exactly that trait of courage in a young Hebrew named Joseph, who endured more than his share of unfair mistreatment.

Joseph didn't suffer at the hands of brutal strangers but as the victim of his ten jealous brothers. Their father, Jacob, had never tried to hide his favoritism toward Joseph, and as a result, the brothers nurtured a smoldering hatred for their younger sibling. When they caught him walking alone in the desert one day, they sold him to a traveling band of Ishmaelite traders and told his father that a wild animal had killed him.

The stories of Paden and Joseph are parallel in a second way. In *Silverado,* Paden's survival plays a major part in the outcome of the story. In a fiery conclusion, Paden liberates a fearful small town from the control of the unambiguously wicked Sheriff Cobb. Similarly, Joseph didn't just survive his brothers' terrible mistreatment; he determined to live for God regardless of his circumstances. That courageous choice made the difference between the survival and the death of his whole family.

The choice to live in a way that pleases and glorifies God doesn't guarantee you problem-free days on earth. It does assure you that whatever happens, God will use your circumstances for your good and the good of God's people.

January 18

The Problem with "Upside"
KING SAUL

As Saul turned and started to leave, God gave him a new heart, and all Samuel's signs were fulfilled that day. 1 Samuel 10:9

If you've ever watched coverage of the NBA draft, you have no doubt heard commentators say that some hot prospect has a "tremendous upside." The commentator means that, although the player may be unpolished and need some seasoning, he has the potential to develop into a fine addition to the team.

Of course, many young players with upside don't reach their potential, and when that happens, a team has wasted its draft pick.

Saul, the man God chose as the first king of Israel, had a lot of "upside," but he is a prime example of tremendous wasted potential.

God had equipped Saul with everything he needed to succeed and had empowered this big, strong man to lead his people. Sadly, however, Saul wasted his talents, his gifts, and his God-given opportunity to achieve greatness.

Since Saul loved his power and position more than he loved God, he was often disobedient and offered lame excuses for his sin. As a result, he lost his power and position well before his time, leaving a sad legacy of failure as a king, father, and man of God.

What might Saul have accomplished if he had loved God wholeheartedly and kept his commandments? Though no one can say for sure, a look at the life of his successor, David, gives us some good clues. Saul is a clear example of what *not* to do with the many gifts God has given each of us.

God has given us many talents and gifts so that we can be everything he wants us to be. That's a lot of upside potential! The question you must answer for yourself is, What will I do with all that God has given me? How can you ensure that your "upside" is developed into realized potential?

January 19

The Most Important Question
SIMON PETER

[Jesus] asked them, "But who do you say I am?" Simon Peter answered, "You are the Messiah, the Son of the living God." Jesus replied, "You are blessed, Simon son of John, because my Father in heaven has revealed this to you. You did not learn this from any human being."   Matthew 16:15-17

The late Robert W. Funk, an American New Testament scholar, founded the infamous Jesus Seminar in 1985. Its sole purpose was to skeptically evaluate Jesus' purported words and deeds as they are recorded in the four Gospels. In other words, the Jesus Seminar tackled the question of Jesus' true identity.

The apostle Peter didn't need to hear the opinions of others—skeptical *or* believing—to know who Jesus was because God had already shown him.

The disciples had heard rumors and conjectures about their Master, and they weren't afraid to tell him that some thought he was John the Baptist resurrected, while others thought he was Elijah or another prophet returned to earth. But one day, Jesus asked them the question that would shape their lives for all eternity: "Who do *you* say I am?"

There was probably a moment of uncomfortable silence as the disciples wracked their brains to figure out how to answer Jesus. It's also not surprising that Peter, the one most willing to say what the others only thought, finally spoke up. Out of his mouth came the most blessed declaration of all time: "You are the Messiah, the Son of the living God."

All twelve apostles were part of a culture and a people who had waited centuries for their promised Deliverer. Peter, a simple fisherman with no formal training or education, knew that Jesus was that man . . . and much, much more.

Peter correctly answered the most important question ever asked.

Who do *you* say Jesus is?

How you answer the question of who Jesus is will shape your entire being. It's not just the question of the historic Jesus who lived two thousand years ago and gave his followers some great teachings. It's the question of whether you know that Jesus is your Messiah and the Son of the living God.

January 20

Keep It Real
NATHANAEL

As they approached, Jesus said, "Now here is a genuine son of Israel—a man of complete integrity." "How do you know about me?" Nathanael asked. Jesus replied, "I could see you under the fig tree before Philip found you." JOHN 1:47-48

Years before he became the twenty-sixth president of the United States, Theodore Roosevelt worked as a rancher in North Dakota. One day, he and one of his hired hands lassoed a steer that lacked a brand. As the cowpoke prepared to brand the animal, Roosevelt stopped him.

"Wait, it should be Lang's brand," he said, referring to his neighbor. Gregor Lang owned the property they were using that day.

"That's all right, boss," the cowboy replied before applying Roosevelt's brand.

"Drop that iron, get back to the ranch, and get out," Roosevelt demanded. "I don't need you anymore. A man who will steal *for* me will steal *from* me."

The Bible praises men of honesty who tell it like it is. Nathanael, one of Jesus' disciples, was that kind of man. He didn't worry about conventions or propriety of speech. When his friend Philip told him he had met the Messiah, a prophet from Nazareth, Nathanael replied, "Nazareth! Can anything good come from Nazareth?" (John 1:46).

Way to go, Nate! Philip must have thought. *I offer to introduce you to our Messiah, and you insult his hometown!*

Nathanael's words dripped with skepticism, and even sarcasm, but they demonstrated a character trait that appealed to Jesus, who seemed to genuinely like Nathanael as soon as he saw him.

What Jesus liked so much about Nathanael was his honesty and integrity!

Nathanael may have been a little rough around the edges when he first met Jesus, but with the polish and refinement Jesus gave him over the next three years, he became a man who made a difference for God's Kingdom.

God blesses you when you speak to him and to others with honesty and integrity—and when you are *real* with him about who you are, what you think, what you struggle with, and what you need.

January 21

Use the Secular for God's Glory
BEZALEL AND OHOLIAB

"The LORD has gifted Bezalel, Oholiab, and the other skilled craftsmen with wisdom and ability to perform any task involved in building the sanctuary. Let them construct and furnish the Tabernacle, just as the LORD has commanded."
EXODUS 36:1

Do you have a difficult time believing that God can make powerful use of a regular working man, such as a truck driver, concrete worker, accountant, or banker? Do you believe that only preachers, teachers, musicians, and missionaries are out there leading people to Jesus and encouraging God's people?

If so, it may be time to adjust your thinking.

Too often, we make unnecessary distinctions between the sacred and the secular. God wants us to understand that he has given us *all* our gifts and talents, even those that don't seem spiritual in nature. God wants you to use whatever gifts you have for his glory.

When the time came for Israel to build a Tabernacle in the wilderness, God had a specific job in mind for two skilled artisans named Bezalel and Oholiab. He called them to use their gifts and skills to build a portable temple, a tentlike structure designed for use in serving and communicating with God.

When Bezalel and Oholiab left Egypt with their Hebrew countrymen as part of the Exodus, did they have any idea that God would use their abilities in that way? How could they? At that point, they had no idea what a tabernacle was, let alone how their skills might contribute to building one. But God had given this pair their skills, and when he asked them to put their abilities into his service, they willingly made them available.

God loves to use unexpected resources for purposes we could never have imagined. Our role in that equation is to do as Bezalel and Oholiab did: make whatever skills, talents, or abilities you have available for the Lord's use.

If you believe that God only uses the pros to do ministry, then it's time to expand your thinking. Put your skills, gifts, and talents in God's hands, realizing that he gave them to you in the first place. Then watch him do amazing things with what you thought of as ordinary, for his glory and the benefit of his people.

January 22

Plan Well
KING SOLOMON

"Now the LORD my God has given me peace on every side; I have no enemies, and all is well. So I am planning to build a Temple to honor the name of the LORD my God, just as he had instructed my father, David. For the LORD told him, 'Your son, whom I will place on your throne, will build the Temple to honor my name.'"
1 KINGS 5:4-5

When George Bernard Shaw visited sculptor Jacob Epstein, he noticed a huge stone block in one corner of the studio. Shaw pointed to the stone and asked Epstein what would become of it.

"I don't know yet," Epstein replied. "I'm still making plans."

"You mean you *plan* your work?" Shaw asked in astonishment. "Why, I change my mind several times a day!"

"That's all very well with a four-ounce manuscript," the sculptor shot back, "but not with a four-ton block."

Many things in life require good planning, a truth the wise King Solomon took into consideration as he prepared to build the Temple in Jerusalem.

Solomon had a consuming passion to bring his father's dream of a permanent house of worship for the Lord to completion, but he tempered his passion with careful planning. He realized that rushing headlong into the construction of such a magnificent, complex structure would mean disaster, so he planned and prepared for the work.

He sought out construction know-how from his neighbors, did some wheeling and dealing with King Hiram of Tyre to acquire the necessary building materials, and enlisted a labor force from around the region. Then he prepared the Temple site.

Only when he had finished all preparations and planning for the construction did Solomon officially begin to build. Seven and a half years from ground-breaking day, this Temple of breathtaking beauty stood on the summit of Mount Moriah.

All of Solomon's wise and careful planning paid off magnificently.

The Bible teaches that we are to submit our plans to the will of God (see Proverbs 16:1; James 4:13-16). If you want to accomplish anything significant in any sphere of life, you must do some careful, prayerful planning.

January 23

Instant Gratification
ESAU

"Look, I'm dying of starvation!" said Esau. "What good is my birthright to me now?" But Jacob said, "First you must swear that your birthright is mine." So Esau swore an oath, thereby selling all his rights as the firstborn to his brother, Jacob.
GENESIS 25:32-33

Experts in human psychology have defined *deferred gratification* or *delayed gratification* as "the ability to wait patiently for something one wants or needs." They recognize that success in most areas of life requires such an ability.

Amazing, isn't it, how modern-day experts so often stumble upon biblical truth?

Whether it's the desire for sex, money, position, or power, the ever-present lure of instant gratification draws men away from their deeper goals and robs them of God's best plans for them. Meanwhile, the Bible repeatedly and consistently urges men to wait patiently, work hard, and trust God for the good things he wants to give them.

If only Esau—Mr. Instant Gratification—had heeded God's instruction!

Esau, Isaac's elder son, was unable to wait patiently for one of the basic necessities of life. Instead, he opted for instant gratification, and it cost him dearly. This man came into the world with the proverbial silver spoon in his mouth. As the firstborn of Isaac and Rebekah's twin sons, he stood to receive all the privileges and inheritances due to the firstborn male.

In a moment of physical weakness caused by hunger, he sold his birthright privileges for a bowl of stew.

Esau's younger brother, Jacob, took his place of greatness in the annals of Israel and in the family tree of Jesus Christ. Esau became the founding father of the Edomites—persistent, bitter enemies of Israel that eventually fell under God's curse (see Malachi 1:3).

How does the lure of instant gratification challenge you? Had you been in Esau's place, how would you have dealt with Jacob's proposition? What things in your present world offer instant gratification that can rob you of better things that God has in store for you? List them. Name them out loud and decide how you are going to deal with them when they come knocking at your door.

January 24

A Spark Becomes a Fire
AENEAS

Peter said to him, "Aeneas, Jesus Christ heals you! Get up, and roll up your sleeping mat!" And he was healed instantly. Acts 9:34

It only takes a spark to get a fire going, and soon everyone around can warm up near its flames.

The old folk chorus "Pass It On" might seem like just a nice campfire song for summer camp, but a brief focus on the lyrics may help us to understand the nature of God's love.

Even the smallest demonstration of that love, the song tells us, can start something that spreads far beyond what we expect or pray for. A bedridden paralytic named Aeneas made that discovery in his hometown of ancient Lydda.

Aeneas had no reason to believe that his miserable lot in life would ever change. After eight years, he had probably resigned himself to life as a beggar. One day, however, he had an encounter with Jesus through Peter's ministry, as the apostle traveled from town to town preaching and healing people in Christ's name.

Peter spent only a few moments with Aeneas, but those precious seconds totally changed the man's life. "Jesus Christ heals you!" Peter said, "Get up! Roll up your sleeping mat!"

After nothing but a verbal command in Jesus' name, Aeneas suddenly felt his body grow strong and whole. As Peter had commanded him, he got up, rolled up his mat, and began walking.

Any encounter with Jesus Christ that so radically changes a man will get people's attention. When the people of Lydda saw Aeneas walking, they knew whom to thank, and *all* of them turned to the Lord (see Acts 9:35).

The spark had become a fire!

People around you need to see God's power working in your life. You could be the spark that ignites a great spiritual fire! Humbly ask God to do something great in your life. Then look for ways to focus attention on the Lord's goodness. He is willing to forgive and restore anyone who comes to him in faith.

January 25

It's Where You're Headed, Not Where You've Been
LEVI

Levi held a banquet in his home with Jesus as the guest of honor. Many of Levi's fellow tax collectors and other guests also ate with them. But the Pharisees and their teachers of religious law complained bitterly to Jesus' disciples, "Why do you eat and drink with such scum?" Luke 5:29-30

How would you respond if you saw someone with an unsavory past put in a position of high leadership? What if a man who had served time for a felony was promoted over you at work or a man with a record of drug and alcohol abuse became a youth leader at church? We normally think that only men of proven character and a clean past should get those higher positions, because we believe that such men are trustworthy.

Jesus didn't always operate by those rules. He often faced questions about his judgment in his choice of friends. After Jesus called Levi (later known as Matthew) to follow him, some Pharisees wondered aloud why he would spend time with such scum as Levi and his villainous friends. Maybe Levi wondered the same thing.

Jews of Levi's day saw tax collectors as the dregs of the earth. The tax men worked for the hated Roman government, and they were notorious for their corrupt business practices.

Jesus' response tells us all we need to know about why he chose to fellowship with a sinner such as Levi: "Healthy people don't need a doctor—sick people do. I have come to call not those who think they are righteous, but those who know they are sinners and need to repent" (Luke 5:31-32).

Levi fit *that* bill perfectly. He wouldn't even call himself a righteous man, never mind what his neighbors thought. He knew that he was a sinner who desperately needed the compassion and forgiveness of Jesus Christ. Once he opened his heart to receive Jesus, his past ceased to matter. Jesus set him on a new course of service to God and his countrymen.

As you consider this story, do you most naturally put yourself in Levi's place or in the place of his accusers? Your answer probably depends on your background. Jesus wants you to know that background means little to him. In his eyes, we are all corrupt, and he loves us anyway.

What counts is where you're headed, not where you've been. Regardless of your past, God wants to use you as a conduit of his love to your family, your coworkers, your church, or anywhere else he might direct you.

January 26

The Real Deal
DEMETRIUS

Everyone speaks highly of Demetrius, as does the truth itself. We ourselves can say the same for him, and you know we speak the truth.   3 John 1:12

The men who have played for Hall of Fame college basketball coach John Wooden remember him as a great coach and as a teacher of important life lessons. Wooden, who led the UCLA Bruins to ten NCAA championships in twelve years, including seven in a row from 1967 to 1973, repeatedly taught the importance of character. "Be more concerned with your character than your reputation," he said. "Your character is what you really are, while your reputation is merely what others *think* you are."

Can people say of you that your reputation, your conversation, and your behavior all demonstrate good character? Demetrius, a little-known believer briefly mentioned in John's third epistle, apparently had a good reputation based on consistently good conduct. John tells us nothing about Demetrius except that people rightly spoke well of him. The apostle contrasts Demetrius with a would-be leader named Diotrephes, whom he describes as a divisive man who made evil and false accusations against John.

God loves to call men like Demetrius into leadership because there is nothing phony about them, and people see them as the real deal. Though men like Diotrephes often attract a short-term following, sooner or later the truth comes out, and men like Demetrius lead a group to a happier and healthier place.

Are you the *real deal*? Does the character that your wife, children, and close friends see line up with the reputation you enjoy at work or in public? When you nourish your true character, your reputation will take care of itself.

January 27

Unanswerable Questions
HABAKKUK

O LORD, our Rock, you have sent these Babylonians to correct us, to punish us for our many sins. But you are pure and cannot stand the sight of evil. Will you wink at their treachery? Should you be silent while the wicked swallow up people more righteous than they?   Habakkuk 1:12-13

Men throughout history have struggled with seemingly unanswerable questions. Believers and nonbelievers alike have asked,

> If God is so holy, why does he allow evil to continue?
> If God is so loving, why does he allow horrible suffering to persist?
> Why does God allow unrighteous people to harass and persecute
>   the righteous?

Tell the truth. Haven't you, at some difficult point in your life, wanted to protest that God is just not fair? If God *really* loved us, we reason, our marriages would run smoothly, our children would behave perfectly, and our jobs would be enjoyable every day.

An Old Testament prophet named Habakkuk struggled with some tricky theological questions of his own, including this one: Why would a righteous God use such desperately unrighteous people as the Babylonians to bring correction and punishment to those he loves?

Habakkuk readily acknowledged God's right to discipline his wandering people, but he recoiled at the idea that a wicked nation would be the instrument of divine correction. How could a holy God *do* such a thing?

Habakkuk's questions mostly remained unanswered, but God sustained the troubled prophet's faith by reminding him that he remained in control, that he knew what he was doing, and that Habakkuk could trust him. In the end, Habakkuk could only trust God and sing praises to his wonderful, mysterious name.

In your life, you will often face questions that seem to have no answers. Though God may give you some direct insight, more often he seems to leave your questions unanswered for the moment. He wants you to learn to say from the heart, "I trust you, God, for you are my Lord!"

What questions about God most trouble you? In a world wracked by pain and injustice, do you, like Habakkuk, recognize that God's eternal love remains in place?

January 28

Humble Courage
PAUL

"I have done the Lord's work humbly and with many tears. I have endured the trials that came to me from the plots of the Jews. I never shrank back from telling you what you needed to hear, either publicly or in your homes." Acts 20:19-20

What image comes to mind when you think of courage? A Rambo-esque soldier who seems impervious to pain or injury? A strong leader such as the great British statesman Winston Churchill? Someone who successfully fights a life-threatening disease and goes on to live a long, healthy life?

When most men think of courage, they don't also think of humility. A hero, they believe, steps up to the plate during a difficult time with an independent, "I *can!*" attitude. He is strong, self-reliant, and ready to take the weight of the world on his shoulders.

The Bible's portrait of a courageous hero looks markedly different. He is confident, all right, but also humble. A biblical hero knows that his courage flows from the One he serves and not from his personal reserves of strength.

The apostle Paul had both qualities. He never seemed to concern himself with the personal consequences of his often unpopular preaching. He *knew* that lifting up the name of Jesus Christ meant trouble and persecution, but he preached anyway.

Paul didn't seem too concerned with whether individuals would like his message. He knew that they needed to hear it, so he preached it. His courage flowed from his conviction that God wanted him to share the truth of forgiveness and restoration from God through Jesus Christ.

You have probably never met anyone as courageous as Paul, but he would be the first to tell you that his courage was dependent on his humble reliance on God's strength and protection, not on his own abilities.

Wimps do not trust, rely on, or obey God. That requires courage and humility that wimps lack. When you are humble and rely on God in everything you do, you will model courage and humility—and no one will mistake you for a *wimp*.

January 29

A Heart for Intimacy
KING DAVID

O LORD, you have examined my heart and know everything about me. You know when I sit down or stand up. You know my thoughts even when I'm far away. You see me when I travel and when I rest at home. You know everything I do.
PSALM 139:1-3

In the dark days of World War I, a British soldier caught creeping back to his quarters from the nearby woods was taken before his commanding officer and accused of passing information to the enemy.

"What were you doing out in the woods alone?" his commander barked.

"I went to find a quiet place to pray," he answered.

"Have you been in the habit of spending hours in private prayer?" his CO demanded.

"Yes, sir!" the accused replied.

"Then down on your knees and pray now!" the officer growled. "You've never needed it so much."

Believing he didn't have long to live, the soldier knelt and poured out a heartfelt prayer based on his long-standing, intimate relationship with God.

"You may go," his commander said. "I believe your story. If you hadn't been often at drill, you couldn't have done so well at review."

King David enjoyed an intimate relationship with God. In Psalm 139, he expressed his understanding of God's omniscience (he knows all), omnipotence (he has power over everything), and omnipresence (he is everywhere).

How did David know these things?

He knew God intimately through spending much time with him!

David had read about God in his written Word, had learned his own need for God's forgiveness and mercy, and had often enjoyed God's protection and blessing.

In his intimacy with God, David invited God to know him in the same way: "Search me, O God, and know my heart; test me and know my anxious thoughts. Point out anything in me that offends you, and lead me along the path of everlasting life" (Psalm 139:23-24).

Nothing shapes your life like an intimate, growing relationship with God. When you cultivate that kind of relationship with your heavenly Father, you can fully enjoy his goodness and love.

January 30

Finding Hope
JOB

"As for me, I know that my Redeemer lives, and he will stand upon the earth at last. And after my body has decayed, yet in my body I will see God! I will see him for myself. Yes, I will see him with my own eyes. I am overwhelmed at the thought!"
JOB 19:25-27

Nelson Mandela, who fought bravely to end South Africa's system of racial segregation known as apartheid, spent much of his life in a seemingly hopeless situation. In an effort to stop his "subversive" activities, the South African government sentenced Mandela to life in prison, where he remained for twenty-six years.

Even as he sat day after endless day in his cell, Mandela never gave up hope. When he finally won his release in 1990, he continued to work against apartheid, and four years later, he became South Africa's first black president.

Nothing more than hope keeps a man going during difficult times. That is especially true when the circumstances *seem* hopeless.

Job clung to that kind of hope.

Job was a good man who suffered terribly and apparently without cause. The Bible says that he lived and walked in complete integrity. For much of his recorded story, Job lamented his misery, fell into discouragement, and asked God, "Why?" Job became so deeply depressed that at one time he wanted to stop breathing just so he could find some peace.

How did Job get through it?

Even in the midst of his suffering and despair, Job found comfort and encouragement in God's promise that he would one day meet his Maker and Redeemer. "I am overwhelmed at the thought!" Job said of the day when his faith would become sight.

That kind of hope can sustain a person even in the dark.

From what do you draw hope during difficult times? Remember that your worst days won't last forever and better days are coming. Remember also that you will one day see your Redeemer, Jesus Christ, face to face. That promise can get you through anything!

January 31

Seeking Divine Approval
EZEKIEL

"Son of man, do not fear them or their words. Don't be afraid even though their threats surround you like nettles and briers and stinging scorpions. Do not be dismayed by their dark scowls, even though they are rebels. You must give them my messages whether they listen or not."   Ezekiel 2:6-7

Imagine a help-wanted ad with the following job description: Wanted—Young man to deliver speeches to stubborn, hostile, and sometimes violent crowds. Must be willing to travel and endure vicious insults and threats to personal safety.

Would you expect an ad like that to flood the personnel manager's desk with résumés? Probably not, but that is the very job God called the Old Testament prophet Ezekiel to do.

God directed Ezekiel to preach an unpopular message to a rebellious audience during a very dark time in Israel's history. He would take heat from all directions. Even worse, God told Ezekiel that he wouldn't see any positive results: "They won't listen, for they are completely rebellious!" (Ezekiel 2:7).

So what was the point in preaching? Ezekiel must have wondered why he should put his health and his life in danger if no one was going to listen. Why not just stay home, keep his mouth shut, and let God do what he was going to do, anyway?

A man concerned with his own reputation and popularity might have opted out, hoping that God would send someone else or just deal with it himself. Ezekiel went where God told him to go and preached the message God told him to preach. He would leave the results—and the personal consequences—up to God.

Do you worry more about the approval of God or of man? Does your obedience depend upon a divine guarantee that you'll see tangible results? Do you see Ezekiel as a hero to be emulated or as a fool to be pitied?

God never promises us popularity or this world's approval as we faithfully follow Jesus Christ. What he does promise is his approval and a great reward if we faithfully serve him regardless of others' responses.

February 1

Ask Directions
MANOAH

Manoah prayed to the LORD, saying, "Lord, please let the man of God come back to us again and give us more instructions about this son who is to be born."
JUDGES 13:8

Okay, maybe—just *maybe*—it's a stereotype, but conventional wisdom says that we men strongly resist asking for directions.

We'll drive around forever looking for an address when we could have arrived in a few minutes simply by asking for directions. We stumble around and sometimes fall, trying to please our wives when we only needed to ask them what they really wanted. We make false assumptions about our children's needs when a little listening to them would erase all doubt.

Manoah, the father of the Israelite judge Samson, gives us a good example of a man who was humble and smart enough to ask for directions and some divine confirmation.

An angel had appeared to Manoah's childless wife, informing her that she would give birth to a very special son who should be dedicated to the service of the Lord and his country. The angel also laid out the ground rules for raising the boy.

No doubt Manoah felt apprehensive about the birth of his son. Even after hearing his wife repeat the angel's instructions, he wanted to know more. Instead of just wondering and worrying, he did what any man in need of directions should do: He asked God for help.

God answered Manoah's prayer of faith. The angel soon returned to give him the directions and the confirmation he needed to take on the task of fathering such a special little boy.

Does anything in your walk with Christ—or in your marriage, family, or work life—make you wonder which way to turn? Do you require a little confirmation for some plan you have in mind? If so, take the time to earnestly seek the Lord and ask for what you need. He will never disappoint anyone who sincerely asks in faith.

February 2

Stability
REUBEN

"Reuben, you are my firstborn, my strength, the child of my vigorous youth. You are first in rank and first in power. But you are as unruly as a flood, and you will be first no longer."   Genesis 49:3-4

A few years back, television-news viewers saw for themselves the destructive power of floodwater as Hurricane Katrina devastated the Gulf Region. The city of New Orleans, in particular, lay under several feet of water for many days.

Hurricanes show us how water, which does so much good for humankind, can become a source of wild destruction and even death when it is out of control.

Reuben, the firstborn son of Jacob and Leah, did some very good things in life; he also made some horrible mistakes. As his father said, he was "as unruly as a flood."

Reuben spoke up on behalf of his brother Joseph and probably saved the boy's life when his other brothers leaned toward murdering him (see Genesis 37:21-22). He later pledged his own sons' lives when Jacob at first refused to allow Reuben's brother Benjamin to travel to Egypt (see Genesis 42:37).

Reuben committed a terrible sin against Jacob when he slept with one of his father's concubines, an act that Jacob never forgot. As the firstborn son, Reuben *should* have received special privileges and promises, but Jacob pronounced, "You will be first no longer" (Genesis 49:4).

Reuben tragically illustrates a fate of unfulfilled potential and missed opportunity. The tribe that bore his name was of relatively little importance in God's plan of redemption.

No one can say what would have happened to Reuben's family had he conducted himself as a man of stability and not become "unruly as a flood." We can take his story as both an encouragement and a warning about the importance of the stability that we and our families need.

Would you call yourself a stable man? Or are you "unruly as a flood"?

As a man of God, a husband, and a father, people look to you for stability. Work diligently at those things that will bring you to spiritual maturity.

February 3

Suffering Has Benefits
PAUL

I am glad to boast about my weaknesses, so that the power of Christ can work through me. That's why I take pleasure in my weaknesses, and in the insults, hardships, persecutions, and troubles that I suffer for Christ. For when I am weak, then I am strong. 2 Corinthians 12:9-10

Vance Havner, a twentieth-century preacher and writer, once reported that, of the 318 delegates who attended the Nicene Council (an important church meeting of the fourth century), fewer than twelve had no visible evidence of persecution or torture. One had a missing eye, another a crippled hand, and yet another a noticeable limp. All had suffered for their faith.

While believers in the Western world currently enjoy relative safety from most severe forms of persecution, followers of Christ during the first three or four centuries after Christ's death and resurrection commonly faced the loss of property, livelihood, health, and even their lives.

The apostle Paul had firsthand knowledge of these things.

Paul did much of his writing from a prison cell and endured many arrests, beatings, imprisonments, threats against his life, and other hardships, solely on account of his loyalty to Christ. He never complained, and he claimed to actually take pleasure in those things.

Pleasure in suffering?

If you knew someone who claimed to enjoy suffering, you would probably advise—maybe even *beg*—that person to get help. But Paul gave a specific reason for his pleasure in suffering for the name of Christ: "When I am weak, then I am strong" (2 Corinthians 12:10).

Paul didn't enjoy suffering for suffering's sake. He knew that his suffering wouldn't last forever and that God had prepared something far better for him. He also understood that in the context of eternity, his suffering would last but a moment, while the glory to come would last forever.

God can use the difficult things in your life to build endurance and maturity into your faith. He can also use those things to remind you of your own weakness and bring you to a point of complete dependence on him.

February 4

It's No Contest
DAVID

David replied to the Philistine, "You come to me with sword, spear, and javelin, but I come to you in the name of the LORD of Heaven's Armies—the God of the armies of Israel, whom you have defied." 1 Samuel 17:45

An old saying in the world of competitive sports goes like this: "The only thing better than a good little man is a good big man." Indeed, all else being equal, the bigger, stronger man almost always wins out.

Fortunately, a young shepherd by the name of David didn't concern himself with such sayings.

The Bible paints a terrifying picture of the giant Goliath. This remorseless killing machine was huge, strong, and highly skilled as a warrior. He also had quite a mean streak. No one in Saul's army had the nerve to confront him.

When no one else would accept Goliath's challenge, David stepped into the fray, almost certainly as a last resort. We can imagine Saul thinking, *At least the kid's pretty good with a slingshot. And didn't he say he once killed both a lion and a bear?* Still, to most observers, this spirited shepherd boy was a decided underdog.

David didn't see himself that way at all. He spoke words of confidence as he confronted the vile Philistine warrior. David knew that *God* had sent him on this mission, and God never sends a man to fight without equipping and guiding him to accomplish his purposes.

Goliath had size, armor, weapons, and a hard heart on his side. David had nothing but a slingshot, a handful of stones, and his absolute faith in a God who delights in enabling his people to do the impossible.

It was a hopeless situation—for the giant. The moment David accepted God's call to the fight, Goliath was as good as dead. Why? David explained it simply and accurately by saying, "This is the LORD's battle!" (1 Samuel 17:47). For a man of faith, that kind of battle is always "no contest."

What "giants" in your life—at home, at work, or in other areas—make you feel like the underdog? If you have chosen to follow Christ, you serve the very same God who made a small shepherd boy's confrontation with a cruel, bloodthirsty giant not just a win, but an absolute rout.

February 5

It Isn't Over until God Says It's Over
PETER

Suddenly, there was a bright light in the cell, and an angel of the Lord stood before Peter. The angel struck him on the side to awaken him and said, "Quick! Get up!" And the chains fell off his wrists.   Acts 12:7

Some observers called it a historic collapse. Others saw it as a historic comeback. With just seventeen games left in the 2007 Major League Baseball season, the Philadelphia Phillies trailed the New York Mets by seven games in the National League East Division standings.

Yet the Phillies eventually won the division.

No team had overcome such a large lead so late in the season, but the Phillies overtook their rivals on the last day of the regular season and headed into the play-offs. As the great Yogi Berra of the New York Yankees once said, "It ain't over till it's over!"

The apostle Peter could say a hearty amen to that statement. The time came when, humanly speaking, it seemed that his life had come to an abrupt end. Herod wanted Peter dead and had already murdered other believers. As Peter sat in a jail cell awaiting a rigged trial that would be followed by a quick execution, he must have wondered how many hours he had left.

God had another plan.

On the night before Peter's trial, an angel appeared in his prison cell, awakened him, released him from his chains, and led him past sixteen armed but unseeing guards to freedom.

At first, even Peter couldn't fully grasp what had happened. As he came out of his stupor, he realized that his "dream" was real: God had set him free!

Peter's experience shows that none of the enemy's chains are strong enough to hold down a man whom God has called to complete a specific purpose and mission. It's true: The man of God is immortal until God chooses to take him home.

Are you facing what seems like an impossible situation, whether at home, at work, in your marriage, or somewhere else? If so, remember that it's not over until God says it's over. He will never abandon you, but he will enable you to complete whatever he has planned for you.

February 6

Rising to the Bottom
SHEBNA

"Who do you think you are, and what are you doing here, building a beautiful tomb for yourself—a monument high up in the rock?" Isaiah 22:16

In a culture where ambition is praised as a man's highest virtue, far too many Christian men adopt a "whatever it takes" attitude toward rising up the ranks.

Whether it's the CEO who cooks the books (just a little!) to make himself and his company look better to investors, the low-level business executive who bad-mouths his peers to make himself look better to his superiors, or the church member who creates problems in the congregation to further his own agenda, people take advantage of opportunities for self-promotion that abound in this world.

God takes a dim view of such strategies.

A man named Shebna held a good deal of power in the administration of King Hezekiah, but pride and vanity ruled his heart. He used his high position to promote himself by beginning to construct an extravagant tomb for his eventual burial.

In so doing, Shebna wrote his own ticket out of town.

Although he sought personal glory, Shebna discovered the quickest way to the bottom. The Lord put a stop to his plans, removed him from office, and exiled him far from Judah (see Isaiah 22:17-18). God had given Shebna everything he needed to become a great servant, but the foolish man squandered those good gifts by trying to rise to the top in his own selfish way.

No doubt you have some goals that you want to reach and the talents and gifts you need to make them happen. God wants to be at the center of *all* your plans. Your part in the equation is to use all he has given you for his glory and the good of others.

Regardless of your specific circumstances, God has put you in a place of leadership and authority so that you can selflessly and humbly serve others. Remember—as Shebna did not—that God bestows his gifts so that you may exalt him, not yourself.

February 7

Revenge Is Costly
JOAB

When Abner arrived back at Hebron, Joab took him aside at the gateway as if to speak with him privately. But then he stabbed Abner in the stomach and killed him in revenge for killing his brother Asahel.   2 Samuel 3:27

"Revenge is a dish best served cold," said Khan, an old enemy of the fictional Admiral James T. Kirk. Khan wanted to avenge a perceived wrong done to him in the 1982 movie *Star Trek: The Wrath of Khan*.

Revenge can cost both parties dearly. As an example, look at the life of Joab, the nephew and army commander of King David. Joab had served the king faithfully and had enjoyed success in his military career, rising to the office of top general. He failed because he used his high position to settle old scores—namely, the death of his brother Asahel at the hand of Abner, the uncle of Saul, the former king of Israel (see 2 Samuel 2:18-32).

At an opportune time, Joab lured Abner—once an enemy of David but now ready to make peace—to the gate of Hebron and murdered him, thus avenging his brother's death while eliminating a potential rival.

Joab had his revenge, but it came at a steep price. When word reached David about what had happened, the king praised Abner but cursed Joab and his family (see 2 Samuel 3:28-29).

Although Joab continued to serve David, when he indulged in vengeance instead of using his position appropriately, he lost an important part of himself. He also planted the seeds of his own eventual destruction (see 1 Kings 2:5-6, 28-35).

Every act of vengeance you ponder and every plan you make for getting even costs you part of who God made you to be. When someone does you wrong, even intentionally, make it your business to forgive that person and to move on so that you can continue to pursue the good things that God has placed before you.

February 8

Follow Instructions
NOAH

Noah did everything exactly as God had commanded him.   GENESIS 6:22

A businessman purchased a credenza with "some assembly required" and transported it to his office. He knew his way around a tool set, so he cracked open the box with its dozens of wooden and metal parts and immediately recognized a problem. Here were the parts—but where were the instructions?

After scattering parts all over his office, the man finally found the assembly instructions at the bottom of the now-empty box. There, in giant letters across the top of the instruction sheet, he read the following warning:

> PARTS ARE ARRANGED IN BOX IN ORDER OF ASSEMBLY.
> DO NOT REMOVE FROM BOX UNTIL THEY ARE NEEDED.

A job that should have taken him forty-five minutes cost him four long, frustrating hours.

Good things come to men who fully and completely follow instructions! A man named Noah found out that this is especially true when constructing a huge boat that was to be home for him—along with his family and who knows how many animals—for several months.

Noah left nothing to chance as he prepared himself and his family for the coming Flood. He had heard God's instructions, and he followed them to the letter, leaving nothing undone.

Though God called Noah a righteous man because of his obedience, Noah obeyed because he was a righteous man. Obedience is a two-way street that both flows from and produces righteousness.

Noah received good things from God because he faithfully followed the Lord's clear instructions. The same can be true for you. When you follow God's instructions in every area of life, you position yourself to receive good things from him.

Think of an area of life in which you believe that God has given you some pretty clear instructions, whether at work, at church, in your family, or in your neighborhood. Can he say of you, as he did of Noah, that you "did everything exactly as God had commanded"? If not, what remains undone that you can begin doing today?

February 9

What's on Your List?
JESHUA AND ZERUBBABEL

Jeshua son of Jehozadak joined his fellow priests and Zerubbabel son of Shealtiel with his family in rebuilding the altar of the God of Israel.... Even though the people were afraid of the local residents, they rebuilt the altar at its old site.
EZRA 3:2-3

Have you ever considered how much of life is a series of lists? You have lists of things to do at home before you go to work and lists of things to do at work before you can go home. Come the weekend, there are more lists.

Sometimes, it's good to stop and ask yourself what tops your list of things to do. If time with God fails to appear, then it is time for an adjustment.

You know the things that hinder you from spending time with God: chores to do, kids to spend time with, ball games to attend, calls to be returned. Then, of course, there's your wife, who needs at least some of your undivided attention.

Jeshua and Zerubbabel were called to lead a remnant of Jews back to Jerusalem following the Babylonian captivity. They created a buzz when they insisted on making provisions for worship *before* preparing to rebuild the city's walls. It's not hard to imagine the worry setting in as the people gazed upon the devastated city—or the questions that followed.

"Can't the altar wait? We'll have plenty of time to build an altar and worship after we get the wall built."

"Don't these guys understand the danger we face? Our enemies want to kill us!"

The people had legitimate concerns that Jeshua and Zerubbabel shared, but these two godly leaders knew what they were doing. They understood that unless they placed the worship of God at the top of their "to do" list, nothing else would matter. Without God's protection, their enemies would destroy them, wall or no wall. They remembered that the people who built the original walls had forgotten to put God at the top of their list—and that's how their walls had come tumbling down.

Does anything on your own "to do" list come before spending time with God? How do you deal with voices that cry, "That can wait—we have more pressing issues to take care of"? When you make time with God your top priority, you invite him to bless all the other things on your list.

February 10

Defending the Faith at Home
JUDE

Dear friends, I had been eagerly planning to write to you about the salvation we all share. But now I find that I must write about something else, urging you to defend the faith that God has entrusted once for all time to his holy people.
JUDE 1:3

At some point, most fathers have had to stand up, "lay down the law," and say no to dangerous things that could harm the spiritual lives of their loved ones. If you've ever had to stand up in this way, then you have followed the example (and the command!) of the New Testament author of the epistle of Jude, who challenged believers to "defend the faith that God has entrusted once for all time to his holy people."

In Jude's day, challenges to the Christian faith came from all directions. While outsiders opposed and persecuted the church, false teachers infiltrated its ranks, spreading poisonous ideas about the relationship between sin and God's grace.

Jude was no wimp. He recognized these things, understood the danger they posed to the church, and stood ready to confront them head-on. He challenged his fellow believers to do the same.

What voices in your own day attempt to drown out sound biblical teaching concerning godliness and morality? You needn't look any further than your local television listings. Like Jude, you have the opportunity—and the responsibility—to stand against those things, beginning at home. Though no confrontation feels pleasant, even on behalf of your faith, it sometimes becomes as much a necessity in today's world as it did in Jude's.

How can you best prepare for the challenge?

God calls you to stand firm and defend your faith against its many modern-day enemies. Do you recognize those enemies? Do you know their tactics? Do you know how to oppose and defeat them? What stand do you believe God is calling you to take in your own home right now?

February 11

Lead by Example
JONAH

The king and his nobles sent this decree throughout the city: "No one, not even the animals from your herds and flocks, may eat or drink anything at all. People and animals alike must wear garments of mourning, and everyone must pray earnestly to God. They must turn from their evil ways and stop all their violence."
JONAH 3:7-8

Can you name one of the biggest enemies of godly leadership, whether at home, on the job, or in ministry? It's this warped attitude: "Do as I say, not as I do!"

On the other hand, a willingness to lead *by example* has always been one of a leader's greatest tools. For example, if you want your children to speak kindly to one another, then speak kindly to them, to your wife, and to others. If you want your coworkers or employees to become more conscientious about their work, then show up on time every day and work to the best of your ability until you go home.

The unnamed king of Nineveh is a model of leading by example.

Like the rest of his people, the king had heard prophecies of doom from the Hebrew prophet Jonah, who didn't call the Ninevites to repentance but warned them of God's coming judgment and wrath.

What does a smart man do when he knows that God stands ready to annihilate his kingdom? The king could have laughed off the warning, given up, resigned himself to his fate, or left the city to its ruin, but this king chose none of the above. He instructed his people to observe a time of fasting, prayer, and repentance, in hoping that God would change his mind and spare the city (see Jonah 3:6-9).

The king did more than *talk* a good game of repentance and prayer. He set an example for all the people by stripping off his royal robes, dressing in burlap, and sitting on a heap of ashes, which were Old Testament signs of humble, deep repentance. The king's humility made a difference! Before long, the whole city followed his example, and God spared the repentant citizens of Nineveh.

God wants you to lead through your example even more than through your words. When you do as you say in every area of life, you make it far easier for everyone around you, including your family, to follow your lead.

February 12

Love Means Giving
JACOB

Jacob worked seven years to pay for Rachel. But his love for her was so strong that it seemed to him but a few days. Genesis 29:20

Remember when you felt that flush of first love? There seemed nothing you wouldn't do and no expense you wouldn't incur just to draw near to the object of your affections. Your heart fluttered and your stomach turned to butterflies just at the thought of her!

True love has the power to transform burdens into almost nothing. No amount of time seems too long, no amount of effort too strenuous, and no expense too costly if these things make the one we love happy, healthy, and comfortable.

For a picture of self-sacrificing love, consider the story of Jacob and Rachel.

Jacob fell so deeply in love with Rachel that he would do anything to have her hand in marriage. This love story took place in a culture where a prospective bridegroom had to bring a costly gift or endowment to the male head of his beloved's family. The problem was that Jacob had nothing to give Laban except time, and his future father-in-law exacted seven years' worth.

You might think that those were the slowest seven years of Jacob's life. Day after day he worked for Laban, longing for a glimpse of Rachel's beauty. Yet the Bible says that for Jacob those years seemed like just a few days.

That is what real love does. When a man genuinely loves his wife, his children, and his God, even things that otherwise might seem burdensome become occasions of true joy because they accrue to the benefit of the ones he loves.

How would you describe your love for God? The Lord gives you the privilege of loving him in a joyful way, not as a burden. How can you best share that joy with those he has placed in your life? How can you give to them and love them today without regard for the cost to yourself?

February 13

Tap into Your Power Source
JESUS

Before daybreak the next morning, Jesus got up and went out to an isolated place to pray. Mark 1:35

Suspense movies have the dramatic formula all figured out: The story's villain chases the hero or heroine, who breathlessly jumps into a car and turns the key . . . only to discover a dead battery or a gas gauge on empty.

The car that won't start, at the worst possible time, is one of many worn-out movie clichés, but it illustrates our common need for power and energy.

This also applies to the spiritual realm.

The Son of God came to earth as a man, so Jesus understood better than anyone else the importance of tapping into the heavenly Power Source by spending unhurried time with his Father. Despite full days of teaching, preaching, doing miracles, and meeting people's needs, Jesus didn't allow anything to get in the way of his prayer times.

Though busy men often complain of burnout, Jesus never did. He kept up an amazingly packed schedule without losing his focus or his energy. How did he manage it? The Gospels reveal that he was energized and empowered through regular times spent with his Father.

If Jesus, the Son of God and the only perfect man who ever lived, made a priority of spending time alone with his Father, how much more should we spend time daily with the One who empowers us to do everything on our plates?

Busy schedules and multiple commitments can make us suppose that we don't have time for spiritual activities such as prayer. Jesus' example teaches us otherwise. It proclaims that time alone with our heavenly Father gives us the energy and power we need to accomplish whatever lands on our "to do" lists.

Jesus considered regular prayer vital to his personal well-being and effectiveness in ministry. How much time are you spending with your heavenly Power Source?

February 14

Praise Your Wife
SOLOMON

You are beautiful, my darling, like the lovely city of Tirzah. Yes, as beautiful as Jerusalem, as majestic as an army with billowing banners.
SONG OF SOLOMON 6:4

Many longtime wives complain that their husbands take them for granted. They worry that the excitement has vanished from their marriage and that the passion, spontaneity, and fun have faded away. The mundane and day-to-day routines have taken over.

Solomon understood the value of speaking passionately to his beloved Shulamite woman. He knew that in expressing his deepest feelings for her, he could bless her and stir up passion between them.

The Song of Solomon overflows with words of love, affection, intimacy, and passion. Precious terms of endearment flew back and forth between Solomon and his beloved. The words that Solomon and his lover spoke to one another model the kind of intimate communication you can enjoy with your wife.

Of course, it's probably a good idea to speak your *own* words as you express how much your wife means to you, but take careful note of the poetic, sensual, concrete way in which Solomon spoke words of love to his mate. Such words are personal and thoughtful.

Take the lead, husband! Ponder what you find most valuable, beautiful, admirable, and sexy about your wife, and then make a point of telling her how much you like what you see.

As the old song goes, "Accentuate the positive . . . eliminate the negative." You won't regret it!

How do you rate the passion and fun in your marriage? Would you say that it's red hot, still glowing, a fading ember, growing cold, or a pile of ashes? To help bring back the flame, regularly speak words of appreciation and love to the wife God has given you. Take time to compliment her, and affirm her inward and outward beauty. Make doubly sure that you speak those words out of genuine desire to affirm her and build her up.

February 15

Our Source of Joy
HABAKKUK

Even though the fig trees have no blossoms, and there are no grapes on the vines; even though the olive crop fails, and the fields lie empty and barren; even though the flocks die in the fields, and the cattle barns are empty, yet I will rejoice in the LORD! I will be joyful in the God of my salvation!   HABAKKUK 3:17-18

In his classic 1952 book *The Power of Positive Thinking,* author Norman Vincent Peale insists that maintaining a positive attitude is the key to a happy, successful life. Many Christian leaders denounced aspects of Peale's still-popular book, but its premise has undeniable, biblical truth. What we think about and focus on really does affect our attitude, especially when things go wrong.

The Old Testament prophet Habakkuk lamented the deteriorating spiritual condition of his people and the consequences of that malaise—namely, the coming destruction of Jerusalem and the Babylonian captivity that would follow. Habakkuk grieved over this situation, but he didn't sink into despair or allow his circumstances to rob him of his joy in serving and loving God. To him, joy in God was a choice, Babylonians or no Babylonians.

"Yet I will rejoice in the LORD!" he cried. "I will be joyful in the God of my salvation!"

To maintain his joy, Habakkuk counted on a couple of basic truths:

> His difficult times wouldn't last forever, and
> his source of joy lay in the God who loved him, not in his outward
>   circumstances.

Habakkuk focused on the positive, not on the deplorable situation around him. His loving God was the one constant in his life.

Face it—life isn't always easy. When God allows times of difficulty into your life, you can always rest in and rely on his constant love and provision. How can you best focus on God's gifts rather than the challenges that threaten to overwhelm you?

February 16

The Right Man for a Tough Job
TITUS

Even one of their own men, a prophet from Crete, has said about them, "The people of Crete are all liars, cruel animals, and lazy gluttons." This is true. So reprimand them sternly to make them strong in the faith. Titus 1:12-13

Ken Carter, a high school basketball coach, made national news in 1999 when he locked out the players from his undefeated and highly ranked Richmond High School varsity basketball team. He canceled all practices and games until his players improved their grades.

What prompted this unusual action? It turned out that a third of Coach Carter's players had failed to keep up their grades as they had agreed to do early in the basketball season. Although Coach Carter received some criticism, he has also been praised as the right man to handle a difficult, and all too common, situation.

God often calls men of character and commitment to handle his more difficult ministerial assignments. Only such men come prepared to handle them.

Among this group was a young man named Titus, a protégé of the apostle Paul. Paul sent Titus to minister for a time in Crete, a place notorious for its lack of discipline, untruthfulness, excessive gluttony, and cruelty.

This was no assignment for the faint of heart!

Only a man of strong character who could solve problems, confront, and love God and his Word would be qualified for such a charge. Titus walked into this difficult assignment and got the job done!

What kind of "Cretans" lie in your path? How do you respond to others' habitual lies, laziness, and cruelty? How can you be God's man in a tough situation, whether at home or at work?

If God calls you to handle a difficult situation, he will equip and empower you to get the job done. Like Titus, you can be eager to depend on God in such situations.

February 17

Behind-the-Scenes Service
EPAPHRODITUS

I thought I should send Epaphroditus back to you. He is a true brother, coworker, and fellow soldier. And he was your messenger to help me in my need. I am sending him because he has been longing to see you, and he was very distressed that you heard he was ill.   Philippians 2:25-26

Ask the typical football fan to tell you who played the key roles in last Sunday's game, and he will probably talk about the stars of the contest—the quarterback who threw for three hundred yards, the tailback who scored two touchdowns, the wide receiver who caught eight passes, or the linebacker who made thirteen tackles. For the most part, even the most rabid football fans don't pay enough attention to know the names of the players who do the little things that make their team successful.

The same thing is true of believers who do the little things necessary to make the church function effectively.

Consider the example of Epaphroditus, a New Testament–era follower of Jesus. If you were to ask most believers of his day to identify him, you might get that faint look of partial recognition you wear when you can sort of recall a name but can't for the life of you place the person.

Although Epaphroditus remains in relative obscurity due to his brief mention in Scripture, Paul considered him an important part of his ministry. Epaphroditus was Paul's "brother, coworker, and fellow soldier," as well as his trusted messenger when the apostle languished in prison.

Many believers, like Epaphroditus, played key roles in beginning the early church. We may not know their names or their stories, but we know that these supporting players now walk the streets of heaven with Jesus Christ, enjoying the rewards of their faithful service.

Not everyone is called to be a star in the Lord's service, but that doesn't mean that what you do for his Kingdom doesn't catch God's eye. It does! Your work is also important to those you have the privilege of serving.

February 18

A Difference Maker
KING HEZEKIAH

Hezekiah was twenty-five years old when he became the king of Judah, and he reigned in Jerusalem twenty-nine years....He did what was pleasing in the LORD's sight, just as his ancestor David had done. 2 Chronicles 29:1-2

In a television commercial for the Lincoln Navigator, NBA superstar Dwyane Wade says, "My dream is to leave the world a better place than I found it."

How refreshing and encouraging it is when a man of Wade's professional stature understands that life is about more than gaining fame, money, and superstardom! You can't help applauding celebrities who want to make a real difference in the lives of real people living in the real world.

A strong sense of conviction motivates many men to dream of making a difference in their world. That is the character quality most prominently displayed in the life of Hezekiah, the thirteenth king of Judah.

Hezekiah stood out as a real difference maker at a time of rampant idolatry. This godly king was a reformer who guided his nation in eliminating idol worship and repairing the Temple in Jerusalem. He also reinstated the Passover feast.

As a result of Hezekiah's work, a spiritual revival flourished in Judah for a time. Hezekiah reigned for twenty-nine years, during which he cemented his status as one of the few righteous kings to rule either Judah or Israel.

When Hezekiah assumed the throne, he clearly stated his intention to make a difference in his world. With God's help, he made those differences. He loved God deeply and remained committed to turning his people back to the Lord.

Have you ever considered that God has put certain people in your life so you can make a specific difference in their lives? He calls you to be the presence of Jesus to all of them. Whether you are a clerk at the corner 7-Eleven or a professional sports superstar, dream of making an impact on your world for God's glory.

February 19

A Spirit of Encouragement
BARNABAS

When the church at Jerusalem heard what had happened, they sent Barnabas to Antioch. When he arrived and saw this evidence of God's blessing, he was filled with joy, and he encouraged the believers to stay true to the Lord.   Acts 11:22-23

You've heard it said that you can't judge a book by its cover, but people who work in bookselling know that a great title or jacket design can spell the difference between a best seller and a pallet of books headed for the bargain bin.

The nickname *Barnabas* means "Son of Encouragement" in New Testament Greek, and it accurately expresses the kind of man he was.

Barnabas specialized in encouragement.

On one of his first missions, Barnabas persuaded the understandably cynical believers in Jerusalem to accept the violent Pharisee named Saul as one of their own. He convinced them that this man had genuinely converted to faith in Christ and that God had begun to prepare him for divine service (see Acts 9:26-28). Saul eventually became the apostle Paul.

Later, Barnabas encouraged the believers in Antioch to remain true to the Lord (see Acts 11:22-23). He encouraged Paul as they traveled together on their long missionary journeys (see Acts 13–14). He invested in a young believer named John Mark, who struggled at the beginning of his life of ministry (see Acts 15:36-39).

Obviously, the name *Barnabas* tells a story all its own!

Barnabas was drawn to those who needed a positive word. What made him such a great source of encouragement? Scripture answers that Barnabas was "a good man, full of the Holy Spirit and strong in faith" (Acts 11:24).

Could your friends and loved ones use the nickname "Barnabas" to describe *you*? Do they see you as a good man, full of the Holy Spirit and strong in faith? If they don't, you can choose now to follow Barnabas's splendid example.

The men and women around you need you to be a twenty-first-century Barnabas. No one ever gets too much encouragement! Walk daily in the power of the Holy Spirit so that God can do Barnabas-size miracles through you.

February 20

Just Enough
AGUR

First, help me never to tell a lie. Second, give me neither poverty nor riches! Give me just enough to satisfy my needs. For if I grow rich, I may deny you and say, "Who is the LORD?" And if I am too poor, I may steal and thus insult God's holy name. Proverbs 30:8-9

A man became envious of some friends because they had nicer homes in better neighborhoods. Always interested in keeping up with the Joneses, he listed his house with a real estate firm and began looking for a bigger, better home.

Shortly after putting his house on the market, the man saw an ad in the newspaper's classified section for a home that seemed just right. He called the realtor, asked a few questions, and began making arrangements to meet the agent and see the house. When the agent told him the address, the man suddenly canceled the appointment and hung up the phone in embarrassment.

He had just inquired about his own home.

Feelings of discontentment will cause a man to do strange things. An Old Testament character called Agur (perhaps a nickname for Solomon) demonstrated that he understood "The Law of Just Enough."

Having too much can cause problems, Agur wrote, because the rich tend to be self-sufficient, self-indulgent, and self-satisfied, and such people easily forget their need for God. Agur also saw dangerous pitfalls in poverty. If things got desperate enough, he might do foolish things that would dishonor himself and God. Agur advised his readers to have just enough to feel satisfied but not so much that they neglected their Provider.

The Bible encourages hard work and lists several rich men in its "Hall of Faith" in Hebrews 11. As you work to pursue a good life for yourself and your family, nurture an attitude of gratitude. Failure to be content with whatever God gives you can lead to a boatload of trouble (see 1 Timothy 6:6-10).

February 21

Moving Past the Past
JOHN MARK

Barnabas agreed and wanted to take along John Mark. But Paul disagreed strongly, since John Mark had deserted them in Pamphylia and had not continued with them in their work.   ACTS 15:37-38

The great inventor Thomas Edison performed some ten thousand experiments before he succeeded in developing a workable electric lightbulb. When a reporter asked Edison if he ever felt discouraged about working so many hours and trying so many things without results, he replied, "Results? Why, man, I have gotten a lot of results. I know several thousand things that won't work."

Everyone fails at one time or another, but if you regard failure as an opportunity for growth, you might be encouraged to keep going and keep trying—and just possibly succeed.

Without question, the Christian life thrives on this principle, and a young man named John Mark (probably the Mark who wrote the second Gospel) illustrates how it works.

John Mark had accompanied Paul and Barnabas on their first missionary journey through Asia Minor, only to leave the team and return home, possibly because he was frightened, discouraged, or homesick (see Acts 13:13). Three years later as Paul and Barnabas were preparing for another missionary journey, Barnabas wanted to give John Mark another chance, believing that the young man had the right stuff to make an effective missionary. Paul disagreed and the two parted ways, with Barnabas taking John Mark and Paul taking Silas as companions in ministry (see Acts 15:36-40).

Barnabas remembered that John Mark had left the team, but he also saw something worth developing in him and became his mentor. John Mark matured, and eventually even Paul recognized him as an effective minister of the gospel (see 2 Timothy 4:11).

Do you believe that past failures disqualify you from effective service in God's Kingdom? Some of the greatest ministers of all time failed early on but later grew to be solid men of God.

February 22

A Dependent Attitude
MOSES

"Listen, you rebels!" he shouted. "Must we bring you water from this rock?" Then Moses raised his hand and struck the rock twice with the staff, and water gushed out. So the entire community and their livestock drank their fill.
NUMBERS 20:10-11

A rookie construction worker couldn't get one of his power tools to work properly. Finally, after struggling with it all morning and falling way behind in his work, he called his foreman.

"I did the best I could," he told his supervisor.

"No, you didn't," the foreman replied. "To do your best, you should have called me sooner."

An independent spirit often comes in handy, but sometimes it keeps us from our best, especially in the spiritual realm.

Moses had faithfully and sacrificially served God ever since the Lord called his name from a burning bush in Midian. This hero of the faith obeyed God's instructions and accurately relayed God's messages to Pharaoh and to the people of Israel. Moses became a humble, obedient servant, yet in a moment of anger and self-reliance, he lost everything that he had worked so hard to gain.

Wandering in the desert made the Israelites thirsty and cranky. When they complained about their lack of water, God gave Moses a strange-sounding command: "As the people watch, speak to the rock over there, and it will pour out its water" (Numbers 20:8). Simple enough—but instead of following God's instructions, Moses angrily rebuked his countrymen and struck the rock twice.

God supplied water as he had promised, but Moses' rash act landed him in *big* trouble. His prideful self-reliance cost him the opportunity to lead his people into the Promised Land.

Self-reliance or God-reliance? That's the choice each of us must make every day of our lives. What would it mean for you to rely on God at work, at home, at church, and even at the gym? What does prideful self-reliance look like in each of those areas?

Growing children need to stretch their wings and assert their independence, but as you grow spiritually, you must remain dependent on God in all things. Certainly he calls you to step out in faith, exert great effort, and take risks for his name. Even then, he calls you to move forward with him, not on your own.

February 23

Mixed Reviews
KING JEHU

Jehu did not obey the Law of the LORD, the God of Israel, with all his heart. He refused to turn from the sins that Jeroboam had led Israel to commit.
2 KINGS 10:31

A father walked into his two sons' bedroom one morning and observed dirty clothes and toys strewn from wall to wall.

"When I get home from work," the father sternly told his sons, "I want to be able to see the floor!" Believing that he had communicated his desire to see the boys' room cleaned up, he went to work. When he got home, he found that his sons had picked up everything from the floor, only to transfer the dirty clothes and toys to their beds and shelves.

Fathers want wholehearted obedience from their children. They want their kids to observe the spirit of what they say, not just the letter. The same is true of our heavenly Father.

Jehu, a king of the northern kingdom of Israel, did some great things for the Lord, but he didn't follow and obey God with his whole heart. That left him with a tarnished legacy. If Jehu's life were a play, his performance would have garnered mixed reviews.

Jehu succeeded brilliantly as he followed God's specific instructions to rid Israel of the house of Ahab and end the worship of Baal. His thorough work earned Jehu commendations from God and won his descendants positions of royalty for generations to come.

Jehu's tolerance of other forms of idolatry, especially the worship of golden calves at Dan and Bethel, cut short his reign and brought about his personal destruction. Jehu learned that halfhearted obedience amounts to disobedience. As the apostle Paul would later write, "Sin is like a little yeast that spreads through the whole batch of dough" (1 Corinthians 5:6).

What does wholehearted obedience to God mean to you? If you want to receive all the blessings God has for you, don't settle for mixed reviews regarding your willingness to go the distance with God.

February 24

Unwavering Faithfulness
URIAH

Uriah replied, "The Ark and the armies of Israel and Judah are living in tents, and Joab and my master's men are camping in the open fields. How could I go home to wine and dine and sleep with my wife? I swear that I would never do such a thing." 2 Samuel 11:11

In one 1950s *Looney Toons* cartoon, Sylvester the Cat is befriended by a big, slow-witted tabby whose loyalty knows no bounds. However cruelly or condescendingly Sylvester treats his wannabe friend, his new companion doesn't withdraw his friendship, loyalty, or protection.

It is admirable when a friend remains loyal and faithful even when treated shamefully. An Old Testament figure named Uriah the Hittite, one of King David's mighty men, provides an example.

Uriah had no way of knowing that his master, King David, had already wronged him by seducing and impregnating his wife. David's invitation for Uriah to stay home, take it easy, and spend the night with Bathsheba was just an attempt to cover David's own appalling sin.

Uriah knew that he couldn't in good conscience stay home with his wife while his men were fighting during the day and sleeping in tents at night. Uriah's loyalty to David and his men cost him dearly because the guilt-ridden David hatched another plan to cover his sin and had Uriah killed in battle.

Uriah did his duty and demonstrated the godly traits of faithfulness and loyalty. His life honored King David and the men he fought alongside. His faithfulness and loyalty cost him his life on earth, but he continues to encourage us from his honored place in heaven to make faithfulness and loyalty high priorities.

God never promises that faithfulness and loyalty will be rewarded or even recognized in this life. Uriah encourages us to think beyond human history. We can cast our lot with the God who never fails to reward those who honor him. The people in your life need you to remain faithful and loyal to them, to God, and to his Word.

February 25

The Savior's Love
JOHN

The disciple Jesus loved was sitting next to Jesus at the table.   John 13:23

An elderly wife once turned to her equally seasoned husband and asked him, "Why don't you tell me you love me anymore?" Her mate looked at her in exasperation and replied, "I told you I loved you on our wedding night. If anything changes, I'll let you know."

All of us need to know that we are loved and valued. It's the cornerstone of security and happiness in any human relationship and the basis of our relationship with God.

The apostle John (who wrote the Gospel that bears his name, three epistles, and probably the book of Revelation) had a keen appreciation for his Savior's love. He referred to himself as "the disciple Jesus loved."

Does it seem odd to you that John would speak of himself in such exclusive terms? If so, stop for a moment and think about the nature of God's love. John understood that Jesus' love for him was God's love, a devoted one-on-one relationship in which Jesus loved him so that he could love others.

Though Jesus certainly loved *all* his disciples, and had chosen each one to carry his message of salvation and forgiveness to the world, John apparently had the most acute awareness of his Master's love. As he understood the depth and breadth of Jesus' love for him, John found the motivation and the empowerment to do courageous, selfless things in Christ's name.

John had no doubts about the Savior's love for him, so he could freely give everything he had to Jesus and to those God had called him to serve.

Do the men and women, boys and girls in your innermost circle know beyond all doubt that you love them? Do they experience your love for them as the love of God? You can offer others the deepest form of love only when you grasp the depth and breadth of Jesus' love for you.

February 26

God Enables Us
JEREMIAH

The LORD replied, "Don't say, 'I'm too young,' for you must go wherever I send you and say whatever I tell you. And don't be afraid of the people, for I will be with you and will protect you. I, the LORD, have spoken!" Jeremiah 1:7-8

Crossing one of life's milestones can excite and frighten you. Maybe the day you left home for college, you realized that life would never again be as simple as it once was. When you stood at the altar, you suddenly realized that life would no longer be just about *me,* but about *us.* When your first child entered the world, it may have registered that you had become responsible for the health, safety, and security of another human being.

Life features many moments that can make you feel inadequate or unqualified. If you can remember one of those moments, you can probably identify with how a young prophet-to-be named Jeremiah may have felt when God called him to preach and prophesy in God's name.

When the Lord called Jeremiah to prophesy against the rebellious nation of Israel, he informed the young man that even before his mother gave birth to him, he had been chosen to serve as God's mouthpiece. We can imagine Jeremiah's mouth going dry, his hands trembling, and his stomach turning to mush as he heard the voice of the Lord calling him to do these things.

"I'm too young to speak for you!" Jeremiah protested.

Jeremiah lacked the confidence to eagerly accept God's call mostly because he hadn't grasped the simple truth that God never calls anyone to do something without first equipping that person to do it successfully. In truth, God had Jeremiah right where he wanted him, in a place where he could clearly see his own weakness and his need for God's empowerment. Jeremiah was the right man for the job for two reasons: God *called* him and God *enabled* him.

The next time you feel overwhelmed or unqualified to carry out what God has called you to do—congratulations! The Lord has you right where he wants you, in a place of humility and dependence on him for the empowerment you'll need for success.

February 27

A Powerful Testimony
PETER

Peter took the lame man by the right hand and helped him up. And as he did, the man's feet and ankles were instantly healed and strengthened. He jumped up, stood on his feet, and began to walk! Then, walking, leaping, and praising God, he went into the Temple with them. Acts 3:7-8

At the Easter service of a West Coast church, the pastor delivered his shortest sermon of the year. Following his sermon, several dozen people walked one by one to the front of the congregation, each carrying easy-to-read, hand-written placards identifying the sin or bondage from which Jesus Christ had released them:

> bitterness . . . violent anger . . . self-condemnation . . . addictions

After the service, many observers said, "I may not remember what the preacher said, but I won't forget what God had helped those people with."

That's the power of a transformed life.

"*No longer lame*" could have been on the placard of a first-century man whose crippled legs were healed the day he met two men named Peter and John. This man wasn't looking for a miracle. He only wanted a few coins so he could get a bite to eat. Though the apostles had no money to give him, they didn't leave him empty handed.

"In the name of Jesus Christ the Nazarene, get up and walk!" Peter said (Acts 3:6), then he took the man by the hand and helped him up.

He could walk! More than that, he could run and leap *and praise God*!

A once-handicapped man walking around and praising God's name is sure to get people's attention. It did, and after *seeing* the reality of Christ's power and *hearing* Peter preach, hundreds, if not thousands, turned to Jesus Christ from the personal testimony of one man! (See Acts 4:4.)

A changed life gives mighty testimony to the reality and power of the gospel. You may not feel qualified to speak to others about Bible doctrines or deep theology, but you can certainly testify to what God is doing in your life. How is God transforming you into a brand-new person?

February 28

Contentment
PAUL

Not that I was ever in need, for I have learned how to be content with whatever I have. I know how to live on almost nothing or with everything. I have learned the secret of living in every situation, whether it is with a full stomach or empty, with plenty or little. Philippians 4:11-12

In one episode of the long-running television comedy *The Simpsons,* the oafish Homer Simpson says to his filthy-rich boss, C. Montgomery Burns, "Ya know, Mr. Burns, you're the richest guy I know—way richer than Lenny."

"Yes," replies Burns, owner and operator of the infamous Springfield Nuclear Power Plant, "but I'd trade it all for a little more."

Though a character like Mr. Burns knows something about making money, he doesn't understand the first thing about contentment, a state of mind the apostle Paul had *learned.*

Paul didn't learn the value of contentment in some kind of vacuum but through his own difficulties. Paul set out on his missionary journeys with little in hand to cover the necessities of life. On many occasions—most notably as he sat in prison for preaching the gospel—he had to do without even the basics. There's nothing like sitting naked and in pain in a bare jail cell to focus your attention on what's really important!

How does a man of God learn contentment? He focuses on the goodness of God in providing him with every breath he takes. Contentment comes when he learns to feel satisfied with whatever provisions God makes for him. Though many would say, "I'll be content once I . . . ," the apostle Paul said, "I will be content in whatever situation God places me and with whatever he provides me."

When you learn to live in this way, you will defeat the spiritual enemies of envy, pride, and greed. As a magnificent side benefit, you will more fully enjoy what God has already so generously given you.

You won't meet a lot of people who truly feel content with what they have. You can find the key to true joy and happiness when you learn contentment, which means living with an attitude of gratitude for all that God has given you.

March 1

A Heart for Worship
ABRAHAM

The LORD appeared to Abram and said, "I will give this land to your descendants." And Abram built an altar there and dedicated it to the LORD, who had appeared to him. Genesis 12:7

What do the angels think when they see you singing hymns with your family at a Sunday morning church service? Do they think, *Wow! That man has learned how genuine worship connects him to the very Power of the universe!* Or do they mutter, "That pathetic human stands there moving his lips, but he has *no clue* what's really happening here"?

Have you ever thought about the power that is available through praise and worship of our heavenly Father?

King David wrote, "You are holy, enthroned on the praises of Israel" (Psalm 22:3). The sentence can be translated, "God inhabits the praise of his people." The Bible makes it clear that praise and worship are avenues through which we enjoy fellowship with God.

We have many biblical examples of men who understood the importance of worship and made it a regular part of their lives. Abraham, the man God called to be the father of his chosen people, may be one of our best examples.

Abraham was a rich man who obeyed God's call to take his family, pull up his stakes, and leave his home in Haran to travel to an unknown land. Wherever Abraham settled, even temporarily, he always took the time to build an altar and worship God.

We don't build altars to God today because the Holy Spirit lives within the bodies of all who place their faith in Jesus Christ. However, God still wants us to follow Abraham's marvelous example regarding the importance of worship.

Have you learned the importance and power of making praise and worship a key component of your daily life? If you want to enrich your prayers and see God working in your life more consistently and miraculously, then follow the example that Abraham set for his family. Cultivate a heart that loves to worship God!

March 2

From the Mountaintop
ELIJAH

"I have had enough, LORD," he said. "Take my life, for I am no better than my ancestors who have already died." 1 Kings 19:4

When you come away from a great experience such as getting married or becoming a father, how do you feel? Excited? Jubilant? Joyful? All of the above? Usually when we receive a great blessing from the Lord, we bask in the positive feelings it brings.

At other times, God takes us to a spiritual or emotional mountaintop and then drops us into a darker time in the valley.

Elijah had just seen God's mighty hand at work in successfully confronting the prophets of Baal. He had ended a long drought in Israel by calling rain from the sky. You would think that Elijah would be on an extended spiritual and emotional high, but that's not what happened.

Just days after the drought ended, Elijah received word that Jezebel, the Baal-worshiping wife of King Ahab, had vowed to kill him. "You killed the prophets of Baal," she declared, "and you're next."

Elijah could stay and trust God to miraculously protect and deliver him or hightail it out of town before Jezebel found him. Emotionally and spiritually spent, the prophet headed for the woods, lay down under a broom tree, and poured out his heart to God.

In just a few days, Elijah had gone from the mountaintop of ecstasy to a valley of depression, but God had no intention of allowing him to stay in that valley. God was about to pick Elijah up, dust him off, and send him back to living and enjoying his life of faith.

Though Elijah confessed that he had had enough and wanted to die, God said, "Let's talk, Elijah." God then restored him.

God may take you through places of difficulty where it doesn't seem that your faith works as it once did. He will never allow you to stay there, though. As he did for Elijah, he will give you just what you need to continue your life of faith.

March 3

Staying within Reach
KING REHOBOAM

The king paid no attention to the people. This turn of events was the will of God, for it fulfilled the LORD's message to Jeroboam son of Nebat through the prophet Ahijah from Shiloh. 2 Chronicles 10:15

"What we've got here . . . is a failure to communicate," the captain famously tells the inmates at a southern prison work camp in the classic movie *Cool Hand Luke*. As repeated escapee Lucas Jackson lies on the ground after being roughed up, the captain tells the other inmates, "Some men you just can't reach."

In truth, there had been no failure to communicate. Luke fully understood the risks and consequences of an escape attempt, but he stubbornly refused to listen.

Rehoboam, King Solomon's son and successor, also refused to be reached. He paid no attention to the people God had put in his life to direct and guide him. These were men who had served his father well and who had acquired wisdom through years of faithful service. They had offered the young king some simple advice: "Lighten up on the people, or there is going to be trouble."

Instead of heeding and applying this counsel, Rehoboam sought out younger, less-experienced men to be his advisers. As you might guess, they counseled him to take the opposite approach and tell the people, "If you think my father was tough, just watch me."

Rehoboam's refusal to listen to godly wisdom resulted in all-out hostility between the northern and southern portions of Israel. The rift quickly hardened into a permanent division that resulted in two distinct nations: the northern kingdom of Israel and the southern kingdom of Judah.

Rehoboam illustrates what can happen to those who stubbornly refuse to listen—to be reachable and teachable. He could have heeded the sage advice of experienced and proven counselors, but he chose to go on a power trip that put him in hot water and ripped his nation apart.

What experienced and proven counselors has God put in your life? Are you listening to them? Do you prefer the counsel of those who tell you only what you want to hear?

God can speak to you through a variety of means—a spiritual leader, your wife and children, a friend. Your job is to remain teachable and reachable.

March 4

Love like a Man
JESUS

Husbands, ...love your wives, just as Christ loved the church. He gave up his life for her to make her holy and clean, washed by the cleansing of God's word.
EPHESIANS 5:25-26

Ulysses S. Grant once took his beloved Julia Dent out for a buggy ride. As they came to a rickety bridge over a flooded creek, Grant assured the nervous Julia that they could cross safely.

"Don't be frightened," he said. "I'll look after you."

"Well," replied Julia, "I shall cling to you whatever happens." True to her word, Julia clung tightly to Grant's arm as they crossed the bridge.

Grant drove on in thoughtful silence for a few minutes then cleared his throat and said, "Julia, you said back there that you would cling to me whatever happened. Would you like to cling to me for the rest of our lives?"

She did, and they married in August 1848.

God created man to look after his wife, to love her perfectly. In Paul's letter to the Ephesian church, the apostle gives men a simple (yet decidedly difficult) instruction about loving their wives: *Love as Jesus loved!*

If you want to know how to love your wife and children, look no further than the perfect-in-every-way example of Jesus Christ. He loved us

—*sacrificially* when he gave up his own life so that we could live;
—*selflessly* as he did everything his Father sent him to do;
—*patiently* in teaching the flawed people whom he asked to follow and serve him;
—*forgivingly* when he asked the Father to forgive those who had crucified him; and
—*generously* in giving us far more than we deserve.

Jesus is our perfect example of love in action. He shows husbands that love is not primarily a feeling but a willing and even eager decision to put specific actions behind the words *I love you.*

Try an experiment this week. Every time you tell your wife, "I love you" (which had better be more than once or twice!), say to yourself, "And that means I'm going to ... take out the garbage ... help put away the dishes ... bring home some groceries ... (fill in the blank)." Put some shoe leather under your love this week!

March 5

A Negative Example
DIOTREPHES

I wrote to the church about this, but Diotrephes, who loves to be the leader, refuses to have anything to do with us. When I come, I will report some of the things he is doing and the evil accusations he is making against us. 3 John 1:9-10

When General George C. Marshall took command of the Infantry School at Fort Benning, Georgia, he immediately began leading by example. Although the post's physical condition had deteriorated badly, Marshall didn't issue any orders for improvements. Instead, he took out his own lawn equipment, paintbrushes, and other tools and went to work on his own quarters.

Soon other officers and enlisted men—beginning with those who lived closest to Marshall—did the same thing, and in the span of just a few weeks, Fort Benning's appearance had brightened up considerably.

When John wrote his third epistle to a church leader named Gaius, he issued a strong warning about a man named Diotrephes, who was a very poor leadership model.

Apparently Diotrephes was a gifted man, but he seemed most interested in moving himself up the church's pecking order. Jesus taught, "Whoever wants to be a leader among you must be your servant" (Matthew 20:26). The proud, arrogant, self-important Diotrephes asserted his own misguided brand of leadership over the church.

John didn't beat around the bush. He simply told Gaius, "Dear friend, don't let this bad example influence you. Follow only what is good" (3 John 1:11).

The Bible tells scores of inspiring stories about men of genuine faith. It also recounts examples of men we should go far out of our way to avoid emulating. Diotrephes certainly fits the latter category. His "me first" mentality put him last in God's scheme of things.

Jesus taught that any man who wants to be great in God's Kingdom must see himself as less important than others. Such a man must find ways to serve others in love. What kind of example are you? Whom are you serving?

March 6

Earnest Prayer
EPAPHRAS

Epaphras, a member of your own fellowship and a servant of Christ Jesus, sends you his greetings. He always prays earnestly for you, asking God to make you strong and perfect, fully confident that you are following the whole will of God.
COLOSSIANS 4:12

Early African converts to Christianity became known for their commitment to regular times of private prayer. They made daily visits to the same spots near their village for their devotional times.

Over time, the paths from the villages to the places of prayer became well worn unless a believer neglected his time of prayer. When that happened, someone would kindly tell the negligent believer, "Brother, the grass grows on your path."

Epaphras, a relatively obscure New Testament character, had a passion for prayer. As an associate of the apostle Paul, he apparently played a big role in establishing the Colossian church (see Colossians 1:7). Epaphras demonstrated such genuine love for the Colossians that Paul told them, "He always prays earnestly for you."

In praying for the Colossians, Epaphras practiced two important elements of prayer: consistency and sincerity. He never let the grass grow on his path, and he always prayed from the heart, which is how a man with a heart for prayer behaves toward those he claims to love.

Can you, like Epaphras, make room for a regular time of prayer on behalf of those you love? If grass has grown on your path, what alterations can you make in your schedule to make prayer a more regular priority?

Nothing makes more of a difference in your walk with Christ than regular times of prayer. With all the people who daily pass through your world, surely there are at least a few whom God has laid on your heart. Pray for them—beginning with your own family.

March 7

High Visibility
CRISPUS

Crispus, the leader of the synagogue, and everyone in his household believed in the Lord. Many others in Corinth also heard Paul, became believers, and were baptized. Acts 18:8

Several studies over the past few years have suggested that the color of a vehicle plays an important part in determining whether or not the vehicle will be involved in an accident. The studies show that brighter cars—silver or yellow, for example—have fewer mishaps because they stand out and are more easily seen.

High visibility can have its rewards.

The Bible cites dozens of examples of men who stood out in a crowd. One such man was Crispus, a Corinthian who heard and accepted Paul's message of salvation through Jesus Christ. Of all those who believed, only Crispus is mentioned by name in the book of Acts.

Why does the Bible mention Crispus and no one else? It is probable that when Luke sat down to write the book of Acts, it seemed noteworthy to him that Crispus led the Corinthian synagogue.

Luke doesn't tell us a lot about Crispus or his background. We know only that he was the synagogue leader in the city of Corinth, that Paul baptized him into the Christian faith (see 1 Corinthians 1:14), and that his family members also became believers in Jesus.

What makes this man noteworthy is his willingness to take a stand in a place where doing so could cause him big problems. Crispus lived in a time and place where professing faith in Jesus Christ was very dangerous. Ordinary Jews who accepted Jesus as Lord could be in for a rough time, and Jewish Christian *leaders* could expect big trouble. Crispus is an excellent example of a man willing to stand out for his faith regardless of the cost.

Do you have the courage to stand out in your world as a man committed to following Jesus Christ? That kind of courage will make a big difference in your life—and in the lives of those God has placed close to you.

March 8

A Great Approach to Life

PAUL

For to me, living means living for Christ, and dying is even better.
PHILIPPIANS 1:21

A bank in New York State once asked a florist to send a card and flowers to a competitor who had recently moved into a new building. Somehow, the florist sent the wrong arrangement and a card that read, "With our deepest sympathy."

If the florist felt embarrassed over his error, he felt even worse when he realized where he had sent the flowers and card intended for the bank. That card went to a funeral home preparing for a memorial service. It read, "Congratulations on your new location!"

Though most people put death near the top of their list of fears, death for the believer is nothing more than moving on to a new location—their eternal home in heaven. The apostle Paul took that approach to both death and life.

As he wrote to the Philippian church from a Roman prison cell, Paul faced the distinct possibility of death, but there is no hint of fear in his letter to the Philippians, only declarations of love, joy, peace, and celebration.

Paul knew the benefits of both life and death. He knew that if he lived, he could continue his work and fellowship with the Philippians. If he died, he would simply move on to his new location, the eternal home that God had prepared for him (see Philippians 1:21-24).

Paul couldn't decide which of those options he preferred.

Although he suffered immensely for the cause of Jesus Christ, Paul never feared anything that life threw his way. He had been threatened with death, beaten to within an inch of his life, and arrested, but he never forgot that God superintended everything that happened to him and that life and death held equally wonderful advantages.

What a great approach to living!

When you live free from fear of death or life, you never have to worry about what lies ahead. Instead, you get to enjoy both the earthly and the heavenly benefits of fellowship with Jesus Christ.

March 9

A Basis for Courage
JOSHUA

"Be strong and courageous, for you are the one who will lead these people to possess all the land I swore to their ancestors I would give them. Be strong and very courageous. Be careful to obey all the instructions Moses gave you. Do not deviate from them, turning either to the right or to the left. Then you will be successful in everything you do." Joshua 1:6-7

What do you think frightens most men? Recent polls and surveys tell us that more men fear professional failure than anything else. Fear of financial failure comes next, followed by the fear of making a serious mistake in their professional or family lives.

Can you identify with any of these fears? Have you ever found yourself awake at night thinking about your professional life, your family's financial security, or whether you are making the right decisions regarding your work and family?

God called Joshua to lead the people of Israel into the Promised Land. He certainly struggled with such fears, but he is a great example of how to make fear a nonissue.

We remember Joshua as a fearless leader. What gave him such courage? It doesn't appear that he started out that way. Otherwise, why would God repeatedly have to tell him to "be strong and courageous"?

Joshua's courage came first from his strong sense of purpose. God had called him to lead saying, "You are the one who will lead these people to possess all the land I swore to their ancestors I would give them" (Joshua 1:6).

Second, Joshua completely obeyed God's instructions: "Be careful to obey all the instructions Moses gave you. Do not deviate from them, turning either to the right or to the left" (Joshua 1:7).

Joshua went down in history as one of Israel's most courageous leaders for a very simple reason: He was determined to go where God called him to go and to do what God called him to do. That's a sure recipe for courage in any age and place.

Where has God called you to go? What has God called you to do? Have you determined to go there and do that? When you combine a God-given sense of purpose with a commitment to obedience, courage results. God will enable you to defeat your enemies and will give you all he has promised.

March 10

All Good Things
KING DAVID

"Wealth and honor come from you alone, for you rule over everything. Power and might are in your hand, and at your discretion people are made great and given strength." 1 Chronicles 29:12

A man nearing retirement knew that he had things pretty good. He had worked hard, made an excellent living, and had the common sense to squirrel away enough funds so that he and his wife could live out their golden years in comfort—and even take some trips now and again.

Though this accomplished man had an industrious streak and a knack for making money, when the time came for his retirement, he gratefully accepted his gold watch, thanked his business partners, and told them, "I'm pleased with what I've been able to accomplish during my years of hard work. At the same time, I'm aware that none of this could have happened without God's blessings. He is the One who allowed me to do everything I've done."

This man "got it"! He understood that although he had worked hard, God was the source of all his accomplishments.

King David also understood that every blessing he had ever enjoyed came from God's open hand. That included the humble realization that no one, whatever his station in life, ever receives anything good apart from God.

As David prepared to hand over the reins of power to his son Solomon, he looked back on his time as Israel's second and greatest king and humbly acknowledged that all his wealth and power, and the wisdom to know what to do with them, came directly from God's generous hand.

The Bible says that David "died at a ripe old age, having enjoyed long life, wealth, and honor" (1 Chronicles 29:28). That was because he never forgot the source of all good things.

God loves hearing you declare him as your source of all good things. When you acknowledge his goodness and generosity, you allow others to see God at work in your life and open yourself to additional blessing.

March 11

The Right Weapon
PETER

Simon Peter drew a sword and slashed off the right ear of Malchus, the high priest's slave. But Jesus said to Peter, "Put your sword back into its sheath. Shall I not drink from the cup of suffering the Father has given me?" John 18:10-11

Author Craig Brian Larson cited a *National Geographic* article about Alaskan bull moose, which go head-to-head in a battle for dominance during the fall mating season. A bull's antlers are its only weapon, and they often get broken during the battle, dooming the bull to defeat. Without exception, the biggest moose, with the largest and strongest antlers, dominates.

Bull moose fight with their antlers because they have no other weapons, but when you fight spiritual battles, you have a variety of resources available. Your choice will always determine whether you win or lose.

Peter's brashness and courage as he tried to protect Jesus by using his sword is admirable on some levels. As Peter saw it, there was nothing else he could do to keep the mob from arresting his Leader. Peter did the best he could that morning, but he went wrong by putting his confidence in his own strength and ability to get things done.

Peter's problem wasn't a lack of willingness to follow Jesus to the bitter end. As Jesus once put it, his spirit was willing (see Matthew 26:41). Peter's problem was that he was fighting the battle before him with the wrong weapon.

Peter really believed that his own courage and willingness to fight would carry him and his Teacher unscathed through the night.

It didn't turn out that way.

Peter was a strong man who meant well, but when he put his confidence in his own abilities and strength—as he often did—he fell flat on his face. Only when he received the Holy Spirit's empowerment did he became the fearless preacher of the gospel that Jesus had called and prepared him to be.

What weapons do you use to fight your spiritual battles? Your human reasoning? Your personal strength? When you rely on God's empowering Holy Spirit, you put yourself in a position to win every battle the devil wages against you.

March 12

When to Retreat
TIMOTHY

You, Timothy, are a man of God; so run from all these evil things. Pursue righteousness and a godly life, along with faith, love, perseverance, and gentleness.
1 TIMOTHY 6:11

Many times throughout history, an overmatched military force failed to retreat when conditions required it. As one modern example, think of Saddam Hussein's refusal to order the retreat of Iraqi forces from Kuwait in the face of certain destruction by the vastly superior U.S.-led coalition. When the megalomaniac Hussein refused to retreat, untold Iraqi deaths resulted.

Every competent military strategist needs to understand when to retreat. Retreat does not mean defeat; it simply makes room for a later victory.

Do you realize that wise believers must also learn when to retreat? That's the lesson the apostle Paul taught his young protégé Timothy.

Paul's "battle plan" called for Timothy to handle certain kinds of temptation by a strategic retreat. "Run from all these evil things," Paul instructed Timothy. Don't just avoid them, don't bargain with them, and don't stand and fight them . . . *run!* As an experienced man of faith, Paul knew the wisdom of his counsel.

From what evil things was Timothy to run? Paul warned him to flee the love of money, for one thing. Those who make earthly riches their life's goal often find themselves involved in spiritually destructive activities (see 1 Timothy 6:9-10).

Paul didn't just counsel retreat, however; he also directed Timothy to counter with something good. He urged the young man to seek righteousness, a godly life, faith, love, perseverance, and gentleness. A diligent pursuit of such things would shelter Timothy from the temptations of the world and equip him to enjoy a spiritually successful life.

God instructs you to beat a hasty retreat from certain kinds of temptation, the love of money being just one example. Instead, pursue things that hold out the promise of a spiritually productive future. When you pursue a godly life, you protect yourself from temptations that the devil intends to use to trip you up.

March 13

The Right Voice
SAMUEL

The LORD came and called as before, "Samuel! Samuel!" And Samuel replied, "Speak, your servant is listening." 1 Samuel 3:10

A Christian man having breakfast with a fellow believer sat in stunned silence as his friend and brother announced, "The Lord has told me that he wants me to leave my wife and marry another woman." Within a few weeks, this deceived man acted on what he had "heard" with predictable results. His family life, his financial life, and his spiritual life all went up in flames.

Though this foolish man no doubt heard *some* voice telling him to follow his fleshly desires, the voice he heard could not have belonged to God. Samuel, the young future prophet whom God had set aside for a life of service and leadership, is an example of a man who learned to hear the *real* voice of God.

One night as he tried to fall asleep, Samuel heard the voice of someone calling his name. Believing that he had heard Eli's voice, he arose to find out what his mentor wanted. Eli denied calling Samuel and sent him back to bed. When the same thing happened again, perhaps the confused Samuel thought, *Maybe it was something I had for dinner.*

Again, for the third time, came the voice.

This time Eli knew that something was up, so he instructed his protégé: "Go and lie down again, and if someone calls again, say, 'Speak, LORD, your servant is listening'" (1 Samuel 3:9).

Samuel did as he was told, and before long, he heard his heavenly Father's voice again, giving him instructions for his first act as a prophet. That night, Samuel began a long and fruitful life of listening for God's voice, as distinguished from the other voices whispering, shouting, and clamoring around him.

Though God doesn't often speak to his children in an audible voice, he still regularly communicates with those who belong to him. How do you learn to hear God speak? It's as simple as opening your Bible, humbling yourself, reading, making yourself available, and letting God know that you are actively listening.

March 14

No-Compromise Faithfulness
SHADRACH, MESHACH, AND ABEDNEGO

Shadrach, Meshach, and Abednego replied, "O Nebuchadnezzar, we do not need to defend ourselves before you. If we are thrown into the blazing furnace, the God whom we serve is able to save us." Daniel 3:16-17

Though you can safely compromise on a lot of things—such as tactics, timing, tastes, and preferences—you had better not compromise your deepest convictions. Compromise in the first category of items can help you move ahead and get things done, but compromise in the second category can lead to utter disaster.

Shadrach, Meshach, and Abednego were Hebrew youths living under Babylonian captivity. They faced one of those choices. Along with Daniel, they had freely altered some things to please their Babylonian masters, but when they received an order to compromise their commitment to God, they adamantly refused.

Nebuchadnezzar, king of Babylon, flaunted some seriously misplaced religious values. He erected a huge gold statue (perhaps of his own image) and decreed that everyone in Babylon, including the captive Hebrews, should bow to it as their god. Anyone who refused would immediately be thrown alive into a blazing furnace.

For the people who worshiped the true God—including Shadrach, Meshach, and Abednego—the time for compromise had passed. They had to make a stand.

If you faced such a deadly threat, wouldn't you want some time to discuss how you should respond? These three men didn't need to discuss anything; for them, there was no decision to be made. Furnace or no furnace, they could not bow down to Nebuchadnezzar's idol. They respectfully but firmly told the king that whether or not God delivered them from almost certain death, they refused to worship his statue.

True to his word, the king threw the trio into the furnace, and true to his character, God miraculously kept them from harm. After the king saw these three young men so amazingly delivered, he began singing a different tune, praising the God these three young men so faithfully served (see Daniel 3:28).

Compromise can be a positive and necessary part of life, but any time such a compromise would distance you from God or encourage you to disobey his Word, a faithful follower of Jesus can only say no.

March 15

A Generous Man
CORNELIUS

In Caesarea there lived a Roman army officer named Cornelius, who was a captain of the Italian Regiment. He was a devout, God-fearing man, as was everyone in his household. He gave generously to the poor and prayed regularly to God. Acts 10:1-2

Researchers at the University of Bern in Switzerland have found that under some circumstances, rats demonstrate a type of generosity. When Professor Michael Taborsky trained his rodents to pull a lever to produce food for other rats but not for themselves, the lab rats demonstrated a phenomenon known as "generalized reciprocity." The rats that had benefited from this kind of charity in the past were found to be 20 percent more likely to help another rat acquire food than the ones that hadn't.

Life lessons from the world of nature!

Scripture recognizes Cornelius, a Roman army officer, as a man of great generosity. He gave richly to others out of what he had received.

As captain of a Roman regiment and head of his family, Cornelius was a busy man. Apparently, he also provided strong spiritual leadership for the members of his household, and he always made generous giving to the poor a lifelong priority.

God honored Cornelius's generosity. The Lord sent an angel to visit Cornelius, which both terrified and encouraged him. The angel acknowledged his openhanded giving to those in need: "Your prayers and gifts to the poor have been received by God as an offering!" (Acts 10:4).

Although Cornelius hadn't yet come to faith in Jesus, this man foreshadowed the teachings of the apostle Paul, who later wrote, "Don't give reluctantly or in response to pressure. 'For God loves a person who gives cheerfully'" (2 Corinthians 9:7). God saw to it that Cornelius heard the gospel, and as soon as he did, he became the first known Gentile convert to Christ.

When you give generously to those in need, you put yourself in a position to receive from God and to set an important example for your family and others. How can you demonstrate cheerful generosity today?

March 16

Going Golden
NABAL

This man's name was Nabal, and his wife, Abigail, was a sensible and beautiful woman. But Nabal, a descendant of Caleb, was crude and mean in all his dealings. 1 Samuel 25:3

You check your mail, and among all the bills, periodicals, and junk mail, you find a fund-raising letter for a local homeless shelter. Or you hear an appeal at church for gifts to assist those overseas who don't have enough to eat. You see a television commercial asking for donations to care for African children orphaned by AIDS.

How do you respond? Life will present you with countless opportunities to extend kindness to those in need and set an example for your family and others.

Examples, of course, can be either negative or positive. Into the former category goes the sad case of Nabal, a wealthy but stingy rancher.

What's in a name? A lot, in this guy's case! The name Nabal means "fool," and his boorish, selfish behavior perfectly fit his name.

Years before God placed him on Israel's throne, David apparently felt confident in sending some of his men to ask Nabal for a few much-needed provisions. "Peace and prosperity to you, your family, and everything you own!" they greeted Nabal (1 Samuel 25:6), and then asked if he would extend kindness to David and his men by sharing food and water with them. Surely Nabal knew that they had been protecting his sheep and other property interests.

Nabal's response was anything but neighborly: "Who is this fellow David? . . . Who does this son of Jesse think he is?" (1 Samuel 25:10). He then insulted David's young servants and sent them rudely away.

Nabal, the fool, missed out on God's blessing when he refused to assist the Lord's servant David. Just a few days later, in what seems no accidental end to the story, Nabal also missed out on a long life when he died of an apparent heart attack.

When you make good use of the opportunities God gives you to extend kindness to others, you live by the Golden Rule and encourage anyone who is watching to follow your example.

March 17

Object Lessons
KING BELSHAZZAR

"You are his successor, O Belshazzar, and you knew all this, yet you have not humbled yourself." Daniel 5:22

In an uncomfortable conversation with his teenage son, a father recounted in detail some of the mistakes he had made in his youth. He described his former days of drug and alcohol use, troubles with the law, and immorality.

After a moment of awkward silence, the youth asked, "Why are you telling me this stuff, Dad?"

"Because, Son," the father replied, "I don't want you to make the same mistakes I've made."

The mistakes of others, including those close to us, can be object lessons for what does and does not work in life. The Old Testament book of Daniel contains the account of Belshazzar, a foolish king who refused to learn from his grandfather's mistakes.

Belshazzar, successor to the Babylonian throne of Nebuchadnezzar, had surely heard stories of how his grandfather long refused to bow before the Lord. He had also heard how God humbled this once-great king by causing him to live like a wild animal. He had listened to reports of how Nebuchadnezzar had finally repented and spoken words of praise for the God of Israel.

Yet the pride-filled Belshazzar dishonored God when he brought out gold cups from the Temple in Jerusalem for use at a drunken, idol-worshiping party at his palace. As Daniel solemnly explained to him, his days as king had come to an end (see Daniel 25:30).

Belshazzar knew the stories and their characters. He knew that the God of Israel honored humility and opposed pride, but he refused to learn anything from it. Perhaps he thought of it as myth or as coincidence, or perhaps he didn't think of it at all. God saw to it that he learned, and it was the last thing Belshazzar ever did.

History can yield valuable object lessons of mistakes to avoid and examples to follow. Though it doesn't help to dwell in the past, it is a good biblical idea to learn from it. What lessons from the past jump out at you?

March 18

Overcoming Inadequacy
ISAIAH

Their voices shook the Temple to its foundations, and the entire building was filled with smoke. Then I said, "It's all over! I am doomed, for I am a sinful man. I have filthy lips, and I live among a people with filthy lips."   Isaiah 6:4-5

There is a joke about a man who visited his psychiatrist one day and complained of an inferiority complex. He told the shrink that no matter what he tried, all he could focus on were his own inadequacies. After listening to the man for a while, the doctor gave him a good news/bad news diagnosis: "The good news is that you don't have a complex. The bad news is—you *are* inferior!"

Do you ever feel inferior or inadequate to serve God as a man, husband, father, businessman, or friend? If so, then you can probably identify with the prophet Isaiah.

Standing in the Temple in God's presence, Isaiah looked into the mirror of God's perfection and saw his own inadequacy staring back at him. *I'm dead,* he thought.

Isaiah knew he wasn't fit to serve God, much less stand in his presence, but God had a plan and purpose for Isaiah. He would send him out to speak his message of wrath and judgment—and of love, forgiveness, and mercy.

Isaiah entered the Temple that day feeling completely inadequate for God's purposes. Something had to be done about that, and only God could do it.

An angelic creature called a seraph approached Isaiah with a burning coal that he had taken from the heavenly altar, touched Isaiah's lips with it, then pronounced his guilt removed and his sins forgiven (see Isaiah 6:6-7).

Something immediately changed within Isaiah. This man of God who only moments before had thought himself as good as dead heard the voice of God asking for someone to go and speak his message. Isaiah boldly called out, "Here I am. Send me" (Isaiah 6:8).

God had made Isaiah fit to serve, and the prophet knew it.

Do you ever feel inadequate to accomplish even the everyday things that God asks you to do? If so, remember that it's not about your qualifications, but about the God who declares you fit to serve him wherever he has placed you.

March 19

Irrelevance
THE TEN SPIES

"The land we traveled through and explored will devour anyone who goes to live there. All the people we saw were huge. We even saw giants there, the descendants of Anak. Next to them we felt like grasshoppers, and that's what they thought, too!"
NUMBERS 13:32-33

Read this list of biblical names and see if you can remember who they were: Shammau, Shaphat, Igal, Palti, Gaddiel, Gaddi, Ammiel, Sethur, Nahbi, Geuel.

Hint: Ten names appear in this list.

These ten men went out as spies from the Israelite camp and returned to their countrymen with negative, discouraging reports.

Sure, they had plenty of good things to say about the land of Canaan. It would make a wonderful home for the people of Israel. But what about those giants—those huge men with bad dispositions who made them feel like grasshoppers?

If you know the story, you know that Moses sent out twelve spies, not ten. Two of them, Joshua and Caleb, encouraged the people to enter the land and take possession of it—*right then!* Alone among the dozen spies, they would one day possess the Promised Land.

Twelve men left the Hebrew encampment to spy out Canaan, but only two of them earned a reputation as men of faith. The others froze in their tracks the first time they perceived an obstacle, and we barely remember them at all.

Faith is a major element in our relationship with God. In its most basic form, this means believing that God always keeps his word and then acting on that belief. The story of the twelve spies gives us ten examples of crippling doubt and two examples of enabling faith.

Which example will you follow as you face your own giants?

When you focus on God and his ability to overcome obstacles, no giant will seem too big and no barrier too strong. That doesn't mean that you won't have to fight any battles! But when you enter the fight armed with the sword of God's Word and the shield of faith, victory will be nearby.

March 20

Pragmatism
ABRAM AND KING BERA

Abram replied to the king of Sodom, "I solemnly swear to the LORD, God Most High, Creator of heaven and earth, that I will not take so much as a single thread or sandal thong from what belongs to you. Otherwise you might say, 'I am the one who made Abram rich.'"   Genesis 14:22-23

The Salvation Army of Naples, Florida, made the news in 2002 when it rejected a check for $100,000 from a local man who had won $14.3 million from the state lottery. Army Major Cleo Damon explained his decision by telling news outlets that he sometimes counseled families made homeless by gambling. He considered it hypocritical to accept money won through gambling of any kind.

In a time when many would have taken a more "pragmatic" approach— "Hey, I don't approve of gambling, but this money can do a lot of poor people a lot of good"—Damon stood out as a man who stuck to the values he and the Salvation Army held dear.

Abram would have applauded his decision.

Abram found himself in uneasy alliance with King Bera of Sodom, a man whose very name meant "wicked." Bera's adversaries routed his forces and captured Abram's nephew Lot (see Genesis 14:8-12). When Abram learned of Lot's capture, he called together a band of men to mount a rescue mission. The raid succeeded, as Abram's men defeated Bera's enemies, rescued Lot, and recovered all the spoils taken from Sodom and Gomorrah.

The king of Sodom offered Abram a generous reward for defeating his foes. In effect, he was saying, "Let me have my people, and you keep the spoils" (see Genesis 14:21). Abram would have none of it. He gave Bera his men back and refused any further compensation. He also cut all ties with Bera.

Abram refused Bera's gesture for one reason: He didn't want the wicked Bera, or anyone else, to believe that the king had made him rich.

Though pragmatism is not all bad, it becomes problematic when you try to get ahead by violating your conscience and God's standards. You'll get much further in the long run by sticking to what you know to be right and by setting an example that others can see.

March 21

A Heart in the Right Place
ABEL

Abel also brought a gift—the best of the firstborn lambs from his flock. The LORD accepted Abel and his gift. Genesis 4:4

The famed U.S. aviator and engineer Alexander de Seversky once tried to encourage a hospitalized friend and fellow pilot who had lost a leg. "The loss of a leg is not so great a calamity," said de Seversky, who sported an artificial leg himself. "If you get hit on a wooden leg, it doesn't hurt a bit! Try it!" His friend obediently raised his walking stick and struck de Seversky's leg as hard as he could.

"You see," he beamed, "if you hit an ordinary man like that, he'd be in bed for five days!"

De Seversky left his friend's room with a smile, but as soon as he reached the hospital corridor, he collapsed in agony.

The young man had struck de Seversky's good leg.

You have to hand it to Alexander de Seversky—he had his heart in the right place even if his wooden leg didn't follow suit.

The Bible has much to say about the importance of having your heart in the right place. Abel, for example, brought his very best firstborn lambs to God as a willing sacrifice.

What did God find so acceptable about Abel's sacrifice?

The writer of the Epistle to the Hebrews explains, "It was by faith that Abel brought a more acceptable offering to God than Cain did. Abel's offering gave evidence that he was a righteous man, and God showed his approval of his gifts. Although Abel is long dead, he still speaks to us by his example of faith" (Hebrews 11:4).

Abel had something his brother did not—a grasp of the faith that pleased God. He understood that any right standing he enjoyed before the Lord came from his abiding faith in a God who rewards those who trust him. He could present his offering of a firstborn lamb, trusting that the sacrifice became holy through his faith.

Anything that you do for God becomes an acceptable offering when you do it with a heart full of faith. Had Cain presented his grain offerings with the same heart of faith as his brother, God would gladly have accepted his sacrifice. Faith is the key, then and now.

March 22

Show Compassion
JESUS

One day Jesus called together his twelve disciples and gave them power and authority to cast out all demons and to heal all diseases. Then he sent them out to tell everyone about the Kingdom of God and to heal the sick.   Luke 9:1-2

Lifestyle evangelism promotes the idea that many nonbelievers are more receptive to the message of salvation through Jesus Christ if they first see believers living good lives. Critics believe that such evangelism leans too much on demonstrating the faith and not enough on speaking about it.

During his earthly ministry, Jesus sent his twelve apostles to cast out demons and heal the sick, but his ministry didn't stop there. Jesus also commanded these men to tell people about the Kingdom of God. He didn't want them to just show people the good news of salvation; they were to tell them about it as well.

These men had seen a close, personal example of One who struck a perfect balance between good works and effective words. Jesus fed the hungry, healed the sick, cast out demons, raised the dead, and offered tenderness and compassion to everyone in need. He also spoke the message that fueled his acts of compassion, even when those words alienated some in the crowd.

The apostles never forgot the example Jesus set for them. After he returned to heaven, they carried on his work of healing the sick and lame, casting out demons, and raising the dead, but they also preached the message of eternal life through faith in the resurrected Jesus Christ.

That's the same message people today need to both see *and* hear!

What acts of compassion and practical help do the people around you most need? What specific good news do they most need to hear from your lips? Take some time to pray about this, asking God to lay on your heart both what you are to do and say and who stands in most need of your God-empowered words and deeds.

March 23

The Cost of Bitterness
ASAPH

I realized that my heart was bitter, and I was all torn up inside. I was so foolish and ignorant—I must have seemed like a senseless animal to you.
PSALM 73:21-22

Though comedian Buddy Hackett openly confessed that he'd had a few arguments with people in his day, he maintained that he had never indulged in bitterness or grudge holding. The reason? "While you're carrying a grudge," he said, "they're out dancing."

Bitterness causes more damage to our relationships, health, and souls than almost anything else. Bitterness tears down the best human relationships. It damages and destroys friendships, family relationships, business partnerships, marriages, and Christian ministries.

Asaph, a leader of David's choir and the author of Psalm 73, well understood the destructive power of bitterness.

Asaph had seen plenty of evil and violence in his day, and what he saw angered him so much that he complained to God asking why he allowed evil people to prosper. He felt angry and frustrated and wondered if there was any point in living a righteous life.

Even as he complained about the injustices he saw, Asaph had a moment of clarity. He realized that he had become bitter over everything he had seen, and it embarrassed him: "I was so foolish and ignorant," he confessed. "I must have seemed like a senseless animal to you" (Psalm 73:22).

Asaph realized that his bitterness had cost him—if only temporarily—part of his humanity.

Asaph rightly felt a sense of righteous indignation at the evil he saw all around him, but he realized that he had crossed a dangerous line when he allowed the wicked things he saw to consume him and bring him to a point of bitterness.

Even the people you love the most will sometimes do and say things that anger you. When that happens, you have a choice either to deal with the anger wisely and righteously or to allow it to grow into bitterness. Bitterness may feel good for a moment, but it always consumes the one who indulges in it. Respond to life's injustices with forgiveness and compassion, and you'll cut out the cold, black heart of bitterness.

March 24

Opposition
SANBALLAT

Sanballat was very angry when he learned that we were rebuilding the wall. He flew into a rage and mocked the Jews, saying in front of his friends and the Samarian army officers, "What does this bunch of poor, feeble Jews think they're doing?" Nehemiah 4:1-2

When a reporter asked a Vietnam-era fighter pilot how he could know that he was attacking the correct targets, the man replied, "You always know you're over the right target because you're being shot at."

In the same way, spiritual opposition often confirms that you're headed in the right direction in your life of faith. The Bible warns us to expect opposition when we move against spiritual enemies bent on opposing our efforts to live a godly life, be a godly husband and father, and be a godly influence on those around us.

Nehemiah endured this kind of opposition as he worked to rebuild the ruined city walls around Jerusalem after the Babylonian captivity. Much of that opposition came from a Samaritan leader named Sanballat, a sworn enemy of the Jewish people who opposed the repopulation and rebuilding of the Holy City. Sanballat did everything he could to thwart Nehemiah's work. First, he mocked and ridiculed the Jews. When that tactic failed, he turned to the sharper weapons of fear, entrapment, and political maneuvering.

Because Nehemiah first dedicated himself and his cause to God, and then proceeded in his work as wisely and practically as he knew how, Sanballat's efforts failed miserably. The city steadily grew in size, mirroring the height of the rebuilt walls, and the residents remained resolute in seeing the task to its completion.

For every project God assigns you, expect a corresponding "Sanballat" to be working behind the scenes to discourage you and keep you from enjoying all God has for you and the people you love. The main question is not whether such opposition will appear, but how you will you respond when it arrives. Will you choose discouragement or strengthen your sense of resolve?

Don't give in to discouragement when you face opposition and setbacks in completing whatever task God gives you. Instead, see them as confirmation that you are "flying over the right target."

March 25

Hope
JEREMIAH

The faithful love of the LORD never ends! His mercies never cease. Great is his faithfulness; his mercies begin afresh each morning. I say to myself, "The LORD is my inheritance; therefore, I will hope in him!" Lamentations 3:22-24

The Irish-born author and playwright George Bernard Shaw made no secret of his liberal thinking and atheism. Late in life, he wrote, "The science to which I pinned my faith is bankrupt. Its counsels, which should have established the millennium, led, instead, directly to the suicide of Europe. I believed them once. In their name I helped to destroy the faith of millions of worshipers in the temples of a thousand creeds. And now they look at me and witness the great tragedy of an atheist who has lost his faith."

You can't be too careful about putting your hope in the right things, as the prophet Jeremiah understood well.

Jeremiah surveyed the ruins of the once-great city of Jerusalem, seeing little to spark his hope. Babylonian invaders obliterated the city, killing tens of thousands (including women and children) and marching thousands more off to Babylon, where they faced decades of slavery.

Jeremiah saw the death and destruction all around him and felt a pain we can only begin to imagine. With raw emotions, a broken heart, and a shocked mind, he stood numbly amid the horrible devastation and the smoldering rubble.

Still, Jeremiah found it within himself to speak to his one Source of hope. From his trembling lips came words of praise: "The faithful love of the LORD never ends! His mercies never cease. Great is his faithfulness; his mercies begin afresh each morning" (Lamentations 3:22-23).

Despite the stench of death hanging in the air, Jeremiah recognized that God had granted him life and that he loved the prophet and his people, despite all appearances. Jeremiah could hope for better things from the hand of his heavenly Father.

Where do you place your hope when you or your loved ones encounter pain and difficulty? By placing it squarely in a faithful, loving God—whatever the evidence might seem to suggest—you connect yourself to life, blessing, and hope.

March 26

Bucking the System
MORDECAI

The palace officials at the king's gate asked Mordecai, "Why are you disobeying the king's command?" They spoke to him day after day, but still he refused to comply with the order.   Esther 3:3-4

On December 1, 1955, a then-unknown Rosa Parks unintentionally made a national name for herself. When a public bus driver ordered her to give up her seat in the first row of the "colored" section to a white passenger, this young black woman from Montgomery, Alabama, refused. Her unplanned act of civil disobedience marked the beginning of the Montgomery bus boycott and helped to launch the career of celebrated civil-rights activist Dr. Martin Luther King Jr. Parks's single act of courageous noncompliance earned her a lasting legacy in the U.S. civil rights movement.

Though the Bible teaches believers to obey those in authority and comply with the laws of the land, it also recognizes that some situations call for bucking the system.

Mordecai, a Jewish man living in Persia following the Babylonian captivity, had unbending integrity, courage, and faithfulness, all of which were tested when King Ahasuerus ordered his officials to bow before Haman, the king's chief agent (see Esther 3:2).

Mordecai had repeatedly proved his loyalty to the king, but as a man who served the true and living God, he would not bow before any human, especially one as wicked as Haman. Though it meant potentially grave consequences for all Jews living in Persia at the time, Mordecai took a courageous stand *against* the king's decree and did what was right in the Lord's eyes.

God took over from there, orchestrating events behind the scenes so that the crisis actually *advanced* the well-being of the entire Hebrew people.

You may hear voices encouraging you to lighten up on your commitment to God and instead "go with the flow." Those voices may seem quite sensible. But when you take a stand, you demonstrate the ultimate value of your commitment to God, and you encourage secret believers to declare their allegiance to the Lord.

March 27

Crying, "Help!"
MOSES

The LORD said to Moses, "Gather before me seventy men who are recognized as elders and leaders of Israel....I will take some of the Spirit that is upon you, and I will put the Spirit upon them also. They will bear the burden of the people along with you, so you will not have to carry it alone." Numbers 11:16-17

"I've just hit a wall!" complained the overworked and burned-out accountant as April 15th approached. The man, with a wife and three young children at home, had put in twelve- to sixteen-hour days for many weeks and had reached the point where he just couldn't work one more hour of overtime.

Do you know the feeling? If you've ever hit a point of burnout, you know the unsettling feeling of losing enthusiasm for work that once meant so much to you or of wanting more than anything to go on vacation and never return.

Moses once reached the point of burnout. He had enjoyed incredible fellowship with God, had felt encouraged and challenged by the Lord, and had received good assistance from Aaron and others. But after so brilliantly leading, providing for, and listening to the fickle people of Israel, Moses had no more to give. Moses honestly complained to God, "If this is how you intend to treat me, just go ahead and kill me. Do me a favor and spare me this misery!" (Numbers 11:15).

Moses had lost the joy of serving simply because he had too much to do and not enough help to get it done. Thankfully, God sent help his way.

When you allow others to help you bear your burdens, you receive great blessings for yourself and for those who help you. You know what that takes, though, don't you? You have to humbly admit your need and stand ready to accept whatever help others can give you.

Think of the last time you felt burned out—overwhelmed with family, over your head at work, fed up with life. Whom did God place in your life to give you the help you needed? Allow your brothers to share your burdens so that you can keep moving forward in the race God has assigned to you.

March 28

Courage to Cry Out
BARTIMAEUS

When Bartimaeus heard that Jesus of Nazareth was nearby, he began to shout, "Jesus, Son of David, have mercy on me!" "Be quiet!" many of the people yelled at him. But he only shouted louder, "Son of David, have mercy on me!"
MARK 10:47-48

Babies cry—that's just their thing. They cry when they are hungry and when they don't feel well. They cry when they want some affection. It comes to them naturally.

When babies cry, do you suppose they ever worry about etiquette or decorum? Do they fret about good manners or respectability? Never. They simply want their needs to be met.

In a simple but profound way, a baby's crying can point out an important part of our relationship with Jesus Christ, just like the story of a blind man named Bartimaeus.

Bartimaeus had apparently heard stories of Jesus' miraculous healings and somehow knew that the Teacher planned to visit his hometown of Jericho. As far as he knew, this would be a one-shot deal. He *had* to get Jesus' attention.

As Jesus and his followers left Jericho, Bartimaeus committed a breach of etiquette by crying out so loudly to Jesus that it annoyed those in the crowd. They all told him to pipe down.

But like a crying baby who screams even louder when its needs don't immediately get met, Bartimaeus shouted at the top of his lungs for Jesus' attention. He didn't care what others thought; he simply wanted Jesus to meet his need.

Bartimaeus made a spectacle of himself. He didn't care about decorum or how he looked or sounded to onlookers—he only cared about getting a chance to tell Jesus what he wanted. Because of his loud persistence, Jesus turned his attention to him.

In one instant and with one command, Bartimaeus's blind eyes could suddenly see. At that moment, the direction of his life changed forever. He left behind his days as a blind beggar and exchanged them for a new identity as a follower of Jesus.

Never let decorum or etiquette stand in the way of crying out to Jesus Christ to meet your pressing needs. Your efforts may annoy others, but a genuine cry of faith never annoys Jesus. It simply attracts his attention.

March 29

Peer Pressure
MICAIAH AND KING AHAB

The messenger who went to get Micaiah said to him, "Look, all the prophets are promising victory for the king. Be sure that you agree with them and promise success." But Micaiah replied, "As surely as the LORD lives, I will say only what the LORD tells me to say."   1 Kings 22:13-14

At one time or another, most parents have said something like this to their kids: "If your friends all drove off the edge of a cliff, would you do it too?"

If you ever heard your parents say this, you probably thought they were more than a little out of touch for saying it. When you became a parent yourself, you probably recognized it as pretty good advice for handling peer pressure.

Peer pressure doesn't stop when you leave adolescence behind. If anything, it intensifies, and the stakes get higher. As one classic example, consider Micaiah, a prophet of God during the reigns of King Jehoshaphat of Judah and King Ahab of Israel. He faced some heavy-duty peer pressure.

The wicked King Ahab had asked Jehoshaphat to send Judah's army into battle with his own in order to defeat Ben-hadad, the king of Syria. Jehoshaphat tentatively agreed to join Ahab, but only after he sought the Lord's will on the matter. Ahab's prophets—more "yes men" than actual prophets—approved the agreement, but Jehoshaphat wanted some confirmation.

Enter Micaiah.

Ahab reluctantly called for Micaiah, who was in prison at the time, and pressured him to agree with his prophets. Micaiah courageously refused. After sarcastically repeating the party line, he spoke the plain truth: This battle would mean Ahab's humiliation and death.

Micaiah resisted Ahab's pressure and faithfully spoke what God had communicated to him. He refused to drive off the edge of a cliff and instead set an example of faithfulness in the face of pressure.

Standing up to peer pressure never feels comfortable, but when you refuse to yield to ungodly pressures, you greatly encourage and bless those who look up to you as an example of faithfulness.

March 30

A Woman's Place
JESUS

"Mary!" Jesus said. She turned to him and cried out, "Rabboni!" (which is Hebrew for "Teacher"). "Don't cling to me," Jesus said, "for I haven't yet ascended to the Father. But go find my brothers and tell them, 'I am ascending to my Father and your Father, to my God and your God.'" John 20:16-17

Several years ago, the Harry S. Truman Library made public more than thirteen hundred letters the late president wrote to his wife, Bess, during their times apart. As president of the United States, Truman traveled frequently, but he never failed to write Bess to let her know he loved her and was thinking of her.

You don't have to be a licensed marriage counselor to understand that the women in your life—your mother, wife, daughters, sisters—need to know you love, value, and respect them, just as Jesus loved, valued, and respected the women in his life.

Though Jesus chose twelve men to be his apostles, he treated women with a then unheard-of respect. He valued their fellowship and friendship and included them in the work that he did. Consider these examples:

> The woman at the well announced the Messiah to the Samaritans (see John 4:1-41).
> Mary and Martha enjoyed a close personal relationship with Jesus (see John 11:5).
> Mary, Martha's sister, anointed Jesus prior to his crucifixion (see Mark 14:3-9).
> Mary Magdalene discovered Jesus' empty grave (see Matthew 28:1-6) and first saw the resurrected Jesus (see John 20:16-18).

Why did women become some of Jesus' closest followers? One simple answer is that he lovingly and respectfully included them in his work.

In extending such respect to women, Jesus swam strongly against the tide of popular culture. Though most men of Jesus' day treated women as possessions, Jesus showed how much he valued the women who followed him.

If you want to know how to treat the women in your life with more love and respect, spend some time examining Jesus' example as described in the Gospels. Jesus, the man perfect in every way, treated the women who faithfully followed him with great dignity and honor.

March 31

The Eyes Have It!
JOB

"I made a covenant with my eyes not to look with lust at a young woman....For lust is a shameful sin, a crime that should be punished."   Job 31:1, 11

If you play with fire, you're going to get burned.

This old expression isn't really a warning not to play with fire but a caution against putting yourself in places where you could endanger your health or life.

Suppose you were to speak to someone who had been badly injured through his own carelessness at home or behind the wheel. Do you think you would find that he had planned to hurt himself that day? Would you not more likely discover that carelessness or lack of preparation led to his disaster?

Sexual temptation burns many men simply because they are careless and unprepared. Even thousands of years ago, Job knew how this worked.

In Job 31, Job takes some time for self-examination. He knew that he hadn't engaged in the sins of lust, lying, or adultery. But he didn't look only at his actions; he also looked at what lay behind them.

Job knew that God's gaze penetrated far deeper than his own. He knew that God saw the thoughts that a man allowed his mind to entertain. He knew the importance of keeping his body away from sexual sin as well as the necessity of not even *looking* lustfully at a woman other than his wife.

Modern men have even more reason than Job to keep a tight guard on what they allow their eyes to take in. Those who have no interest in pleasing the Lord will say, "Hey, there's no harm in looking," but the man committed to God knows better. Every instance of adultery or illicit sexual contact begins with a look not a touch. Follow Job's advice if you want to keep your body and mind pure: Don't even look!

It's a simple equation: God wants to bless you, and the devil wants to steal everything you have. Though it's nearly impossible in today's image-driven world to avoid glimpsing scenes that can trip you up sexually, it's important that you take what precautions you can to keep them as far from eyeshot as possible! A shield that keeps out 95 percent of the arrows is better than no shield at all.

April 1

The Request God Honors
KING SOLOMON

"Give me an understanding heart so that I can govern your people well and know the difference between right and wrong. For who by himself is able to govern this great people of yours?" 1 Kings 3:9

Life can feel overwhelming. Everything comes at you so fast that sometimes you don't know what to do. Bills, appointments, accidents, meetings, illnesses, travel, and maintenance can all start piling up and threatening to bury you under a mountain of responsibilities. How can you cope?

The newly crowned King Solomon knew the feeling.

As Solomon prepared to succeed his father, David, as king of Israel, he knew that he couldn't handle the task. As he prayed, he openly acknowledged that he felt like a lost child. The responsibilities before him looked too great.

Solomon didn't have to think twice when God asked him what he most wanted for himself. He could have asked for anything—a long life, riches, revenge on his enemies. Instead, he focused on his most immediate need for wisdom and understanding.

God liked what he heard and gave Solomon exactly what he had asked for—and more. God gave Solomon wisdom and understanding beyond that of any other man, and then he gave him riches, fame, respect, and a long life (see 1 Kings 3:11-14).

Solomon's request for wisdom pleased God beyond measure, and such a request still pleases him today. When you feel overwhelmed with life, just remember the example of Solomon, who once felt the same way and knew what he needed if he wanted to handle the job before him.

Business responsibilities, home requirements, family commitments, neighborhood activities . . . what usually causes you to feel you might be going under? If you want to please God in every area of your life, you have a critical need for wisdom. Fortunately, your loving, generous God is always happy to give you that gift as long as you place your faith firmly in him when you ask for it (see James 1:5-6).

April 2

Who Is *Really* in Control?
JOSEPH

God has sent me ahead of you to keep you and your families alive and to preserve many survivors. So it was God who sent me here, not you! Genesis 45:7-8

When Frank hopped in his car one Monday morning and headed for work, he had no idea that another commuter would run a red light and broadside his car, sending him on an ambulance ride to the local emergency room. However, Frank's injuries didn't put his life in danger.

Instead, they saved his life.

When the ER staff checked Frank's vital signs, they discovered that he had unusually high blood pressure, an irregular heartbeat, and other telltale symptoms of heart disease. Frank's condition, though treatable with medication, could have taken his life if it hadn't been detected in time. Frank felt sore and tired after his accident, but he thanked God for his discomfort. He firmly believed that the Lord had used the accident to save his life.

The patriarch Joseph would have smiled at Frank's story.

When Joseph's brothers saw him alive and well years after they had sold him into slavery, they quite naturally were stunned and frightened. They knew that he held their lives in his hands.

But long before, Joseph's heart and mind had made peace with his treacherous brothers. He had no more animosity toward them. How could he when he firmly believed that the God who remains in control of all things had sent him to Egypt with a special calling in mind?

How do you respond when difficulties come your way? When you and your wife have a blowout argument, when one of your kids defies everything you say, when an important deal at work falls through, when you have some real questions about a new direction at church, how do you typically react? Do you allow negative emotions to rule the day, or do you take refuge in God, knowing without a doubt that he remains in control? If you follow Joseph's example, you will know the joy of serving a God who uses *all* things for your good.

God has an amazing way of using even the worst circumstances for your good. Will he tell you what he's up to in the middle of your difficulties? Not likely. We have no record that he ever told Joseph about his plans ahead of time. That means that Joseph had to move forward by faith—just as you do.

April 3

God's Tools of Intervention
DAVID

David replied to Abigail, "Praise the LORD, the God of Israel, who has sent you to meet me today! Thank God for your good sense! Bless you for keeping me from murder and from carrying out vengeance with my own hands."
1 SAMUEL 25:32-33

Has life ever pushed you so hard that you felt on the verge of an explosive emotional outburst? Whether you have an argument with your wife, a problem with one of your children, or issues at work, life offers many moments for you to lose it and do or say things you might consider out of character.

Before he took the throne of Israel, David, a man of considerable passion and emotion, found himself on the verge of committing a terrible sin because of human anger. On the run from a jealous and unbalanced King Saul, he found himself badly in need of provisions. He sent ten of his men to ask a wealthy man named Nabal to help him. Nabal refused to help David and insulted him and his men as if they were common criminals.

When David heard about it, he should have stopped, taken a deep breath, and *responded* to the situation in a way befitting a man anointed to be king. Instead, he *reacted* in rage, ordering four hundred of his men to kill Nabal and all his people.

Only the intervention of Nabal's wife, Abigail, kept David from committing a terrible sin. She didn't defend her worthless husband, but she reminded David that killing the man would perpetrate a grave sin against God (see 1 Samuel 25:24-31). Her wise words prevented David from doing something he knew to be wrong. He humbly listened to her correction and turned away from an ungodly plan that would have dishonored him and God.

God calls you to provide your family with spiritual leadership, encouragement, correction, and direction. To do this job well, God has given you ears to hear what your loved ones have to say to you. It might be that God wants to use them to say something important to you.

April 4

God's GPS
PAUL AND SILAS

Next Paul and Silas traveled through the area of Phrygia and Galatia, because the Holy Spirit had prevented them from preaching the word in the province of Asia at that time. Acts 16:6

Who would have thought, even ten years ago, that so many new automobiles would have global positioning systems (GPS) as standard equipment? These electronic devices tell a driver at the push of a button exactly where he is and how to get where he wants to go. Today, drivers who even a short time ago didn't know what a GPS was, depend on these devices to arrive on time at their chosen destinations.

When you're driving, it's important to know where you are going and how to get there. It's far more important to know where God wants you to go, how to get there, and what to do once you arrive.

How does God direct you? He does it in the same way that he did in the time of the apostle Paul and his companion in ministry Silas: through the Holy Spirit's leading.

The Bible tells us that the Spirit of God "prevented them from preaching the word in the province of Asia" and instead sent them to preach in places called Phrygia and Galatia. The Bible doesn't say *why* God didn't want Paul and Silas in Asia at that time or *how* the Holy Spirit prevented them from going. The important part of this account is that these men were so tuned-in to the Holy Spirit that they knew exactly where God wanted them to go.

The Holy Spirit faithfully guided Paul, Silas, and the rest of those he had called to preach, and he wants to guide your life today. The key is to remain in tune with him by faithfully following the guidance he has already made clear to you.

There is no better place to be in life than in the place where God has put you. When you follow the leading of the Holy Spirit, you can know without a doubt that you are right where he wants you.

April 5

A Perfect Servant
JESUS AND PETER

Jesus replied, "You don't understand now what I am doing, but someday you will."
"No," Peter protested, "you will never ever wash my feet!" Jesus replied, "Unless I
wash you, you won't belong to me." John 13:7-8

During the American Revolution, a stranger in civilian clothes rode past a
group of exhausted soldiers who were repairing a small barricade. Their leader
made no attempt to help them but instead stood by, barking orders.

When the rider asked the leader why he wasn't helping his men, he
retorted with great dignity, "Sir, I am a corporal!" The stranger apologized,
dismounted, and began helping the soldiers himself. The job done, he turned
to the corporal and said, "Mr. Corporal, next time you have a job like this
and not enough men to do it, go to your commander-in-chief, and I will
come and help you again."

With that, General George Washington mounted his steed and rode off.

Jesus taught his disciples a valuable lesson about servanthood shortly
before his arrest and crucifixion. He did something that the Jewish people
considered demeaning even to the lowliest servant: He washed their feet.

Though all twelve felt uncomfortable at having their Master wash their
feet, Peter finally protested: "No! You will never wash my feet," but Jesus
wanted to teach Peter and the other apostles an important lesson, and Peter's
protests weren't going to stop him. "Unless I wash you, you won't belong to
me," he warned.

Peter yielded and allowed his Master to be his Servant.

When Jesus had finished washing the disciples' feet, he put on his robe and
asked them if they understood what had just happened. When they met his
question with silence, he explained that he had set an example of how they
were to treat one another when he had returned to his Father.

This example is for us, too.

**God put us on earth to serve others, even those we don't personally know. Serving is a
privilege because it builds up other believers and gives them a chance to see God's love
in action.**

April 6

Rightly Placed Confidence
ELIJAH

*Ahab summoned all the people of Israel and the prophets to Mount Carmel.
Then Elijah stood in front of them and said, "How much longer will you waver,
hobbling between two opinions? If the LORD is God, follow him! But if Baal is
God, then follow him!"* 1 Kings 18:20-21

Walking through the front door one evening after a long day's work, a man
glanced up just in time to see his four-year-old son flying at him. The boy
wanted to greet Dad (and have some fun doing it), so he jumped off the
family sofa into his arms.

The boy had played "jump and catch" with his father many times before,
and Dad had never failed to catch him. He knew that Dad would never drop
him, even when he added this new twist.

That's confidence!

Elijah demonstrated that kind of confidence in his heavenly Father when
he challenged 450 priests of the pagan idol Baal to call on their god to match
the power of the true and living God. Elijah had grown tired of the waffling
going on around him. He wanted the people to decide once and for all whom
they would serve—God or Baal. To give them a clear choice, Elijah challenged the priests of Baal to make a sacrifice in front of everyone and see what
happened.

They did, and nothing happened.

Now it was time for the *real* God to show what he could do.

When Elijah had seen the sad spectacle of Baal's priests, he set up an altar
and made things a little more interesting by saturating the altar, the sacrifice,
and the ground around it with water. At just the right moment, he called on
God to remind the people who he was.

Elijah never had a doubt about what would happen next.

With the people *and* the prophets of Baal looking on, God sent down a
fire that consumed the soaked offering, the wood, and the stones of the altar.
After seeing that demonstration, the people of Israel had no doubt about who
the *real* God was.

**Place your complete confidence in the one true God. You can count on him to step up and
be God in every one of life's situations.**

April 7

A Clear Conscience
JOB

I will never concede that you are right; I will defend my integrity until I die. I will maintain my innocence without wavering. My conscience is clear for as long as I live. Job 27:5-6

A man ridden with guilt walked into his pastor's office, hoping to find relief. "Pastor," he confessed, "I've been misbehaving a lot lately, and my conscience is killing me."

"Well, let's talk about that," the pastor offered. "And then let's pray that God would strengthen your resolve."

"Actually," the man interrupted, "I was hoping you could pray that my conscience wouldn't bother me so much."

How often do we long for a *quiet* conscience when what we really need is a *clean* conscience? The Old Testament story of Job shows us the crucial difference.

God allowed Satan to attack Job on several fronts at once, including his family life. Thereafter, three well-meaning but misguided friends offered Job their counsel as to what had gone wrong. One of those friends, named Eliphaz, offered this gem: "Is it because you're so pious that he accuses you and brings judgment against you? No, it's because of your wickedness! There's no limit to your sins" (Job 22:4-5).

There is no doubt Job did a quick personal inventory to see if Eliphaz's words had any merit, but he already knew better. He had a completely clean conscience, and though he was suffering greatly, guilt over some hidden sin wasn't one of the reasons.

Though Job didn't know why he was suffering, he knew that it hadn't come about as a result of his sin. Even God had called Job "blameless—a man of complete integrity" (Job 1:8).

Difficult times are bound to come, but when you keep your conscience clear, you can find the same comfort that Job knew. A clean conscience provides relief that no medicine can touch.

Do you enjoy a clean conscience? Do you keep short accounts with God? The best thing about a clear conscience is knowing that you are at peace with God and with other people, regardless of what happens to you.

April 8

Conditional Blessings
SAMUEL AND KING SAUL

"How foolish!" Samuel exclaimed. "You have not kept the command the LORD your God gave you. Had you kept it, the LORD would have established your kingdom over Israel forever." 1 Samuel 13:13

Arabian horses go through rigorous obedience training in the Middle Eastern deserts, including a test that seems harsh to people who don't understand the demands of desert life.

The trainer deprives the horse of water for several days before turning it loose. The thirsty horse naturally runs toward water, but just as it bends down for a drink, the trainer blows his whistle. If the horse has learned obedience, it stops and returns to the trainer. Only when the trainer feels sure that he has the horse's full obedience does he allow it to go back for a much-needed drink.

Does such training seem cruel to you? If so, remember that a rider on the desert sands of Arabia depends on his horse to obey his every command. His life and that of his horse depend on it.

Just as a Middle Eastern rider depends on his horse's obedience for survival, our receiving God's full blessing depends on our obedience. That is where Saul, Israel's first king, fell flat on his face.

Samuel had given Saul clear instructions as he prepared for battle: *"Go ahead to Gilgal and wait for me"* (see 1 Samuel 13:8). But Saul didn't wait for Samuel. Instead, he foolishly decided to play the role of a priest and performed sacrifices in a way that clearly violated God's law.

This act of disobedience marked the beginning of the end of Saul's reign. Had Saul kept God's commandments, the Lord would have established his "kingdom over Israel forever" (1 Samuel 13:13).

God laid out simple conditions for Saul's blessing, but Saul squandered his chance at greatness because he lacked the courage and wisdom to obey.

The Bible is chock-full of promises for blessing if you obey God's simple commands. When you live according to his Word, you put yourself in a perfect position to receive all he has for you and your family.

April 9

Credit Where Credit Is Due
NEHEMIAH

On October 2 the wall was finished—just fifty-two days after we had begun. When our enemies and the surrounding nations heard about it, they were frightened and humiliated. They realized this work had been done with the help of our God. Nehemiah 6:15-16

When asked how he remained humble and likeable in the face of so much success, the immensely talented and popular entertainer Jackie Gleason said, "The way I see it, God gave me the talent I have, so I have no reason to be arrogant about it."

Nothing keeps a man's feet on the ground like remembering that every blessing he has, including his own skills and talents, comes from the hand of a gracious and generous God. Nehemiah understood the importance of giving God the credit in all things. He put that understanding into practice as he oversaw the rebuilding of the walls around Jerusalem after the Babylonian captivity.

When Nehemiah learned that the city's walls lay in ruins, leaving the city vulnerable to attack, he sprang into action. He surveyed the problem, prayed about it, and came up with a plan to rebuild Jerusalem's defenses. It took an astonishingly short fifty-two days to reconstruct the walls.

Some residents of Jerusalem might have expected Nehemiah to indulge in a little self-congratulation, but he had no interest in such things. Nehemiah knew that the swiftness of the rebuilding project would be a warning to Jerusalem's enemies only if he made sure that God received the credit.

He was entirely happy to do so.

Nehemiah is a good example of a man who understood the importance of having a vision and working hard to see it become a reality. More importantly, he gave credit where it was due. There are no self-made men—only men who recognize the God who made them.

When you go out of your way to give God the credit for any good thing you accomplish, you give honor where it is due. What good thing is God doing in your life right now? Have you given him the credit?

April 10

Reporting What They Had Seen
PETER AND JOHN

They called the apostles back in and commanded them never again to speak or teach in the name of Jesus. But Peter and John replied, "Do you think God wants us to obey you rather than him? We cannot stop telling about everything we have seen and heard."   Acts 4:18-20

Years ago, people attending training sessions for the Billy Graham crusade in Detroit, Michigan, were asked the question, What is your greatest hindrance to witnessing? The respondents gave several reasons for their lack of personal evangelism, but the number one hindrance by far was fear. More than half of the people said that they were afraid of how others would react if they were to tell them about Jesus.

Peter and John, two of Jesus' closest disciples during his earthly ministry, didn't have that problem. They had heard exceptional preaching and teaching. They had seen impressive miracles—demons cast out, the sick healed, the dead raised, storms calmed. And, of course, they had seen the empty tomb and the resurrected Jesus.

They had heard Jesus say, "Go into all the world and preach the Good News to everyone" (Mark 16:15).

Seeing and hearing all these things had lit a fire of passion within them to tell others all about it.

Peter and John spoke respectfully, even humbly, to the religious authorities who had thrown them into prison for preaching the gospel. Because of what they had seen and heard, they continued to give a clear and unequivocal message: "No matter what you do to us, we *can't* stop preaching; however you threaten us, we *won't* stop preaching."

After what they had seen and heard, there was no way they *could* stop.

What keeps you from telling your friends, neighbors, coworkers, and family members about Jesus today?

One of the great privileges of following Jesus is the opportunity of telling those around you about him—what he has done for you and what he can do for them. Use the opportunities you are given to share your faith with those God has placed in your life.

April 11

Are You Reliable?
BARUCH

Jeremiah sent for Baruch son of Neriah, and as Jeremiah dictated all the prophecies that the LORD had given him, Baruch wrote them on a scroll. Then Jeremiah said to Baruch, "I am a prisoner here and unable to go to the Temple. So you go to the Temple on the next day of fasting, and read the messages from the LORD that I have had you write on this scroll."   Jeremiah 36:4-6

If automobile manufacturers want consumers to see one quality in all their products, it is reliability. They know that people won't buy that sexy sports car if it sits lifeless on its chassis when someone turns the key in the ignition.

People value dependability. They want dependable cars that always start, cell phone service that never drops a call, insurance that always covers them when they have an accident, and friends who never fail them in a time of need.

Baruch, a relatively obscure scribe who served the prophet Jeremiah, earned a reputation for being reliable. As Jeremiah's secretary, Baruch had to accurately record (and sometimes speak aloud) his mentor's prophecies, including those of the coming invasion and destruction of Jerusalem and the national captivity that would follow.

Baruch demonstrated his reliability by

—coming when Jeremiah called on him from inside a prison cell (see Jeremiah 36:4);
—accurately writing down Jeremiah's prophecies (see Jeremiah 36:4);
—reading the prophecies aloud as Jeremiah instructed him (see Jeremiah 36:8-9); and
—remaining committed to Jeremiah's message even in the face of serious opposition and setbacks (see Jeremiah 36:32).

Baruch was completely reliable for his friend Jeremiah and for God. He is an example of the kind of friend we all want and of the kind of friend, husband, father, and servant we should all be.

Are you reliable? Can people count on you to do what you say you will do? Do you make a habit of following through on what you start even when it becomes an unexpected burden? Solid relationships require the quality of reliability, just as much as a car needs gas or a plant needs light. Are you providing it?

April 12

Honest Self-Examination
THE PHARISEE AND THE TAX COLLECTOR

"The tax collector stood at a distance and dared not even lift his eyes to heaven as he prayed. Instead, he beat his chest in sorrow, saying, 'O God, be merciful to me, for I am a sinner.' I tell you, this sinner ... returned home justified before God. For those who exalt themselves will be humbled, and those who humble themselves will be exalted." Luke 18:13-14

Jim Fixx, author of the 1978 best seller *The Complete Book of Running* and a man who himself ran eighty miles a week, seemed a marvel of physical conditioning.

He died of a heart attack at age fifty-two while running alone on a Vermont road. Fixx's wife, Alice, later said that Jim had no idea that he had a heart problem because he refused to get regular checkups.

Just as you need regular physical checkups to accurately assess your physical condition, you need regular "spiritual checkups" to assess your relationship with God.

Jesus once told a story of two men who visited the Jerusalem Temple, one a self-righteous Pharisee who had no idea of his desperate spiritual sickness, and the other a common sinner who, after some painful soul-searching, found himself in desperate need of mercy and forgiveness.

"Common sinner" might not be the best description of the latter man, however. Jesus called him a tax collector, an agent of the Roman government, and a scoundrel well-known for ripping off his own people. As this man entered the Temple, his thoughts turned to the awful things he had done, the people he had defrauded, and the hatred and scorn he had earned from his despicable behavior.

He could only say, "O God, be merciful to me, for I am a sinner."

True confession before God means being honest enough to admit who you are and being humble enough to realize that you can never earn God's forgiveness. Such honesty allows you to speak the truth that God requires of you and gives you the humility of a contrite heart.

April 13

A True Friend
JONATHAN AND DAVID

Jonathan made a solemn pact with David, saying, "May the LORD destroy all your enemies!" And Jonathan made David reaffirm his vow of friendship again, for Jonathan loved David as he loved himself. 1 Samuel 20:16-17

What character qualities do you desire in a good friend? I'm not talking about just a buddy or an acquaintance, but the kind of friend who "sticks closer than a brother" (Proverbs 18:24). George Washington once said of true friendship, "Be courteous to all, but intimate with few, and let those few be well tried before you give them your confidence. True friendship is a plant of slow growth, and must undergo and withstand the shocks of adversity before it is entitled to the appellation."

David, the man God chose as Israel's second king, had that kind of friendship with Jonathan, the son of King Saul, whom David would one day replace on the throne.

After God told the prophet Samuel to anoint David as Saul's successor, the jealous King Saul made several attempts on David's life. Jonathan stood up for his friend, warning and encouraging him whenever his father sought to harm David. As Saul's eldest son, Jonathan would normally have ascended the throne upon his father's death, which makes his support of David all the more remarkable.

Who wouldn't value a friend like *that*?

Jonathan "loved David as he loved himself." As his close friend, he knew David's character and his heavenly calling. He sacrificed himself for his friend David, even though doing so cost him everything.

Could David ever have risen to become Israel's greatest king without Jonathan? David owed his friend so much that even years after Jonathan's untimely death, the king still honored his friend's memory by treating his children and descendants with respect.

Do you have a friend like Jonathan? More importantly, *are* you a friend like Jonathan?

To become a friend like Jonathan is costly, but who can calculate the rewards of such an enduring friendship? Who in your circle of friends might be a good candidate for a "Jonathan-David" friendship? What would it take for you to develop such a relationship?

April 14

Where to Go in Your Suffering
HEMAN

O LORD, God of my salvation, I cry out to you by day. I come to you at night. Now hear my prayer; listen to my cry. Psalm 88:1-2

As World War II ended and the horrors of the Nazi Holocaust became more evident, someone found a message scrawled on the cellar wall of a concentration camp in Cologne, Germany: "I believe in the sun when it isn't shining. I believe in love even when I don't feel it. I believe in God even when he's silent." This writer somehow found hope in the face of unspeakable suffering.

During difficult times, it is easy to wonder if God is listening to you, much less speaking. Samuel's Levite grandson Heman wondered the same thing.

Heman had a leading role in conducting the sacred service of rededicating the Temple during Hezekiah's reign. At another time in his life, when he wrote Psalm 88, he offered only words of suffering and doubt, not of praise and thanksgiving.

You won't be singing this psalm at your Sunday church service!

No one knows the life circumstances that motivated this psalm, but Heman clearly felt distraught and completely abandoned: "O LORD, I cry out to you. I will keep on pleading day by day. O LORD, why do you reject me? Why do you turn your face from me?" (Psalm 88:13-14).

Though Heman suffered tremendously, hope never completely left him. He wrote only one statement of comfort in his entire psalm, but what a powerful one it is! Heman declared that the Lord was the God of his salvation.

Where could Heman turn for comfort and salvation during those dark days? An unnamed prisoner found this same place in a German concentration camp. Like Heman, the prisoner somehow looked past his broken heart and sickly body, past what he perceived as absolute silence on God's part, and declared that the Lord alone remained the source of everything good.

The times will come when you will wonder where God has gone in the midst of your personal difficulties and suffering. You may find yourself questioning whether he hears you or has anything comforting to say to you. Even when God remains silent, he is still God, and he still loves you!

April 15

Moved by What He Saw
THE ROMAN OFFICER

When the Roman officer who stood facing him saw how he had died, he exclaimed, "This man truly was the Son of God!" MARK 15:39

Rembrandt's painting *The Three Crosses* depicts Jesus' crucifixion. If you look closely, you can see a solitary human figure almost lost in the shadows at the edge of the painting.

Experts on Baroque art believe that this solitary figure is a Rembrandt self-portrait. They think that he included it because he recognized the part his own sins played in nailing Jesus to the cross.

Nothing touches a man like recognizing his part in putting the Son of God to death. A nameless Roman officer stood by watching and listening as the Savior completed the most important act in human history, his sacrificial death on the cross.

This soldier had taken part in some of the most barbaric, brutal executions imaginable, but everything seemed different this time. He had overseen Jesus' crucifixion; he had stood by as the nails pierced Jesus' hands and feet. He listened as Jesus silently endured shouted angry cursing and jeering beyond what any common criminal might expect. He had heard Jesus cry out in agony and had felt the ground beneath his feet tremble at the very moment this Messiah breathed his last.

The Roman soldier, a man of war whose own acts of cruelty and violence had surely seared his conscience and hardened his heart, witnessed all this from the foot of the cross. He concluded, "This man truly was the Son of God!"

Although Scripture gives us no further account of this soldier's life, it is hard to imagine his life not changing for the good. He had seen, at close range, the man he identified as the Son of God willingly pouring himself out as an offering for sin. No wonder he openly declared what so few others dared to say.

What does Jesus being the true Son of God mean to you? Nothing changes, moves, motivates, or transforms us like this realization. When you understand and admit your part in his sacrificial death, you take the first step toward becoming the kind of man God made you to be.

April 16

Godly Enthusiasm
ZERUBBABEL

"This is what the LORD says to Zerubbabel: It is not by force nor by strength, but by my Spirit, says the LORD of Heaven's Armies. Nothing, not even a mighty mountain, will stand in Zerubbabel's way; it will become a level plain before him!"
ZECHARIAH 4:6-7

We all dread failure, and who among us hasn't experienced it?

Think of the last time you planned, prepared for, and were passionate about something that just didn't happen. Maybe a project at work began well but got stuck on your "things to do later" list. Perhaps you planned to make family Bible study a priority only to find that you couldn't fit it into everyone's busy schedules.

Zerubbabel, who led the first band of Jews back to Judah following the Babylonian captivity, probably felt a similar sense of failure. He oversaw the reconstruction of the Jerusalem Temple that the Babylonians had leveled seven decades earlier. Though the project began well enough, over a period of sixteen years, the people's enthusiasm for it waned, leaving an unfinished, useless shell of a building sitting on the Temple mount.

It's not hard to imagine that Zerubbabel felt a deep sense of discouragement over the stalled project. God had personally chosen him to oversee the task, yet the Temple just sat there, mired in the quicksand of a thousand excuses.

Into this disheartening situation came the prophet Zechariah, who carried a simple but vital message: "Don't depend on your own strength or that of the people to get the job done, Zerubbabel. Instead, depend on God and his ability to empower you for the task."

Zechariah's message couldn't have come at a better time. It renewed Zerubbabel's faith and passion for completing what he had started. With that renewed sense of enthusiasm, he united the people of Jerusalem and got them back to work.

God has the same message for you today. No worthy project is about human force or strength; it must be about his mighty Spirit. Trust that God will give you everything you need in order to complete the tasks he sets before you.

Everyone is disappointed now and then, but discouragement is a choice. Do you genuinely believe that God's Spirit holds the key to your success, or do you think that you or someone else does? Discouragement cannot hold you in its icy grip if you allow the Spirit of God to burn brightly in your soul.

April 17

A Deal Breaker
THE RICH YOUNG MAN

Jesus told him, "If you want to be perfect, go and sell all your possessions and give the money to the poor, and you will have treasure in heaven. Then come, follow me." But when the young man heard this, he went away sad, for he had many possessions. Matthew 19:21-22

Think of the last time you came face-to-face with a "deal breaker." It looked as if all systems were go in some area of your life, and then you discovered some detail or condition you found unacceptable. Take these, for example:

> You are offered a great job with better pay, but it requires more travel and being away from your wife and kids more than you would like.
>
> Your daughter asks you if she may go to the party of a friend you really like, but you find out there will be no adult supervision.
>
> Your neighbors ask you and your wife to "double" with them, but you find out that they plan to attend an event that includes heavy drinking.

Into every life, some deal breakers, situations with specific terms and conditions that require you to say no, must fall.

Sometimes God presents some deal breakers of his own. Jesus once met a wealthy young leader who had to decide if he could accept Jesus' conditions for discipleship. He was a good man who kept God's commandments, yet he was aware of an empty place in his life.

"What else must I do?" he asked Jesus, who genuinely loved the man and wanted to add him to his growing number of followers.

Jesus called him to do what his apostles had done, which was to leave everything behind and follow him.

That was the deal breaker!

This rich, powerful young man wanted to follow Jesus but not as much as he wanted to hang on to his stuff. The men who had given up everything to follow Jesus shook up the world for God's Kingdom, while this reluctant young man ended his life as a sad case of unfulfilled potential.

Never see Jesus' call to follow him unreservedly as a deal breaker. Consider it an opportunity to make a difference in the lives of those around you. What could keep you from following him completely? What would you struggle to give up?

April 18

What Pleases God
MOSES

Moses again pleaded, "Lord, please! Send anyone else." Then the LORD became angry with Moses. Exodus 4:13-14

Hall of Famer Connie Mack, who set the all-time record for wins by a Major League manager, once said, "I've seen boys on my baseball team go into a slump and never come out of it, and I've seen others snap right out and come back better than ever. I guess more players lick themselves than are ever licked by an opposing team."

As in sports, ordinary life presents you with opportunities to accomplish great things. What you succeed in doing often depends on your attitude.

When God first appeared to Moses in the desert and informed him that he would lead the people of Israel out of Egyptian captivity, Moses' attitude was negative and self-defeating. Most believers probably think that a miracle such as the one Moses saw that day—God's voice booming out of a bush that was burning but not burning up—would have them ready to move mountains. They think that they would just be asking, "When do we get started?"

Moses' response was quite different. Instead of focusing on the awesome task that lay before him, Moses narrowed his focus to his own human frailty. Humility is a good thing in God's eyes, but when humility turns into an "I can't" attitude, it can keep you from enjoying the good things that God has for you. If God says that you can do something, you can do it.

Moses found himself in desperate need of an attitude adjustment and a radical change of focus. Once he negotiated those things, he set off on an adventure in which he could accomplish everything God had arranged for him to do.

God loves it when you turn your focus toward him and away from your own fears, frailties, and doubts. True humility sees itself in relation to God's greatness. It doesn't say, "That's too big for me," but rather, "If God wants me to do it, then with his help, I can certainly do it." Is there anything too hard for you to accomplish today?

April 19

Loyalty
ITTAI

Ittai said to the king, "I vow by the LORD and by your own life that I will go wherever my lord the king goes, no matter what happens—whether it means life or death." 2 Samuel 15:21

A humorous cartoon depicts two men paddling a canoe down a remote river. As the man in the rear of the canoe looks back, he sees a dog following them in a miniature canoe of his own, grinning widely at the prospect of spending some time with his master. The caption reads, "Yes, I do own a dog . . . why do you ask?"

A good dog is a great example of unconditional love and loyalty. Most dogs will do anything for a chance to spend more time with their masters.

Such was the personal loyalty of an Old Testament man named Ittai. He was one of six hundred Gittites who were natives of the Philistine city of Gath. They had accompanied King David out of Jerusalem as he fled from his treasonous son Absalom. As David stopped at the outskirts of the city and allowed his loyal servants to pass ahead of him, he stopped Ittai and suggested that he return home to Jerusalem. After all, this wasn't Ittai's fight.

Ittai wouldn't hear of it. He vowed in the name of God that he, his men, and their families would follow the deposed king wherever he went, even if it meant their deaths.

Ittai knew the risks of following David, and he certainly knew what he was giving up. Following David meant trading the safety and comforts of Jerusalem for the uncertainties and dangers of the desert.

Still, he followed, and he remained loyal to the man he recognized as his rightful king.

In the end, David richly rewarded Ittai's loyalty. When David returned to the throne of Israel, he made Ittai commander of one-third of Israel's army (see 2 Samuel 18:2-5).

Do you consider personal loyalty an important trait? To whom do you owe your loyalty? From whom do you expect it? Though loyalty doesn't rank as high on some men's lists as it once did, God promises to bless your loyalty to Jesus Christ. In what ways can you demonstrate that loyalty this week?

April 20

Gratitude
THE DEMON-POSSESSED MAN

The man who had been freed from the demons begged to go with him. But Jesus sent him home, saying, "No, go back to your family, and tell them everything God has done for you." Luke 8:38-39

In their study of the effects of personal gratitude, Dr. Michael McCollough of Southern Methodist University and Dr. Robert Emmons of the University of California at Davis found that people who expressed daily gratitude reported higher levels of alertness, enthusiasm, determination, optimism, and energy, as well as lower levels of depression and stress. The study also showed that those who expressed gratitude were more likely to feel loved and to reciprocate acts of kindness.

Had they been able to study the life of a needy man in Jesus' day, their conclusions would have been confirmed. The Gospels contain a beautiful story about the effects of gratitude in the life of a troubled man whose life Jesus touched.

As Jesus and his disciples arrived at a shoreline town on the Sea of Galilee, they encountered a violent demon-possessed man who lived in a cemetery. He was naked, out of his mind, and completely alone. When he saw Jesus, he ran toward him and threw himself at his feet, shrieking and begging Jesus not to torture him. Jesus calmly and purposefully took control of the situation. He spoke to the man and delivered him from his life of torment.

As Jesus and the disciples prepared to reboard their boat, the deeply grateful man *begged* Jesus to allow him to travel with them. Jesus had other plans. He told the man to go home and tell his family and friends what had happened to him.

Though Jesus didn't allow the man to go with him, he still gratefully followed Jesus' instructions. When he returned to his home, he told everyone he knew that Jesus had set him free.

True gratitude does that to a man. When you think of everything that God has done for you, what other response is there but to follow him?

A grateful heart is the best witness to the goodness and power of God. Gratitude has an infectious quality, so count your blessings today and express your gratitude in your words and actions.

April 21

A Good Choice
KING AHAZ

Later, the LORD sent this message to King Ahaz: "Ask the LORD your God for a sign of confirmation, Ahaz. Make it as difficult as you want—as high as heaven or as deep as the place of the dead." But the king refused. "No," he said, "I will not test the LORD like that." Isaiah 7:10-12

Two hunters came across a bear so big that they dropped their rifles and ran. One of them climbed a tree while the other hid in a nearby cave. The bear was in no hurry to eat, so he sat down between the tree and the cave and patiently waited.

Suddenly, the hunter in the cave rushed out, almost ran into the waiting bear, then dashed back in again. When the same thing happened again, his companion frantically called out from the tree, "Are you crazy? Stay in the cave till he leaves!"

"I can't! There's another bear in there—and he's bigger than *this* one!"

Sometimes life presents true dilemmas as it forces choices between two equally difficult or even impossible alternatives. Ahaz, the ungodly king of Judah, once found himself in just such a situation.

Ahaz had brought the religious, political, and social climate in Judah to a point of crisis. And things would soon get much worse for Ahaz and Judah.

Assyria, the dominant world military power of the day, was on the move and posed a growing threat to Judah, Israel, and Syria. Israel and Syria were both Judah's enemies, but they tried to persuade Ahaz to join them in standing up to Assyria.

Ahaz knew that there was probably only one plan worse than siding with Assyria against Israel, and that was to side with Israel and Syria against Assyria. He seemed to have no other alternative other than one that he had no interest in—the *right* one. He simply couldn't get himself to trust God and allow him to take care of the situation (see Isaiah 7:11).

Rather than make the wise choice, Ahaz chose what he saw as the lesser of two evils. His choice to join forces with Assyria had disastrous consequences for the nation of Judah (see 2 Kings 16:7-9).

Life will sometimes present you with what seem to be equally difficult or impossible choices. When you can't figure out what to do next, the one right alternative is to trust God and allow him to get you through such troublesome times.

April 22

A Friend Indeed
AHIMELECH

David asked Ahimelech, "Do you have a spear or sword? The king's business was so urgent that I didn't even have time to grab a weapon!" "I only have the sword of Goliath the Philistine, whom you killed in the valley of Elah," the priest replied. "It is wrapped in a cloth behind the ephod. Take that if you want it, for there is nothing else here."   1 Samuel 21:8-9

Jackie Robinson, the first African-American to play Major League baseball, often endured brutal insults and racial slurs at every stadium he played in, even at his home field in Brooklyn. In one memorable game, Robinson, who played second base, committed an error, which gave Dodger fans all the ammunition they needed to ridicule him.

As Robinson stood in the infield, hearing words of hatred shouted from the stands, his close friend and teammate shortstop Pee Wee Reese made what was then an amazing gesture of friendship and loyalty. Reese walked over to Robinson, put his arm around his shoulder, and faced the crowd, which immediately grew quiet. Robinson later said that Reese's act of friendship had saved his career.

A true friend gives of himself, and even *sacrifices* himself, for the good of another when he is in need. Ahimelech, the chief priest in Nob, was this kind of friend to David.

When David arrived in Nob, he was a fugitive on the run from an angry and jealous King Saul. Ahimelech met David's immediate needs with food for him and his men and a weapon for battle. Ahimelech didn't know that Saul wanted to kill David. He only knew that his friend was in need of help.

His act of kindness and friendship came at a heavy price.

When Saul received word that Ahimelech had assisted David, he summoned the high priest into his presence, accused him of treason, and ordered his execution. Then he ordered the execution of Ahimelech's fellow priests and their families (see 1 Samuel 22:9-19).

Being a true friend in another's hour of need often means making personal sacrifices. Do you have that kind of friend? *Are* you that kind of friend?

April 23

Use Your Gifts
THE FAITHFUL SERVANT

"The servant to whom [the master] had entrusted the five bags of silver came forward with five more and said, 'Master, you gave me five bags of silver to invest, and I have earned five more.'" Matthew 25:20

You pay an investment broker to invest your hard-earned money and earn you more money. A good investment broker takes factors such as the amount of money you entrust to him and the amount of time you want to wait before getting some returns into account.

When you entrust your money to an investment broker, you don't just give it to him; you leave it in his care so that he will take wise steps to increase your wealth. You hire him as a steward of your money.

The Bible explains the importance of good stewardship and contains at least one story of a servant who took his role as a steward very seriously.

This servant's master entrusted him with five bags of silver, then left on a long trip, confident that his servant would use his abilities to maximize his profits (see Matthew 25:14-15). The servant didn't wait around but immediately invested the silver in a way that he knew would pay off handsomely. Upon his return, the master couldn't contain his delight at learning that his faithful servant had *doubled* his money.

Try earning that kind of return with a passbook savings account!

"Well done, my good and faithful servant," his master exclaimed. "You have been faithful in handling this small amount, so now I will give you many more responsibilities. Let's celebrate together!" (Matthew 25:21).

This wise and faithful servant received a handsome reward for his good stewardship because he understood that the wealth he had been using belonged to his master, not to himself.

One reason that God entrusts you with spiritual gifts is so that you can produce fruit for him. What spiritual gifts has he presented to you? How are you using the gifts God has entrusted to your care to give him a good return?

What makes it difficult for you to see yourself as a steward? What can you do to place this reality at the forefront of your thinking? As God's good and faithful servant, you have the privilege of using what he has given you for his good, for the good of those close to you, and for your own good.

April 24

Don't Make a Vow
JEPHTHAH

Jephthah made a vow to the LORD. He said, "If you give me victory over the Ammonites, I will give to the LORD whatever comes out of my house to meet me when I return in triumph. I will sacrifice it as a burnt offering."
JUDGES 11:30-31

As a wealthy businessman lay dying, his pastor visited him in his hospital room to speak of God's healing power. "Pastor," he wheezed, "if God heals me, I'll give the church a million dollars."

Several months later, the pastor visited the now miraculously recovered businessman in his office. After exchanging pleasantries, the pastor uneasily broached the subject of the businessman's vow.

"You know," the pastor said, "when you were dying in the hospital, you promised to give the church a million dollars if God healed you. We haven't received it yet."

The tycoon felt shocked. "Did I say that?" he asked. "I guess that shows how sick I really was!"

Jephthah—a skilled, courageous warrior who valiantly delivered the nation of Israel from the tyranny of the Ammonites—once made a vow that he had no business making. He gets high marks for following through on his word, but he utterly fails for the kind of word he uttered.

Jephthah promised God that he would make an altar sacrifice of whatever came out of his home to greet him following his victory. No doubt he thought a sheep or a goat would wander out of the door. As it turned out, his daughter was the first to leave the house to greet him.

Though we don't know for sure whether Jephthah sacrificed his daughter as a burnt offering (the text seems to suggest that she was forced to live as a virgin apart from her family for the rest of her life), his foolish vow certainly caused him trouble.

The Bible contains hundreds of God's conditional promises of blessing. Jephthah went terribly wrong when he tried to set *his* conditions for blessing rather than approaching God in faith to ask him what offering he wanted.

Have you ever felt that you needed to offer God something to receive his promised blessings? God is passionately interested in blessing you with one condition: Go to him and ask in faith. You can't buy what God already wants to give you!

April 25

The Gift of Time
ETHAN

Remember how short my life is, how empty and futile this human existence! No one can live forever; all will die. No one can escape the power of the grave.
PSALM 89:47-48

"Life's Paces," a poem by Henry Twells, makes several observations about the passage of a man's days on earth:

> *When as a child I laughed and wept, time crept.*
> *When as a youth I waxed more bold, time strolled.*
> *When I became a fullgrown man, time RAN.*
> *When older I still daily grew, time FLEW.*
> *Soon I shall find, in passing on, time gone.*
> *O Christ! wilt Thou have saved me then? Amen.*

Perhaps the essence of godly wisdom is realizing that we are mortal and that God numbers our days. Our time on earth will eventually come to an end.

Ethan, a Levite and court musician, made a similar observation in his own day. Acknowledging that no one had yet figured out how to live forever, he wrote, "No one can escape the power of the grave" (Psalm 89:48).

Ethan was obviously in touch with his own mortality; he was also in touch with his own *immortality:* "I will sing of the LORD's unfailing love forever!" (Psalm 89:1).

Ethan grasped the truth that each day he lived on earth was a gift from God. He also knew that the grave would not be his end. He knew how to put his time on earth to the best use by openly praising the God whose love never failed him. Everyone around him heard of God's goodness: "Young and old will hear of your faithfulness" (Psalm 89:1).

The American poet Carl Sandburg wrote, "Time is the coin of your life. It is the only coin you have, and only you can determine how it will be spent."

How are you spending the time God has given you?

God has given you the privilege of living each moment of your life with the knowledge that time is a gift and an opportunity. It's a gift to enjoy and an opportunity to make a difference in the lives—and the eternities—of those around you.

April 26

Sage Advice
JETHRO AND MOSES

When Moses' father-in-law saw all that Moses was doing for the people, he asked, "What are you really accomplishing here? Why are you trying to do all this alone while everyone stands around you from morning till evening?" EXODUS 18:14

From its inception in 1946 until its launch in 1990, the Hubble Space Telescope was beset with delays, budget problems, and design flaws. An official who prepared a presentation on the lessons of Hubble's problems placed the following at the top of his list: "In naming your mission, never use a word that rhymes with trouble."

Someone once said, "A wise man learns from the mistakes of others. Nobody lives long enough to make them all himself."

Jethro, Moses' father-in-law, wanted to prevent Moses from making enough mistakes to bury the newborn nation of Israel. Like so many zealous leaders, Moses filled his plate to overflowing. He often worked from dawn till dusk, just listening to and settling his people's legal disputes.

Into this state of affairs came Jethro, who told Moses, "This is not good! You're going to wear yourself out—and the people, too. This job is too heavy a burden for you to handle all by yourself" (Exodus 18:17-18). Jethro then offered Moses some sage advice: Slow down and let someone else do part of the work!

As a priest of Midian and a successful businessman, Jethro had a lot of wisdom to share. Very likely, in his long-past youthful zeal, Jethro had learned the value of seeking help when his load became too heavy.

Jethro advised Moses to select men who loved and feared God as arbiters and leaders of the people. To qualify, they had to demonstrate high character and integrity in every area of their personal lives. Moses was more than happy to follow his father-in-law's advice.

Sometimes God allows you to earn some wisdom through your mistakes. When he does that, a time may come when you can impart some of those hard-earned smarts. By tapping into your own experience, you can encourage others to avoid the things you already know won't work.

April 27

Watch, Listen, and Learn
DANIEL

"Look at this great city of Babylon! By my own mighty power, I have built this beautiful city as my royal residence to display my majestic splendor."
DANIEL 4:30

Study after study indicates that people learn through various kinds of observation. One study presented a remarkably detailed breakdown of how much we learn through our different senses:

> One percent of what we know comes through taste; 1.5 percent through smell; 1.5 percent through touch; 3.5 percent through smell; 11 percent through hearing; and 83 percent through sight.

Nebuchadnezzar, the prideful king of Babylon, failed to learn from what he observed through his eyes, so he had to learn his lesson the hard way, through taste and smell.

Nebuchadnezzar had a frightening dream that he asked the prophet Daniel to interpret. Daniel told him the dream meant that the king's pride would result in a severe bout of divine discipline. He told the king that he could avoid the chastening if he would humble himself before the God of heaven. Daniel begged the king to give up his pride so that God could relent.

The king thanked Daniel for his help, but what he heard didn't translate into a changed heart or life. That happened only after Nebuchadnezzar took some hard blows from God's hand.

A full year after seeing and hearing of God's greatness—and even paying lip service to God—Nebuchadnezzar proudly looked out at the great city of Babylon and sang his own praises. God had given Nebuchadnezzar an opportunity to humble himself the easy way, but he refused. Now God would teach him the hard way.

God immediately announced that Nebuchadnezzar would lose his kingdom and be sent out to live like a wild animal. He spent some time smelling and tasting the grass until he humbled himself and listened to the word of the Lord. Were Nebuchadnezzar alive today, he might give anyone who cared to listen this simple advice: Watch, listen, and learn!

Are you willing to watch, listen, and learn when God instructs you? Are you teachable? When God speaks to you, take it to heart.

April 28

Created for a Purpose
ADAM

God created human beings in his own image. In the image of God he created them; male and female he created them. Genesis 1:27

In February 1980, the U.S. Olympic hockey team earned the gold medal at Lake Placid, New York, with a 4-2 win over Finland. Not many people remember that game, however. A semifinal game three days earlier still holds the limelight.

In one of the greatest upsets in sports history, the young Americans defeated a veteran Soviet team that most everyone saw as unbeatable. Before his team's game against the Soviet Union, U.S. coach Herb Brooks told his players, "You are born to be a player. You are meant to be here at this time. This is your moment."

Nothing defines and motivates a man like a sense of purpose and a reason for being.

Adam never questioned his purpose in life. He had an innate sense that the Lord had put him on earth for one reason: to enjoy fellowship with God. Adam belonged to God, and God belonged to Adam.

Adam reveled in the wonders of God's creation. He tended the Garden of Eden, named all the animals that lived there, and began to care for the earth around him.

Adam also reveled in God's presence.

God created Adam "in his own image" so that he could occupy a place of special honor and privilege. Out of all the creatures God had created, Adam alone could intentionally respond to God in obedience and love and relate to him as his heavenly Father.

Sadly, Adam's sin threw all creation into chaos and spoiled that perfect relationship between the Creator and his creatures. The "Second Adam," Jesus Christ, came to earth to give us the opportunity to enjoy the kind of fellowship Adam had originally enjoyed with God (see 1 Corinthians 15:45-49).

Do you ever wonder why God created you and put you where you are? God created you with a special purpose in mind: to enjoy a relationship with him in which you choose to love and obey him and enjoy his presence daily.

April 29

In Suffering
JESUS

[Jesus] went on a little farther and fell to the ground. He prayed that, if it were possible, the awful hour awaiting him might pass him by. "Abba, Father," he cried out, "everything is possible for you. Please take this cup of suffering away from me. Yet I want your will to be done, not mine."   Mark 14:35-36

How do you typically respond when you face difficult circumstances? What do you do when your marriage is in trouble or you're suffering serious physical difficulties? How do you grieve the loss of a loved one?

A man facing all of the above had a difficult time reconciling the idea of a loving God with everything that was happening to him. "I didn't sign up for this!" he said in exasperation.

If you're honest, you would probably admit that you would prefer a life without suffering and that you would do anything you could to avoid it. However, as Augustine once said, "God had one Son on earth without sin, but never one without suffering."

Jesus faced suffering that no human being had ever experienced. He had before him a terrible death on a cross and the prospect of becoming sin so that we could inherit God's righteousness.

Jesus knew that all those things were coming, and he begged his Father to take away the cup from which he was about to drink. But even as Jesus prayed for relief, he remained completely and single-mindedly submitted to his Father's will.

Though he suffered anguish that we can't imagine, at the moment of truth, he was willing to go through with the appointment God had made for him. "I want your will to be done, not mine," he prayed.

Jesus maintained his attitude of humble submission that night because he had spent his entire life on earth yielding himself daily to his Father's will.

Nothing tests your submission to God's will and plans like adversity. You will pass that test when you maintain an attitude of continual submission to God, even when times are easy and seem good.

April 30

Inner Conflict
PAUL

I know that nothing good lives in me, that is, in my sinful nature. I want to do what is right, but I can't. I want to do what is good, but I don't. I don't want to do what is wrong, but I do it anyway.   Romans 7:18-19

The recent ESPN miniseries *The Bronx Is Burning* tells the story of the 1977 New York Yankees, a team whose inner turmoil threatened to tear them apart before reaching their full potential.

Filled with strong personalities such as Reggie Jackson, Thurman Munson, manager Billy Martin, and owner George Steinbrenner, the Yankees nearly imploded on several occasions. In the end, however, their superior talent won them the 1977 World Series.

Like the 1977 Yankees, we face our own inner conflicts between our desires to live godly lives and our inability to do so in our own strength. The apostle Paul understood that conflict well.

As a spiritual man, Paul loved God and desired to follow the law of God perfectly. As a fleshly man prone to sin, Paul found himself unable to always do what he knew was right. He was equally unable to always avoid doing what he knew was wrong.

Can you identify?

In his letter to the Romans, Paul revealed his genuine conflict over his desire to obey God perfectly and his inability to do so. He knew that he hadn't achieved sinless perfection. He was keenly aware of his own imperfections and wanted more than anything to have victory over sin.

Paul knew what we need to know: We are sinners who must daily tap into God's grace and forgiveness.

When you finally stand in Jesus' presence, you will have absolute and eternal victory over sin. Until then, you will find consistent success in avoiding sin only as you walk daily in the power of the Holy Spirit.

May 1

On Track
ACHAN

The LORD said to Joshua, "Get up! Why are you lying on your face like this? Israel has sinned and broken my covenant! They have stolen some of the things that I commanded must be set apart for me."   Joshua 7:10-11

In December 2004, the world looked on in horror at news reports of a giant tsunami. It was triggered by a powerful earthquake in the Indian Ocean off the northwest coast of Sumatra, Indonesia. The tsunami devastated the coastal areas of the region and killed nearly three hundred thousand people. The whole world felt its effects.

Though most observers found it incredible that a relatively localized underwater earthquake could cause such destruction and death, scientists had known for decades that such a catastrophe was not only possible but probably inevitable. As soon as a mountainous underwater shelf gave way and crashed to the ocean bottom, havoc would follow on the surface.

This tragic event dramatically illustrates the terrible ripple effect of sin. We must stay on track with the Lord lest some mountainous part of our lives gives way and devastates others. The story of Achan illustrates such a tsunami of sin.

God gave crystal-clear instructions for the invasion of Jericho. He promised to give the Israelites a miraculous, crushing victory over the city. In return, he told the people to put aside for him *all* the gold, silver, and other valuables they would seize during their raid.

Achan paid no attention to God's instructions. He secretly kept some choice loot for himself, and just like that, a mountainous shelf broke loose and crashed into the ocean floor. A spiritual tsunami immediately followed.

Israel should easily have conquered the little hamlet of Ai, their next target, but the Hebrew attack ended in humiliating defeat. Achan's sin had removed God's hand of blessing from the Israelite army, and three dozen innocent soldiers died in the resulting upheaval.

Even sin that you might regard as secret affects you and those closest to you, including your family. When you feel tempted to stray, remember that those you love most depend on you to stay on track.

Where do you most feel the tug to stray? Where in your life does it feel toughest right now to stay on track? Take these concerns specifically to God in prayer, and enlist the help of a faithful friend to encourage you to stay the course.

May 2

A Passion for Justice
ELIJAH

Elijah answered, "I have come because you have sold yourself to what is evil in the LORD's sight."   1 Kings 21:20

Standing before Judge Horace Gray, who would one day serve on the United States Supreme Court, a man who had escaped conviction on a technicality listened as Gray told him, "I know that you are guilty and you know it, and I wish you to remember that one day you will stand before a better and wiser Judge, and that there you will be dealt with according to justice and not according to law."

Horace Gray achieved greatness as a judge because he had a passion for justice. Gray also understood that ultimate justice remained in God's hands. The prophet Elijah also had that kind of passion; it was part of what made him one of the Bible's true heroes of faith.

Elijah courageously and steadfastly pronounced judgment on Ahab, the king of Israel, for conspiring with his wife Jezebel to have an innocent man named Naboth stoned to death on trumped-up charges of blasphemy. Ahab wanted Naboth's family vineyard for himself, and he would stop at nothing to get it. In his mind, being king entitled him to whatever he wanted, so he misused his position of authority to take it.

When God informed Elijah of what had happened, the prophet grew so angry and indignant that he confronted Ahab face-to-face as the king stood in the very vineyard that he had acquired by committing murder. There Elijah courageously pronounced God's judgment on Ahab for concocting such an evil scheme.

Elijah was a good man with a passionate sense of commitment to God's justice. That included standing up on behalf of those who couldn't stand up for themselves. When he saw such a terrible wrong committed against an innocent man, he could not stand by and do nothing.

Are you willing to stand up for those who can't stand up for themselves? God blesses those who act from a sense of true justice. The world needs more Elijahs!

May 3

The Importance of Insight
DANIEL

As I, Daniel, was trying to understand the meaning of this vision, someone who looked like a man stood in front of me. And I heard a human voice calling out from the Ulai River, "Gabriel, tell this man the meaning of his vision."
DANIEL 8:15-16

A college student faced with a difficult two-part economics exam went to great lengths to understand all the terminology and theories the professor had taught that semester. A few days after taking the exam, he found out that he had failed it.

The student had a perfect score on the first section, which consisted of multiple choice and true/false questions. Unfortunately, he bombed on the second, which asked him to apply what he had learned to a real-world situation.

His experience illustrates that though head knowledge is fine, it is of little value without the deeper understanding required to apply that knowledge to real life. The same holds true in the spiritual realm.

God gave Daniel a mysterious vision concerning future events, but at first he didn't let the prophet understand its meaning. Daniel realized that a vision without a satisfying interpretation would do him no good. He needed to know the vision's meaning.

As Daniel struggled to decipher the vision, an angel named Gabriel appeared to him and explained it. Daniel finally understood the puzzling vision but only because he had set his heart on grasping its strange and terrifying images. Daniel genuinely wanted insight into the vision, so God freely gave it to him, but not all at once.

Knowledge of God's Word is good, but such knowledge doesn't have life-changing impact without the practical understanding needed to apply it. Fortunately, God promises to give understanding to *anyone* who earnestly seeks it, just as Daniel the prophet did.

How often do you study the Bible so that you can know what it takes to be a godly man, husband, father, and employee? Do you seek the wisdom and understanding you need to apply God's Word to every area of your life? What is God saying to you today?

May 4

Are You Worthy?
PAUL

I am the least of all the apostles. In fact, I'm not even worthy to be called an apostle after the way I persecuted God's church. But whatever I am now, it is all because God poured out his special favor on me. 1 Corinthians 15:9-10

This country has only one medical national honor society: Alpha Omega Alpha Honor Medical Society, founded in 1901. It is sometimes called the "Phi Beta Kappa" of medical societies. Its mission is to recognize and enhance outstanding professionalism and leadership in the medical field and academic excellence and service within medical schools. Its name is derived from the initials of a Greek motto: "Worthy to serve the suffering."

The Bible includes several examples of men who, humanly speaking, didn't seem worthy to serve God. In his grace and mercy, God nonetheless *called* them, enabled them to serve, and *declared them worthy.*

Such was the case with the apostle Paul.

In his many epistles, Paul often referred to his own checkered past, which included violent persecution of those he would later call his brothers and sisters (see 1 Timothy 1:13). Paul acknowledged that it was only "because God poured out his special favor" on him that he was fit to serve the Kingdom of God by preaching in the name of Jesus Christ.

Why did God make Paul worthy to serve? It wasn't because of the man's talent or background or because he felt sorry for him. It was due entirely to God's grace, generosity, and goodness. The Lord took a man that believers did their best to avoid and transformed him into the world's best-known ambassador for Jesus Christ.

Do you consider yourself worthy to serve?

Your worthiness to serve God doesn't come from any special talents, abilities, or credentials you have. God made you worthy to serve him when he gave you his Holy Spirit as your source of love and power.

May 5

An Unshakable Foundation
ABRAHAM

Abram believed the LORD, and the LORD counted him as righteous because of his faith. Genesis 15:6

If you were to ask ten churchgoing men how to please God, you might get ten different answers, much like the following:

—Read the Bible and pray more.
—Do more to bring family, neighbors, and friends to Christ.
—Be more attentive to your wife and kids.
—Be honest in all business dealings.
—Give more money to your church and missions.

No doubt each of these is an important priority for any man of faith. All of them please God. But to have the impact God intends, they must join forces with faith. Faith is foundational to everything you want to do.

The Bible extols Abraham as a man of incredible faith. Though far from perfect, he habitually took God at his word and believed that he would do just what he promised.

Because of Abraham's faith, God made him the father of many great nations. Through Israel, God promised to bless the entire world with the coming of the Messiah, Jesus Christ. On a more personal level, God blessed Abraham by calling him a man in good standing with his Creator.

God made Abraham some big promises, and Abraham had no way of knowing *how* he would keep them. Through his deep and abiding faith, Abram (or Abraham in later years) remained more focused on God's nature than on how he would bring things about. He simply believed that he served a faithful and true God who *always* did what he promised to do.

That's the kind of faith God loves to see operative in your life. It's the kind of faith you need as the foundation for everything you do.

You please God most not just by doing things that the Bible instructs you to do, but by doing them out of a joyful heart of faith. Such a heart knows that God is who he says he is and that he rewards those who believe him when he says, "I will."

May 6

Standing In for Those Who Can't Stand
THE FOUR FRIENDS

While he was preaching God's word to them, four men arrived carrying a
paralyzed man on a mat. They couldn't bring him to Jesus because of the crowd, so
they dug a hole through the roof above his head. Then they lowered the man on his
mat, right down in front of Jesus.   Mark 2:2-4

Mother Teresa, the Nobel Prize–winning nun who spent her life assisting
the desperately poor in Calcutta, India, once said, "It is a kingly act to assist
the fallen."

Mother Teresa did more than her share of "kingly acts" in her eighty-seven
years of life on earth. She became famous worldwide as an advocate for the
desperately poor and helpless, and she inspired countless others to give of
themselves in service to God and humanity.

Four unnamed men in the second chapter of Mark's Gospel demonstrated
this kind of compassion. They went to extraordinary lengths to assist the
fallen and thus manifested the kind of compassion God asks us to extend to
the world around us.

The Bible doesn't tell us what these men might have said to one another or
to the people around them. We can only imagine their thoughts as they tore a
hole in a roof and lowered their friend down on a mat to rest directly in front
of Jesus.

Sometimes a man's words count a great deal less than what he does on
behalf of another. These four men didn't ask Jesus for anything for themselves. Rather, they selflessly did something extraordinary to bring a needy
friend before Jesus, who gladly responded to their faith and compassion.
These men acted out of a willingness to stand for someone who couldn't stand
for himself.

Who in your world needs you to perform the same kind of act on his or
her behalf? Genuine faith doesn't just think kind thoughts or feel warm emotions toward someone in need; it acts out of faithfulness to God.

You can perform no greater act of compassion than to stand for someone who can't stand
for himself or herself. Who in your life needs you to stand in the gap for them today?
Perhaps it is someone living under your own roof.

May 7

A Burden Becomes a Calling
GIDEON

"Sir," Gideon replied, "if the LORD is with us, why has all this happened to us? And where are all the miracles our ancestors told us about? Didn't they say, 'The LORD brought us up out of Egypt'? But now the LORD has abandoned us and handed us over to the Midianites." Judges 6:13

What do people like William Wilberforce, Martin Luther King Jr., and Desmond Tutu have in common? They were all burdened enough about some injustice to get up off their knees and do something about it.

Wilberforce took action against his nation's abominable slave trade, King fought the lack of civil rights for African-Americans, and Tutu worked hard to relieve the suffering he witnessed in South Africa.

The Old Testament prophet and judge Gideon would have felt very much at home in their company.

In Gideon's day, the people of Israel had drifted so far from God that he gave them over to the oppression of the Midianites, who mistreated and persecuted the helpless Hebrew population. As you might expect, that didn't sit well with Gideon.

One day, Gideon had an encounter with one of God's angels—really, with God himself—as he wondered aloud where all of God's miraculous works had gone. God had acted powerfully in the past, but how and when would he free his people from their current oppressors?

Funny you should ask, Gideon!

God had a specific plan in mind for Gideon, but before he divulged it, he put within Gideon a burden for his oppressed people. At first, Gideon questioned his ability to take on such a huge task, but in the end, he brilliantly led his people to throw off the Midianites' yoke of oppression.

That kind of thing often happens when someone's burden becomes their calling.

When you begin praying for God to send someone to accomplish something significant for his Kingdom—say, introducing a neighbor or coworker to Jesus—be ready for him to call you to play a part yourself. God often puts those burdens within you so that you will feel moved to step out and speak up.

May 8

A Passionate Life
DAVID

David danced before the LORD with all his might, wearing a priestly garment. So David and all the people of Israel brought up the Ark of the LORD with shouts of joy and the blowing of rams' horns. 2 Samuel 6:14-15

Though a man can hide some things deep within his soul, passion isn't one of them.

When a man passionately loves his wife, it shows in how he speaks *to* her, talks *about* her, and treats her. When he feels passionate about his children, he gives everything he has for them. When he approaches his work with passion, he produces a steady stream of excellence.

When he feels passionate about God, everyone around him sees a heavenly flame in his eyes.

David was a man who expressed his passion. Though at times his passion got the better of him, everyone knew that he put his whole heart, mind, and body into everything he did.

Soon after David ascended the throne of Judah, he demonstrated his passion for God and his people. He immediately worked to reunite the battered kingdom of Israel that was almost torn apart by Saul's godless leadership. He went to extraordinary efforts to bring the Ark of the Lord to its rightful place in Jerusalem, and as the Ark made its way into the city, David couldn't contain his enthusiasm. He began dancing before the Lord "with all his might." Most observers who saw his passion cheered him on.

David's wife Michal also saw David's display of unbridled passion, but she ridiculed him for it and questioned his motives.

David didn't care. He knew that he acted out of deep love for the Lord, and he had no reservations about appearing a little foolish in his devotion to God. He intended to worship God with all his heart, soul, mind, and strength.

Most of us are probably more like Michal than like David. We need to ask ourselves what kind of passion we have for God.

Serve, love, fear, and worship God with all the passion you can muster. So what if someone thinks you're overdoing it? Who cares if someone makes fun of you? The only important audience is God.

May 9

Watch and Pray
JESUS AND PETER

[Jesus] returned and found the disciples asleep. He said to Peter, "Simon, are you asleep? Couldn't you watch with me even one hour? Keep watch and pray, so that you will not give in to temptation. For the spirit is willing, but the body is weak."
MARK 14:37-38

In his younger days of working as a door-to-door salesman, Alfred C. Fuller, founder of the Fuller Brush Company, called upon a woman who invited him into her home with the words, "Lead me not into temptation." Without missing a beat, Fuller replied, "Madam, I am not leading you into temptation but delivering you from evil!"

He sold the woman three brushes that day.

Peter, James, and John—Jesus' three closest friends during his earthly ministry—once spent a night in the devil's crosshairs. They were in very real danger of giving in to the worst temptation—and they didn't even know it.

Jesus invited these three to wait with him in the garden of Gethsemane. He instructed them to keep watch and pray. "So that you will not give in to temptation," he said. "For the spirit is willing, but the body is weak."

Jesus knew these three men intimately, so he knew their weaknesses. He also knew that they were about to endure a terrible morning that would fulfill centuries-old prophecies concerning his arrest, trial, and death.

Jesus had told his disciples earlier that evening that they would all abandon him in his hour of need. Peter proudly proclaimed that he would never leave Jesus' side no matter what happened.

As Jesus prayed in the garden that night, Peter fell fast asleep. The man who felt so sure that he would stand up to whatever came his way neglected to keep watch and pray, thus leaving himself defenseless against the coming temptation.

Peter wanted more than anything to stand by Jesus that evening, but at the moment of truth, the big fisherman failed Jesus miserably because he relied on his own strength and courage. He forgot that real power comes from watching and praying as Jesus instructed.

No one can completely avoid temptations to sin, but when you remain prayerfully on the alert for those temptations, God can give you the strength and wisdom you need to enjoy victory even when the devil throws his worst at you.

May 10

A Cure for Disappointment
TWO MEN OF EMMAUS

They said to each other, "Didn't our hearts burn within us as he talked with us on the road and explained the Scriptures to us?" LUKE 24:32

Someone once anonymously wrote about the ultimate source of encouragement: "If I look at myself, I am depressed. If I look at those around me, I am often disappointed. If I look at my circumstances, I am discouraged. But if I look at Jesus, I am constantly, consistently, and eternally fulfilled!"

Depressed. Disappointed. Discouraged. Those words only begin to describe how Jesus' disciples felt during those days after he died on the cross. They had put so much hope in this Man, believing him to be the long-awaited Messiah that God had promised centuries before.

Now he was gone, and with him went all hope of better things.

Luke records an account of two despondent disciples. These men lived in Emmaus, a town about seven miles from Jerusalem, where their hopes for a better life had vanished three days earlier. Into this pit of despair stepped Jesus.

The men didn't instantly recognize Jesus as he walked next to them on their trek back to Emmaus. Yet they felt mesmerized by his discourse about what had happened and what it all meant.

At just the right moment, Jesus revealed himself to them. When he disappeared from their sight, he took with him all the pain, despair, and disappointment that had been their constant companions over the previous three days.

As long as these two men spent their days looking at themselves, at others, and at their circumstances, they felt nothing but hopelessness. When they looked at Jesus—the resurrected, once-dead-but-now-alive Jesus—they remembered his promises, and hope that he really was the One they had been hoping for flamed anew.

Their disappointment, despair, and discouragement vanished for good, for despite whatever heartaches lay ahead for them, *they had seen Jesus*!

How do you handle discouragement? When you face situations that leave you feeling depressed, disappointed, and discouraged, look to Jesus. He left the glories of heaven to live on earth, die on a cross, and rise from the grave so that you could enjoy the abundant life he came to bring you.

May 11

A Shining Lamp
STEPHEN

The Jewish leaders were infuriated by Stephen's accusation, and they shook their fists at him in rage. But Stephen, full of the Holy Spirit, gazed steadily into heaven and saw the glory of God, and he saw Jesus standing in the place of honor at God's right hand. Acts 7:54-55

During the Nazi occupation of Denmark, King Christian X was horrified to see a Nazi flag flying over a Danish public building. He immediately called the German commandant and demanded that the flag be taken down at once. The commandant refused.

"Then a soldier will go and take it down!" promised the king.

"He will be shot," the commandant threatened.

"I think not," the king replied, "for I shall be the soldier."

Within minutes the Nazis took the flag down.

Nothing prompts change like a man's courage in the face of potential personal loss. Stephen had that kind of courage.

Stephen was an outspoken believer at a time when being a Christian could cost a man everything, including his life. That's exactly what happened to Stephen, whom Jewish religious leaders stoned to death for his "blasphemy."

Though the religious leaders in Jerusalem hoped that persecuting Christians would put a stop to this new religious movement, exactly the opposite happened. Because Stephen willingly died for what he believed in, he contributed greatly to the spread of the gospel message. Stephen's violent death touched off a firestorm of brutal persecution against the first-generation believers, many of whom fled Jerusalem for the surrounding areas, taking the Good News with them.

But there was more.

At the scene of Stephen's murder stood a young Pharisee named Saul— the same Saul that God miraculously converted, renamed Paul, and sent to preach to the non-Jewish world. Stephen's courage and faith in the face of death apparently made a lasting impression on Paul, whose bold preaching would change the world forever (see Acts 22:19-20).

Someone once said, "I would not give much for your religion unless it can be seen. Lamps do not talk, but they do shine." Is your lamp shining today?

May 12

True Kindness
BOAZ

Boaz went over and said to Ruth, "Listen, my daughter. Stay right here with us when you gather grain; don't go to any other fields. Stay right behind the young women working in my field." Ruth 2:8

An exceptionally beautiful woman, the mother of British writer W. Somerset Maugham had married an exceptionally homely man. When a family friend asked her why she picked such an ugly husband, she replied, "He has never once hurt my feelings."

Kindness in word and deed is a powerful equalizer!

Boaz, a wealthy and influential farmer in Bethlehem, was consistently kind and compassionate.

"The LORD be with you!" Boaz greeted his harvesters in the morning. "The LORD bless you!" the workers answered back (Ruth 2:4). Goodwill flowed between Boaz and his servants. They had seen for themselves that he cared about others and extended kindness and respect to everyone he met.

The generosity and kindness of Boaz came into play when he asked about Ruth, a transplanted Moabite widow who had come to his field to gather bits of grain left behind by his harvesters.

When Boaz heard Ruth's story, he was moved with compassion. He told her not to glean from anyone else's field but to stay on his property where he could guarantee her personal safety and give her enough water to drink. He invited Ruth to eat with him (see Ruth 2:14) and commanded his reapers to leave some bundles of grain for her to find (see Ruth 2:15-16).

Do you know anyone like Boaz? If so, what makes him special? How do people respond to him? How can you be more like him?

Do the people closest to you think of you as a kind person? What can you do today to extend to others the same kindness that God has extended to you? Even if you don't believe that you have much to offer others, keep in mind that simple kindness is a great equalizer.

May 13

Wise and Humble Leadership
KING UZZIAH

When he had become powerful, he also became proud, which led to his downfall.
He sinned against the LORD his God by entering the sanctuary of the LORD's
Temple and personally burning incense on the incense altar.
2 CHRONICLES 26:16

In a speech to the Corps of Cadets at the U.S. Military Academy, General
H. Norman Schwarzkopf said, "I've met a lot of leaders in the Army who
were very competent—but they didn't have character. And for every job
they did well, they sought reward in the form of promotions, in the form of
awards and decorations, in the form of getting ahead at the expense of someone else, in the form of another piece of paper that awarded them another
degree—a sure road to the top. You see, these were competent people, but
they lacked character."

It takes a man of true humility to keep his feet on the ground over the
long haul when he is given power or authority over others.

Uzziah, Judah's tenth king, was not such a man.

Uzziah ascended to the throne at age sixteen. He led his people to several
military victories and restored his nation to almost unprecedented levels of
prosperity and power.

Uzziah's long and sometimes distinguished reign came to an unfortunate
end because of his arrogant thirst for power. One day he expressed his arrogance by entering the sanctuary of the holy Temple and burning incense on
the altar, which was a job God had reserved for his priests.

No doubt Uzziah was a strong and able leader. Unfortunately, he failed to
understand and accept his place in God's plan for the nation of Judah. Had
Uzziah remained humble and led as God had called him to do, he might have
become one of the nation's greatest kings. Rather than end his career as magnificently as it had begun, he spent his later years shut away from people in a
leper colony.

**Do you understand your place in the big picture? How would you describe it? What kind of
leader are you in your home, workplace, or church? As a man of God, you are called to be
a leader who understands your place in the universe. That means leading with humility.**

May 14

Know Your Identity
SAMUEL

All the elders of Israel met at Ramah to discuss the matter with Samuel.... They told him,... "Give us a king to judge us like all the other nations have."
1 SAMUEL 8:4-5

In his book *The Mask behind the Mask: A Life of Peter Sellers,* biographer Peter Evans reports that the comedic actor played so many roles that he sometimes lost his own identity. When a fan approached Sellers one day and asked him, "Are you Peter Sellers?" he tersely answered, "Not today," and walked on.

During the time of Samuel, Israel's high-ranking political and religious leaders somehow lost their identities.

God wanted Israel to be different from any other kingdom on earth, and he wanted his chosen leaders to instruct the people in his ways. Still, Israel's elders clamored for Samuel to give them a human king so that they could fit in with the pagan nations around them.

When God responded to Samuel's announcement that the elders of Israel wanted a king, he sounded like a brokenhearted father: "It is me they are rejecting, not you. They don't want me to be their king any longer. . . . Do as they ask, but solemnly warn them about the way a king will reign over them" (1 Samuel 8:7-9).

Samuel did as God had told him. He warned the people of the consequences of rejecting their true King, but it made no difference. Israel's elders had convinced the people that they needed a human king. Consequently, Israel became "like all the other nations," relying on a flesh-and-blood king rather than on the King of kings.

When Israel's elders looked at the nations around them, they lost sight of their own identity. They forgot that God was their King and that they were his children. Things would never be the same for the nation.

They never are when you lose sight of your real King.

Who is your king? Whom do you trust to guide and lead you in every area of your life? If God is your King, you have firmly established your identity as a child of the King of kings.

May 15

Knowing Jesus
NICODEMUS

There was a man named Nicodemus, a Jewish religious leader who was a Pharisee. After dark one evening, he came to speak with Jesus. "Rabbi," he said, "we all know that God has sent you to teach us. Your miraculous signs are evidence that God is with you." John 3:1-2

Think back to when you first courted your wife. You probably wanted to find out everything you could about this exciting young woman, so you asked questions. You asked her about her faith, her beliefs, her background, and about what she enjoyed. There was no end to the questions you wanted to ask.

If you *really* want to get to know someone, you have to ask lots of questions. A Pharisee named Nicodemus wanted to know Jesus, so that's what he did.

Most of the Jewish religious leaders in Jesus' day showed little or no interest in truly knowing him. Nicodemus was an exception. He came to visit Jesus at night, probably so that he could have some uninterrupted time to find out more about the man who had created such a stir in his hometown.

He also didn't want anyone to see him in case the meeting didn't go well.

Unlike most of his associates, Nicodemus acknowledged that God had sent Jesus to teach them if they would only listen (see John 3:1-2).

Nicodemus learned a lot more about Jesus that night than he probably expected. Jesus taught him that he wasn't just a teacher but the Messiah his people had waited so long to see. He was the Savior of the entire world who came to bring salvation to anyone who would believe in him.

Hearing these things changed Nicodemus's life and his eternal destiny.

Before the evening ended, Nicodemus *knew* Jesus. No longer just a curious bystander, he had become a true disciple who stood up for Jesus when his associates wanted to do away with him (see John 7:50-52). He even took part in Jesus' burial (see John 19:39).

Do you really want to know Jesus? Getting to know him more deeply and intimately means spending time with him. It means asking questions, observing his life, and hearing his words. When you do these things, you will learn more about him than you expect.

May 16

Need Faith?
JESUS AND THE DESPERATE FATHER

"What do you mean, 'If I can'?" Jesus asked. "Anything is possible if a person believes." The father instantly cried out, "I do believe, but help me overcome my unbelief!"   Mark 9:23-24

Standing outside his burning house, a man looked up in horror to see his son standing on the roof, waiting for help. Knowing he had little time to rescue his son, the man stretched out his arms and called, "Jump! I'll catch you."

The boy knew that he had to get out of the house and that the only way to do it was to jump. But all he could see, other than the dark night, were the flames and billowing smoke. He was too afraid to jump.

"I can't jump," the boy protested. "I can't see you."

"But I can see you," the dad called back, "and that's all that matters."

At times, we need some assurance before we can take a leap of faith. The unnamed father of a demon-possessed boy needed that kind of assurance. He had already seen Jesus' disciples fail miserably at casting out the evil spirit that had tormented his son for most of his life. Now he wondered if the Master could do anything for him.

"Have mercy on us and help us, if you can," he begged Jesus.

Jesus fully intended to heal the boy, but first he dealt with the man's doubts. "Anything is possible if a person believes," he told him, intending to build the man's faith.

This desperate father had no doubt heard about Jesus and the amazing miracles he had performed, but for some reason, he couldn't bring himself to fully believe that Jesus could do what others had tried and failed to do.

"I do believe," he told Jesus, "but help me overcome my unbelief!"

Though this man may not have had enough faith to completely believe Jesus could help him, he had more than enough faith to go to the One who generously gives the faith we need to see a miracle.

If you want God to do great things in your life, you will need faith. During times of doubt, when you wonder if he really can do anything to help you, don't be afraid to ask God to assure you and strengthen your faith. He is more than willing to do that!

May 17

What's Inside Counts
PAUL AND TIMOTHY

Don't let anyone think less of you because you are young. Be an example to all believers in what you say, in the way you live, in your love, your faith, and your purity. 1 Timothy 4:12

On his daughter's sixteenth birthday, a father got the wheels rolling on his promise to buy her a used car. That morning, the two headed out to visit some local lots to see if they could find a car that she liked and he could afford.

As they passed one used-car lot, a car caught the daughter's eye, and she excitedly asked her dad to stop so they could check it out. At a glance, it looked like a great deal. The paint was in excellent shape, and the car had no dents.

When they prepared to take a test drive, they noticed the heavy smell of cigarette smoke, the tears in the front seats, the badly stained carpet, and the sun-faded dashboard. The test drive ended before it began.

"Wow, Dad!" the daughter said as they left the lot. "That car looked great on the outside, but the inside was a total mess!"

What really counts is on the inside.

That was the essence of the apostle Paul's message to Timothy, the young pastor of the Ephesian church. Timothy had doubts about his ability to lead. He wondered if some of the church's older saints might look down on him as a wet-behind-the-ears kid who became their pastor only because he was Paul's friend.

Paul wanted Timothy to understand that his fitness to serve had nothing to do with his age or experience. It had everything to with what lay within him—godly character and an understanding of God and his Word.

If people could look inside of your soul, what would they see? Would they come away from the experience encouraged, impressed, or aghast?

What do you think qualifies you to serve God as a leader in your home, workplace, or church? In God's mind, your qualifications have nothing to do with your appearance, youth, charm, or any other external feature. You lead best when you understand that what is on the inside—strong character and a passion for God and his Word—is what really counts.

May 18

Wisdom to Listen
PHARAOH AND JOSEPH

Joseph's suggestions were well received by Pharaoh and his officials. So Pharaoh asked his officials, "Can we find anyone else like this man so obviously filled with the spirit of God?"   Genesis 41:37-38

A talented but stubborn high school basketball player began his senior season as a starter, only to find himself riding the bench by midseason. At an especially competitive game one Friday night, the player couldn't take it anymore. He blurted out, "Coach, why aren't you playing me anymore?"

As though he had been expecting the question, the coach replied, "Since you couldn't listen to me while you were on the floor, I thought you might be able to hear a little better sitting next to me."

The young man learned his lesson. He started listening to his coach, and a few games later he was back on the floor.

One of a man's most important traits is his willingness to listen. The Pharaoh who ruled Egypt during Joseph's lifetime had the humility to listen and thus saved countless lives.

Some very disturbing nightmares awakened Pharaoh one night, and he desperately wanted to know what they meant. When none of his advisors could tell him, one of his high-ranking officials remembered meeting a man named Joseph who had an amazing ability to interpret dreams.

Pharaoh sent for Joseph, who was in prison at the time, and asked him what the dreams meant. The news behind the dreams wasn't good, Joseph warned. There would be seven years of prosperity in Egypt, then seven years of severe famine. Joseph suggested that Pharaoh appoint someone to oversee the gathering of food during those seven years of plenty so that the people wouldn't starve during the seven lean ones.

Pharaoh listened to Joseph, and then he appointed him to administer a food program that would keep that part of the world from starving. Pharaoh's willingness to listen to a man "obviously filled with the spirit of God" saved his nation and probably his monarchy.

Have you learned to listen? God places people in your life with the purpose of giving you wisdom and direction you might not otherwise have. The art of listening is rare these days, but it's vital to receiving God's very best for you.

May 19

Believe and Receive
ZECHARIAH

Zechariah said to the angel, "How can I be sure this will happen? I'm an old man now, and my wife is also well along in years."   Luke 1:18

A seminary professor traveling by airplane sat next to a young boy reading a Sunday school take-home paper. Thinking he could have some fun with the boy, he nudged him and said, "Young man, if you can tell me something God can do, I'll give you a big, shiny apple."

The boy thought for a moment and then replied, "Mister, if you can tell me something God *can't* do, I'll give you a whole *barrel* of apples!"

Faith is based on the fact that God keeps his promises, especially the ones that seem humanly impossible.

Zechariah was an elderly priest serving in Jerusalem just prior to the birth of Jesus. His wife, Elizabeth, had no children. They had prayed for a child, but now, in their old age, they expected to live out their lives together without children.

God hadn't forgotten Zechariah's prayers! One day, he sent the angel Gabriel to tell him that he and his wife would have a son. God had already appointed this child to prepare the Jewish people for the arrival of their Messiah.

You would think that the appearance of an angel of the Lord would be enough to convince a man of God like Zechariah. However, instead of thanking Gabriel for the message, praising God with every fiber of his being, and running home to tell his wife the amazing news, Zechariah spoke words of unbelief (see Luke 1:18).

This was unfortunate.

God wasn't about to allow Zechariah's unbelief to get in the way of what he was doing. God keeps his promises, but because Zechariah had spoken words of unbelief, God struck him speechless.

He missed out on the opportunity to praise God and tell his friends and family the wonderful news.

How do you respond when God makes you a wonderful promise? God loves to show you his goodness and power by doing what is humanly impossible. You receive every blessing he has for you when you respond to him in faith.

May 20

Loving When It Hurts
HOSEA

When the LORD first began speaking to Israel through Hosea, he said to him, "Go and marry a prostitute, so that some of her children will be conceived in prostitution." Hosea 1:2

In 1943, as World War II hit its full stride, 903 troops and four chaplains—George L. Fox, Alexander D. Goode, John P. Washington, and Clark V. Poling—boarded the USAT *Dorchester* on a dreary winter day and headed across the frigid North Atlantic where German U-boats prowled.

Just past midnight on February 3, a German torpedo ripped into the ship's side, sending the men scrambling for the lifeboats. As the *Dorchester* began to founder, someone discovered that there weren't enough life jackets to go around.

In a wonderful picture of self-sacrifice, the four chaplains stripped off their own life jackets and gave them to other men. Then they linked arms and lifted their voices in prayer as the *Dorchester* went down.

Apart from Jesus, there may be no better biblical example of sacrificial love than the Old Testament prophet Hosea.

You wouldn't wish Hosea's family life on your worst enemy. God commanded him to marry a prostitute named Gomer as an object lesson of God's love for the wayward nation of Israel.

It's hard to imagine how a man of God like Hosea felt as he looked at his dimming prospects for a happy family life, but Hosea heard God and obeyed.

Before long, Gomer left Hosea and returned to her old ways, but Hosea, who obeyed God even when it meant agonizing self-sacrifice, refused to let Gomer go. Instead, he pursued her and brought her back home.

Hosea sacrificed himself to love someone completely unworthy of his love. In so doing, he painted a real-life picture of God's love for his rebellious people and set an example of the love we should have for the unlovable.

Sooner or later, you're going to meet someone who is, in human thinking, "unlovable," but God calls us to be vessels of his self-sacrificing love to such people. Sometimes that means giving and loving until it hurts—just as God loved you when he sent his Son to die.

May 21

Opportunities to Speak
SHEMAIAH

The prophet Shemaiah then met with Rehoboam and Judah's leaders, who had all fled to Jerusalem because of Shishak. Shemaiah told them, "This is what the LORD says: You have abandoned me, so I am abandoning you to Shishak."
2 CHRONICLES 12:5

Part of the training of a young circus elephant is teaching it to stay put. Trainers put its leg in a stock and chain it to a deeply rooted stake. At first, the young elephant strains against the chain, trying to gain freedom, but once it realizes that it can't uproot the stake, it gives up.

From then on, the animal can be "chained" with nothing but a slender rope that it could easily snap with one movement. The elephant stays put because it believes that it can't pull free.

The Bible includes many examples of God sending men to free his people from their sin and rebellion. One of those people was the prophet Shemaiah, who took a message of freedom to his people. All that was required was for them to turn back to God.

Shemaiah's message for Rehoboam and the other leaders of Judah was hard to swallow. Shemaiah told Rehoboam that the people of Judah had abandoned God, so he was giving them over to their mortal enemy, King Shishak of Egypt.

It's difficult to imagine that Shemaiah felt anything but heartache over having to deliver such a message. Judah was his country, too, after all. He loved his people and wanted God's best for them.

But Shemaiah's willingness to speak God's message made a difference.

The leaders of Judah listened to what Shemaiah said, and they humbled themselves. Though their sin would still have consequences, God relented on his plan to destroy Judah (see 2 Chronicles 12:6-8).

Shemaiah knew the conditions for Judah's freedom, and because he believed God and obediently spoke that message, his nation and its people avoided certain death.

When you have that kind of courage, you can make a difference in your world.

Listen to the inner promptings that tell you to share your faith. God may want to use you to free someone you care about from the power of sin and bring him into his eternal Kingdom.

May 22

Infectious Enthusiasm
PHINEHAS

The LORD said to Moses, "Phinehas son of Eleazar and grandson of Aaron the priest has turned my anger away from the Israelites by being as zealous among them as I was." Numbers 25:10-11

Eugene Ormandy, the world-renowned violinist and conductor, was well-known for his enthusiasm for music. Ormandy was so zealous that he once dislocated his shoulder while conducting the Philadelphia Orchestra.

An Old Testament character named Phinehas, the grandson of Aaron the priest, demonstrated this kind of zeal for God.

Phinehas had seen the immorality going on around him. His people committed sexual acts with the women of Midian, and many of them had begun worshiping the Midianites' false gods.

Phinehas could not stand idly by and allow his people to defile themselves. Neither could he allow God's judgment to continue falling without trying to bring it to an end. He had already seen twenty-four thousand of his brothers and sisters die, and it broke his heart.

Finally, Phinehas had his "last straw" moment, and it was time for him to act.

When Phinehas witnessed one of his Hebrew brothers shamelessly taking a Midianite woman into his tent, he had seen enough. His zeal for God kicked in, and he passionately executed the man who had so openly sinned against God. In doing so, he distinguished himself as a man who was willing to take a strong stand for what was right. Because he did so, the people of Israel were spared, and Phinehas's descendants received God's special blessing (see Numbers 25:12-13).

God doesn't want you to take the law into your own hands, but he challenges you to approach your relationship with him with Phinehas's zeal.

When you are enthusiastic about your relationship with God, you are bound to affect those around you. Your family doesn't need to see you acting out of vengeance, but they need to see you as a man of passion for God.

May 23

Influence from Within
KING JOSIAH

Never before had there been a king like Josiah, who turned to the LORD with all his heart and soul and strength, obeying all the laws of Moses. And there has never been a king like him since. 2 Kings 23:25

Missionary John Geddie arrived on the island of Aneityum in 1848 and worked there for twenty-four years, making a huge impact for the Kingdom of God. After his death, a tablet erected in his memory read,

> In memory of John Geddie, D.D., born in Scotland, 1815, minister in Prince Edward Island seven years, Missionary sent from Nova Scotia to Aneityum for twenty-four years. When he landed in 1848, there were no Christians here, and when he left in 1872 there were no heathen.

Josiah had the same kind of influence on the world around him. The Bible says that Josiah "did what was pleasing in the LORD's sight and followed the example of his ancestor David. He did not turn away from doing what was right" (2 Kings 22:2).

When you look at Josiah's background, not much appears to point toward greatness. His father and predecessor was Amon, a wicked king who helped drag Judah back into idolatry. For Josiah, it wasn't a matter of where he came from but of where he was headed.

Josiah took the throne at age eight, following his father's assassination. In the eighteenth year of his reign, he instructed the high priest, Hilkiah, to begin repairing the Temple, which had been damaged and badly neglected during the reigns of the previous two kings. And that was only the beginning.

After hearing a reading of the long-lost Book of the Law, the young king compared what he had heard with what he saw around him. Josiah knew that the time for change had come. He gathered the people together and led them in a renewal of their covenant with God.

Josiah influenced others for God because he followed the Lord with all his heart. Scripture remembers him as a man who "turned to the LORD with all his heart and soul and strength" and as a man whose humility and heart for God led to changes in others.

Making a difference in the lives of people around you begins with changes within yourself. When those changes take place, you can't help but influence others for the better.

May 24

Defend What Is Right
MOSES

Israel, listen carefully to these decrees and regulations that I am about to teach you. Obey them so that you may live, so you may enter and occupy the land that the LORD, the God of your ancestors, is giving you. Deuteronomy 4:1

"To each his own."
   "Different strokes for different folks."
   "We all march to the beat of a different drummer."
   "Whatever works for you . . ."
   Each of us naturally tends to think that we have the right to adopt our own set of morals, standards, and spirituality apart from any absolute standard. Believers in Christ must reject such a belief. In your home, especially, it's your job to set godly standards and follow through by living up to them.
   Moses, the man God called to deliver the Hebrews out of Egyptian slavery, accepted such a responsibility when he became the leader of his people. He delivered an uncompromising message of strict obedience to God with no tolerance for sin. His message called for full compliance with the Word of God and the rejection of any kind of idolatry.
   It also included the promise of reward for full obedience.
   Moses understood the importance of setting righteous standards for the people he led. Though no one would call him perfect, he faithfully walked the path of obedience to God without fear of being labeled inflexible, intolerant, dogmatic, or, worst of all, judgmental. He could bear the name calling so long as he focused on the God who had called him and on his God-given goal.
   Do you have that kind of courage and conviction? Are you willing to risk anger, resentment, opposition, or insults to follow God with a clear conscience? You're not perfect, but God doesn't ask for perfection. He asks for simple, Spirit-empowered obedience.

God wants you to speak and live in a way that reflects the truth of his Word, beginning with your own home. God promises countless blessings to those whose words and deeds reflect an uncompromising commitment to him and to his truth.

May 25

A Humble, Suffering Servant
ISAIAH

He was pierced for our rebellion, crushed for our sins. He was beaten so we could be whole. He was whipped so we could be healed. All of us, like sheep, have strayed away. We have left God's paths to follow our own. Yet the LORD laid on him the sins of us all. Isaiah 53:5-6

Arthur H. Rostron, the skipper of RMS *Carpathia*, was asleep the night of April 14, 1912, when one of his crew burst into his cabin to inform him of a distress signal from the RMS *Titanic*. The celebrated ship had struck an iceberg and was in trouble.

Rostron, one of that awful night's true heroes, raced at nearly full speed toward the *Titanic's* last reported location. As a devout man of faith and prayer, Rostron never hesitated but issued orders for the *Carpathia* to head toward the iceberg-infested waters some sixty miles away—the *Titanic's* last known position. At 4:00 AM, the *Carpathia* reached the *Titanic* and rescued more than seven hundred people from the icy waters.

Rostron gave everything at his disposal to save others.

As a man, Jesus Christ was the *perfect* example of that kind of giving. From the moment he entered the scene in the little Mediterranean land of Palestine two thousand years ago, Jesus began giving.

He hasn't stopped.

The prophet Isaiah, who lived and ministered almost eight centuries before Jesus' birth, saw this humble, suffering Servant from his own time. Isaiah depicts a man who willingly subjected himself to unspeakable suffering on behalf of others in love, humility, and self-sacrificial giving.

Knowing what Jesus has given you, what can you give back to him and to those who also serve him or need to know him?

How does Jesus' selfless giving motivate you? When Jesus saved you, he reserved a place for you in his eternal Kingdom. He also set you on a new life course of humble giving to him and to those he has placed in your life. You bless him, bless others, and bless yourself when you make it your goal to give as he gave to you.

May 26

Nothing to Fear
JESUS

Soon a fierce storm came up. High waves were breaking into the boat, and it began to fill with water. Jesus was sleeping at the back of the boat with his head on a cushion. The disciples woke him up, shouting, "Teacher, don't you care that we're going to drown?"   Mark 4:37-38

A military governor once met with General George Patton in Sicily at the height of World War II. When the man praised Patton for his courage, the general replied, "Sir, I am not a brave man. . . . The truth is, I am an utter, craven coward. I have never been within the sound of gunshot or in sight of battle in my whole life that I wasn't so scared that I had sweat in the palms of my hands."

Years later, Patton wrote in his autobiography, "I learned very early in my life never to take counsel of my fears."

Few things in life test a man's mettle like fear. During times of fear, a man's faith is put to its sternest test.

Jesus' disciples faced such a test.

As Jesus and his disciples crossed the Sea of Galilee, a storm came up that deeply worried even the experienced fishermen onboard. With their nerves jangling and their faith shaken, they felt sure the end had come.

As the disciples did everything they could to keep their boat from sinking, Jesus remained so calm that he slept through the worst that the Sea of Galilee could deliver. The disciples, by now gripped with utter terror, wondered how anyone could possibly sleep through it all.

The disciples didn't yet have Jesus' sense of a God-ordained destiny. He knew that he had a purpose for coming to earth and that nothing could keep him from fulfilling it.

Jesus calmed the storm by speaking to it. Still wide-eyed with fear and amazement, the disciples learned something that is still true today: When Jesus accompanies you, you have nothing to fear. ·

Fear is an unavoidable aspect of life, but you don't have to allow your fears to rule you or keep you from enjoying all that God has for you. When you put your focus on Jesus instead of on the storms of life, you can triumph over fear time after time.

May 27

Always Prepared
THE ETHIOPIAN EUNUCH

The eunuch asked Philip, "Tell me, was the prophet talking about himself or someone else?" So beginning with this same Scripture, Philip told him the Good News about Jesus. Acts 8:34-35

Eight Boy Scouts who lost their way in September 2007 while camping in a heavily wooded area of the North Carolina mountains turned up safe and sound, but one day late. The boys and their three leaders had lost the trail leading out of the woods and decided to set up camp and wait for daylight rather than try to make their way out in the dark.

An assistant Scoutmaster, whose son had accompanied the group, later told news reporters, "Everybody's in good shape, a little tired. . . . As the Scout motto says, they were prepared."

"Be prepared" is also good advice when you meet someone who wants to know what your life of faith is about.

Philip, a believer whose story is found in the book of Acts, was a good example of that kind of preparation. Philip met an Ethiopian eunuch of some standing with Candace, the queen of Ethiopia. He had some very direct questions concerning the writings of the prophet Isaiah, and Philip was ready with the answers.

He explained to the Ethiopian that Isaiah, like many other Old Testament prophets, had written about Jesus Christ, who had recently lived, died, and been raised by God so that all who believed in him could be saved.

The man from Ethiopia, like so many people in our world, wanted answers regarding God and his own destiny. Philip modeled the kind of preparation advocated by the apostle Peter: "If someone asks about your Christian hope, always be ready to explain it" (1 Peter 3:15).

Are you prepared?

If you're living the Christian life, it's only a matter of time before someone asks you questions about your faith. Be ready to give clear and concise answers that demonstrate genuine care and concern for that person's eternal destiny.

May 28

Contrary to Popular Opinion
KING JOASH

The leaders plotted to kill Zechariah, and King Joash ordered that they stone him to death in the courtyard of the LORD's Temple. 2 Chronicles 24:21

It may be hard to believe, but at one time, *potatoes* were the object of scorn, hatred, ridicule, and fear. When Sir Walter Raleigh first introduced potatoes to England, the Brits wouldn't touch them, believing that they caused all sorts of illnesses and death. British newspapers ran scathing editorials against them, and ministers preached against their evil.

According to public opinion, it was only through the hard work of a few courageous souls that the humble potato earned its legacy as a food staple.

Sometimes we must stand against even the strongest public opinion. Zechariah, a prophet who ministered in Judah during the reign of King Joash, illustrates the point.

Early in his life, Joash served God faithfully, but after the death of the priest Jehoiada, he followed public opinion and joined the masses in abandoning God and worshiping man-made idols.

Zechariah encouraged Joash and the people to return to the Lord and warned them of the consequences of their idolatry. The message from God that Zechariah repeated was simple and straightforward: "Why do you disobey the LORD's commands and keep yourselves from prospering? You have abandoned the LORD, and now he has abandoned you!" (2 Chronicles 24:20).

That wasn't what the king or his subjects wanted to hear.

Zechariah paid with his life for his willingness to buck public opinion. The people ignored what he told them and stoned him to death in the Temple courtyard.

Sometimes you may have to stand against the tide of opinion in your home, at work, or among friends. A key to receiving God's blessing for yourself and others is being faithful to him and his Word even when others don't want to hear about it.

May 29

When Opportunity Knocks
JESUS AND THE SAMARITAN WOMAN

Jesus, tired from the long walk, sat wearily beside the well about noontime. Soon a Samaritan woman came to draw water, and Jesus said to her, "Please give me a drink." He was alone at the time because his disciples had gone into the village to buy some food. John 4:6-8

After running some particularly successful ten-cent sales of outdated items, a young hardware store employee approached his boss with a business proposal: open a store that sold only nickel and dime items. The young man said he could run the store if his boss would supply the capital.

"The plan will never work," his boss said, "because you can't find enough items to sell at a nickel and a dime."

Though the young employee was disappointed at the time, he later tried out his idea and made millions. His name was F. W. Woolworth.

Years later, his old boss lamented the fact that he had turned down such a good opportunity: "As near as I can figure it," he said, "every word I used in turning Woolworth down has cost me about a million dollars."

Jesus understood the importance of making the best use of every opportunity to preach and teach his message. His encounter with a Samaritan woman is an example.

There was bad blood between Jews and Samaritans, and most Jews avoided traveling through Samaria at all costs. One day, Jesus walked through Samaria with his disciples on the way to Galilee.

Jesus was ready for an opportunity to share his message with the people of Samaria, and that opportunity came as he waited at a well near the Samaritan village of Sychar.

Around noon, a Samaritan woman happened by, and Jesus asked her for a drink of water. An in-depth conversation about who Jesus was and what that meant to her followed his request. Jesus' words made a lasting impression on this woman, who immediately returned to her village and stunned her neighbors with the news that she had met the Messiah.

Because Jesus made the very best of his opportunity to speak to the Samaritan woman, "many Samaritans from the village believed in Jesus" (John 4:39).

Life will present you with opportunities to serve God through serving others. You bless others and yourself when you watch for those opportunities and make the most of them.

May 30

Passion for God's Word
APOLLOS

A Jew named Apollos, an eloquent speaker who knew the Scriptures well, had arrived in Ephesus from Alexandria in Egypt. He had been taught the way of the Lord, and he taught others about Jesus with an enthusiastic spirit and with accuracy. However, he knew only about John's baptism.   Acts 18:24-25

In his book *The Wonders of the Word of God,* evangelist Robert L. Sumner tells the story of a new Christian who lost his eyesight and both hands in an explosion.

One of the man's greatest disappointments was that he could no longer read the Bible. Then he heard about a woman in England who read Braille with her lips. Hoping he could do the same, the man sent for some books of the Bible in Braille, but he was bitterly disappointed to find that the explosion had also damaged the nerve endings in his lips.

One day, as he brought one of the Braille pages to his lips, his tongue touched a few of the Braille characters, and he realized that he could use his tongue to read the Bible. By the time Sumner wrote his book, the man had read the entire Bible four times.

What a passion for the Word of God!

Apollos had that kind of passion. As a gifted, educated Jewish man from Alexandria, he loved to teach the Word of God in the synagogues, but he had one limitation: Apollos didn't fully understand the significance of Jesus' death and resurrection. He finally received that understanding when he visited Ephesus and came under the teaching of Aquila and Priscilla, a married couple who lived in the city.

From then on, Apollos couldn't be stopped. He moved from Ephesus to Corinth, where he met the apostle Paul and made such an impression on the church there that some of the believers credited him with starting their church (see 1 Corinthians 1:10-17). Apollos was an eloquent speaker, but he became a great teacher and preacher because he had the passion for God's Word that all men of God need.

The Bible contains everything you need for living a victorious, powerful life of faith. If you have a passion for that kind of life, you will need a passion for God's Word.

May 31

A Thorn of Humility
PAUL

To keep me from becoming proud, I was given a thorn in my flesh, a messenger from Satan to torment me and keep me from becoming proud.
2 CORINTHIANS 12:7

Former baseball great Ralph Kiner had a great season for the Pittsburgh Pirates in 1952. Unfortunately, the Pirates didn't return the favor. They finished 42-122 and dead last in the National League.

When the season ended, Kiner approached Pirates general manager Branch Rickey and asked for a raise, reminding him that he had led the league with thirty-seven home runs.

"Where did we finish?" Rickey asked.

"Last," Kiner replied.

"Well," said Rickey, "we can finish last without you."

There's always something to humble even the most accomplished man.

The apostle Paul, a man of considerable humility, well understood the importance of keeping his pride in check. He actually thanked God for sending some unidentified problem—one he referred to as a "thorn"—to keep him in his place. Whatever Paul's "thorn in [the] flesh" was, he continually thanked God for it because it reminded him that without the constant empowerment of God's Holy Spirit, he had nothing to offer the Kingdom of God.

"That's why I take pleasure in my weaknesses," he wrote, "and in the insults, hardships, persecutions, and troubles that I suffer for Christ. For when I am weak, then I am strong" (2 Corinthians 12:10).

It takes a lot of courage to thank God for something that appears to be a problem or hindrance, but that's what Paul did. He understood that character qualities such as patience and humility don't just happen; they develop over time, and often through difficult life experiences.

Do you have that kind of courage?

Instead of seeing your difficulties as hindrances to your life of faith, look at them as opportunities that God allows into your life to keep you humble. Let them remind you that your strength is in him alone.

June 1

Honesty's Rewards
SAMUEL

"Testify against me in the presence of the LORD and before his anointed one. Whose ox or donkey have I stolen? Have I ever cheated any of you? Have I ever oppressed you? Have I ever taken a bribe and perverted justice? Tell me and I will make right whatever I have done wrong." 1 Samuel 12:3

An armored car once spilled two million dollars on a busy freeway in Columbus, Ohio. Officials recovered only four hundred thousand dollars of the funds; most of the rest disappeared with the throngs who scooped up the loose cash. Only a few were honest enough to return what clearly did not belong to them.

Life presents us with many opportunities to choose right or wrong, integrity or deceit, truth or lies. Who doesn't fudge a little in business dealings? Who doesn't tell his spouse the occasional white lie?

After all, that's better than creating more conflict, right? Who doesn't once in a while give in to his buddies and do sleazy things? Hey, we're only human.

Samuel, a prophet and judge, earned a reputation for unimpeachable honesty that served him well throughout his long public career. At the coronation of Saul, Israel's first king, Samuel had something important to say regarding the people's demand for an earthly king to rule over them, but first he challenged them to tell him if he had ever stolen anything, cheated or oppressed anyone, taken any kind of bribe, or perverted justice in any way.

Samuel was asking the people to declare their opinion of him. Did they know him as a man of honesty and integrity? Was he a thief and a robber, or a fair and trustworthy leader? Everyone knew the answer and didn't hesitate to give it: Yes, Samuel was honest; yes, he lived with integrity; yes, he always treated the people fairly; yes, they could trust him. Samuel could speak to the people that day with great authority because he had carefully maintained his reputation as an honest man over many years.

Can you speak with the same authority?

We choose every day whether we will deal in truth or in lies. Regardless of your past, you can start choosing right now to be a man of integrity, honesty, and truth. What temptations in your life urge you to bend the truth? How can Samuel's example help you to choose honesty instead?

June 2

Desperate Faith
JAIRUS

A man named Jairus, a leader of the local synagogue, came and fell at Jesus' feet, pleading with him to come home with him. His only daughter, who was about twelve years old, was dying. Luke 8:41-42

When the young daughter of Princess Alice of Hesse fell ill with diphtheria in 1878, doctors told Princess Alice not to come close to her daughter lest she endanger her own health. One evening as the child struggled to breathe, Alice forgot her doctors' orders and took her child into her arms in a desperate attempt to keep her from choking to death. A short time later, Alice also fell ill, and she died within days.

Desperation has a way of making people forget about themselves and take unusual risks.

Jairus, a synagogue leader in Capernaum, knew the risks when he fell at Jesus' feet and begged him to heal his deathly ill daughter. Jairus knew that his Jewish countrymen wouldn't take kindly to his approaching Jesus in that way. By falling at his feet, Jairus acknowledged that Jesus was everything he said he was—and everything the Jewish religious establishment said he was not.

Jairus needed more than faith to come to Jesus; he also needed courage.

He had probably watched in agony as his daughter fell ill and then descended toward death. As a synagogue leader, he had access to the very best care available in those days, but none of that would keep his daughter alive.

Jairus had one final hope: Jesus!

Jairus had heard of Jesus' miracles, and he *knew* that Jesus could heal his daughter.

Jairus's need was so profound and his situation so desperate that he risked everything to take a huge step of faith. He cried out to Jesus for help, and the Savior who never turns down a humble man gave him exactly what he needed.

Where do you turn when you're in desperate need? Turn to Jesus with all your faith and passion. Don't worry if others think that your crying out to him seems like a desperate last resort. Sometimes it is! Turn to Jesus, who gives you what you need when you have the faith to humbly ask him for it.

June 3

No Rocking Chair in Here!
CALEB

"Give me the hill country that the LORD promised me. You will remember that as scouts we found the descendants of Anak living there in great, walled towns. But if the LORD is with me, I will drive them out of the land, just as the LORD said."
JOSHUA 14:12

Some men age gracefully.

You know the type. They may *look* younger than their age, and they certainly *act* it. They remain youthful in their attitude and energetic in their disposition. These active men continue to accomplish significant things, even when others believe they should be living out their golden years in a rocking chair.

Fast-forward forty-five years from the time that Caleb and Joshua urged their countrymen to possess Canaan. The two led a younger generation into the Promised Land, and the Lord granted many victories over warlike enemy tribes. Now Caleb was eighty-five years old.

You might think that such a veteran soldier would welcome a rocking chair, but not Caleb! He had yet to take possession of the land the Lord had promised him more than four decades earlier, and he intended to see that promise fulfilled.

Caleb's courage sprang from his unshakable belief that God keeps his promises. He knew that giant Anakites lived in the hill country, but he exclaimed, "If the LORD is with me, I will drive them out of the land, just as the LORD said" (Joshua 14:12).

Like Caleb, Joshua had absolute faith in the reliability of God's promises. Several years earlier, the Lord had told him to be strong and courageous and not to be afraid or discouraged because the Lord would be with him wherever he went (see Joshua 1:9). When Joshua eagerly acknowledged Caleb's God-given right to Hebron (see Joshua 14:13), his octogenarian friend heartily engaged the enemy and drove them out, just as God had promised!

What sort of hill country has the Lord set before you? It may seem impossible to accomplish and daunting to ponder, but if God goes with you into the battle, the outcome is certain before the arrows even begin to fly. Of course, you won't grasp the victory if you don't enter the battle.

You may live to age eighty-five or one hundred, but you will never outlive tough challenges. So get that rocking chair out of there! You have battles to win and blessings to impart to the next generation.

June 4

Saying Thank You
THE TEN LEPERS

As they went, they were cleansed of their leprosy. One of them, when he saw that he was healed, came back to Jesus, shouting, "Praise God!" He fell to the ground at Jesus' feet, thanking him for what he had done.   Luke 17:14-16

In one episode of the television comedy *Seinfeld*, Jerry and his friends become the beneficiaries of an acquaintance's generous gift of hockey tickets. *Play-off* hockey tickets, no less.

Though Jerry also had the promise of tickets for the next game, he and his friends missed out because Jerry *refused* to call and thank their hockey ticket source, who gave the next game's tickets to someone else.

Sometimes expressing gratitude means going out of your way to let the other party know how thankful you feel. The Bible illustrates this principle in the story of ten men that Jesus healed of leprosy.

When these men saw Jesus approaching, they cried out, "Jesus, Master, have mercy on us!" (Luke 17:13). So far, so good, but after these men received their miraculous healing, only one of them returned to give thanks. You can hear the surprise in Jesus' voice when he says, "Didn't I heal ten men? Where are the other nine?" (Luke 17:17).

All ten lepers received physical healing that day, but only one man was changed for good. His heart was so filled with gratitude that he had to go back to Jesus and thank him. He had already received one special blessing that day, and because he went out of his way to thank Jesus, he received something even greater.

The same goes for you when you make that special effort to say thank you.

It's always good to have an attitude of gratitude for the things God has done for you. Take the time to say so. Go out of your way to openly praise and thank God.

June 5

Persecution or Blessing?
SAUL OF TARSUS

He fell to the ground and heard a voice saying to him, "Saul! Saul! Why are you persecuting me?" "Who are you, lord?" Saul asked. And the voice replied, "I am Jesus, the one you are persecuting!"   Acts 9:4-5

Ronald Reagan, the fortieth president of the United States, had his share of critics, but even his staunchest political enemies understood the wisdom of Reagan's "Eleventh Commandment": Thou shalt not speak ill of a fellow Republican.

Reagan believed deeply in party unity. He held that when just one GOP member tore down or criticized another, his words hurt the entire party.

The same could be said about how you treat fellow believers. When you bless them through your words and actions, you bless Jesus. When you tear them down, criticize them, and hurt them through word and deed, you persecute the Savior who calls them his brothers (see Matthew 12:49).

That was the first lesson Jesus taught Saul, the man who would become the apostle Paul. Saul believed in his heart that he was doing God's work as he tried to shut down a new religious movement. He believed that in persecuting individual believers, he was ridding the world of threats to the Jewish faith.

All of that changed when Saul heard Jesus' voice telling him that his persecution hurt Jesus as well as individual Christians and Christian communities.

Saul's encounter with Jesus on the road to Damascus changed everything about him. He no longer persecuted Christ and his followers but loved, blessed, and served them.

Think about that the next time you feel like persecuting your Christian brother or sister.

When you feel tempted to speak harshly or do something hurtful to a fellow believer, remember that Christ calls him his own brother. Instead of cursing that person in word and deed, bless him in everything you say and do.

June 6

A Man of Hope
ABRAHAM

Even when there was no reason for hope, Abraham kept hoping—believing that he would become the father of many nations. For God had said to him, "That's how many descendants you will have!"   Romans 4:18

A father arrived late to his son's Little League baseball game, missing the entire top half of the first inning. When he sidled up to the dugout and asked his son for the score, the boy beamed, "We're behind 16-0. But that's okay. We haven't even had a chance to bat yet!"

That boy demonstrated a biblical idea of hope by maintaining a sense of expectancy even when the circumstances suggested packing it in and giving up.

Abraham knew a lot about hope.

At the ripe old age of seventy-five, Abraham clearly heard God's voice promising to make him the father of many nations and countless descendants. Yet almost a quarter of a century later, Abraham and his wife, Sarah, still had no children.

What would *you* think if you had been Abraham?

Humanly speaking, Abraham had every reason to wonder if God had forgotten his promise. He was closing in on his hundredth birthday, and his wife trailed him by only a decade. It's not hard to imagine Abraham asking God, "Say, Lord, did you overlook something here?"

Somehow, Abraham didn't lose hope but steadfastly clung to the faith that justified him before God, according to the Bible. He remained utterly convinced that the God he had faithfully followed and served would keep *all* his promises.

True to that expectation, God blessed Abraham and his wife with a son named Isaac. In so doing, he made the father of the Israelites into an example of the hope that never disappoints a man. As God later said through Isaiah, "Those who trust in me will never be put to shame" (Isaiah 49:23).

Has God given you an as-yet-unfulfilled promise in some area of your life? Have you grown weary in waiting? The Bible encourages you to have hope, which means to believe firmly in the God who always keeps his promises. Continue to trust in him and persevere in all he has called you to do until he fulfills that promise.

June 7

Learn to Listen
KING SOLOMON

Fools think their own way is right, but the wise listen to others.   Proverbs 12:15

> *A wise old owl lived in an oak;*
> *The more he saw the less he spoke;*
> *The less he spoke the more he heard.*
> *Why can't we all be like that wise old bird?*

This anonymous poem echoes some of Solomon's thoughts about wise counsel. In several of his proverbs, Solomon advises his readers to listen carefully to those who have gone before them because they have the wisdom acquired by a long walk with God.

Solomon offered a lot of advice on heeding the wise counsel of mature leaders. Sadly, however, he didn't always do as he said.

As Solomon prepared to ascend the throne as king of Israel, his father, David, who was close to death, advised him: "Observe the requirements of the LORD your God, and follow all his ways. Keep the decrees, commands, regulations, and laws written in the Law of Moses so that you will be successful in all you do and wherever you go. If you do this, then the LORD will keep the promise he made to me" (1 Kings 2:3-4).

Solomon may have spoken words of wisdom, but his life ended in foolishness. He knew God's clear warning against taking many wives, but that's exactly what he did. In all, he took seven hundred wives and three hundred mistresses, some of them women from outside his own nationality and faith.

Solomon's failure to practice what he preached led to his downfall. His wives turned his heart away from God and toward idol worship, which scuttled what could have been a legacy of unparalleled greatness.

You will save yourself a lot of trouble by knowing the Word of God and doing what it says. That's a good way to avoid heartache and the only way to receive every blessing God has for you.

June 8

Letting Go
JOSEPH

Joseph replied, "Don't be afraid of me. Am I God, that I can punish you? You intended to harm me, but God intended it all for good. He brought me to this position so I could save the lives of many people." Genesis 50:19-20

It probably shouldn't surprise anyone, but the consensus among psychological experts is that emotional maturity is a key to living a healthy, happy, productive life. This includes handling emotions in a healthy way when life throws a curveball.

Unfortunately, we naturally tend to hang on to negative emotions such as anger, bitterness, fear, resentment, and anxiety. We may *say* that we don't feel those things when life doesn't go as we think it should, but deep inside, we churn with every negative feeling imaginable.

Joseph didn't seem to have that problem. Scripture portrays him as a man of amazing kindness, forgiveness, courage, and faith. He had plenty of opportunity to demonstrate these qualities throughout his difficult life.

Even after his brothers sold him into Egyptian slavery, Joseph thrived in every situation because God oversaw everything that happened to him. God used Joseph's circumstances for his own purposes, for Joseph's good, and for the benefit of others.

Joseph's story contains an important lesson that Paul neatly summarized in his letter to first-century Roman believers: "We know that God causes everything to work together for the good of those who love God and are called according to his purpose for them" (Romans 8:28).

Are you holding on to negative emotions? Are you bound by an unfair past? When you understand that God can use everything that happens to you for his purposes, those things will begin to lose their grip on you.

Just ask Joseph!

It's far easier to let go of negative emotions when you remember that God uses everything that happens to you to accomplish his purposes. You don't always know when and how he will do this, but that he will do so is a biblical promise.

June 9

A Walk with God
ENOCH

After the birth of Methuselah, Enoch lived in close fellowship with God for another 300 years, and he had other sons and daughters. Enoch lived 365 years, walking in close fellowship with God. Then one day he disappeared, because God took him.   Genesis 5:22-24

A senior citizen who had walked with God for decades made a mistake when taking his medications and quickly wound up in the hospital. When it became clear that the error might cost him his life, his whole family gathered to say good-bye.

Many tears mixed with much joy as sons, daughters, grandchildren, and the man's faithful wife remembered his legacy and how he was the only member of his family of origin to make the choice to follow Christ.

After less than a week in the hospital, he fell into a light coma and said nothing for a couple of days. With his eldest son in the room, he suddenly opened his eyes, smiled, and exclaimed, "Wow!" Then he fell back into a coma and died a short while later.

Had this man enjoyed a vision of heaven? His son thinks so, and the thought gives him deep comfort. He says that it was as if God and his father had walked together for so many years that on that day the Lord said, "Joe, we're a lot closer to my house than yours. Why don't you just come home with me?"

Enoch walked with God and simply disappeared into heaven one day. The writer of Hebrews pointed out a benefit of walking with God when he wrote, "Before [Enoch] was taken up, he was known as a person who pleased God" (Hebrews 11:5).

Enoch pleased God because he walked with him daily. He relied on him, enjoyed his companionship, obeyed his commands, and put him at the center of everything he said and did.

Would you like to be known as a man who pleases God? If so, walk with him as Enoch did.

When you walk with God, you please God. When your life pleases him, you know the blessed assurance of your place in his eternal Kingdom.

June 10

Respect the Office
DAVID AND KING SAUL

"Surely the LORD will strike Saul down someday, or he will die of old age or in battle. The LORD forbid that I should kill the one he has anointed!"
1 SAMUEL 26:10-11

You've probably heard it said of high-ranking elected officials that even if you disagree with the man, you should still respect the office he holds. In other words, though you may not personally like or endorse the political positions of your mayor, governor, or president, those people still occupy God-ordained positions of leadership and thus deserve our honor and respect.

God chose David to succeed Saul as Israel's king. David demonstrated that kind of respect for his predecessor . . . and then some.

David's popularity among the people soared after his successful confrontation with the Philistine Goliath, and Saul didn't like it. In his jealousy and anger at David's popularity, he tried to kill David. From a strictly human standpoint, David might have been justified in standing up to Saul and ending a very real threat to his personal well-being.

David *couldn't* do that.

David had two opportunities to kill Saul, and twice he refused to do so. He knew that Saul's day of reckoning would come, and that he could not in good conscience bring that about himself. David knew that God alone had the authority to remove Saul because he was the Lord's anointed.

David respected Saul's office. More than that, he respected God's office as the One whose sovereign will works everything out in his own good time.

David's mercy toward Saul demonstrated his unbending faith that God had appointed him as Saul's successor. David knew better than to run ahead of God and take matters into his own hands.

When you understand that God remains at the helm of the universe and that he actively works to bring about his perfect will at the right time, you can relax. Wait on him to move on your behalf instead of trying to make things happen in your own way and time.

June 11

Make the Most of It
PAUL

Near the shore where we landed was an estate belonging to Publius, the chief official of the island. He welcomed us and treated us kindly for three days. As it happened, Publius's father was ill with fever and dysentery. Paul went in and prayed for him, and laying his hands on him, he healed him. Acts 28:7-8

A woodsman wished to break up the monotony of his workday, so he challenged one of his coworkers to an all-day wood-chopping contest. The challenger worked his hardest all day, stopping only for a quick bite to eat, while the other contestant took a leisurely lunch and several breaks during the day.

At the end of the day, the challenger was shocked and more than a little annoyed to see that his opponent had chopped substantially more wood than he had.

"I don't get it," he complained. "Every time I looked, you were taking a rest, yet you chopped more wood than I did."

"What you didn't notice," the winning woodsman retorted, "was that every time I sat down to rest, I sharpened my ax."

The apostle Paul was once in a place where he could have used some rest and relaxation. As he traveled to Rome to plead his case before Caesar, a vicious storm wrecked his ship, landing him and the other passengers on the small Mediterranean island of Malta.

Malta is a beautiful place that remains a popular tourist destination. After all the work Paul had done over many years, you might think he would just bide his time on the island, but Paul's commitment motivated him to make the best use of every moment God gave him, including his three months in Malta waiting for a ship bound for Rome.

During those three months, Paul did the same things he had done on his missionary journeys. He healed the sick, preached the Word of God, and planted seeds of faith that would grow into a thriving church.

Whether you are working, spending time with your family and friends, or resting, time is a precious commodity. Make the best use of every moment God gives you, whatever your situation.

June 12

It's about Love
JESUS

[Jesus] turned to his critics and asked, "Does the law permit good deeds on the Sabbath, or is it a day for doing evil? Is this a day to save life or to destroy it?" But they wouldn't answer him. Mark 3:4

In his 1996 book *Surprised by the Power of the Spirit,* Jack Deere tells the story of a pastor who found himself in hot water with his church's elders.

One icy Sunday morning, the pastor awoke to find that the roads to church had become impassable. Instead of staying home, he put on his ice skates and skated over the river that ran between his home and the church. When he arrived, the elders were horrified to learn that their preacher had skated on the Lord's Day. When the pastor explained that it was either skate or miss church, one of elders asked, "Did you enjoy it?" When the preacher replied that he hadn't, the board of elders decided that he hadn't done anything wrong.

Nothing gets the attention of a religious old guard faster than trying something new and different. If you want a good example of that, look no further than Jesus' life on earth.

When Jesus came into the world, the Jewish religious leaders had weighed down both themselves and the people with so many rules and regulations that no one could keep them all, and certainly not while joyfully serving and loving God.

Jesus' wisdom and compassion steered the people back toward the spirit of the Law, which was rooted in love for God and neighbor. He demonstrated that principle, and further shook up the religious leaders of his time, when he walked into a synagogue one Sabbath, found a man in need, and "worked" by healing him.

How do you approach Christianity? Are you a legalist, or do you enjoy the freedom Jesus came to give you?

Jesus came to free you from the chains of legalism and give you a life of liberty and love. You can enjoy walking in his Spirit without making overly strict religious observances.

June 13

Second Chances
NAAMAN

Naaman became angry and stalked away. "I thought he would certainly come out to meet me!" he said. "I expected him to wave his hand over the leprosy and call on the name of the LORD his God and heal me!" 2 Kings 5:11

In one infamous play, Roy Riegels established himself as a legend in college football. In the first half of the 1929 Rose Bowl, Riegels, a lineman for the University of California, scooped up a fumble and headed for Georgia Tech's end zone. Inexplicably, Riegels reversed field and ran the wrong direction, leading to Tech's two-point safety.

Despite his teammates' encouragement to head back out after halftime, the despondent Riegels told his coach, Nibs Price, "Coach, I can't do it. I've ruined you, I've ruined myself, I've ruined the University of California. I couldn't face that crowd to save my life."

But Price wouldn't have it. "Roy," he instructed, "get up and go back out there—the game is only half over!" Nibs Price obviously believed in the biblical principle of second chances, a principle also operative on behalf of a highly decorated Syrian officer named Naaman.

Naaman had a serious infectious skin disease. When the prophet Elisha heard of his condition, he sent for Naaman, but when Naaman arrived at Elisha's home, he was disappointed and angered when the prophet just sent a messenger telling him that if he washed in the Jordan River seven times, he would be healed.

Naaman stormed away from Elisha's home, but his servants encouraged him to do as Elisha had said. When he obeyed, his disease disappeared.

Naaman found out that day that the God of Israel is a God of second chances.

Because of his humble, if reluctant, obedience, Naaman found healing. More importantly, he found salvation in the only place it could be found. "Now I know that there is no God in all the world except in Israel," he exclaimed, and then Naaman began serving him (see 2 Kings 5:15-18).

You may have really messed up your past life of faith, but you don't have to live in the past. God believes in second chances!

June 14

Blessed Assurance
THE CRIMINAL ON THE CROSS

He said, "Jesus, remember me when you come into your Kingdom." And Jesus replied, "I assure you, today you will be with me in paradise."   Luke 23:42-43

A middle-aged man with inoperable cancer did everything his doctors suggested in an attempt to extend his life. Despite his enduring months of pain and the discomfort of chemotherapy and radiation treatment, his cancer continued to spread. He was using the best options available for recovery, but he was dying.

As a man of faith, he knew that Jesus had the power to heal. He knew that the many people who loved him prayed passionately that he might get well.

He also knew one other thing: Everyone that Jesus healed died eventually.

Was this fatalism or resignation toward what appeared to be his too early death? Hardly. He knew that whether or not Jesus healed him physically, he would soon hear Jesus' voice welcoming him to his eternal home in heaven.

A blessed assurance indeed!

One of the last voices Jesus heard in his final moments of agony on the cross was that of a man who shuddered at his eternal prospects. He was dying painfully on another cross at Jesus' side when he found hope.

He knew that he deserved his earthly fate as a criminal whose own choices had put him on death row. Somehow, he also knew that something better could be waiting for him if he could just summon the strength to speak to Jesus.

"Jesus," he gasped, "remember me when you come into your Kingdom."

He listened as Jesus labored to speak those sweet words of comfort, "I *assure* you, today you will be with me in paradise."

Though he had only minutes to live, this condemned criminal knew that in a short time he would hear that same voice welcoming him into an eternal home whose wonder and beauty were beyond imagining.

When you have faith in Jesus Christ, you have the blessed assurance that you are guaranteed an eternal home in heaven regardless of what happens to you.

June 15

Intentions Matter
BALAAM

Balak's messengers, who were elders of Moab and Midian, set out with money to pay Balaam to place a curse upon Israel. They went to Balaam and delivered Balak's message to him. "Stay here overnight," Balaam said. "In the morning I will tell you whatever the LORD directs me to say."   Numbers 22:7-8

Did you ever know a married coworker who avoided an adulterous affair only because he feared being caught and losing everything he had worked for? Are you acquainted with a stingy believer who gives generously because someone told him that giving guarantees more financial blessings?

Motives can be everything.

The Bible insists that God sees not just what we do but also *why* we do it. In other words, it's not just the actions that count but the motivation behind those actions.

Take Balaam, for example. He was a Midianite sorcerer, a "prophet for hire" who three times spoke a blessing on the nation of Israel. He is still denounced in Scripture as an evil man with a corrupt heart.

Wait a minute, you might be thinking. *How can a man who blessed God's people not once, but three times, be such an evil man?*

The book of Joshua tells us that the only reason Balaam didn't curse Israel as the Moabite king Balak requested was that God stopped him and *made* him speak blessings (see Joshua 24:1-13). Later, the apostle Peter classified Balaam with false teachers who "lure unstable people into sin" (2 Peter 2:14) and wrote that he "loved to earn money by doing wrong" (2 Peter 2:15). In Jesus' words, Balaam "showed Balak how to trip up the people of Israel" (Revelation 2:14).

Balaam spoke blessings on God's people when he intended to speak curses. Clearly, he lacked a true heart for God.

Do you obey God from the heart? Do you find yourself doing the right thing for the wrong reasons? God honors and blesses you when you have an obedient heart. What comes from the heart is what matters!

June 16

Restored and Ready
PETER

Peter swore, "A curse on me if I'm lying—I don't know the man!" And immediately the rooster crowed. Suddenly, Jesus' words flashed through Peter's mind: "Before the rooster crows, you will deny three times that you even know me." And he went away, weeping bitterly.   Matthew 26:74-75

A middle-aged Vietnam veteran weighed down with guilt listened intently as a friend explained God's plan of salvation through Jesus Christ.

When his friend finished, the vet nodded in agreement, but in his mind, one big problem loomed. "Man, you don't even want to know the things I've done in the past," he said. "I know this Jesus stuff works for a lot of people, but I don't think it will work for someone who's done the kind of things I've done."

The world bursts with people weighed down with sins, some so serious that they doubt they can ever find forgiveness. The Bible teaches that God offers forgiveness for even the worst of sins and the worst of sinners.

Peter learned this truth firsthand.

Two men sinned terribly during the final hours before Jesus' death: Judas Iscariot, who betrayed him, and Peter, who denied even knowing him. Theories abound as to Judas's motivation for betraying Jesus, but few experts question why Peter denied him. He was afraid.

Judas and Peter both failed Jesus miserably, and both men immediately knew they had done wrong and felt the pangs of guilt. Judas was so ashamed that he tried to return the money he had received for betraying Jesus, hoping to undo the wrong he had committed. Peter wept bitterly over his denial and felt so ashamed that he disappeared from the scene.

That's where the similarities end.

Of these two remorseful sinners, only one turned back to the Lord. Judas took his own life, but a repentant Peter returned to Jesus, who set him on a course of courageous preaching and teaching.

God extends his forgiveness for the very worst sins and to the very worst of sinners. When you fail Jesus in any way, he invites you to follow Peter, who found forgiveness and restoration when he turned back to his Master.

June 17

Words of Correction
JOAB AND KING DAVID

The king said to Joab and the commanders of the army, "Take a census of all the tribes of Israel—from Dan in the north to Beersheba in the south—so I may know how many people there are." 2 Samuel 24:2

In poll after poll asking what people find most annoying, constantly correcting others is almost always near the top of the list. People don't generally like being corrected.

Sometimes, however, it's appropriate and even necessary to speak words of correction, even when those words are not warmly received.

Joab, David's top military leader, dutifully listened as the king ordered him to take a census of the people of Israel to determine the number of fighting-age men he had. The idea didn't sit well with Joab.

"May the LORD your God let you live to see a hundred times as many people as there are now! But why, my lord the king, do you want to do this?" (2 Samuel 24:3). In another biblical account of the same incident, Joab adds, "Why must you cause Israel to sin?" (1 Chronicles 21:3).

Doesn't it make sense for a king to want to know how many potential soldiers he has? What was so sinful about taking a census?

Joab apparently understood that David's orders came out of his reliance on superior military strength rather than on the might of heaven. In other words, David trusted in his own power instead of God's.

Joab did his duty. Though he warned David not to go through with the census, the king ordered it anyway. He paid a terrible price for failing to heed Joab's simple words of correction.

There may come a time in your life when you'll have to speak words of correction. When that happens, check your motivation and choose your words carefully.

June 18

One-on-One Evangelism
ANDREW AND SIMON

Andrew went to find his brother, Simon, and told him, "We have found the Messiah," (which means "Christ"). Then Andrew brought Simon to meet Jesus.
JOHN 1:41-42

A man in his late twenties knew that his good friend and fishing buddy needed to come to Jesus Christ for salvation. Without being preachy or badgering his friend, the man began to talk about his own life-changing experiences with God.

Eventually, the man's friend wanted to know more.

The young man, excited and confident, talked about how he had come to know Jesus Christ as his Savior and how much he wanted his friend to know him also.

Ultimately, the man's friend came to Christ, and neither of them ever forgot how their friendship changed his life and his eternal destination.

Not everyone gets to preach to mass audiences as Billy Graham and Luis Palau do, but everyone can make an eternal difference in the lives of people around them.

That's exactly how the apostle Andrew got his start.

If you're looking through the book of Acts to see which of the apostles first brought an outsider into the fold, you need to back up one book and look at the first chapter of John's Gospel. There you will see that the apostle-to-be Andrew introduced his brother Simon, whom Jesus called Peter, to Jesus.

When Andrew first met Jesus and realized his identity, he couldn't contain his excitement. He had to tell *someone,* and that someone was his own brother. Andrew and Peter had grown up together, played together, and worked together as adults.

Andrew's one simple act of personal evangelism—inviting his brother to come and see the Messiah—altered the course of Peter's life forever. Peter, in turn, influenced the lives of millions who would come to faith in Jesus Christ through his work as an *apostle.*

You may not have the mass appeal of Billy Graham, but you can still make a difference in the eternal life of someone close to you. It isn't about training or credentials; it's about telling your friends and loved ones that you have found the Messiah!

June 19

The Courage to Reconcile
JACOB AND ESAU

Jacob insisted, "No, if I have found favor with you, please accept this gift from me."… And because Jacob insisted, Esau finally accepted the gift.
GENESIS 33:10-11

At a New Year's Eve party at London's Garrick Club, British actor Seymour Hicks approached playwright Frederick Lonsdale and suggested that he reconcile with a fellow member who had been Lonsdale's friend in the past before a falling-out.

"It is very unkind to be unfriendly at such a time," Lonsdale said. "Go over now and wish him a Happy New Year."

Lonsdale crossed the room and coldly said to his former friend, "I wish you a Happy New Year, but only one."

Whether because of human pride, fear of rejection, or some other emotional issue, we struggle to reconcile with someone who has hurt us—or someone we've hurt.

Take the example of Jacob and his brother, Esau. After so many years apart from his brother, Jacob felt terrified at the prospect of seeing him again. He knew that Esau was angry with him for bilking him out of his birthright, and he wondered if he was going to live through this reunion.

Jacob and his family had returned to the land of Canaan, where Esau lived. By now, Esau was a successful, wealthy businessman, and as Esau and four hundred of his men approached Jacob and his family, Jacob wondered if he had done the right thing.

As Esau came closer, Jacob trembled. Would Esau kill him and everyone in his family?

No, he wouldn't.

Esau ran to Jacob and embraced him, forgave him, and invited him to bring his family to Seir and set up their homes there. Though years of rancor and hatred stood between Jacob and Esau, their brotherhood enabled them to reunite peacefully and lovingly in the end.

Is there an estranged friend or family member with whom you need to seek reconciliation? You can never completely avoid conflict in your life, but you can take steps to be reconciled with a person you have disagreed with. Take the first step. It might be easier than you think!

June 20

Two Are Better Than One
AQUILA

Give my greetings to Priscilla and Aquila, my coworkers in the ministry of Christ Jesus. In fact, they once risked their lives for me. I am thankful to them, and so are all the Gentile churches.   Romans 16:3-4

Many men today choose to stay single longer, but study after study shows that married men tend to live longer, healthier, and happier lives than those who remain single.

How's that for a ringing endorsement of marriage?

There's another benefit of marriage that was experienced by a Jewish believer named Aquila. Having a spouse encourages a stronger spiritual life and a more effective ministry.

Having a partner in ministry can make the work go more smoothly and efficiently. In New Testament times, preachers and apostles often traveled in pairs. Peter and John, Paul and Barnabas, and Paul and Silas were good traveling teams.

Then there was Aquila and his wife, Priscilla.

The Bible never mentions Aquila without also mentioning Priscilla. These two were united in marriage, and they were partners in ministry.

Aquila and Priscilla first appear in Scripture in Acts 18, which reports that the couple shared their home in Corinth with the apostle Paul. They had been forced to flee Rome due to the Roman emperor Claudius's decree commanding all Jews to leave the city. They took with them their hearts for service.

Aquila and his wife later traveled with Paul to Ephesus, where they continued their ministry as Paul's helpers. That help included meeting with an impressive man of God named Apollos to explain the significance of Jesus' death and resurrection to him more completely.

Aquila made a difference in his place and time in the world. He could work more effectively because he had a wife who was a partner in his ministry.

Aquila's marriage to Priscilla was a source of strength and encouragement for him and for everyone they met, especially those God had called to preach for Jesus.

Marriage has many benefits, and one of the best is receiving and giving encouragement and strength. When these qualities spill over to others, the blessings multiply.

June 21

Recognize Your Smallness
HEROD

Herod put on his royal robes, sat on his throne, and made a speech to them. The people gave him a great ovation, shouting, "It's the voice of a god, not of a man!"
ACTS 12:21-22

American naturalist and author William Beebe was a close friend of Theodore Roosevelt and often spent time at his home in Cove Neck, New York. The two would go out on the lawn at night and search the skies for a certain spot of light. Roosevelt would then recite, "That is the Spiral Galaxy in Andromeda. It is as large as our Milky Way. It is one of a hundred million galaxies. It consists of one hundred billion suns, each larger than our sun."

Having made that observation, Roosevelt would grin and say, "Now I think we are small enough! Let's go to bed."

It's easy to recognize a man who does not realize his own smallness. He's the one with an air of self-sufficiency and self-satisfaction. He's just like Herod Agrippa I, who paid dearly for his arrogance.

Herod, the grandson of Herod the Great, was known for his terrible treatment of his subjects and his uncontrolled egotism. The latter quality cost him everything.

When a delegation of men from Tyre and Sidon arrived in Jerusalem to meet with Herod, he appeared to them wearing his royal robes, sat on his throne, and began speaking to them. These men either liked what Herod had to say, or more likely, they intended to stroke his massive ego. "It's the voice of a god, not of a man!" they cried out, and Herod gladly accepted their adulation.

That day, Herod usurped the worship that God had reserved for himself. Had he been able to give God what was rightfully his, his story would have ended in blessing. Instead, it ended in his death. The last bow he took sent him on a one-way trip to his grave.

God loves to bless you when you give him the praise and worship due to him. That happens more easily when you recognize your own smallness . . . and God's greatness.

June 22

Acknowledge Your Limitations
THE MAN AT THE POOL OF BETHESDA

*When Jesus saw him and knew he had been ill for a long time, he asked him,
"Would you like to get well?" "I can't, sir," the sick man said, "for I have no one
to put me into the pool when the water bubbles up. Someone else always gets there
ahead of me."*   John 5:6-7

In the 1973 action thriller *Magnum Force,* San Francisco Police Lieutenant
Briggs boasts to detective Harry Callahan that he has been on the force for
a long time without ever having to take his gun out of its holster. Without
a moment's hesitation, "Dirty Harry" fires back, "Well, you're a good man,
Lieutenant, and a good man always knows his limitations."

That's a pretty good observation.

An unnamed sick man who met Jesus one day knew his limitations. When
Jesus asked him if he wanted to get well, he responded, "I can't."

Something about the words "I can't" offends the sensibilities of most
Christians. Haven't we been taught that we can do all things through Christ
because nothing is impossible for him? But for this man, "I can't" was the
truth. He had been unable to walk for thirty-eight years. He couldn't make
his own way through the crowds of infirm people hoping to bathe in the
healing waters of the pool of Bethesda. So he waited for someone to help
him get in.

What he obviously couldn't do, Jesus did.

Jesus knew the man's problem and realized what he wanted. He also knew
that on his own, the man had no hope of changing his situation.

"Stand up, pick up your mat, and walk!" Jesus commanded, and in an
instant, the man's body strengthened and he began walking.

I can't!

Sometimes those are the very words Jesus wants to hear. When they come
from the lips of someone who understands his own limitations, there's a good
chance that this person will realize his need for complete dependence on
Christ.

When life stretches you beyond your limitations, you are right where God wants you.
God loves to do his most spectacular work at such times. Who knows what might happen
for those who humbly acknowledge their weakness and inability and cry out to God for
a miracle?

June 23

Put Off Procrastination
FELIX

A few days later Felix came back with his wife, Drusilla, who was Jewish. Sending for Paul, they listened as he told them about faith in Christ Jesus. As he reasoned with them about righteousness and self-control and the coming day of judgment, Felix became frightened. "Go away for now," he replied. "When it is more convenient, I'll call for you again." Acts 24:24-25

Do you know anyone who appreciates the mantra "Never do today what you can put off until tomorrow"? Do you have unfinished projects at your home? Are there stacks of paper on your desk that you haven't gotten around to reading? Any phone calls that you haven't managed to return?

Procrastination is a great enemy of accomplishment. Procrastination keeps you from success at home and at work, and it prevents you from being all that God wants you to be.

Felix was a procrastinator. He was the Roman governor of Judea during the time of the apostle Paul, and he had an opportunity to respond to the message of salvation through Jesus. Paul told him and his Jewish wife, Drusilla, of their need for faith in Christ so that they could one day inherit the Kingdom of Heaven.

As Felix listened intently to Paul's message, it frightened him so badly that he put off hearing more. Felix allowed his fears to drive him away from Christ instead of toward him. "Go away for now," Felix told Paul. "When it is more convenient, I'll call for you again."

Tragically, that "more convenient" time never came. Though the governor talked to Paul again on several occasions, he never again brought up the subject of God or salvation. Instead, he focused on seeking bribes and thus missed out on God's greatest gift of an eternity with him in heaven.

Ask yourself what blessings you might be missing because you choose to put off your responsibilities and do them at a "more convenient" time. Every day that you live is a gift from God. Use that gift to do the things God has directed you to do. Never put off until tomorrow what you can do today!

June 24

God's Presence
MOSES

Moses said, "If you don't personally go with us, don't make us leave this place."
EXODUS 33:15

The renowned British writer C. S. Lewis once wisely said, "He who has God and many other things has no more than he who has God alone."

Have you ever been in a situation that made you realize how much you needed God's personal presence? Sometimes life comes down on us so hard that we can do nothing but cry out, "I can't do this without you!"

Moses had an acute sense of his need for God's presence as well as his provision, promises, and power.

Experience brought him to that conclusion.

Moses had already endured a lot in his walk with God. He had fled for his life from Egypt, spent forty years living in Midian, faced down a stubborn Pharaoh, and seen God's magnificent power in freeing his chosen people from Egyptian slavery.

Moses knew that none of those things could have taken place if God had not been with him, and the thought of doing anything without God terrified him.

God called Moses to lead the people of Israel *out* of bondage and *into* the Promised Land. As Moses considered the enormous task before him, he knew that he didn't want to take a single step further without the assurance of God's continued presence. If God wouldn't promise Moses that, then this shepherd-turned-leader preferred to remain in the wilderness. Moses felt that the Promised Land without the Promise Giver didn't hold much promise.

Moses thus arrived at precisely the place where God had wanted him all along. He realized that he wanted nothing more than to have God with him everywhere he went and in everything he did.

How much does the presence of God mean to you?

Think of someone that you believe clearly enjoys the presence of God. What makes this person different? Do people enjoy being around him or her? Why? What would it take for you to be someone who also clearly enjoys God's presence?

June 25

Taking Stock
KING MANASSEH

While in deep distress, Manasseh sought the LORD his God and sincerely humbled himself before the God of his ancestors. And when he prayed, the LORD listened to him and was moved by his request. 2 Chronicles 33:12-13

At his yearly physical, a middle-aged man who had always thought of himself as healthy was stunned to learn that all was not well with his body. Somehow, twenty-five pounds of extra weight had crept up, he had dangerously high blood pressure, and his years of smoking had damaged his lungs.

If he didn't make some changes, his doctor told him, he was a prime candidate for a stroke. In the days that followed, the man began to take stock of what he had allowed to happen to his body and what it might mean to him, his wife, and his children if he didn't make some changes.

He made those changes.

Times of stress can motivate a man to do a little self-examination. Manasseh, the evil king of Judah, had that experience.

Manasseh was the righteous King Hezekiah's son and successor, but he was hardly a "chip off the old block." Manasseh made sinning into a personal art form by persecuting those who worshiped the true God, reestablishing the idolatry his father had abolished, and practicing soothsaying and sorcery.

God warned Manasseh that he would pay a price for his sins, but Manasseh refused to listen. Finally, Assyrian forces invaded Judah and took him away to Babylon, where he remained for twelve years suffering atrocious treatment at his captor's hands.

God had given Manasseh a chance to take stock of his life.

This once proud, idolatrous man humbled himself before God and repented of all his evil. The light came on as Manasseh finally realized, "The LORD alone is God!" (2 Chronicles 33:13).

God returned Manasseh to Jerusalem, where he did his best to undo the damage he had done. He was a changed man, from the inside out.

Has God shown you things about yourself that need to change? Our loving, gracious God reveals our imperfections in order to change and transform those who surrender to him.

June 26

Say Something Good
TERTULLUS

When Paul was called in, Tertullus presented the charges against Paul in the following address to the governor: . . . "We have found this man to be a troublemaker who is constantly stirring up riots among the Jews all over the world. He is a ringleader of the cult known as the Nazarenes." Acts 24:2, 5

During Winston Churchill's last year as British prime minister, he attended an official ceremony where he heard, from several rows behind him, a man whispering to his friend, "That's Winston Churchill. They say he is getting senile. They say he should step aside and leave the running of the nation to more dynamic and capable men."

When the ceremony concluded, Churchill, known for his sometimes sarcastic wit, turned to the gossip and the man's friend and said, "Gentlemen, they also say he is deaf!"

Sadly, too few people today live by the adage "If you can't say something good, don't say anything at all." Though the Bible repeatedly enjoins believers to use words that build others up rather than tear them down, it's very easy to find excuses to speak ill of another.

Tertullus, a Jewish advocate before the Roman government, was an extreme example of someone who went out of his way to tear another man down. The apostle Paul was one of his victims. Like many others of his day, Tertullus wanted to stop all the preaching about Jesus, and he intended to do what he could to make that happen.

Standing before Felix, the Roman governor of Judea, Tertullus accused Paul of disturbing the peace throughout the Roman Empire and preventing Jewish people from exercising their religion. Though Tertullus's accusations were far more than just a spin on the facts, his words made a big difference in Paul's life. Tertullus intended to have Paul imprisoned—or worse—but Paul continued his preaching, now in the presence of Roman leaders.

Words have real power to harm your brother or sister in Christ, including the ones in your own home. Before you say something about another person, ask yourself if what you're about to say builds that person up or tears him down.

June 27

The Path to Greatness
JAMES AND JOHN

[James and John] replied, "When you sit on your glorious throne, we want to sit in places of honor next to you, one on your right and the other on your left."
MARK 10:37

At a time when people are leaving the corporate world in droves to pursue their own businesses, many people ask, "What do I need to do in order to be successful?" One of the most frequent answers is simply to serve—to put the customer's or client's needs and desires ahead of one's own. As one business adviser put it, "The greater the quality and quantity of your service, the greater the reward."

Our culture doesn't always value putting others' needs and desires first, but as the apostles James and John learned, that is exactly what they needed to do to achieve greatness.

One day, James and John sidled up to Jesus and made an audacious request. They wanted Jesus to give them the two highest seats of honor when Jesus assumed his throne. James and John's request didn't sit too well with the rest of the disciples, probably because they had similar ambitions. That day, Jesus taught all of them what it takes to assume a position of greatness in God's Kingdom.

James and John had the noble goal of being great in God's Kingdom. Jesus didn't scold them for asking, but he taught them and the other disciples that the path to greatness is found by serving others.

Does achieving greatness by putting others first seem a little backward? It does to a lot of folks today, but that's just what God calls you to do. Your humility will be richly rewarded!

Do you want to be great in God's Kingdom? To be the kind of leader, husband, father, and worker he calls you to be, make serving others your life's ambition.

June 28

Make a Lasting Impression
KING DARIUS

King Darius sent this message to the people of every race and nation and language throughout the world: "Peace and prosperity to you! I decree that everyone throughout my kingdom should tremble with fear before the God of Daniel. For he is the living God, and he will endure forever."   Daniel 6:25-26

What would you do if you knew that by demonstrating your faithfulness to God through simple acts such as attending church regularly and talking about your faith at home, you could have a lasting influence on your children?

In a recent article in *Kindred Spirit,* Dr. Michael Green cites a study that found that the sons of fathers who frequently attended church, discussed religion at home, and were committed to their faith tended to follow that same pattern throughout their lives.

How you live and how you demonstrate your faith can make a big impression.

Darius the Mede is a great example of what can happen when a man sees the fruit of true faith. Opponents of Daniel duped Darius into sending the prophet into a den of lions. Darius knew that he had sent Daniel to a horrible death, and it tore him up so badly that he spent the night fasting.

More than ever, Darius wanted to see the power of Daniel's God put on display. That's what happened as Daniel emerged from the lion's den the next morning without so much as a scratch.

What an impression this made on Darius! He had just seen a miracle, and he had no other explanation for it. This was the work of a mighty God! Darius praised the name of Daniel's God.

Our world is full of men like Darius who need to see the truth and goodness of God demonstrated openly in the lives of those who faithfully and wholeheartedly serve him.

What can you do to impress a Darius in your own world?

As a believer, you are called to make an impression on the world around you. You do that when your life, words, and attitudes set you apart among people that desperately need to see God's power at work.

June 29

Great for the Soul
THE PRODIGAL SON

"I will go home to my father and say, 'Father, I have sinned against both heaven and you, and I am no longer worthy of being called your son. Please take me on as a hired servant.'" Luke 15:18-19

In the 1884 presidential race, Republican candidate James G. Blaine believed that he had Democrat Grover Cleveland on the ropes. It had been revealed that Cleveland, then a bachelor, had fathered a son with the widow Maria Crofts Halpin. In an attempt to paint Cleveland as an immoral man, Republicans distributed leaflets showing an infant with the label "One more vote for Cleveland." Blaine's supporters paraded and chanted, "Ma, ma, where's my pa? Gone to the White House, ha ha ha!"

These moves backfired badly.

Cleveland came out and confessed his indiscretion, which took the issue off the table for Blaine. His openness apparently won over the American people, who elected him president.

The Bible repeatedly teaches the importance of confession and tells us that God is "faithful and just" to forgive those who humbly confess their sins (see 1 John 1:9). Jesus illustrated this point by telling the story of a young man who left a good life on his father's farm to pursue a life of sin.

Once he had run out of money and had to take work tending the pigs—despised animals who ate better than he did—the young man came to his senses and decided to return home, confess his sins, and humbly ask his father if he could stay on as one of the hired hands (see Luke 15:14-19). His father wouldn't hear of hiring his own son. Instead, he welcomed his boy back into his home with a celebration (see Luke 15:22-24).

The father's willingness to welcome his son back into his family showed his love for his son and his son's willingness to leave the way he had been living.

This is just like our heavenly Father.

Your heavenly Father is more than willing to forgive you when you confess your sins and return home to him. Confession, to God and to others hurt by your actions, is good for the soul. It is the key to reconciliation.

June 30

Risk Assessment
ANANIAS

"But Lord," exclaimed Ananias, "I've heard many people talk about the terrible things this man has done to the believers in Jerusalem! And he is authorized by the leading priests to arrest everyone who calls upon your name." Acts 9:13-14

If you have ever started a new business or expanded an established one, you know the importance of risk assessment. Simply put, that means examining the risks involved in launching a new venture and determining whether the payoff is worth the risk.

Ananias, a prominent believer living in Damascus, once received a very risky command from God and had to decide what he would do about it.

God had given Ananias an assignment that made him very uncomfortable. He was to look after Saul, a young Pharisee notorious for his cruel treatment of Christians in Jerusalem. Ananias knew Saul as a sworn enemy of the church. His sole purpose in coming to Damascus had been to persecute him and other believers.

Ananias must have wondered if God was talking about the same Saul he had been hearing about.

Just to find out, Ananias reminded God of the terrible things Saul had done to believers in Jerusalem. Saul was even authorized to arrest Christians, but God didn't relent. He intended for Saul to take his message of salvation to both Gentiles and Jews (see Acts 9:15).

Ananias knew the risks of reaching out to a man like Saul. Nevertheless, he was confident that God knew what he was doing and had a good purpose for bringing Saul to Damascus. This overshadowed his trepidation.

Ananias weighed the risks and knew that the benefits of obedience far outweighed anything he feared. Because he obeyed, he was able to play a supporting role in God's plan to spread the gospel throughout the world.

God may one day call you to do something that seems risky to your human thinking. When you have the faith to understand that God is in control and has your path mapped out, you can confidently go wherever he calls you, knowing that he has your best interests in mind.

July 1

Passionate Intercession
ABRAHAM

Will you sweep away both the righteous and the wicked? Suppose you find fifty righteous people living there in the city—will you still sweep it away and not spare it for their sakes? Surely you wouldn't do such a thing, destroying the righteous along with the wicked. Genesis 18:23-25

Have you ever felt a sense of sorrow and powerlessness as a family member or someone else you care deeply about makes a life choice that you know will lead to trouble? Perhaps the son you love deeply enters into a life of addiction. A friend may decide to leave his wife and pursue another woman.

Abraham was face-to-face with such a situation.

Abraham's heart sank when God announced that he would destroy Sodom. His nephew Lot and his family lived in that city, and Abraham possibly knew other people there as well. Abraham took this news hard and personally, so he couldn't just stand back and watch God destroy Sodom without trying to intercede on its behalf.

Abraham knew and trusted God. He understood that he could count on God's assessment of Sodom to be just and righteous. He also knew something of God's mercy, so Abraham pleaded Sodom's case by appealing to God's righteous character. Despite the flagrant sin of its residents, Abraham asked God if he would spare the city if he could find fifty righteous people living there.

God acknowledged that he would.

Emboldened by this success, Abraham took his passionate plea several more steps. He asked God if he would spare the city for the sake of forty righteous men—then thirty, twenty, and, finally, ten.

"I will not destroy it for the sake of the ten," the Lord told Abraham (Genesis 18:32).

As Abraham pleaded with God on Sodom's behalf, he showed his confidence that God loved him enough to hear him out.

God didn't want it any other way.

Are you a man of persistent, passionate prayer? God loves it when you care enough to pray with passion for those who need his love and mercy. They may never know how zealously you prayed for them, but you and God will know.

July 2

Get Up and Go!
JOSHUA

Moses my servant is dead. Therefore, the time has come for you to lead these people, the Israelites, across the Jordan River into the land I am giving them.
JOSHUA 1:2

When the 2007 college football season opened, nobody gave tiny Appalachian State University any serious chance of challenging mighty Division I University of Michigan in the season opener for both teams.

So much for expectations!

In one of the biggest upsets in sports history, the little Division I-AA school from Boone, North Carolina, shocked the football world when it defeated the Wolverines—in Ann Arbor, no less—by a score of 34-32.

The Mountaineers spent several months preparing for their big game with Michigan, but all that preparation would have meant nothing had they failed to show up! Their fans were very happy that they did.

Sometimes, experiencing the good things in life is just a matter of getting up, going out, and showing up. That's as true in the spiritual realm as it is in sports.

Throughout Scripture, God attaches promises to his commands. He says, "If you do this, I will do that." Joshua, the man God chose to succeed Moses and lead Israel into the Promised Land, heard exactly that kind of divine promise and command.

Shortly after Moses' death, God said to Joshua, "The time has come for you to lead these people, the Israelites, across the Jordan River into the land I am giving them." He followed that instruction with a promise: "Wherever you set foot, you will be on land I have given you" (Joshua 1:3).

Joshua is one of the greatest examples in the Bible of how "showing up" at God's command leads to victory. Joshua would have left us a very different example had he failed to do that one simple thing: *Go!*

God gives many conditional promises in the Bible; his promises are often contingent upon our taking steps of obedience. If you want to accomplish great things in your life and for his Kingdom, then take those first steps. Show up and go!

July 3

Righteous Anger
JESUS

Jesus made a whip from some ropes and chased them all out of the Temple. He drove out the sheep and cattle, scattered the money changers' coins over the floor, and turned over their tables. Then, going over to the people who sold doves, he told them, "Get these things out of here. Stop turning my Father's house into a marketplace!" John 2:15-16

Someone once anonymously stated, "A person who is angry on the right grounds, against the right persons, in the right manner, at the right moment, and for the right length of time deserves great praise."

No man has ever expressed "praiseworthy anger" quite like Jesus.

On several occasions, Jesus became angry over something he saw or heard. He angrily confronted the Jewish religious authorities over their lack of love and true faith in his heavenly Father.

On one of his visits to Jerusalem, Jesus responded in violent anger when he saw people using the Temple for improper purposes. At that time, money changers and other businessmen often set up shop in and around the Temple during Passover. They exchanged foreign currencies for Jewish money (for a hefty surcharge) so pilgrims could purchase sacrificial animals for the Passover celebration.

Jesus didn't get nearly as angry with the business practice as he did with the money changers who did their greedy gouging in the place where people prayed and worshiped God.

All of this was done with the approval of the Temple priests.

Jesus always directed his anger at things that stood in the way of God's purposes for humankind. Jesus loved God and his righteousness, and he effectively expressed his anger at unrighteousness.

Do you express your anger over the same kinds of issues that angered Jesus?

Anger is as much a part of the human condition as love. When you become angry, stop and ask yourself if it's for the right reason, at the right people, and at the right moment. Are you angry in the way that Jesus would be angry?

July 4

Infectious Faith
ELIJAH

Elijah said to her, "Don't be afraid! Go ahead and do just what you've said, but make a little bread for me first. Then use what's left to prepare a meal for yourself and your son. For this is what the LORD, the God of Israel, says: There will always be flour and olive oil left in your containers until the time when the LORD sends rain and the crops grow again!" 1 Kings 17:13-14

Don't you just hate it when you're on your way to work and you hear a song on the radio that you can't get out of your head? You might not even like the song, but somehow it just keeps rattling around in your brain.

An infectious tune like that has real staying power.

Faith is often like that. When you speak about it and demonstrate your faith openly, it is bound to infect others. That's the kind of faith the prophet Elijah had.

At times, it seemed to Elijah that he was the only man of faith left in Israel. That didn't stop him from speaking God's Word to those who desperately needed to hear it. One of those people was a widow in a little village named Zarephath. God directed a hungry Elijah to visit her one day.

Times had grown harsh in Israel. Drought had led to famine and famine to desperation, especially for the poor. When God sent Elijah to Zarephath, the prophet probably assumed that he would meet a *wealthy* widow with a heart for service. The woman he met was so destitute that she was facing the likelihood of death.

As a man of faith, Elijah didn't allow a little thing like this woman's poverty to keep him from seeing God's hand at work. Elijah looked at the woman's desperation and saw someone who needed a boost of faith.

Elijah persuaded the woman to share what little she had with him. Because she did, faith won out that day. She never again lacked food for herself or her son.

God doesn't give you faith so you can keep it to yourself. Faith isn't real unless you put it to work. Don't worry about running out—God will always give you more just when you need it.

July 5

Bottom-Line Wisdom
SOLOMON

That's the whole story. Here now is my final conclusion: Fear God and obey his commands, for this is everyone's duty. God will judge us for everything we do, including every secret thing, whether good or bad. ECCLESIASTES 12:13-14

The seventeenth-century French mathematician and philosopher Blaise Pascal once said, "There is in the heart of every man a God-shaped void." There truly is a space in each of us that only God can fill.

Solomon learned that bit of wisdom the hard way.

Some believe that the book of Ecclesiastes contains Solomon's observations and his warnings for people to avoid the mistakes he made as he allowed power, wealth, and lust to take God's rightful place in his heart. Solomon had it all, but he eventually concluded that those things weren't enough. When he looked at what he had accomplished, Solomon saw that everything—even the rich blessings God had sent his way—amounted to exactly nothing. His life was empty and meaningless.

Early in his life, Solomon asked God for wisdom, and thereafter the Bible refers to him as the wisest man who ever lived. In his later years, however, he made some very unwise choices.

Despite God's repeated warnings to keep him at the center of his life, Solomon drifted from the Lord and turned to other gods. After spending a great deal of time chasing power, wealth, pleasure, and respect, Solomon abandoned the God who had so faithfully and richly blessed him.

Without God at the center of your life, Solomon warns, life becomes meaningless. Without him, life amounts to nothing but birth, a lot of hard work, and death. When you make Jesus Christ central to everything, even everyday events have meaning and significance.

Have you made your relationship with God central to everything you do?

God loves to richly bless those who place him at the center of their lives. That's the one and only way to find fulfillment and enjoyment, even in the everyday events of your life.

July 6

The Effects of Jealousy
KING SAUL AND DAVID

The very next day a tormenting spirit from God overwhelmed Saul, and he
began to rave in his house like a madman. David was playing the harp, as he did
each day. But Saul had a spear in his hand, and he suddenly hurled it at David,
intending to pin him to the wall. But David escaped him twice. Saul was then
afraid of David, for the LORD was with David and had turned away from Saul.
1 SAMUEL 18:10-12

After performing with fellow Russian ballet dancer Vaslav Nijinsky one evening, Anna Matveyevna Pavlova was so overcome with jealousy and anger
that she fainted behind the curtain. Pavlova's problem? After their performance, she heard the audience shouting Nijinsky's name louder than hers.

Jealousy—the emotion we feel toward someone who has something we
believe should be ours—has the potential to wreck human and divine relationships and turn otherwise healthy people into emotional basket cases.

That, in a nutshell, was the story of King Saul and his jealousy toward
David. The young man did nothing but serve the king faithfully, but Saul
grew angry with him because of his growing popularity.

When Saul promoted David to the position of army commander, he
served with distinction, defeating the dreaded Philistines and leading his victorious men home. Saul should have celebrated his army's victory, but when
he heard the people singing songs that celebrated David's return, jealousy
took over. Saul went insane and made it his life's goal to kill David, the man
God had already chosen to succeed him.

Saul's story reminds us that jealousy doesn't get us one step closer to enjoying God's blessings. Instead, it will steal the joy and contentment the Lord
wants us to experience.

Knowing that, we can come to no other conclusion but that jealousy is
totally crazy!

Who is most likely to make you feel jealous? How can you turn that jealousy into gratitude
for what God has done in the life of another and for what he wants to do in your life? Rest
content in the knowledge that God has mapped out a life of blessing specifically for you.

July 7

Seeing as God Sees
PETER AND CORNELIUS

Peter told them, "You know it is against our laws for a Jewish man to enter a Gentile home like this or to associate with you. But God has shown me that I should no longer think of anyone as impure or unclean." Acts 10:28

As a young student, Mahatma Gandhi spent time reading the Gospels and seriously considered converting to Christianity. One Sunday, he walked to a nearby church, planning to attend the service and talk to the minister about becoming a Christian. When he entered the sanctuary, the usher refused to seat him and suggested that he worship with his "own people."

Gandhi left the church and never returned.

Sadly, people are good at making distinctions about race, social status, religion, and other factors. The apostle Peter learned that those things mean nothing to God.

As Peter prayed one day before lunch, he saw a strange vision of a sheet holding all sorts of animals that were considered unclean according to Jewish law. Then came the voice: "Get up, Peter; kill and eat them" (Acts 10:13). As a devout Jew, Peter would have none of it, but the voice insisted: "Do not call something unclean if God has made it clean" (Acts 10:15). The vision repeated itself three times, and the sheet disappeared into heaven.

The vision left Peter scratching his head.

As Peter puzzled over what he had seen and heard, some men representing a Roman officer named Cornelius asked him to come with them to Caesarea and visit their commander, who had seen a strange vision of his own. By the time Peter arrived at Cornelius's house the next day, something had clicked inside him.

Peter knew that it was unlawful for a Jew to enter a Gentile's home. He also understood the message of his vision: "God has shown me that I should no longer think of anyone as impure or unclean" (Acts 10:28).

God doesn't look at a person's race, social standing, or anything else besides their need for a Savior. He sent Jesus to draw *all* men to himself.

Do you approach people of every race, color, national origin, and social class in the same way? God calls you to embrace them and welcome them as people Jesus came to save. He calls us to love everyone.

July 8

Anticipation Rewarded
SIMEON

At that time there was a man in Jerusalem named Simeon. He was righteous and devout and was eagerly waiting for the Messiah to come and rescue Israel. The Holy Spirit was upon him and had revealed to him that he would not die until he had seen the Lord's Messiah.   Luke 2:25-26

There may be no better picture of the excitement of anticipation than your family dog when you walk through the door at the end of the day. He runs to you wagging his tail, in anticipation of spending some quality time with his master. When you pick up his food dish, he dances around in anticipation of dinner.

Humans are also creatures of anticipation. Several studies have suggested that even the expectation of something good benefits our health and sense of well-being.

Anticipation can also have a positive effect on your walk with the Lord!

Simeon, an aging saint still alive when Jesus was born, illustrates what the anticipation of a blessing can do to a man. Simeon had lived a long life of such close fellowship with God that the Holy Spirit had told him that he wouldn't die before he had seen the Messiah. Imagine the anticipation that filled Simeon's every day!

Then one day, Simeon heard that still, small voice of the Holy Spirit telling him to go to the Temple. His heart probably pounded as he thought about what that might mean. *This has to be the day,* Simeon thought as he hurried from his home to his people's place of worship.

When Simeon saw the baby Jesus, he knew immediately that this was the One he had been waiting for. He reacted with a mixture of joy, contentment, and relief at the fulfillment of the prophecy: "Sovereign Lord, now let your servant die in peace, as you have promised. I have seen your salvation, which you have prepared for all people" (Luke 2:29-31).

You can receive God's best blessings when, like Simeon, you listen to God, believe him, and wait expectantly for him to keep his promises.

July 9

Lead by Doing
EZRA

"O my God, I am utterly ashamed; I blush to lift up my face to you. For our sins are piled higher than our heads, and our guilt has reached to the heavens. From the days of our ancestors until now, we have been steeped in sin." Ezra 9:6-7

When a company vice president learned that many of his best people had developed the habit of arriving late for work, he mapped out a plan of action. Instead of singling out his valuable employees, he decided to call a department-wide meeting and talk about the rampant tardiness, including himself as a part of the problem.

In the following weeks, this VP made sure that he always arrived at work on time. Before he knew it, arriving to work late was a problem of the past in his department.

People usually follow an example better than any amount of talking. If you want people to do what is good and right, do those things yourself.

The priest Ezra led the second wave of Jewish exiles back to their homeland after seventy years of captivity in Babylon. When he arrived in Jerusalem, he didn't like what he saw. Many of the people had directly disobeyed God's law by marrying people outside the Jewish faith. Even worse, they had started living like the pagans they had married (see Ezra 9:1).

For Ezra, what should have been a time of joy and celebration quickly became a time of mourning and repentance. Although he was innocent of any wrongdoing, Ezra led the people in confessing their sins.

In this situation, Ezra might have been tempted to distance himself from the people he loved. He could have just let God deal with them as they deserved. Instead, he prayed in repentance on behalf of all the people and included himself.

Ezra's "repentance by example" moved his people to change their ways. They did as Ezra had done by confessing their sins and turning toward God (see Ezra 10:2, 11-12).

Leading the people who are closest to you toward the right attitudes and actions doesn't begin with telling them what to do, but with doing those things yourself.

July 10

A Man after God's Heart
KING DAVID AND NATHAN

David confessed to Nathan, "I have sinned against the LORD." 2 SAMUEL 12:13

Employers looking for someone to oversee the most important affairs of a company usually look for a man with a proven track record of integrity and high moral character. They normally look for a man who always tells the truth, remains faithful to his wife and children, and always does right by other people. Applicants who lack these qualities are quickly shown the door.

God is not a typical employer.

Consider King David, for example. In the space of a few weeks, David committed some extremely heinous sins. He lusted, committed adultery, lied, and murdered his loyal servant Uriah.

Thanks for coming in, David. The secretary will show you out.

Despite David's high crimes, the same God who knew David's every thought and action as well as his future called David a man after his own heart (see 1 Samuel 13:14).

Did God miss something? Or did he see something that most of us overlook?

When the prophet Nathan confronted David about his sins, the king didn't make excuses. He delivered no "I'm only human" speech. Instead, he humbly acknowledged, "I have sinned against the LORD."

Later, sitting alone in his misery and shame, a broken David wrote, "Wash me clean from my guilt. Purify me from my sin. For I recognize my rebellion; it haunts me day and night. Against you, and you alone, have I sinned; I have done what is evil in your sight" (Psalm 51:2-4).

God didn't call David a man after his own heart because he was perfect, but because David humbly and brokenheartedly recognized his own sin and knew what to do about it.

In your personal, family, and business lives, and in your friendships, you will blow it from time to time, sometimes badly. You prove yourself a man after God's own heart when you humbly confess what is wrong to God and to the people you have hurt and ask them to forgive you.

July 11

Share Another's Joy
JETHRO

Jethro was delighted when he heard about all the good things the LORD had done for Israel as he rescued them from the hand of the Egyptians.   Exodus 18:9

Hearing about someone else's good fortune brings out the best in some people. Most of us like sharing in the joy of a couple's newly announced engagement or the birth of a baby, for example.

The apostle Paul wrote that we are to "be happy with those who are happy" (Romans 12:15). That means joining others in celebrating God's goodness to them.

Jethro, Moses' friend and father-in-law, celebrated with the people of Israel when God had finally delivered them from years of oppression in Egypt. When Moses told Jethro, a Gentile, of the great things God had done, the elderly man couldn't help rejoicing with them. "Praise the LORD, for he has rescued you from the Egyptians and from Pharaoh. . . . I know now that the LORD is greater than all other gods, because he rescued his people from the oppression of the proud Egyptians" (Exodus 18:10-11).

When Jethro heard of God's goodness to the Israelites, he immediately blessed those around him with words of praise. He realized that the true God of Israel was at work in his family.

The same thing can happen when you share in another's joy over God's kindness and blessings. Will you openly praise God when he blesses your family, friends, and others who make up your world?

When God does great things in your life, it's fitting to speak words of praise and thanksgiving. You bless others and yourself when you share in others' joy and speak words of praise.

July 12

Avoid Distractions
DEMAS

Demas has deserted me because he loves the things of this life and has gone to Thessalonica. 2 Timothy 4:10

In an effort to stop a wave of petty theft in the former Soviet Union, authorities placed armed guards around key factories. At one Leningrad plant, a guard stopped a man driving a wheelbarrow containing a suspicious-looking sack.

"All right," the guard said, "what do you have there?"

"Just sawdust," he replied, then emptied a sack to show that he spoke truly. The same scene repeated itself every night for a week until the guard's curiosity got the best of him.

"I know you," the guard said. "Tell me what you're smuggling out of here and I'll let you go."

"Wheelbarrows, my friend," came the answer. "Wheelbarrows."

One of the devil's most powerful weapons is distraction. He used that weapon effectively against a once-faithful believer named Demas.

At one time, Demas was a dependable partner in Paul's ministry. In Paul's brief letter to Philemon from a Roman prison, he wrote, "Epaphras, my fellow prisoner in Christ Jesus, sends you his greetings. So do Mark, Aristarchus, Demas, and Luke, my coworkers" (Philemon 1:23-24).

Paul didn't use the word *coworker* lightly. At some point, Demas had greatly assisted Paul's ministry, and Paul considered him a dependable friend during some of his most difficult times.

But in his letter to the young Ephesian pastor Timothy, Paul's words about Demas convey hurt, betrayal, and abandonment: "Demas has deserted me."

Demas apparently didn't leave Paul to pursue other ministry opportunities or to see his family. He left, Paul wrote, because he loved "the things of this life."

Whatever Demas's reason for deserting Paul, he was distracted from his important work of serving Paul in his ministry and faithfully following Jesus.

What distractions keep you from fully and freely serving Jesus? What will you do about them? The enemy loves to distract you, but when you keep your eyes on Jesus Christ, you will avoid being sidetracked in your life of faith.

July 13

God Won't Give You Up!
ZEPHANIAH

"For the LORD your God is living among you. He is a mighty savior. He will take delight in you with gladness. With his love, he will calm all your fears. He will rejoice over you with joyful songs." Zephaniah 3:17

Have you ever found yourself in a business venture, a home restoration, or some other situation in which you realized that you were throwing good money after bad? When you know that you have to get out before you go completely broke, you can say that you are cutting your losses. You stop wasting your money and time on something that clearly won't pay off.

The prophet Zephaniah understood that God never "cuts his losses" with those who belong to him.

Zephaniah ministered at the time of Judah's King Josiah, who instituted some broad religious reforms in his nation. Though Zephaniah approved of the reforms, he wanted his people to understand their need to make changes within themselves and not just in their external religious practices.

True religion, he taught, is a matter of the heart.

In most of his little book, Zephaniah railed against the immorality, idolatry, and injustice of his times. He decried Judah's sin, proclaimed their need for repentance, and foretold God's wrath against those who refused to stop sinning and turn toward him.

Sounds pretty ominous, doesn't it?

Zephaniah didn't stop there. As gloomy as some of his prophecies may have sounded, the final third of his book turned to a message of hope. God still loved his people and wanted more than anything for them to turn back to him.

Zephaniah understood God's faithfulness and love. He knew God so personally that he sensed God's delight in him and his people. He could thus preach God's message of hope for those who would simply listen, turn from their sin, and bask in his everlasting love.

God takes sin very seriously and will never look the other way when you fail him. Still, he wants you to know with certainty that he will never "cut his losses" by giving up on you. He always finishes what he starts.

July 14

To Forgive or Not to Forgive
PHILEMON AND ONESIMUS

I appeal to you to show kindness to my child, Onesimus. I became his father in the faith while here in prison. Onesimus hasn't been of much use to you in the past, but now he is very useful to both of us. I am sending him back to you, and with him comes my own heart. Philemon 1:10-12

In her book *Clara Barton: Professional Angel,* Elizabeth Brown Pryor recounts how Clara Barton, the founder of the American Red Cross, was reminded about some particularly humiliating treatment she had received years before. When Barton acted as if she couldn't recall the incident, her stunned friend asked, "Don't you remember it?" Barton replied, "No, I distinctly remember forgetting it."

The Bible repeatedly teaches that we are to forgive those who do us wrong and restore relationships injured by those injustices, much as God does for us when we confess our sins.

Philemon, an apparently wealthy and influential believer who lived in Colossae and assisted Paul in starting the church there, faced the same decision we face when someone wrongs us. Do we forgive and restore, or do we withhold forgiveness and allow the relationship to fester and die?

Philemon had a genuine problem with Onesimus, one of Paul's new converts. Onesimus had been Philemon's slave; he had stolen from Philemon, deserted him, and run away to Rome. Paul tactfully and tenderly appealed to Philemon's sense of God's grace and forgiveness as he asked him to deal kindly with his returning slave.

The question wasn't whether Philemon had been wronged—he clearly had—but what he was going to do about it. Legally, he could have had Onesimus punished severely.

How would Philemon handle this new arrangement?

The Bible doesn't directly address what happened between these two men once Onesimus returned to Colossae. Church tradition holds that Philemon welcomed Onesimus back home and used his influence to raise him to a prominent place in his hometown church.

Understanding God's grace and forgiveness is the key to forgiving those who have hurt us. When we extend forgiveness to those who need it, we free them to realize what God intends for them.

July 15

Don't Rock the Boat
KORAH

One day Korah son of Izhar, a descendant of Kohath son of Levi, conspired with Dathan and Abiram, the sons of Eliab, and On son of Peleth, from the tribe of Reuben. They incited a rebellion against Moses, along with 250 other leaders of the community, all prominent members of the assembly. Numbers 16:1-2

A missionary organization once welcomed a young man with a rather inflated view of his leadership ability. As soon as he received an assignment to a foreign mission, he began bucking the established leaders and asserting himself. Within weeks, the mission had to be abandoned as dissension within the ranks became an all-out rebellion.

Rebelling against authorities God has put in place is a great way to scuttle whatever God wants to accomplish in your life. Look at the biblical account of the would-be revolutionary Korah.

Like most overly ambitious people, Korah was a man of strong, if misguided, leadership skills. He organized a corps of leaders with the intention of usurping Moses' authority and installing his own version of the priesthood. Korah apparently hadn't thought his plan through completely, or he forgot what had happened to Aaron and Miriam (Moses' brother and sister) when they challenged Moses' leadership (see Numbers 12).

As a Levite, Korah was already a special leader, but he wanted more than what God had given him. When Korah rebelled against Moses, God removed him and his coconspirators from their positions. In fact, he removed them from the earth altogether.

God makes leaders of people whom he wants in such positions. When we rebel against those leaders, we risk being removed from the place of blessing God has for us, as happened to Korah.

Some of God's greatest leaders have been willing to rock the boat from time to time, but they have usually had a strong grasp of appropriate respect for authority.

The Bible teaches us to submit to earthly authority because our sovereign God places people in positions of leadership. When we submit to those in authority, we demonstrate a key condition for God's blessing: humility!

July 16

True Compassion
THE GOOD SAMARITAN

A despised Samaritan came along, and when he saw the man, he felt compassion for him.   Luke 10:33

Do you enjoy helping out a friend in need? Most of us do. Helping a good friend move or paint his house gives us a chance to enjoy each other's company. Besides, when we help a friend in need, he's likely to return the favor.

What about helping a stranger? Can you extend a hand to someone with whom you've shared conflicts and arguments? What about people who can't help you back?

Jesus taught that acts of love and compassion toward friends don't score a lot of points with our heavenly Father. When we reach out to a stranger—or even an enemy—we will receive a reward from heaven (see Luke 6:35-36).

Jesus told the story of a man who demonstrated true love and compassion by stopping to help a stranger in need. One day, a severely injured Jewish man lay at the side of a road, and a pair of people you might expect to help him—a priest and a Temple assistant—went out of their way to avoid him.

Only when a man we know as the Good Samaritan happened upon the scene did the man receive the care he needed to live through the night.

Here's where the story takes on extra meaning.

Jews and Samaritans didn't care much for one another. Jews saw Samaritans, a mixed-race people whose roots went back several centuries before Christ's birth, as impure and not "one of us." This particular Samaritan didn't see the man lying in a ditch as an enemy or as someone who hated him but as a fellow human in need of a helping hand. He stopped, helped, and went the extra mile by taking him to an inn and caring for him. When he had to leave, he paid the innkeeper to continue taking care of the man.

True compassion is the kind we extend to strangers and even enemies, simply because they are in need.

You prove that your faith is real when you extend to strangers, and sometimes to your enemies, the kind of love and compassion that Jesus has extended to you.

July 17

Seeing Jesus
JOHN

When I saw him, I fell at his feet as if I were dead. But he laid his right hand on me and said, "Don't be afraid! I am the First and the Last." Revelation 1:17

In a Gallup poll conducted several years ago, Americans were asked who they thought Jesus was. Of those interviewed, 70 percent said that he was not just another man; 42 percent stated that he was God among men; and 27 percent believed he was only human but was divinely called.

Throughout history, men have struggled with Jesus' identity and what it means to them. The apostle John had no doubts. He had seen Jesus as a man and as the glorified Son of God who returned to his Father in heaven.

The Roman government had exiled John to a Greek island called Patmos. While there, as John spent time alone worshiping the Lord, he heard and saw things that further shaped his thinking and his ministry. John heard a voice so loud it sounded like a trumpet blast. It told him to write down what he would see and send it to seven major churches of Asia Minor: Ephesus, Smyrna, Pergamum, Thyatira, Sardis, Philadelphia, and Laodicea (see Revelation 1:10-11).

When John turned to see the speaker, he was floored.

John knew that he was seeing Jesus, the "Son of Man" (Revelation 1:13), but he didn't look at all like the Jesus that John had spent three-plus years following. His face shone like the sun, and his head and hair were white as snow. He held seven stars in his hand, and from his mouth came a sharp two-edged sword.

John had the privilege of hearing and seeing Jesus as the King who had taken his throne in heaven. John reacted with both dread and fear, but because John was his faithful servant, Jesus spoke words of comfort to him, saying, "Don't be afraid!"

Jesus has identified himself as your trustworthy friend and Savior; he is also the sovereign King of all creation. When you approach him as both, you can walk confidently in the work he has done on your behalf.

July 18

Don't Panic
PAUL

Just as day was dawning, Paul urged everyone to eat. "You have been so worried that you haven't touched food for two weeks," he said. "Please eat something now for your own good. For not a hair of your heads will perish." Then he took some bread, gave thanks to God before them all, and broke off a piece and ate it.
ACTS 27:33-35

Years ago, during a stressful time in America's history, a bumper sticker quipped, "Anyone who isn't in a state of panic just doesn't understand the situation!"

At a moment of crisis, our emotions easily get the best of us. When problems at home, at work, and with others begin to overwhelm us, we can be tempted to "fly off the handle" or panic.

The apostle Paul had many occasions when he could have given in to anxiety and panic. One of those moments took place on board a ship sailing toward Rome. The journey started off peacefully enough, but soon a vicious Mediterranean storm slammed the ship, convincing even seasoned sailors that they were about to die.

Paul had been through enough in his life of faith to know that God would allow nothing to destroy him until he had completed his appointed mission. He had a battle-tested faith that helped him to keep his head and set a calm example for the crew in the midst of a terrifying storm.

Paul heard God give him the promise of a safe voyage for himself and everyone else on board: "Not a hair of your heads will perish," he declared confidently.

Like Paul, we can find peace in the midst of the worst storms when we understand that *nothing* can happen to us unless our heavenly Father allows it. Our situations may not be easy or fun, but God still remains in control.

Accidents, tragedies, catastrophes, and deep human suffering sometimes make it seem that God has lost control of the big ship we call Earth. When we place our faith in his power to keep and deliver us—however fierce the storms we might have to ride out— we can keep our wits about us even when others are losing theirs.

July 19

Inner Cleansing
HILKIAH

The king instructed Hilkiah the high priest and the priests of the second rank and the Temple gatekeepers to remove from the LORD's Temple all the articles that were used to worship Baal, Asherah, and all the powers of the heavens. The king had all these things burned outside Jerusalem on the terraces of the Kidron Valley, and he carried the ashes away to Bethel.   2 Kings 23:4

If you were about to undergo a risky but needed surgical procedure, what would concern you more, the conditions in the hospital lobby or the conditions in the operating room? Surely you would want to feel confident that the operating room was absolutely sterile.

The same applies when it comes to your spiritual hygiene. When your heart is clean and pure before the Lord, you can be assured of receiving his best for you.

An Old Testament priest named Hilkiah shows the importance of inner cleansing. Hilkiah was God's high priest during the reign of King Josiah, who left a legacy of unbending loyalty to the Lord and a commitment to spiritual renewal among the people of Judah.

Josiah gave Hilkiah an important assignment. He would lead a group of spiritual leaders into the Temple and cleanse it of everything the ungodly priests before him had used for idol worship. Hilkiah approached the job with passion. He removed all the poisonous trappings of idolatry and took them outside the city to burn them. To make sure that nothing remained, he deposited the ashes in Bethel, about ten miles from Jerusalem.

Hilkiah must have felt overwhelming joy when he completed his task. For the first time in years, the interior of God's Temple was completely clean and ready for worshiping God.

Life can sometimes overwhelm us with responsibilities. Don't forget to stop regularly to take out the trash.

You may not think you've committed any big sins, but it's still important to examine yourself from time to time and clean out anything that keeps you from enjoying full fellowship with the Lord.

July 20

Full of Him
KING REHOBOAM

When Rehoboam was firmly established and strong, he abandoned the Law of the LORD, and all Israel followed him in this sin.   2 Chronicles 12:1

You hear a lot about self-fulfillment these days. When you accomplish more, you're told, you'll find fulfillment. You'll have a healthier outlook on life, your relationships, your future, and yourself—*if you can just summon the strength and creativity to accomplish and acquire more.*

The Bible teaches that true fulfillment and strength are found in walking closely with God and humbly obeying his commands. Consistent blessing comes when you give God the credit for everything you are and everything you accomplish.

Rehoboam didn't get that memo.

Rehoboam, the son of Solomon, made a lot of mistakes following his ascension to the throne, and they divided his kingdom. Like his father, Rehoboam took a good look at all he had accomplished in Judah, became self-satisfied, and abandoned God and his law.

Rehoboam was so full of himself that he crowded out God's place in his heart.

The consequences of Rehoboam's self-satisfaction were dire. With Rehoboam leading the way, Judah slipped further away from God until the kingdom was nearly destroyed at the hands of Shishak, king of Egypt. Rehoboam had no choice but to surrender to Shishak, who ransacked the holy Temple and made Judah subservient to Egypt (see 2 Chronicles 12:9).

Rehoboam failed as a leader and as a man of God because he found strength and satisfaction in his own accomplishments rather than in God's power and goodness.

What is your source of satisfaction?

It is easy to be self-satisfied when you look at the things you have accomplished. Lasting blessing comes when you humbly acknowledge that everything you are and everything you accomplish come from God's generosity and kindness.

July 21

Who Are *You* Promoting?
ADONIJAH

David's son Adonijah, whose mother was Haggith, began boasting, "I will make myself king." So he provided himself with chariots and charioteers and recruited fifty men to run in front of him. 1 Kings 1:5

For the past quarter century or so, Jude Werra has spent much of his time documenting résumé fraud, credentials inflation, and the misrepresentation of executive educational backgrounds. Werra and others have found that far too many managers and executives allow their desire for self-promotion to get the best of them. They include false and misleading information in their résumés.

Sadly, many people have no compunction about promoting themselves ahead of others. That is nothing new, of course, as the story of Adonijah, King David's fourth son, demonstrates.

As David's days drew to an end, Adonijah made an incredible boast that he would make himself king. Adonijah didn't hide his selfish ambition or shameless self-promotion. He invited Judah's royal officials and his brothers to join him as he performed animal sacrifices.

Tellingly enough, Adonijah left out Solomon, whom David had already named as his successor. He also failed to invite the prophet Nathan.

Nathan and Bathsheba, Solomon's mother, knew what Adonijah was up to and asked David to give orders at once that Solomon be proclaimed king. When Adonijah heard what had happened, he went to the altar, and Solomon pardoned him. The pardon would last only as long as he showed himself loyal to Solomon (see 1 Kings 1:52-53).

Sadly, Adonijah just couldn't let it go.

In his craving for power and position, Adonijah made a second attempt to take the throne. In the end, his stubbornness and self-promotion cost him his life (see 1 Kings 2:13-25).

Though self-promotion can give you some of what you desire for a time, in the end, only humbly assuming your part in God's plans will lead to blessing. There's nothing wrong with striving for bigger and better things, but remember that it is God's place to promote you, not yours.

July 22

No Mixed Messages
ZADOK

Adonijah took Joab son of Zeruiah and Abiathar the priest into his confidence, and they agreed to help him become king. But Zadok the priest, Benaiah son of Jehoiada, Nathan the prophet, Shimei, Rei, and David's personal bodyguard refused to support Adonijah. 1 Kings 1:7-8

"My door is always open," a company manager told his staff one day. "If you need anything or have any questions, don't hesitate for a moment to stop in and talk to me."

That sounds pretty inviting! most of the staff thought, until they tried to take their boss up on his invitation.

One by one, each of the staff found that though their boss's door was always open and his invitation was sincere, he was rarely in the office. If he was, he was so busy with outside phone calls or e-mails that he had to tell them he'd get back to them. He rarely did.

Talk about mixed messages!

The Bible contains several examples of people whose words and actions sent a message of single-minded devotion. One of these was the high priest Zadok, who time and again proved his faithfulness and affection to God and then to two men God had chosen to serve as kings of Israel, David and Solomon.

Zadok never wavered in his support for the men God anointed king. He joined David at Hebron as a brave young warrior (see 1 Chronicles 12:23-28), took his place as ruler over the Aaronites (see 1 Chronicles 27:16-17), and remained loyal to David when his son Absalom attempted to take the throne.

During David's final days, Zadok refused to support Adonijah, David's fourth son, when he attempted to succeed David on the throne. Instead, he gave his unwavering allegiance to Solomon, the man David had named as his successor.

Zadok's godliness and loyalty were rewarded. Because he remained loyal to God and to his appointed leaders, he was Israel's high priest during both David's and Solomon's reigns.

Does your life send a message of steadfast devotion to God and to the people he has placed in your life? People around you need to see your loyalty in the way you talk, live, and serve God. Make sure that your life and your words don't send mixed messages.

July 23

True Satisfaction
PHILIP

Philip said, "Lord, show us the Father, and we will be satisfied." Jesus replied, "Have I been with you all this time, Philip, and yet you still don't know who I am? Anyone who has seen me has seen the Father! So why are you asking me to show him to you?" John 14:8-9

Bill Hybels, founder and senior pastor of Willow Creek Community Church in South Barrington, Illinois, once wrote of billionaire Howard Hughes, "All he ever wanted was more. He was absolutely convinced that more would bring him true satisfaction. Unfortunately, history shows otherwise. . . . He died a billionaire junkie, insane by all reasonable standards."

There are many reasons why people don't find satisfaction in life, and one of them is that they don't always know what they are looking for.

Philip, one of the twelve apostles, had spent three-plus years following Jesus and had led his fellow disciple Nathanael to him (see John 1:45-48), and he still felt dissatisfied.

As Jesus prepared his disciples for his death, he told them, "If you had really known me, you would know who my Father is. From now on, you do know him and have seen him!" (John 14:7). That statement had all the disciples scratching their heads, but Philip spoke up, saying, "Show us the Father, and we will be satisfied."

Philip firmly believed that Jesus was the Jewish people's promised and long-awaited Messiah, but for some reason it hadn't quite sunk in that Jesus was truly God in the flesh. Jesus gently rebuked Philip. "Have I been with you all this time, Philip, and yet you still don't know who I am? Anyone who has seen me has seen the Father!"

All Philip wanted was to see his heavenly Father. That evening, he learned that he could satisfy that desire by looking at Jesus.

Where do you look to find satisfaction? If that's what you want, you need look no further than Jesus Christ. As the perfect image of his heavenly Father, he can satisfy your craving for God.

July 24

Seeing Is Believing
THE MAN BORN BLIND

"Why, that's very strange!" the man replied. "He healed my eyes, and yet you don't know where he comes from?...Ever since the world began, no one has been able to open the eyes of someone born blind. If this man were not from God, he couldn't have done it." John 9:30-33

Some people have a special talent for missing the point. You know the type. If you told him the fable of "The Ant and the Grasshopper" to illustrate the importance of preparation, he would respond with the oh-so-profound observation that insects don't talk.

Jesus dealt with such men throughout his earthly ministry. The Jewish religious leaders constantly opposed him and couldn't see past their own legalism and tradition long enough to see that this Man was unique. No wonder he raised such a ruckus among the common people.

Others came to understand who Jesus was because they witnessed or experienced his miracles with open minds and hearts.

When Jesus met a man born blind one Sabbath day, he demonstrated God's power to heal. He spit in the dirt, wiped mud over the man's eyes, and told him to go wash. When he did as Jesus said, he received the gift of sight. For the first time in his life, this man could see his own hands, his reflection in the water, and his parents' faces.

He also saw something special about Jesus.

The Jewish religious leaders wanted to take issue with Jesus' "working" on the Sabbath, but the man who received the gift of sight made a profound observation: "If this man were not from God, he couldn't have done it" (John 9:33).

His simple, to-the-point thinking was absolutely correct!

As Jesus' follower, you should always be ready to point to Jesus as your source of spiritual sight. He is the One to whom others must turn to receive eternal life.

People close to you are bound to notice that the spiritual insight Jesus gives you makes a difference in every area of your life. When they do, tell them what he has done for you— that you were once blind but now you can see.

July 25

Forgive and Restore
PAUL

I am not overstating it when I say that the man who caused all the trouble hurt all of you more than he hurt me. Most of you opposed him, and that was punishment enough. Now, however, it is time to forgive and comfort him. Otherwise he may be overcome by discouragement. So I urge you now to reaffirm your love for him.
2 CORINTHIANS 2:5-8

General James Oglethorpe, an English philanthropist who founded the colony of Georgia, once said to his friend John Wesley, the founder of Methodism, "I never forgive." Without missing a beat, Wesley retorted, "Then I hope, sir, that you never sin."

Wesley wanted Oglethorpe to understand the biblical principle that we must be willing to forgive those who sin against us, just as God forgives us.

The apostle Paul told the Corinthian Christians to forgive a man who had caused him and the church a lot of trouble. Paul even wanted them to welcome him back into the fold to comfort and encourage him.

Though the Bible doesn't say what this man had done, the story points out that God's purpose for discipline is to forgive and restore, not to condemn and reject.

Paul apparently shared these believers' sense of injury over what this wayward brother had done, but he eagerly extended forgiveness and restoration to him. He knew that in so doing, he had given this now-repentant man hope and encouragement.

Who in your life needs that kind of forgiveness and encouragement? As a follower of Christ, be willing and ready to completely forgive those who do you wrong, intentionally or unintentionally. When you forgive completely, you encourage the one who has wronged you and restore a damaged or severed relationship.

July 26

Faith, Obedience, Miracles
JEHOSHAPHAT AND JORAM

"This is what the LORD says: This dry valley will be filled with pools of water! You will see neither wind nor rain, says the LORD, but this valley will be filled with water. You will have plenty for yourselves and your cattle and other animals. But this is only a simple thing for the LORD, for he will make you victorious over the army of Moab!" 2 Kings 3:16-18

Humorist and author Jan King told the story of a friend who couldn't get his son to clean his bedroom. The boy always agreed to tidy up but never followed through.

The son's attitude changed when he joined the United States Marine Corps after high school. When he came home on leave after basic training, his father asked him what he had learned in the service.

"Dad," he said, "I learned what *now* means."

Many Christians receive God's commands but wait to see what *he's* doing before obeying. Unfortunately, this "You first, God" approach to obedience often means missing out on his blessings, and maybe a miracle or two.

Jehoshaphat and Joram, kings of Judah and Israel, needed a miracle. Their armies had marched against Moab, but after seven days, the soldiers had run out of water and were in danger of dying of thirst.

Speaking through the prophet Elisha, God sent them word that he would miraculously provide water. There was only one condition: They were to dig ditches in the valley near Israel's camp *and* wait for him to act.

Did that make sense during a long-lasting drought?

Jehoshaphat and Joram were far apart spiritually, but the godly king of Judah and the idolatrous king of Israel had a choice that day—to laugh at Elisha and ignore God's command or to obey and wait for a miracle.

Jehoshaphat and Joram acted in faith and obedience, and God fulfilled his promise with more water than their men and animals could possibly drink.

When God commands you to do something that seems humanly unreasonable, do you act immediately or wait for him to act first? God doesn't call you to blind faith and obedience but to faith and obedience rooted in the knowledge of who he is. He desires to bless you when you trust him enough to obey.

July 27

Intimacy with God
MOSES

When Moses came down Mount Sinai carrying the two stone tablets inscribed with the terms of the covenant, he wasn't aware that his face had become radiant because he had spoken to the LORD. EXODUS 34:29

When you arrive at the office on a summer Monday morning, it's easy to tell which of your coworkers has spent the weekend outside. Even outdoorsy types who carefully apply their sunscreen will have a glow from basking in the sun.

You can't hide a personal encounter with God any more than time spent in the summer sun.

Moses had spent forty days and nights in God's presence, talking with God as he would with his best friend. When the time came for Moses to return to camp, he picked up the tablets of the law and began his descent.

As Moses reached the camp, no one wanted to come near him. The people saw the glow on Moses' face, and it frightened them.

Spending hours of quality time with someone is bound to change you. You maintain your personal identity and nature, but parts of the other person's character, convictions, and even appearance rub off on you and change you to some degree.

That is exactly what happened when Moses enjoyed intimate fellowship with his Creator. The people of Israel that God had called him to lead would never again see him in the same light.

Moses had a glow about him because he spent time getting close to God. What would make people see a similar glow in you?

How much intimate time do you regularly spend with God? Do you know how to speak to him as a friend and as the Creator of the universe? When personal encounters with God are your priority, those around you can't help but see their positive, life-changing effects.

July 28

Feeling Insignificant
KING MELCHIZEDEK

Melchizedek, the king of Salem and a priest of God Most High, brought Abram some bread and wine. Melchizedek blessed Abram. Genesis 14:18-19

When the American astronomer Henry Norris Russell finished a lecture on the Milky Way galaxy at Princeton University, a woman approached him and asked, "If our world is so little, and the universe is so great, can we believe that God really pays any attention to us?" Dr. Russell replied, "That depends, madam, entirely on how big a God you believe in."

Most men want to feel significant. We want to think that we make a unique difference in the world around us. We want our lives to really matter to the God who created a universe so vast that most of it will probably remain forever undiscovered.

Melchizedek, a priest living in the time of Abram (Abraham), is a relatively unknown biblical character whom God used to accomplish great things for his Kingdom. Melchizedek appears almost as a footnote in Genesis 14:18-20, a snapshot account of his meeting with Abram. Then he disappears, not to be heard of again until centuries later when God announces, seemingly out of nowhere, that the Messiah will be "a priest forever in the order of Melchizedek" (Psalm 110:4).

After several more centuries, Melchizedek appears in Scripture again, this time in Hebrews, where the writer likens his ministry to that of Jesus Christ (see Hebrews 5:6-10).

Melchizedek didn't set out to be compared with Jesus; he was just a priest faithfully serving God in the days of Abram. Although he is a mysterious figure mentioned in only four verses of the entire Old Testament, God had a plan that would give him eternal significance.

God is always at work behind the scenes, pulling rabbits out of hats that you never saw coming. He can use anyone, however obscure, to do great things in his Kingdom.

And he probably won't tell you what he's up to!

When you feel small, insignificant, and forgotten, remember Melchizedek. God is equally at work in your life, unfolding a plan for you that he designed long before you were born.

July 29

Unexpected Blessings
KING CYRUS

In the first year of King Cyrus of Persia, the LORD fulfilled the prophecy he had given through Jeremiah. He stirred the heart of Cyrus to put this proclamation in writing and to send it throughout his kingdom. Ezra 1:1

Someone once said that those who follow and serve Christ are "instruments in the hand of God." When we submit ourselves to his will and purposes, he uses us as implements to change our part of the world.

You probably don't have a problem with the idea of being an instrument in God's hand, but what about some of the instruments he uses to bless you, mold you, or correct you? The grumpy, intolerant boss? The family member who wants nothing to do with God? The physical difficulties you can't seem to shake?

Sometimes God uses completely "secular" means in order to bring about his perfect will. He used Cyrus, king of Persia, in that way.

Within a year of Cyrus's conquest of Babylon, the king issued a decree that freed the people of Judah from their seventy years of exile and returned to them the gold and silver articles Nebuchadnezzar had taken from the Temple. Though at first it appears that Cyrus acted out of compassion and love for God, the truth is that Cyrus didn't know or serve God. Cyrus did those things only because God had stirred his heart.

About 150 years before Cyrus issued his decree, the prophet Isaiah wrote of him, "Why have I called you for this work? Why did I call you by name when you did not know me? It is for the sake of Jacob my servant, Israel my chosen one" (Isaiah 45:4).

Cyrus didn't have a life of faith or personal fellowship with God. He was simply an instrument in God's hand as he worked out his will in his people's lives.

God can and may do something like that in your life.

God often blesses and guides his people using unexpected means. When you submit to his will and purposes, he can even use things you consider to be "secular" for your good and for his glory.

July 30

Finding Assurance
JOHN THE BAPTIST

John the Baptist, who was in prison, heard about all the things the Messiah was doing. So he sent his disciples to ask Jesus, "Are you the Messiah we've been expecting, or should we keep looking for someone else?" Matthew 11:2-3

A young man enduring a crisis of faith approached the well-known twentieth-century American clergyman Harry Emerson Fosdick one day and confessed that he no longer believed in God.

"So you are an atheist?" Fosdick asked. "Describe to me the kind of God you don't believe in."

The youth proceeded to do just that. Fosdick listened patiently, then replied, "My boy, that makes two of us. I don't believe in that God either."

Times of doubt can trouble a man who follows Jesus Christ, but you have a place to turn for assurance when you find yourself going through periods of doubt.

John the Baptist, one of the Bible's courageous men of faith, had seen Jesus Christ up close. He had proclaimed him "the Lamb of God who takes away the sin of the world" (John 1:29). He had baptized him and had heard God's voice say, "This is my dearly loved Son, who brings me great joy" (Matthew 3:17).

Yet as he sat in a prison cell for confronting Herod Antipas, the tetrarch of Galilee, about his unlawful marriage to his brother's wife (see Matthew 14:3-4), John began to seriously doubt Jesus' identity. Eventually, John sent his disciples to ask Jesus if he really was the promised Messiah. Jesus sent him back a message of reassurance, telling them to report to John the things they had seen and heard when they had visited him.

For centuries, people have wrestled with *why* John doubted and *what* those doubts meant, but why John doubted is much less important than what he did with his doubts. John didn't just wallow in them; he took them to the Author and Finisher of his faith, Jesus Christ.

Where do you turn when you suffer moments of doubt? When you feel depressed, discouraged, or doubtful, turn to Jesus, the Author and Finisher of your faith. He will never allow those who believe in him to fall away.

July 31

Submission
JESUS

Then [Jesus] returned to Nazareth with them and was obedient to them. And his mother stored all these things in her heart. Luke 2:51

A man with a slightly rebellious streak once learned the value of submission to authority, particularly when behind the wheel of a car. Near his home was a usually quiet intersection with a diamond-shaped yield sign. Because he rarely saw cars coming through the intersection when he left for work early in the morning, he usually ignored the sign and tore through it.

One day as he approached the intersection, he took a sip of coffee from his travel mug and prepared to head on through as he always had. At the last possible moment, he glanced to his left and saw a school bus filled with children approaching.

He slammed on his brakes, narrowly avoiding a horrible accident that could have taken his life and the lives of dozens of kids. He never ignored that yield sign again.

It's easy to ignore the yield signs God puts up for us, but the Bible teaches that we enjoy God's blessing and protection when we heed the warning signs he so lovingly places in our paths.

Even as a young boy growing up in the tiny town of Nazareth, Jesus knew the importance of submission to his Father and to the people he had put in authority over him. As the Son of God, Jesus knew his identity. He also knew that to grow into a perfect man of God, he needed to honor his earthly mother and father.

As a boy, Jesus laid the foundation for a life of perfect submission to his heavenly Father. Everything he did, said, and thought sprang from the fact that he had yielded his own will to his Father (see John 5:30).

Jesus built his life on a solid foundation of submission. On what foundation have you built yours?

Most men don't like the idea of submitting to someone else, but when you intentionally submit to God and follow his leading, you are on your way to a life of blessing.

August 1

Zip It
ELIPHAZ, BILDAD, AND ZOPHAR

They sat on the ground with him for seven days and nights. No one said a word to Job, for they saw that his suffering was too great for words. Job 2:13

After a long day's work and the usual evening activities at home, a man sat down with his wife and listened as she talked about her day. She didn't paint a pretty picture.

"I've been having a lot of problems with my sister," she began. "It seems that no matter what I do, she finds fault and criticizes me. Now I find out she's been saying the same things to our mother!"

"Well, honey," the man offered, "you need to sit down and talk to your sister and tell her —"

His wife's sudden look of disapproval stopped him cold. "What's wrong?" he asked.

"If I had been looking for your advice on how to fix the situation," she said frostily, "I would have asked you for it. Right now, I just need you to be quiet and listen to me!"

Many men struggle with just listening, but there is great wisdom in remembering why God gave you two ears and only one mouth. Eliphaz, Bildad, and Zophar, friends who tried to comfort Job in his suffering, lacked that kind of wisdom.

At first, Eliphaz, Bildad, and Zophar were exactly the kind of friends a suffering man needs. When they first saw Job, they recognized that he just needed to bend some ears. They tore their clothing, put dust on their heads, and sat with him silently until Job spoke.

They should have quit while they were ahead.

Job's three friends meant well when they began speaking, but instead of comforting Job through active listening, they tried to analyze and fix his problems.

Of course, they failed miserably. Eliphaz, Bildad, and Zophar had a chance to make a positive difference in Job's life, but because they couldn't remain quiet and listen, they made a bad situation even worse.

You are probably wired to fix things—the car, the leaky faucet, the water heater. Sometimes when a loved one begins bending your ear, your best course isn't to try to fix their problem but to zip your lips and listen.

August 2

Your Eternal Family
JESUS

Jesus replied, "Who is my mother? Who are my brothers?" Then he looked at those around him and said, "Look, these are my mother and brothers. Anyone who does God's will is my brother and sister and mother."   Mark 3:33-35

What kind of mental picture does the word *family* conjure for you? Is it taking your wife and children out to enjoy time together? Is it spending that too infrequent time with your mother and father? Getting together with your brothers and sisters to reminisce about growing up together?

Family means different things to different men. Jesus gave a new definition of *family* when he taught that his real family was made up of all who sought to do God's will.

Jesus knew that his biological family had concerns about him and wanted to get him away from the crush of eager followers (see Mark 3:20-21). He also knew that his earthly relatives lacked the spiritual eyes to see the truth. He had come to do his Father's will, and anyone who tried to get in his way, even with the best of intentions, would have to take a backseat to his new family.

"Anyone who does God's will is my brother, sister, and mother," he declared.

What a provocative thing to say! Let it become your source of inspiration and comfort. Whatever your earthly family looks like, you have a heavenly family of Jesus' brothers, sisters, and mother —his own eternal family.

Your earthly family is God's gift to you to treasure and love. He has also given you an eternal family of brothers and sisters in Christ whom you have the privilege to treasure and love for all eternity.

As committed as you are to your earthly family, remember that you have an eternal family created through faith in the resurrected Christ. How can you help them to better worship, love, and obey your heavenly Father?

August 3

Ready for Interruptions
SIMON OF CYRENE

A passerby named Simon, who was from Cyrene, was coming in from the country-side just then, and the soldiers forced him to carry Jesus' cross.   Mark 15:21

One stressful afternoon, Bill received a phone call at his office from a close relative with a pressing spiritual need. "Later" wasn't going to work. Instead of continuing to work, he took an hour out of his desperately busy day to talk to his relative about God's love and salvation.

Bill's willingness to be interrupted made a difference in his relative's life . . . and in his eternity.

If you're like most men, you are busy. Work, family, friends, and church all cry out for your time. It's still important to be ready when God sends you an interruption for the good of another person.

A man named Simon faced that kind of interruption.

Jesus was alone in his suffering as he dragged his cross toward a hill out-side the city of Jerusalem. Exhausted from a sleepless night and a morning of brutal treatment at the hands of his Roman tormenters, Jesus sank under the weight of his cross.

Into this scene of suffering and love stepped Simon, a Jewish pilgrim from the North African city of Cyrene (in present-day Libya).

When Simon started his day, he had no idea that he would play an impor-tant part in God's plan to bring salvation to the world. Simon was one of hundreds of thousands of Jewish pilgrims who traveled to Jerusalem annually to honor God in the Passover celebration.

But God interrupted Simon's plans.

The Roman centurion in charge of executions didn't have time to wait for Jesus to gather enough strength to make it up the hill for his execution. He saw Simon in the crowd and conscripted him for the unpleasant job of carry-ing Jesus' cross.

Simon carried a part of Jesus' burden that morning that not even his disci-ples were around to carry. When he did that, he played a small but important part in Jesus' story.

Are you ready and willing to bear the burdens God asks you to carry? Sometimes those burdens mean interruptions from everyday business. God blesses you richly when you are available to bear your part of the load, especially when it means changing your daily schedule.

August 4

Appearance Isn't Everything
JOSEPH, THE HUSBAND OF MARY

As he considered this, an angel of the Lord appeared to him in a dream. "Joseph, son of David," the angel said, "do not be afraid to take Mary as your wife. For the child within her was conceived by the Holy Spirit."   Matthew 1:20

In his biography *Houdini,* author Harold Kellock recounts how the famous magician had himself shackled and locked in a Scottish jail cell. He quickly freed himself from the shackles and then turned his attention to the cell lock. Houdini tried everything he knew, but the lock wouldn't open. Finally, the exhausted Houdini leaned against the door, which opened so suddenly that he fell headfirst into the corridor.

The turnkey hadn't locked it.

The lesson behind this story? It's not good to make assumptions.

It's hard to imagine Joseph, the man God called to fill the role of Jesus' earthly father, as not making some assumptions when his fiancée, Mary, told him she was pregnant with the long-awaited Messiah. Joseph knew only two things as fact: Mary was pregnant, and he wasn't the father. The news of Mary's pregnancy shattered Joseph. *What will my family think? Certainly they won't buy this story. I don't know if I buy this story!*

Still, what if it were true?

Although Joseph loved Mary, he seriously considered ending their engagement. God saw his heart and knew that he was the right man for the job of raising Jesus to adulthood. As Joseph uneasily slept one night, God confirmed Mary's story and told Joseph not to be afraid to marry her.

Joseph must have suffered incredible anguish when Mary told him of her pregnancy, but his heart and mind remained open. God allowed Joseph the privilege of caring for the most important child ever born.

When you receive what appears to be bad news, keep an open mind and heart. God may have a plan to bring blessing out of what you thought was a personal tragedy.

August 5

Shun Evil Alliances
DANIEL AND KING BELSHAZZAR

Daniel answered the king, "Keep your gifts or give them to someone else, but I will tell you what the writing means."   Daniel 5:17

As the power of the media, especially electronic media, has grown, elected officials have increasingly tried to avoid the appearance of impropriety. Politicians generally avoid taking money or other donations when doing so may give the appearance of compromise. Such a practice gives elected officials some cover because it allows them to serve out of a sense of duty to the people and not out of a desire for power or to pad their own bank accounts.

We naturally see something admirable about a man who refuses under-the-table financial reward for public service. That kind of man earns others' trust and proves himself worthy to serve.

That's partly why the prophet Daniel refused Belshazzar's offer of monetary gifts and political status. The Babylonian king wanted a favorable interpretation of a most disturbing vision, and he probably hoped his largesse would secure what he wanted. He obviously didn't know Daniel, an old prophet of God who refused to make a buck with the gift God had given him. Daniel had no interest in clasping hands with a man he saw as committed to evil.

Daniel also knew from the meaning of Belshazzar's vision that the foolish king had just made his final political proposal. He didn't hesitate to give Belshazzar the bad news, nor did he show the slightest vacillation in rejecting the doomed king's gifts. Instead, Daniel let it be known that neither the truth nor his integrity was for sale.

Daniel served God with the integrity of a man who knows his part in the Lord's plans and wouldn't think of doing anything to compromise himself or the truth God had called him to speak. Such a man recoils at the thought of clasping hands with evil, especially for something as paltry as personal gain.

What really motivates you to serve? Do you see yourself as part of God's special forces on earth, as an ambassador in his foreign service, as a servant in his Kingdom? If you serve God and others with a heart of love and commitment to him and others, you're on the right track.

August 6

Hearing God
ELIJAH

When Elijah heard it, he wrapped his face in his cloak and went out and stood at the entrance of the cave. And a voice said, "What are you doing here, Elijah?"
1 KINGS 19:13

Busy restaurants are not good places for meaningful discussions. With the patrons talking, music playing, and waiters taking orders, it's sometimes nearly impossible even to hear your companion's voice.

Hearing God is sometimes like that too. With all the noise life makes, it can be difficult to hear him. Like Elijah the prophet, however, you can learn to hear God's voice above all else.

Although Elijah had given his all, no good seemed to be coming of it. Although he had preached and performed miracles, the people refused to listen to him. Now King Ahab's wife, Jezebel, wanted to kill him. He sat in a cave in fear and despair, wondering where God was in all of his suffering.

Elijah desperately needed to hear from the Lord.

God wanted to speak to Elijah. After telling the prophet to come out of his cave and stand before him on the mountain, God passed by. A windstorm arose, so powerful that it tore rocks loose. After the wind came an earthquake, and after the earthquake there was a fire.

At first, it looked as though God had spoken to Elijah in a spectacular way; but that's not what had happened, and Elijah knew it. God was not in any of those noisy demonstrations; they were just forerunners of the real deal that was to follow.

Finally, Elijah heard it. Still sitting in the cave, wallowing in his misery, he heard a gentle whisper. He knew it was time to come out and listen to God's voice.

This was the voice of the One Elijah loved and served, the One on whom he depended. Elijah heard God's inviting voice, poured out his broken heart, and then just listened.

Can you hear God's voice above life's everyday noise? God wants you to discern his voice, so when you need to hear him, take some time to be alone away from the noise of life . . . and just listen.

August 7

Bonds of Friendship
PETER, JAMES, AND JOHN

He took Peter, James, and John with him, and he became deeply troubled and distressed. He told them, "My soul is crushed with grief to the point of death. Stay here and keep watch with me." Mark 14:33-34

A British publication once offered a prize for the best definition of a friend. Among the thousands of responses the periodical received was this winning entry: "A friend is the one who comes in when the whole world has gone out."

We all need true friendship. All of us need someone with whom we can share our hopes, our fears, our desires, and our suffering. Even Jesus needed close friends in order to complete his assignment on earth.

Jesus had twelve apostles, men he had chosen to remain with him throughout his earthly ministry. Among these men that he called friends, three in particular enjoyed a special bond with Jesus. Peter and the brothers James and John were in the Lord's inner circle as his very closest friends. Jesus allowed them to see and hear things not available to the others.

This trio alone was present at the Transfiguration when Jesus revealed his glory to them (see Matthew 17:1-9). They were the only disciples there when he raised the daughter of a synagogue leader from the dead (see Mark 5:37-42). They accompanied Jesus as he faced his night of anguish and pain in the garden of Gethsemane (see Mark 14:32-34).

After Jesus' return to heaven, Peter and John established a far more amazing legacy of service than the rest. Peter founded and led the fledgling church in Jerusalem and wrote the epistles bearing his name. John, who lived the longest of the twelve, wrote the fourth Gospel, three epistles, and the book of Revelation.

Peter, James, and John were ordinary fishermen when they first met Jesus, but because they enjoyed such a special friendship with him, they made the biggest impact for Christ in the world.

The sure path to receiving the very best God has for you, and to making the biggest impact on your world for him, is to cultivate a friendship with Jesus Christ. Then love will motivate you to obey him.

August 8

Fatherly Love
THE PRODIGAL SON

So he returned home to his father. And while he was still a long way off, his father saw him coming. Filled with love and compassion, he ran to his son, embraced him, and kissed him.   Luke 15:20

Paco ran away from home without even leaving a note. His heartbroken father searched for his son for months, to no avail. In a last-ditch effort to find his boy, he put an ad in a Madrid newspaper: "Dear Paco, Meet me in front of this newspaper office at noon on Saturday. All is forgiven. I love you. Your Father."

That Saturday, hundreds of boys named Paco stood in front of the newspaper office, each waiting to receive his father's love and forgiveness.

A good father loves and forgives like the father Jesus described in his famous story of a father and his wayward son.

It's not hard to imagine this kind of father shedding bitter tears as he watched the son he loved so much taking his inheritance and disappearing from view. It's also easy to imagine him praying passionately every day that the boy would return home and rejoin the family. That was all he *could* do other than watch and wait.

When this father saw his son appear on the horizon, he recognized him instantly. Despite the shuffle and the haggard appearance, he *knew him.* He couldn't just stand and wait for his boy to reach home, so he *ran* to his son and eagerly welcomed him back, not as a servant or as damaged goods, but as a much-loved son in good standing.

By going out of his way to restore a broken relationship, this fictional father became an example of a loving dad's forgiveness and grace. How many other "Pacos" out there need to experience the same thing?

What man or woman, boy or girl close to you needs this kind of love, forgiveness, and grace? Can you provide it? What specifically can you do to make the gift a very special event? When you freely give of yourself in this way, you heal your relationships and set an example for others.

August 9

Just like You
PAUL AND BARNABAS

When the apostles Barnabas and Paul heard what was happening, they tore their clothing in dismay and ran out among the people, shouting, "Friends, why are you doing this? We are merely human beings—just like you!" ACTS 14:14-15

Perhaps you remember the 1980s *Saturday Night Live* character Enid Strict, also known as the Church Lady, the smug, ill-tempered, self-righteous, annoyingly pious host of her own talk show, *Church Chat*. After spending most of her show berating guests that she saw as nothing but nasty sinners, the Church Lady closed her show by doing her "superior dance."

Hit it, Pearl!

The Church Lady spoofed what comedian Dana Carvey, who created and played the character, saw as holier-than-thou churchgoers. She was an example of someone you would never want to be.

Paul and his missionary companion Barnabas demonstrated an attitude of humility and tolerance as they faced sin and idolatry in a city called Lystra. There they healed a crippled man then watched in horror as the locals, who believed them to be the pagan deities Zeus and Hermes, began worshiping them.

That had to be an offensive spectacle to a couple of devout Jews like Paul and Barnabas! They didn't respond in anger, disgust, or with any air of superiority.

Paul and Barnabas continued to love these sinners even though they hated the sin.

The Lystrans' attempts to worship Paul and Barnabas grieved the two missionaries, so they sent a message that they were no better than anyone else there that day. All of them together were sinners saved by God's grace.

What kind of messages are you sending to those around you?

You'll be a more consistent and effective example of Jesus Christ's saving and transforming power when you approach others as a regular human being who is saved only because of God's wonderful grace.

August 10

A True Leader
TIMOTHY

This is a trustworthy saying: "If someone aspires to be an elder, he desires an honorable position."   1 Timothy 3:1

Dwight D. Eisenhower, the thirty-fourth president of the United States, once spoke about the character qualities of a leader: "In order to be a leader, a man must have followers. And to have followers, a man must have their confidence. Hence the supreme quality of a leader is unquestionably integrity. Without it, no real success is possible, no matter whether it is on a section gang, on a football field, in an army, or in an office."

Those are high standards, indeed. The apostle Paul instructed the young pastor Timothy to look for such qualities in those he assigned as elders in his church at Ephesus.

Timothy found himself in a tricky situation as a young pastor serving saints older than he was. Still, he faced the daunting responsibility of picking the right leaders for his congregation.

Paul instructed Timothy to look for leaders who had good personal lives, exemplary family lives, and character qualities such as self-control, wisdom, hospitality, and gentleness.

Timothy understood that God had called all believers to live by a higher standard than the world around them. He also understood that the Lord had set even higher standards for him and his leadership team. He knew that being a church leader meant consistently demonstrating the kind of character he wanted his congregation to emulate and the kind that motivated them to follow.

If you were to join Timothy's church today, would you qualify as one of his leaders?

It is no small thing to be a leader—in your home, at work, or in church. If you aspire to a position of leadership, then you are called to a high standard of conduct. You must make your every step match your every word.

August 11

In Spite of Spin
AMOS AND AMAZIAH

Then Amaziah, the priest of Bethel, sent a message to Jeroboam, king of Israel: "Amos is hatching a plot against you right here on your very doorstep! What he is saying is intolerable. He is saying, 'Jeroboam will soon be killed, and the people of Israel will be sent away into exile.'" Amos 7:10-11

In the days before electronic recording devices could capture every little syllable, politicians didn't have to watch their words with the painstaking care required today. Today, they know their opponents are likely to spin anything they say into something different from what they meant.

That was the tactic a corrupt priest named Amaziah used against the prophet Amos. In an attempt to quiet Amos and his message, Amaziah accused him of treason against Israel and King Jeroboam. The priest saw a chance to shut Amos up when the prophet denounced Jeroboam and pronounced God's judgment on his ancestors.

Amaziah put his own spin on Amos's words, telling the king that the prophet had said he would die by the sword and that Amos had conspired to carry out his own words of judgment.

Amos's prophecies came true, but not in the way that Amaziah had presented them to the king. Jeroboam died a natural death, but his son and successor, Zechariah, died at the hands of Shallum after just six months on the throne (see 2 Kings 15:8-10).

Amos's life and ministry demonstrate the sad truth that some will always attempt to spin the words and actions of godly people. It also demonstrates the blessings of carefully and faithfully speaking God's truth even when others don't want to hear it.

Amos knew he was preaching an unpopular message and that Amaziah would go to incredible lengths to stop him. Amos remained faithful to God and to the message God had called him to speak.

God rewards you when you serve him faithfully in your words and actions. When you face your own Amaziahs, God will bless you when you remain faithful to him and to what he has called you to do and say.

August 12

Access
MOSES

"Only Moses is allowed to come near to the LORD. The others must not come near, and none of the other people are allowed to climb up the mountain with him."
EXODUS 24:2

When you purchase a hot ticket to a popular concert or exclusive dinner party, you guard it with your life. You know the value of that little piece of paper. If you have a ticket, you are welcomed; if you don't have one, you're standing on the street with no hope of access.

One of the greatest benefits you receive when you place your faith in Jesus Christ is that of open and free access to your Creator and heavenly Father.

At one time, only a few select people had direct access to God. One of those people was Moses, the servant God had chosen to lead his people out of Egyptian captivity. At the time of the Exodus, the people depended on Moses as their go-between. Only Moses was permitted to hear God's voice, talk directly to God, plead with God on the people's behalf, receive God's commandments, and obtain God's directions for what to do next.

As Moses prepared to ascend Mount Sinai, God told him specifically that only he—not even Aaron, Nadab, or Abihu, the men he had chosen as his priests—was allowed to come near enough to see God's glory and hear his voice. In granting Moses such close access to him, God gave him a great responsibility and a great privilege.

As amazing as it may seem, that's a privilege you can enjoy today. Though God limited direct access to himself during Old Testament times, you can now freely approach him because of your faith in his only Son, Jesus Christ.

The Bible promises that when you put your faith in Jesus, you can "come boldly to the throne of our gracious God" (Hebrews 4:16). God wants to hear from you and speak to you every day. You can approach him confidently and receive everything you need to be the man, husband, and father he wants you to be.

August 13

He Got It
KING DAVID

His unfailing love toward those who fear him is as great as the height of the heavens above the earth. He has removed our sins as far from us as the east is from the west. Psalm 103:11-12

Men who follow Jesus Christ wholeheartedly after being saved from a life of sin often have a passion for God's love and forgiveness that is far more intense than a man who grew up in the faith and never departed.

King David expressed such passion in Psalm 103.

David had plenty in his life for which he needed forgiveness. At times, he allowed his emotions to overwhelm him, and on several occasions he found himself in trouble because of it. Like us, he was a sinner who needed God's grace and forgiveness.

And he knew it.

David knew when he failed God, and he knew that he deserved to pay the price for his wrongdoing. He also understood that God's love would never fail him. He recognized that God forgave so completely that it was as if he had never committed a sin.

David didn't choose his words at random when he wrote that his sins were separated from him "as far . . . as the east is from the west."

If a pilot were to take off in his airplane and begin to circle the globe, he would eventually find himself heading south if he first headed north. If that same pilot were to circle the globe going east, he would never stop going east for as long as he stayed in the air.

David knew—as should you—that God's love and forgiveness are absolute, even for the worst of sins and the worst of sinners.

Like David, you can know that God's love will never fail you even when you blow it. When you confess your sins, he completely and eternally separates them from you and you from them.

August 14

The Right Direction
ANANIAS

There was a certain man named Ananias who, with his wife, Sapphira, sold some property. He brought part of the money to the apostles, claiming it was the full amount. With his wife's consent, he kept the rest. Acts 5:1-2

Phil was an outstanding youth leader at his church, but he had a lousy sense of direction. One weekend, he headed a caravan of teenagers to a youth conference in St. Helens, Oregon, about twenty-five miles west of Portland. By the time he realized he had taken a wrong turn, he and his charges found themselves in Hood River, a lovely Columbia River Gorge community about sixty miles *east* of Portland.

Part of what makes someone a good leader is his ability to persuade people to follow. That's why it's important that you lead the people God has placed in your life in the right direction.

Ananias, whose sad story appears in Acts 5, was apparently a strong leader at home. Unfortunately, he took his family in a horribly wrong direction and paid a heavy price for it.

Ananias was among the first-generation believers in Jerusalem, many of whom sold their property, pooled their resources, and generously cared for those in need. Ananias sold his property, but instead of bringing all the money to the apostles, he kept some of it for himself.

The apostle Peter pointed out that Ananias had done nothing wrong in keeping some of his own money (see Acts 5:4). Where he failed terribly was in telling the apostles that he had given all of it.

All of this happened with his wife's full cooperation.

As the head of his house, Ananias was responsible for leading his wife, Sapphira, and his children, if he had any, with honesty and integrity. In his vain desire for human praise, he led his wife down a deadly road of deception.

Look at the story of Ananias and ask yourself, *Where am I leading my family?*

Your family will very likely follow wherever you lead them. One of the greatest rewards for leading your wife and children in the right direction is seeing them grow in character and integrity.

August 15

Sexual Temptation
JOSEPH

Joseph was a very handsome and well-built young man, and Potiphar's wife soon began to look at him lustfully. "Come and sleep with me," she demanded. But Joseph refused.   Genesis 39:6-8

Have you ever attempted to drop a few pounds (or more than a few)? If so, you know the stupidity of stocking your freezer with your favorite ice cream, your cupboards with your favorite cookies, or your refrigerator with your favorite cheesecake. Doing so would put you in a place where you felt, in the words of the apostle Paul, "the temptation to be more than you can stand" (1 Corinthians 10:13).

And that, as you may have learned the hard way, is an excellent strategy for keeping those pounds on.

Sometimes God calls us to stand up to temptation and fight it like a man; at other times, he instructs us to run away from it. *Sexual* temptation calls for the latter strategy. God tells us to avoid it; and failing that, we are to run from it.

Enter Joseph.

Wasn't Joseph sexually attracted to the wife of his master Potiphar? It is hard to believe that he wasn't. As the spouse of a high-ranking Egyptian official, she probably used her beauty to get what she wanted.

She *really* wanted Joseph!

What could Joseph do? Because he refused to betray his master or dishonor God, he had only two options left: resist the seduction or flee. When resisting didn't work, Joseph ran, leaving us with an excellent example to follow when sexual temptation tries to catch us in its snare.

Many centuries later, the apostle Paul warned a young pastor named Timothy to "run from anything that stimulates youthful lusts" (2 Timothy 2:22). *Run,* he says, not walk, box, argue, evangelize, flatter, flirt, reason with, or saunter away. Run!

In what situations are you most likely to encounter sexual temptation? Clearly identify them and develop a plan for running away. God never intended for you to put yourself in a position where you may find it easy to fall. Don't reason with sexual temptation or try to stand up to it. Run!

August 16

Unintended Consequences
GIDEON

Gideon made a sacred ephod from the gold and put it in Ophrah, his hometown. But soon all the Israelites prostituted themselves by worshiping it, and it became a trap for Gideon and his family. Judges 8:27

Some ninety years ago, the United States Congress passed the eighteenth amendment, also known as Prohibition. After the amendment was ratified three years later, the law of unintended consequences kicked in. The amendment drove small-time alcohol suppliers out of business and consolidated the business in the hands of organized crime, which flourished during the Prohibition years.

Sometimes our best-intended actions have negative consequences. Even a man of amazing faith like Gideon had to learn that lesson.

Gideon had just led Israel in a rousing victory over Midian. The people showed their appreciation when they elected him as ruler over their nation. Gideon answered that offer with a resounding, "Thanks, but no thanks!"

As a man of God, Gideon knew he couldn't take the office that God had reserved for himself as ruler over his people. Had Gideon stopped there, we could have called him a true success.

Unfortunately, Gideon didn't stop there.

Gideon asked the people to gather up gold collected from their Midianite enemies so that he could make an ephod, a vestment worn by Hebrew priests of the day, probably as a memorial to God's goodness in helping Israel defeat Midian.

There were unintended consequences.

The Bible says that the ephod "became a trap for Gideon and his family." That's because the Israelites didn't use it as an emblem commemorating their victory over Midian but as an object of worship (see Judges 8:27).

After God gave Israel victory over Midian, Gideon could have provided the kind of spiritual guidance his people desperately needed. Though Gideon provided leadership during a time of war, he failed to step up and offer it at a time when the people needed spiritual guidance. Gideon's ephod seemed like a good idea at the time, but it left a stain on his legacy.

How can you avoid the law of unintended consequences? When you set out to do something you see as important, even with the best of intentions, seek God and his approval before you move out.

August 17

Build the Future
PETER

Peter said to him, "We've given up everything to follow you. What will we get?"
MATTHEW 19:27

A company vice president who made very good money surprised at least one guest at his New Year's Eve party. Despite his wealth, the VP, his wife, and their two children lived in a modest three-bedroom house. He drove a ten-year-old SUV.

When the guest asked the VP why he lived in such a humble home and drove an unassuming automobile, he replied, "I want to be able to send my kids to college and take my wife on vacations later. If we spend all our money now, we won't be able to do either."

Jesus taught his followers that those who give up current comfort and status will receive in the years to come and in eternity far more than anything they gave up. After meeting the rich young ruler who couldn't make that connection, Peter wanted to connect some dots of his own.

Peter never had riches, but he gave up everything he had—his business, status in his hometown, the comforts of home—to follow Jesus Christ and become his disciple. Now he couldn't help wondering what he and the other disciples would get out of it. Being Peter, he asked Jesus about it directly.

Jesus wasn't surprised or angered by the question. In fact, he seemed eager to answer. He told the disciples that they would one day judge Israel's twelve tribes and that "everyone who has given up houses or brothers or sisters or father or mother or children or property, for my sake, will receive a hundred times as much in return and will inherit eternal life" (Matthew 19:29).

Sounds like a great trade-off, doesn't it?

Jesus wanted Peter to understand that because he had given up everything to follow him, he could expect something far better in return in this life and in the one to come.

That's a promise for you, too!

What does Jesus' command to "store your treasures in heaven" (Matthew 6:20) mean to you? When you give yourself for God, he notices and will reward you far beyond anything you've given up.

August 18

Receive God's Promises
ISAAC

Isaac pleaded with the LORD on behalf of his wife, because she was unable to have children. The LORD answered Isaac's prayer, and Rebekah became pregnant with twins. Genesis 25:21

Over the past few decades, the world of professional sports has suffered a series of allegations that some of its most notable athletes have knowingly used performance-enhancing drugs.

Though some would argue that those drugs weren't illegal at the time some athletes took them, most observers regard their use as cheating because they give users an unfair advantage.

The world of sports carries incredible pressure to succeed, and some competitors handle that pressure by taking shortcuts. They may achieve success, but they do it in the wrong way.

Isaac probably felt that kind of pressure. After two decades of marriage to his beloved Rebekah, he still had no son to show for it. In those days, a couple married that long without a child considered their lot to be shameful, especially for the wife.

What could Isaac do? Would he give up? Would he father a child with another woman like his father Abraham? Isaac didn't even consider those options. He did what any man should do when his heart is set on something: He got on his knees and prayed.

Finally, God delivered—not just once but twice!

It took twenty years, but one day Isaac opened his eyes to a world that could rightfully call him "father" (see Genesis 25:20-26). For much of the time before the blessed event, Isaac spent long hours on this knees, reminding God of his promises, giving thanks, and begging him for a son.

So Isaac received God's blessings in God's way.

God has an incredible plan to bless you personally. When you feel tempted to run ahead of God and do things in your own way and time, remember that God reserves his best blessings for those who willingly submit themselves to his rule. That means faithfully asking for what you want and then waiting patiently for God to act.

August 19

Called to Stand
AARON

"Don't get so upset, my lord," Aaron replied. *"You yourself know how evil these people are. They said to me, 'Make us gods who will lead us.'"*   Exodus 32:22-23

Eugene Corr was an assistant police chief in Seattle, Washington, during a dark time of corruption in the department. In 1969, when police records revealed payoffs to officers and suspicious political contributions, Corr had no choice but to stand up.

Corr risked his career and even his life when he and two other assistant chiefs demanded that Police Chief Frank Ramon resign. Some officers loyal to Ramon called Corr a snitch, and someone scrawled "Kill Corr" over his parking spot.

Corr refused to back down. Though he took a lot of heat for standing up to corruption, his efforts paid off. He emerged as a hero to many and was later credited with making the SPD a more professional, trustworthy force.

Aaron, Moses' brother and right-hand man, had an opportunity to stand up for God. Unlike Corr, he failed.

Aaron had been with Moses long enough to know better. He knew that God had commanded the Israelites not to make themselves any kind of idol (see Exodus 20:4-5), but as Moses met face-to-face with God on Mount Sinai, the people of Israel had an encounter with an idol made of gold. Aaron had engineered the whole ugly mess.

Aaron should have led the people to serve and worship the real God, but he failed. He couldn't find it within himself to stand up to the people when they clamored for an idol to worship. Worse yet, when Moses confronted him, Aaron claimed to be an innocent bystander (see Exodus 32:22-24).

Aaron failed first when he knuckled under to the people's idolatry. He failed a second time when he refused to accept blame for his part in the people's sin.

As a follower of Christ, you will encounter many opportunities to stand up and be counted. Will you be ready? It's not a matter of chance but of preparation. If you want to be able to stand during a time of crisis, you have to practice standing in the daily routine of life.

August 20

A Balanced Approach
MICAH

Where is another God like you, who pardons the guilt of the remnant, overlooking the sins of his special people? You will not stay angry with your people forever, because you delight in showing unfailing love. Once again you will have compassion on us. You will trample our sins under your feet and throw them into the depths of the ocean! Micah 7:18-19

There may be nothing more difficult than finding balance. Between work, family, church, and friends, it's sometimes hard to know how to divide your time and energy and make the best use of your resources.

The Bible is largely a book about finding balance between work and play, God and other people, faith and deeds—and between God's hatred for sin and his desire to completely forgive the sinner.

The Old Testament prophet Micah had a grasp on that kind of balance.

Most of Micah's message seems anything but pleasant. Micah was a contemporary of Isaiah who called the nation of Judah to repentance. He railed against false prophets, political corruption, and the spiritual apostasy that had overtaken Judah's culture. He preached against greed, selfishness, and exploitation, and he stood up for the poor and the oppressed.

Micah's prophecy balanced the message of judgment with God's promises of blessing and forgiveness. He insisted that God longed to do good to those who would forsake their sin and return to him.

Micah's word from God championed a balanced approach to spiritual things. Though he never shied away from pointing out the consequences of sin, Micah also gave his repentant hearers hope for better things ahead.

Micah had a keen sense of these things because he knew that his heavenly Father loved him and delighted in forgiving his sin.

Are there people in your life who need to see both sides of God's nature? When you point out their need for God's forgiveness, also tell them that your heavenly Father has blessed you and forgiven you completely.

As a man whose sins Jesus has removed for good, you're an example of your heavenly Father's balance in dealing with sin. He didn't have to forgive you, but he did, just because of your faith in his Son, Jesus Christ.

August 21

Credentials
AMOS

Amos replied, "I'm not a professional prophet, and I was never trained to be one. I'm just a shepherd, and I take care of sycamore-fig trees. But the LORD called me away from my flock and told me, 'Go and prophesy to my people in Israel.'"
AMOS 7:14-15

A man walked into a large company's personnel office and handed the human resources manager an envelope containing his résumé. The manager opened the envelope, read for a few moments, then looked up at the hopeful candidate.

"Is this a joke?" he asked.

"Not at all," the applicant answered. "I'm willing to learn and to work hard."

The personnel manager thanked him for coming in and sent him away without any chance of getting a job. Why?

His résumé listed no educational background and no job experience. It simply read, "I'm willing!"

Though simple willingness to learn and work hard might not impress some personnel managers, it's just what God looks for in a servant. Amos didn't claim to be anything special—he wasn't even a professional prophet. By profession, he was a shepherd who also tended a grove of sycamore-fig trees. But Amos had something that God values above any professional credentials: a willingness to follow and obey.

Amos ministered during the reign of kings Uzziah of Judah and Jeroboam II of Israel. Though both kingdoms enjoyed peace and prosperity during this time, they also suffered a period of spiritual superficiality and economic injustice.

Into this dark situation stepped Amos, a humble nothing of a man by human standards. God called him to preach about judgment of the rebellious and the eventual restoration of the repentant.

The people who heard Amos's message told him to hold his tongue, but he simply couldn't stay quiet. God had given him a message to preach, and he preached it with enthusiasm. That tends to happen when you do what you believe God has called you to do.

Most people believe that they need training and credentials to minister to others. God doesn't care about your professional and educational background nearly as much as he cares about your willingness to faithfully serve him. Are you willing?

August 22

Costly Unbelief
ELISHA

The officer assisting the king said to the man of God, "That couldn't happen even if the LORD opened the windows of heaven!" But Elisha replied, "You will see it happen with your own eyes, but you won't be able to eat any of it!" 2 KINGS 7:2

Have you ever known a wet blanket? You know—the guy who never goes anywhere without taking along an attitude of negativity and disbelief? This guy looks at God's promises of blessing and wonders aloud not *when* they'll happen but *if.*

If so, you know a man who regularly misses out on the empowerment, blessing, peace, and joy that God generously gives to those who are willing to ask him and believe him for what they need.

Nothing keeps God from blessing people quite like unbelief. That was certainly the case with the unnamed officer of Samaria's king during the prophet Elisha's time.

Samaria's people suffered a terrible famine following the Aramites' invasion. Starving people spent all their money on items usually considered inedible. Finally, the desperate king sent his officer to ask Elisha to do something. Elisha compassionately pronounced a blessing on Samaria, telling the officer that within one day there would be more than enough flour and barley for everyone (see 2 Kings 7:1).

The king's officer just couldn't believe his ears or God's promises: "That couldn't happen even if the LORD opened the windows of heaven!" he exclaimed.

He was dead wrong.

Elisha once more affirmed God's blessing on Samaria, but he told this unbelieving officer that he wouldn't enjoy so much as one bite of the bounty. Just a few hours later, everything Elisha had predicted came true.

This officer would have received God's blessing along with the rest of his people if he had done just one thing: take God at his word. In what areas of life do you need to take God at his word today?

God promises to bless you richly if you choose to believe him and expectantly wait for him to come through. He has never yet failed a man who placed his full trust in him, and he won't fail you.

August 23

Jesus Replaced *This* Man?
BARABBAS

A mighty roar rose from the crowd, and with one voice they shouted, "Kill him, and release Barabbas to us!"   LUKE 23:18

He felt sure he was about to die.

As the young man headed off for work that morning, he had spilled some scalding hot coffee onto his lap. Distracted, he ran his car off the highway and down a steep hillside. As his car rolled the final hundred-plus feet, powerful forces thrust him through the windshield.

As the man lay on the ground, he knew that he was bleeding badly and that he probably wouldn't live much longer. But as he prepared to die, a passing truck driver appeared on the scene. He bandaged the young man's wounds as best he could and called 911 on his cell phone. They waited together for the ambulance to arrive.

Then the trucker disappeared from the young man's life.

Though this accident survivor never saw his hero again, he knew he would always remember the man who had saved his life.

Barabbas no doubt arose the morning of his scheduled execution and felt a similar sense of consuming dread. He knew how the Romans dealt with criminals like him, and they had an agonizing, humiliating death all planned. What Barabbas didn't know that morning was that he would live to see another day because Someone would save his life and take his place at Calvary.

Jesus understood Barabbas's anguish. He understood because he had been through it himself. He had wept, sweated, and begged. If only there were some other way!

But there was not.

The Roman governor Pilate tried to secure Jesus' release, but the people who brought him in for trial weren't having it. Given the choice between sending the vicious criminal Barabbas to his death or sending Jesus, they chose Jesus. We don't know what Barabbas did following his reprieve, but surely, for the remainder of his life, he remembered Jesus as the One who died in his place.

You should think of Jesus in exactly the same way.

Jesus came to earth and died to save you from the penalty of your sin. When you think of Jesus, don't just remember him as a teacher whose example has changed your life. Honor him as the One who died in your place.

August 24

Set Apart
SAMSON

The LORD said to Moses, "Give the following instructions to the people of Israel. If any of the people, either men or women, take the special vow of a Nazirite, setting themselves apart to the LORD in a special way." Numbers 6:1-2

The United States Marine Corps has one slogan it uses very effectively in its television commercials: The Few. The Proud. The Marines. The idea of being set apart as someone special, a cut above the average, appeals to potential recruits.

The Old Testament also tells us about a class of men who were set apart. The Nazirites had taken special vows of obedience to a set of rules that others didn't have to follow. The vow meant that they had set themselves apart for God's service.

Samson and Samuel were two of the Bible's well-known Nazirites. Both men observed the outer signs of Nazirite spirituality by abstaining from alcoholic beverages, refusing to cut their hair, and avoiding personal defilement by touching a dead body.

That's where the similarities ended.

Samson seldom lived an exemplary life of service, obedience, and faith, but instead used his strength to push his own agenda. Samuel served God and his people selflessly and faithfully.

Samson's Nazirite observances made a difference on the outside only; Samuel's became an outward sign of what God was doing inside him. God had called both men to serve with faith and courage, but only Samuel made a lasting impact for the Lord and his people. Centuries later, they continue to demonstrate that it's not what a man does on the outside that matters to God; it's what is on the inside.

Has your faith changed what is inside of you? Would you say that the greatest changes in your life have taken place on the inside or the outside? When you make it your life's focus to follow Jesus, he changes you from the inside out and sets you apart for a life of obedience to him and service to others.

August 25

Costly Inaction
PONTIUS PILATE

Pilate saw that he wasn't getting anywhere and that a riot was developing. So he sent for a bowl of water and washed his hands before the crowd, saying, "I am innocent of this man's blood. The responsibility is yours!"   Matthew 27:24

Imagine having to decide between various alternatives that would all be costly to you. Would you choose the least costly alternative, do what your conscience told you was right, or wait and allow the situation to sort itself out (in other words, do nothing and let the chips fall where they may)?

Pontius Pilate, the Roman governor of Judea during the time of Christ, was in this situation. Standing before him was Jesus, accused of capital crimes but guilty of nothing except offending the sensibilities of some Jewish religious leaders.

Pilate had never been a friend of the Jews, but despite his low or nonexistent religious convictions, he saw something special about Jesus.

He also recognized Jesus' innocence.

Pilate wanted to let Jesus go. He pleaded repeatedly with the Jewish leaders to relent in their demands that he be crucified, only to hear some not-so-subtle threats about his standing with Caesar.

Pilate knew the right thing to do, but rather than make an unpopular decision, he caved in. He decided by choosing not to decide.

Pilate stood before those who wanted Jesus dead and symbolically washed his hands of responsibility for what would happen to Jesus. Then Pilate sent him away to die.

Though Pilate seemed to understand that Jesus was no ordinary man, his passivity in the face of popular opinion relegated his name as a joke and a curse in history.

That's a legacy that no man can wash from his hands.

Sometimes you may have to make unpopular decisions and take unpopular stands, even in your own home. You demonstrate your courage and convictions when you assume responsibility and do what is right, even when that is risky.

August 26

The Right Reasons
SIMON THE SORCERER

Peter replied, "May your money be destroyed with you for thinking God's gift can be bought! You can have no part in this, for your heart is not right with God. Repent of your wickedness and pray to the Lord. Perhaps he will forgive your evil thoughts, for I can see that you are full of bitter jealousy and are held captive by sin."
ACTS 8:20-23

When the great missionary Hudson Taylor interviewed candidates for ministry in China, he typically asked them, "Why do you wish to go to a foreign mission field?"

One candidate answered, "I want to go because Christ has commanded us to go into all the world and preach the gospel to every creature." Another said, "I want to go because millions are perishing without Christ." Others gave equally good and valid answers.

Taylor responded, "All of these motives, however good, will fail you in times of testing, trials, tribulations, and possible death. There is but one motive that will sustain you in trial and testing; namely, the love of Christ."

Sometimes intense self-examination is needed to know if we are doing things for the right reasons.

Simon the Sorcerer had a big problem with inappropriate motivation. He had heard the apostles' preaching, had accepted their message, and had been baptized (see Acts 8:12-13). Still, he was missing something.

Simon apparently had some very real power, for the people of Samaria called him "the Great One—the Power of God" (Acts 8:10). When the apostles showed up, however, he recognized that his power paled in comparison. After his conversion, Simon approached the apostle Peter and offered him money in exchange for the power to lay hands on people and give them the Holy Spirit.

Simon apparently wanted God's power so he could use it in the same way he had used his own: to make a profit. Peter would have none of it and sternly scolded Simon for believing that money had anything to do with the power of God. Simon remains an example, reminding us that we must be sure to serve God for the right reason—love!

There is no better motivation to serve and follow Jesus than of love for him, for our brothers and sisters in the faith, and for those who need to hear his message of salvation.

August 27

What Goes Around
KING ADONI-BEZEK

Adoni-bezek said, "I once had seventy kings with their thumbs and big toes cut off, eating scraps from under my table. Now God has paid me back for what I did to them." They took him to Jerusalem, and he died there. Judges 1:7

A middle-aged father, disturbed by his children's unkind words and behavior toward one another, asked his pastor to come to his home to talk about it.

"I don't understand why they're so mean and cruel to one another," he lamented. Just then, his son walked up to the table and interrupted his conversation. Rather than gently instructing the boy to go play so he could continue his conversation, the man snapped at him, sending him away hurt and sulking.

The Bible tells us that we always reap what we sow. Or, as the more secular saying has it, "What goes around, comes around."

Adoni-bezek, a Canaanite king during the biblical period of the judges, learned that truth in a gruesome way. His unpleasant story shows the importance of treating others with fairness, justice, and kindness.

Adoni-bezek enjoyed some success as a king and military leader as he defeated and took into captivity seventy nearby kings. He went terribly wrong and sealed his own fate by mistreating these captives. He cut off their thumbs and big toes and forced them to beg for scraps from his table.

When the armies of the tribes of Judah and Simeon attacked Canaan, they took Adoni-bezek into custody and cut off *his* thumbs and big toes—just as he had done to the seventy kings he'd held in captivity—and sent him off to Jerusalem, where he died.

The story of Adoni-bezek reminds us that we do reap what we sow. If you want to reap kindness and love, then sow them in your every word and action.

Remember Jesus' Golden Rule? When you treat others with the same kindness and respect that you want, they will be more likely to treat you that way. When you don't . . . well, that's a different story.

August 28

A Basis for Confidence
AZARIAH AND KING UZZIAH

Azariah the high priest went in after him with eighty other priests of the LORD, all brave men. They confronted King Uzziah and said, "It is not for you, Uzziah, to burn incense to the LORD. That is the work of the priests alone, the descendants of Aaron who are set apart for this work. Get out of the sanctuary, for you have sinned." 2 Chronicles 26:17-18

Like most artists, John Singer Sargent, one of the most gifted and highly renowned portrait painters of his day, went through times when he doubted his ability. When those doubts began to creep in, he would look at one of his most highly praised paintings and remind himself, "I painted that!" Just like that, his confidence would return.

Nothing keeps you from what God calls you to do more than self-doubt and fear. On the other hand, nothing gives you confidence like knowing you have God's full support.

At the pinnacle of his reign, King Uzziah of Judah was arguably one of the most powerful men in the world. Few dared to say no to him or tell him what to do. Yet a high priest with strong convictions—and a lot of courage—did exactly that.

Azariah, the high priest, knew that Uzziah had been out of line. The king had entered the holy Temple and burned incense, a duty that God had reserved for his priests alone. Someone had to say something, and Azariah was just the man to do it.

Azariah knew that confronting the king of Judah entailed a great deal of risk, to put it mildly. Uzziah had the authority, the temperament, and (probably) the inclination to end Azariah's life.

Still, Azariah spoke up.

Did Azariah speak out presumptuously or recklessly? Was he simply "popping off" because he expected his priestly position to protect him? No! Azariah spoke out because he knew that he had God's full support.

Predictably, Uzziah flew into a rage when Azariah confronted him, but in the end it was Azariah, not Uzziah, who continued to stand in the Temple as God's servant.

Are you a confident person? You gain confidence and courage when God gives you his approval and blessing as you do what he calls you to do, regardless of the risk.

August 29

Real Men Do Cry
JESUS AND LAZARUS

Then Jesus wept. The people who were standing nearby said, "See how much he loved him!" John 11:35-36

Did you know that crying can be good for you?

Research suggests that tears of emotion—as opposed to the kind you get in a smoky room or when you slice onions—can rid the body of harmful chemicals built up during times of nervous tension. Some researchers also believe that men are more prone to stress-related illness when they resist crying.

Jesus was never afraid to show his emotions. He was able to weep when appropriate, as it was when he visited the town of Bethany following the death of his close friend, Lazarus.

Jesus knew how the saga of Lazarus's death would end that day. Before he ever arrived in Bethany, he knew that people would witness a spectacular miracle and that his dear friend Lazarus would live again. Yet he cried as he approached his friend's tomb.

Did Jesus cry because he saw and felt others' pain that day? Was he grieved and angry that death had invaded his dear friends' lives? Was he disappointed that the people of Bethany lacked faith?

Whatever the reason for his tears, Jesus remained the perfect man throughout this incident. He was perfect in love, holiness, and his ability to express emotion.

If the only perfect man who ever lived was not ashamed to show his emotions, even to the point of shedding tears, might you consider showing some emotion to those closest to you?

Although many people around you—especially your family—look to you as a source of stability and strength, they also need to see you express what's in your heart. Be the strong leader God calls you to be, and don't be afraid to follow Jesus' perfect example by showing genuine emotion to those you love.

August 30

Show Appreciation
STEPHANAS, FORTUNATUS, AND ACHAICUS

I am very glad that Stephanas, Fortunatus, and Achaicus have come here. They have been providing the help you weren't here to give me. They have been a wonderful encouragement to me, as they have been to you. You must show your appreciation to all who serve so well. 1 Corinthians 16:17-18

"Would it kill you to just once in a while show some appreciation for the things I do around here?" a frustrated wife challenged her loving but sometimes thoughtless husband.

No, it wouldn't have killed him; he just hadn't thought of doing it.

Everyone likes words of thanks and gestures of appreciation. We feel especially blessed when someone takes the time and effort to say thank you for something we've done.

The apostle Paul made a practice of giving and receiving appreciation. He made a point of showing and telling his fellow believers in Corinth how to express their appreciation to those who had faithfully served them.

Paul took the time to praise Stephanas, Fortunatus, and Achaicus, three Corinthian believers who traveled out of their way to encourage and assist Paul in his ministry. He gave these men a verbal pat on the back for their service and used his first letter to the Corinthians to encourage the believers there to show their appreciation for everyone who served them.

This was important enough to Paul that he didn't just *suggest* that people show their appreciation; he *commanded* it, saying, "You must show your appreciation to all who serve so well."

Some men—even some men of God—sometimes forget to express their thanks, but getting into the habit of showing appreciation is as easy as following Paul's example. Why not go out of your way to say thank you to the people who make your life better? You'll be blessed when you offer your thanks, and so will they!

Take time today to show appreciation for the things others do for you. Thank your wife for what she does to make your life more comfortable, your children for something they have done well, and your parents for giving you life.

August 31

Unexpected Wisdom
ELIHU

"I will say my piece. I will speak my mind. For I am full of pent-up words, and the spirit within me urges me on." Job 32:17-18

A father, frustrated by his son's habit of tracking dirt in the house every time he went out to play, snapped at the boy, "Can't you find a place to play that's cleaner?"

The boy looked quizzically at his dad and answered, "Dad, if God didn't want me to play in the dirt, why did he make so much of it?"

Simple wisdom sometimes comes from unexpected places.

Job's three friends—Eliphaz, Bildad, and Zophar—felt sure that God was punishing Job for some hidden sin, a charge that Job flatly rejected. Job saw no purpose for his suffering and thought that God was treating him unfairly.

All four had jumped to some seriously wrong conclusions.

Enter Elihu, who had listened to the four-way conversation but had kept his mouth shut because of his youth. Elihu finally spoke up, telling Job and his three friends that they had it all wrong. God wasn't necessarily punishing Job, and even if he were, he *certainly* wasn't treating Job unfairly.

"Listen to me, you who have understanding," Elihu said. "Everyone knows that God doesn't sin! The Almighty can do no wrong. He repays people according to their deeds. He treats people as they deserve" (Job 34:10-11).

Wise words from an unexpected source!

Like Job's other friends, Elihu made some seriously wrong assumptions about him. But although he misunderstood Job, he displayed a bit of understanding that the four older men either lacked or had temporarily forgotten.

Elihu knew that Job's suffering could not be in vain. He knew that Job shouldn't see his affliction as a sign that God didn't care about him, but rather as a tool in God's hand to teach Job more about his true character.

That's a truth we all need to hear now and then.

Do you need special wisdom and knowledge today? If so, remember that God may use unexpected means to give it to you. Keep your eyes and mind open because you never know how—or through whom—God will speak to you.

September 1

Real-Life Knowledge
JOB

"You asked, 'Who is this that questions my wisdom with such ignorance?' It is I—and I was talking about things I knew nothing about, things far too wonderful for me." Job 42:3

"I thought I really knew Janet when we first got married," a doting husband told his friends and family at his twenty-fifth wedding anniversary party. "But now I realize I didn't know one thing about her. I only got to know her as we went through some ups and downs together. The more I realized I was married to a woman I could always trust and could count on to stick by me when things got rough, the more I loved her."

You can get to know a person in the times when life is easy and enjoyable, but you really find out what he or she is made of when you're not at your best.

After suffering through the loss of his property, wealth, health, and family, Job came to a better understanding of God. God had called Job "a man of complete integrity" (Job 1:8), but this up-close-and-personal understanding of God was new even for him.

Job suffered through a horrible set of circumstances for no apparent reason. When it seemed that things couldn't get any worse, he began questioning God, complaining to God, and even accusing God of treating him unjustly.

When God finally entered into Job's suffering and revealed himself, Job could do nothing but humbly retract the foolish things he had said: "I take back everything I said, and I sit in dust and ashes to show my repentance" (Job 42:6).

Job had seen and heard God as he really is. He had listened as God asked him some pointed questions. When that happened, Job came to the end of himself and began to understand his own smallness compared to God's glory and power: "I had only heard about you before, but now I have seen you with my own eyes" (Job 42:5).

You get to know about God through praying, reading your Bible, and fellowshipping with other believers. You come to know him more fully and personally when you apply your knowledge to real-life situations, especially the difficult ones.

September 2

Overt Love
SOLOMON

He escorts me to the banquet hall; it's obvious how much he loves me.
SONG OF SOLOMON 2:4

If you truly, deeply, madly love someone, then your feelings are bound to show, one way or another. That's part of being made in God's image. We love the way God loves, and God loves in an obvious way, demonstrated openly and outwardly.

Today's Scripture is a staple for those who wish to read about a man's love for his woman in the Bible. It describes the depth and breadth, as well as the specific demonstrations, of a husband's passion for his lady. It also pictures God's love for you.

Wait a minute! you may be thinking. *I thought the Song of Solomon was about a man's love for his wife, not about God's love for us.*

Actually, it's both. The one pictures the other.

Solomon's beloved Shulamite knew how much he loved her. In his words and deeds, Solomon demonstrated his love in ways that everyone could see. When he invited her into the banquet hall where his family, friends, and servants all dined with him, he openly expressed his undying love.

Solomon certainly reaped the rewards of his openness with the Shulamite!

Though the Song of Solomon is a poem about the passionate love between Solomon and his beloved, and a real-life account of a man who knew how to cultivate a mutually satisfying and uplifting relationship with the woman he loved, it's also a model of how you can love others whom God has placed in your life. Love them passionately and openly so that they never have to question how much you love them.

Let your wife, children, family, and friends know how much you love them every day, and in as many ways as you can think of.

After all, that's what God has done for you!

God made it obvious how much he loves you by sending his Son to die for you, among other things. You can be obvious about how much you love those he has placed in your life. Don't make them guess or ask. Show them.

September 3

Hit the Ground Running
JOSHUA

Joshua then commanded the officers of Israel, "Go through the camp and tell the people to get their provisions ready. In three days you will cross the Jordan River and take possession of the land the LORD your God is giving you."
JOSHUA 1:10-11

In the early years of the American Civil War, President Abraham Lincoln became so angered at Union commander George McClellan's inactivity that he wrote the general this one-sentence letter: "If you don't want to use the army, I should like to borrow it for a while. Respectfully, A. Lincoln."

Historians remember McClellan as a talented organizer and strong leader, but they also remember his military operations as a frustrating series of missed opportunities.

Joshua was a strong leader who made the most of his opportunities. After Moses' death, God gave Joshua his marching orders: He would lead the people of Israel into the Promised Land. Joshua didn't hesitate for a moment in following those orders.

In our time, nearly every move people make seems to require planning, risk assessment, and cost analysis. It may seem unthinkable—and even reckless—for a leader to receive orders and move on them immediately. But Joshua knew that God, the operation's real Commander in Chief, had orchestrated all the necessary events. The people of Israel had only to pack up and move out.

"In three days you will cross the Jordan River and take possession of the land the LORD your God is giving you," Joshua confidently told Israel's top leaders. And that's exactly what happened because Joshua didn't hesitate but immediately obeyed God's commands.

Though there are times in the life of faith to wait quietly and patiently, there is also a time to move out immediately. We remember Joshua as a great man of faith because he believed God completely and acted without delay on his directives and promises.

When you believe God and know that he will keep all his promises, you won't wait when God says, "Go now!" Instead, you'll move out and conquer the land he's given you. If God is for you, who can ever be against you? (see Romans 8:31).

September 4

Always Caring
JESUS

When Jesus saw his mother standing there beside the disciple he loved, he said to her, "Dear woman, here is your son." And he said to this disciple, "Here is your mother." And from then on this disciple took her into his home. John 19:26-27

One crisis at a time!

All of us feel that way when we're hurting or stressed. With everything going on in your life, you can easily lose sight of some important details, including the needs of those closest to you, and focus only on the crisis at hand.

Jesus somehow continued to meet the needs of others even as he was taking his last breath. How did he do it?

Imagine the chaotic scene of Jesus' crucifixion. Most of his disciples had deserted him, leaving him, his immediate family, a few women, and the apostle John to face his painful and humiliating death. As Jesus took on the sins of the whole world, pain ripped through every particle of his bleeding flesh. Yet even in the midst of his pain, Jesus remained as obedient to God and as caring toward others as ever.

Jesus' mother, Mary, suffered inconceivable pain and grief as she saw the cruelty her son endured. In his perfect obedience, love, and compassion, a suffering Jesus tended to her needs, giving John the task of taking her into his own home and caring for her.

Imagine the heart of compassion and love a man would need to so tenderly care for another's needs under such agonizing circumstances. Under the weight of such suffering, what man wouldn't forget about everyone around him and just focus on his own pain?

Jesus wasn't just any man. He was the most compassionate man who ever lived, and he spent his last few moments on earth tending to the needs of others.

What kind of stress or pain most often forces you to turn inward? When does it become most difficult for you to show compassion to others? In your times of difficulty and suffering, remember that Jesus has compassion for you, and he genuinely cares about everything that happens to you.

September 5

Sound Judgment
ZERUBBABEL

Zerubbabel, Jeshua, and the other leaders of Israel replied, "You may have no part in this work. We alone will build the Temple for the LORD, the God of Israel, just as King Cyrus of Persia commanded us." Ezra 4:3

If you use a personal computer, you can't be too careful about guarding against viruses and worms, covert files designed to do some serious damage to your computer. That means being careful about what e-mails you open, what files you download, and what Internet links you click on.

It is also important to guard against those who try to lead you away from a strong, biblical faith. That means using sound judgment regarding the outside influences you allow into your home and your life.

Zerubbabel had that kind of good judgment.

After leading a wave of former Jewish captives back to Jerusalem from Babylon, Zerubbabel oversaw the building of an altar to the Lord and the rebuilding of the holy Temple, destroyed some seventy years earlier. As the rebuilding efforts began, weeping and shouts of joy could be heard for miles around. That got the attention of some traditional adversaries who offered—with highly suspect motives—to help reconstruct the Temple.

It was decision time for Zerubbabel and his fellow workers.

After weighing the offer (and the apparent motives behind it), he told their would-be helpers, "Thanks, but no thanks!"

As a Christian man, your world is in some ways very similar to that of Zerubbabel. Your challenge? Make sure that you use the same kind of sound judgment as he did in dealing with outside opposition.

What opposition do you face in your Christian faith? Who seems willing to help—but only because they have subversive motives? You need sound judgment to decide who should spend time with your family, what images you and your kids should view, and what kinds of activities you will choose. Ask God to reveal it to you, and then act upon what he shows you.

September 6

Your Place in the Body
ARCHIPPUS

Say to Archippus, "Be sure to carry out the ministry the Lord gave you."
COLOSSIANS 4:17

As you go to church on Sunday morning, do you recognize that God has a specific purpose and ministry for you that day? Or do you go merely to sing a few hymns, listen to the pastor's sermon, and have lunch with your friends and family?

Don't miss out on the blessings you can receive when you assume your place of service in the body of Christ. The Bible teaches that God has given every believer—including you—a calling to serve in some way and the talents and abilities to serve effectively.

An obscure servant and minister from Colossae named Archippus shows how this works. Though the Bible doesn't spell out the exact nature of Archippus's ministry, it was apparently important enough to the apostle Paul that he encouraged the young man to make sure he got the job done.

Paul's encouragement to Archippus says two important things: First, he didn't want him to see his ministry as a burden or as something he *had* to do. Instead, he was to approach it as a special, one-of-a-kind gift from God's own hand. Second, Archippus was responsible for continuing to put that gift to good use as he served God and his church.

Archippus didn't *have* to serve; he *got* to serve! He *enjoyed the privilege* of playing his own important role in making the Colossian church the thriving congregation God intended it to be.

God has given you a particular ministry and the gifts it takes to effectively and efficiently carry it out. Do you know what personal ministry he has given you? If so, are you pursuing it with your whole heart?

You may not be called or equipped to be a pastor, missionary, elder, or Sunday school teacher, but God has given you a gift and a calling that you can use to bless others in your church. When you faithfully fulfill your divine calling, you bless others and put yourself in a position to receive God's greatest blessings.

September 7

Breaking Barriers
CORNELIUS

"I sent for you at once, and it was good of you to come. Now we are all here, waiting before God to hear the message the Lord has given you." Acts 10:33

You don't have to be more than a casual sports fan to know that Jackie Robinson is credited with breaking down Major League Baseball's long-established color barrier. On April 15, 1947, this skilled African-American played his first game for the Brooklyn Dodgers. Though Robinson endured merciless taunts and insults—even at Ebbets Field, his home ballpark—he opened the door for thousands of African-American players who had dreams of playing in the big leagues.

People tend to honor those who first do something of note, and very often they then follow this leader. A Roman military officer named Cornelius broke a few barriers of his own when he placed his faith in Christ; his conversion made a big difference in his family and community.

The Bible remembers Cornelius as the first Gentile to come to faith in Jesus following the Lord's death and resurrection. Cornelius had a reputation as a generous, devout man who feared the God of Israel. He listened and obeyed when God delivered a personalized message to him, telling him to invite the apostle Peter to his home in Caesarea to more fully explain the way of salvation.

When Peter visited Cornelius, the apostle explained everything to him, and Cornelius accepted his words.

As Cornelius listened to Peter, the Spirit of God fell on *everyone* who heard the message. That amazed Peter's Jewish traveling companions, who saw for themselves that God intended salvation through Jesus for Jews and Gentiles alike (see Acts 10:44-45).

Jesus' death and resurrection broke down the long-standing barrier between God and man *and* between Jews and Gentiles. Because Cornelius heard and obeyed God's instructions, he played a big part in bringing his fellow Gentiles to faith in Christ.

You receive God's personal blessings when you listen, trust, and obey God's Word. God blesses you when you obey, and he uses your obedience to bless those around you.

September 8

Conflict Resolution
ABRAM AND LOT

Finally Abram said to Lot, "Let's not allow this conflict to come between us or our herdsmen. After all, we are close relatives!"   Genesis 13:8

High in the Andes Mountains on the border between Argentina and Chile is a statue called *Christ of the Andes*. It represents a pledge between the two countries that as long as the statue stands, peace will reign between them.

Shortly after the statue was dedicated, the Chilean people began protesting that they had been snubbed because the statue faced Argentina and had its back to their country. As tempers flared in Chile, a Chilean newspaperman soothed their anger by saying, "The people of Argentina need more watching over than the Chileans."

The ability to resolve conflict is an important people skill for any man to have and one that Abram ably demonstrated when he deftly avoided a potentially serious conflict between himself and his nephew Lot.

Lot had accompanied Abram out of Egypt and into Canaan, where they both pitched their tents and began tending their animals. The conflict arose when Abram's and Lot's herdsmen began arguing among themselves. There wasn't enough quality pastureland to support both men's huge herds.

Abram took the first step in resolving this conflict by recognizing the problem and talking to Lot about it. He told him that the bickering between their herdsmen had to stop before it spilled over into their relationship. His second step was to offer Lot the choice of whatever portion of land he wanted. Abram would take what was left.

Abram gave Lot first choice of the land around them. When Lot took the land he wanted, the two went their separate ways for a time.

Problem solved!

Abram gave Lot the first choice because he was more concerned with maintaining a good relationship with his nephew than with building his own wealth. Abram knew that God would continue to bless him—and his relationship with Lot—no matter where he settled.

Conflicts are inevitable in human relationships, but you take an all-important step in resolving them when you recognize that the people close to you are far more important—to God and to you—than the issue that caused you to butt heads.

September 9

Pride's Angry Partner
KING NEBUCHADNEZZAR

Nebuchadnezzar flew into a rage and ordered that Shadrach, Meshach, and Abednego be brought before him. Daniel 3:13

The eighteenth-century British physician John Hunter helped to pioneer the field of surgery, but his intense anger sometimes led to severe chest pains. "My life," he used to say, "is at the mercy of any scoundrel who chooses to put me in a passion."

Hunter's words were prophetic. After a heated argument with a colleague at St. George's Hospital in London, Hunter walked out of the room . . . and dropped dead.

Anger can erupt from a lot of things, but one of the most common is simple, human pride. The proud man tends to believe that he is owed something, such as respect and admiration. When he doesn't get what he wants, he becomes angry.

The powerful Babylonian king Nebuchadnezzar was a man whose pride often led to violent anger.

Nebuchadnezzar's arrogance knew no bounds. Early in the book of Daniel, he showed some signs of humbling himself and turning to God, but his true colors showed when three Hebrew men named Shadrach, Meshach, and Abednego refused to bow before his ninety-foot golden idol.

Nebuchadnezzar wasn't used to hearing people say no to his demands. When these three devout men that he saw as "nothings" defied his order and told him that they would bow before no one but God, his pride kicked in, he flew into a rage, and he had them thrown into a blazing-hot furnace.

God used the incident to humble Nebuchadnezzar. Before that happened, the king made an example of how uncontrolled pride often finds an equally destructive partner: uncontrollable anger.

Are you a humble man? If so, you're probably not given to fits of anger. Humility is like a fire hose on the short fuse of anger. If you want to keep anger from being a problem in your life, put a check on your pride. Don't let pride take you down.

September 10

Take the Lead at Home
ABSALOM AND AMNON

When King David heard what had happened, he was very angry.
2 SAMUEL 13:21

George Steinbrenner, the fiery and sometimes controversial New York Yankees owner, allegedly has a plaque on his desk with this quotation: "Lead, follow, or get out of the way."

The Bible promises blessings when you take your positions of leadership seriously and lead in a godly way. It also includes the story of a man who failed to lead as God intended.

David was often a brilliant leader on the battlefield and in the palace, but he struggled mightily in one key area. Far too often, he defaulted on his God-ordained leadership in his own home. For that reason, his family was *dysfunctional*.

The prophet Nathan warned David about the family consequences of his sin with Bathsheba. Though God forgave the sorrowful and repentant David, the awful repercussions of his folly remained in place.

When Absalom, David's second-oldest son, learned that his half-brother Amnon had raped his sister, he waited to see how David would respond. When David failed to take the lead, Absalom took revenge against Amnon and then fled Jerusalem for his life.

Amnon's murder broke the king's heart, as did Absalom's absence. David eventually restored Absalom, but the young man became embittered against his father and eventually led a nearly successful rebellion.

In many ways, David left behind a legacy of brilliant leadership. Had he been more proactive as a family leader, his legacy would have been even greater.

Are you ready and willing to establish a legacy of strong, godly leadership at home? David would tell you, "Don't default on your responsibility here. Other things may seem more important, but I can tell you categorically that they are not."

As a husband, father, and man of God, you have the privilege and responsibility of leading others toward godliness. Of course, that kind of leadership costs you something, but it will cost you more to leave it to someone else. Remember David, and honor God by leading your own home with skill and passion.

September 11

Face the Music
ONESIMUS

I am sending him back to you, and with him comes my own heart. I wanted to keep him here with me while I am in these chains for preaching the Good News, and he would have helped me on your behalf. Philemon 1:12-13

At one time, Steve described himself as a hard-working, hard-fighting, hard-drinking construction worker. Through the witness of a caring friend, he found salvation in Jesus. As he began to grow in his faith, God brought to his mind a wrong he had once committed. Years before he had stolen some tools from a construction company.

One Saturday morning, he packaged up every tool he had taken (worth about four hundred dollars) and sent them back to the company's last-known address. He wrote a note explaining that he had become a Christian and wanted to make things right. He included his phone number and address, should the company want to take additional action.

Sometimes God brings to mind past wrongs we have committed so that we can make amends and seek forgiveness. Onesimus, a runaway slave, took that course of action.

Onesimus had deserted his master, Philemon, a wealthy believer in Colossae, and had headed for Rome, probably to find a little anonymity. While there, he met the apostle Paul, who brought him to faith in Christ.

Now Onesimus had a decision to make.

Onesimus knew he had wronged his master; he had deserted him and stolen from him. He also knew that under Roman law his crimes carried potentially frightful penalties. Still, despite his own fears, Onesimus returned to Philemon.

Why would a man who knew the risks of returning to Colossae willingly go back? Wouldn't it have been safer just to remain in Rome and continue serving Paul?

Onesimus had become a new man in Christ, and he knew that God wanted him to return to Philemon and make amends for his actions. As a believer, he also understood that God would be with him regardless of the consequences he faced.

Confessing your sins against another person—and making amends when necessary—is seldom easy. God always honors you when you go out of your way to seek another's forgiveness, even if you committed the wrong long ago.

September 12

Get into the Action
LUKE

That night Paul had a vision: A man from Macedonia in northern Greece was standing there, pleading with him, "Come over to Macedonia and help us!" So we decided to leave for Macedonia at once, having concluded that God was calling us to preach the Good News there.   Acts 16:9-10

Michael Yon, a former Green Beret and an author, was once a freelance journalist covering the war in Iraq. He reported on the car bombings, skirmishes, and fallen soldiers that have become daily news.

One day, Yon crossed the line from reporter to combatant.

In an August 2005 firefight in Mosul, Yon put down his pen, picked up an M4 rifle, and fired at insurgents who had wounded two leaders of the First Battalion, Twenty-fourth Infantry Regiment. He went from recording history to making it.

Luke, who wrote the book of Acts, was a lot like Michael Yon. At one point in the apostle Paul's story, Luke became part of the team that *was making* history.

In Luke's narrative in Acts 16, look especially for a change in language from third person to first person. Luke didn't just tag along with the group that traveled with Paul; he took an *active* part in their ministry. For example, he wrote, "*We* decided to leave for Macedonia at once, having concluded that God was calling *us* to preach the Good News there" (Acts 16:11).

Luke was not content to just sit back and observe other people's experiences of faith. He became an integral part of things by doing the same work, taking the same risks, preaching the same message, and reaping the same rewards as Paul, Barnabas, and Peter.

Christian growth is not just about learning more, praying more, and enjoying other people's faith experiences; it's about throwing yourself into the work of the Kingdom. It's about putting down the devotionals and partnering with God in your home, workplace, neighborhood, community, and church.

September 13

Alert and Ready
PAUL'S NEPHEW

Paul's nephew—his sister's son—heard of their plan and went to the fortress and told Paul. Paul called for one of the Roman officers and said, "Take this young man to the commander. He has something important to tell him."
ACTS 23:16-17

Johann Gottlieb Rall was a German colonel in command of Hessian troops in Trenton, New Jersey, during the Revolutionary War. One day, one of Rall's loyalists brought him an urgent message: General George Washington and his men had crossed the Delaware River that morning and were on their way to attack Trenton.

The spy, who had seen Washington's forces gathering, was never given access to Rall, so he wrote the important message on a piece of paper, and one of Rall's porters took it to him. The story says that Rall, playing poker with some of his men, stuffed the message in his pocket without bothering to read it.

In a surprise attack on December 26, 1776, Washington's men won what is considered a key victory in the Revolutionary War—and mortally wounded Rall.

The Bible counsels us to be alert and ready to move when God gives us a message of blessing, teaching, or warning. The apostle Paul's nephew saved his uncle's life because he remained alert and ready to act on what he knew.

God had chosen Paul to speak his message of salvation "to the Gentiles and to kings" (Acts 9:15). As he waited in jail for his opportunity to speak to Caesar, his nephew alerted him and his guards of a plot against his life.

The Bible doesn't say how Paul's nephew received this information, only that he acted immediately on what he knew. He kept his head about him and took action as soon as he gained the key information, and God used him to play a part in completing Paul's divinely appointed mission.

You can't always anticipate how God will speak to you. He might speak through a miracle, the words of a family member or friend, simple life circumstances, or his written Word. When you remain alert and step out in faith at the opportune time, the Lord can use you to alter the course of history.

September 14

Maintain Your Guard
NOAH

After the flood, Noah began to cultivate the ground, and he planted a vineyard. One day he drank some wine he had made, and he became drunk and lay naked inside his tent.   Genesis 9:20-21

The prebout conference between two opposing boxers and the referee usually includes these important instructions: "Obey my commands at all times and protect yourself at all times."

In other words, Listen up . . . and keep up your guard!

Does that sound at all like God's instructions for your life?

Noah, despite his reputation as the only righteous man on earth in his day (according to Genesis 6:9), once failed to keep his guard up. His mistake had serious repercussions for his family.

Eight people survived the cataclysmic global flood. God used them to give humanity a new start with a clean slate. Unfortunately, sin soon began to take root again.

One day Noah, who began a vineyard after the Flood, violated the biblical principle of moderation in his drinking. After a glass of wine or three too many, Noah became so drunk that he passed out in his tent.

As Noah lay drunk, his youngest son, Ham, entered his father's tent and sinned when he "saw that his father was naked" (Genesis 9:22). Though scholars debate what specific sin Ham committed, it seems clear that Ham didn't conduct himself in a godly way.

When Noah realized what Ham had done, the consequences of the sin—his own and his son's—took effect. He pronounced a curse on Ham's son Canaan that had repercussions for thousands of years.

Noah let his guard down for only a moment, but his sin led to dire consequences for his family. He is an example of the importance of obeying God's commands and keeping your guard up at all times!

Though God is more than willing to forgive and restore you when you confess your sin, you avoid the consequences entirely when you keep your guard up. "Protect yourself at all times" is good advice for the ring and for life.

September 15

Redemption through Obedience
BOAZ

Ruth told her mother-in-law about the man in whose field she had worked. She said, "The man I worked with today is named Boaz." "May the LORD bless him!" Naomi told her daughter-in-law. "He is showing his kindness to us as well as to your dead husband. That man is one of our closest relatives, one of our family redeemers." Ruth 2:19-20

A man riding some dangerous rapids at work felt tempted one day to just leave his job and let the chips fall where they would, but after thinking of his wife and children, he couldn't do it.

"If it weren't for my wife and kids," he said, "I'd find something else to do. But I can't do that now. I'm going to stick it out and do what I have to . . . for them."

That's a man who puts action behind his love!

A man who truly loves his family will do almost anything to make sure they feel safe, comfortable, and blessed. When he also loves God, he realizes that meeting his family's greatest needs begins with the simple obedience that characterized a man named Boaz.

Ruth, a young Moabite widow, must have wondered why the wealthy, influential Boaz would show her such kindness. Her mother-in-law, Naomi, recognized Boaz as what Old Testament law called a "family redeemer," a close relative who had the option of purchasing family land, as well as marrying a poor and needy widow within his own family (see Leviticus 25:25-28).

When Ruth's husband died, she traveled with Naomi to Bethlehem. There she met Boaz, who compassionately cared for her. Eventually he married her and brought her into the lineage of King David (Ruth and Boaz were David's great-grandparents), a direct ancestor of Jesus.

The kindness of Boaz toward Ruth did not come from romantic love, at least at first, but from his love for God. When Boaz extended his extraordinary kindness, courtesy, and hospitality to Ruth, he acted out of obedience to the God he so faithfully served.

God blesses nothing more completely than eager obedience. Like Boaz, you can bless yourself and your family when you live with a heart attitude of love and obedience to your heavenly Father.

September 16

A Foresightful Man
PAUL

No, dear brothers and sisters, I have not achieved it, but I focus on this one thing: Forgetting the past and looking forward to what lies ahead, I press on to reach the end of the race and receive the heavenly prize for which God, through Christ Jesus, is calling us. Philippians 3:13-14

Harry Truman, the thirty-third president of the United States, was a forward-looking man. He likened men who focused too much on the past to a "Floogie Bird," a wooden toy with a label on its neck, reading, "I fly backwards, I don't care where I'm going. I just want to see where I've been."

Though it may sometimes be tempting to live in the past, God promises to bless you when you focus on what he calls you to do today and in the future. The apostle Paul lived by this biblical truth.

Paul remembered the past and the lessons he had learned from it. In fact, he often referred to his past, but he didn't live there. He preferred looking forward to the things God had for him—namely, finishing the race that was set when God first called him to devote his life to serving Jesus Christ.

That's a great lesson for everyone who follows Jesus.

God has a wonderful plan for your future. Don't focus so much on where you've been that you lose sight of where you are headed.

Though it's great and helpful to remember your past and the lessons it teaches, God wants you to become a forward-looking man who continually presses on with an eye for the great things the Lord will do for you today and in the future.

September 17

What Say You?
ELIEZER

The man bowed low and worshiped the LORD. "Praise the LORD, the God of my master, Abraham," he said. "The LORD has shown unfailing love and faithfulness to my master, for he has led me straight to my master's relatives."
GENESIS 24:26-27

Moments after the toddler received some much-needed liquid refreshment at his grandmother's hand, the boy's mother spoke up.

"Now, what do you say?" she asked.

"Ank oo!" came the toddler's response.

Teaching children basic manners is an essential part of parenthood. That's especially true for Christian parents who want their children to learn the importance of verbally thanking those who help them—including God.

Gratitude should flow naturally from the Creator-creature relationship. God wants you to make gratitude a big part of your relationship with him. He wants you to bring your needs and desires to him in prayer so he might meet them, and then he wants you to thank him for answering your prayers. You also have many good things that you didn't even think to ask for.

Abraham's servant Eliezer went to God and asked very specifically and directly for a sign that would show him which woman he was to take back to Abraham to become Isaac's wife.

When God gave Eliezer exactly what he had asked for, he remembered to turn to him immediately to praise and thank him for his goodness and faithfulness.

God gives you the wonderful privilege of serving him in many capacities and also gives you everything it takes to do the job successfully.

Now . . . what do you say?

When God gives you a mission to undertake or a goal to accomplish, remember to pray for specific blessings regarding those things. When he answers that prayer—and he always will, although maybe not in the way that you expect—go back and thank him for everything he has done.

September 18

God's Kindness
KING HEZEKIAH

About that time Hezekiah became deathly ill. He prayed to the LORD, who healed him and gave him a miraculous sign. But Hezekiah did not respond appropriately to the kindness shown him, and he became proud. So the LORD's anger came against him and against Judah and Jerusalem. 2 Chronicles 32:24-25

Most history buffs remember industrialist John D. Rockefeller Sr. as one of the richest men in American history. They may also remember him as the man who revolutionized the petroleum industry after founding the Standard Oil Company in 1870.

Rockefeller also earned a reputation for generosity. He believed that God had blessed him with every dollar he had earned and that the Lord had called him to be a good steward of that money. He gave to countless worthy enterprises, including many Christian ministries.

In the Bible, the word *stewardship* means making good use of everything God has given you, including your money, talents, and time.

Though the Bible calls Hezekiah a godly king, he didn't make good use of an amazing gift God had given him: fifteen years of additional life (see 2 Kings 20:1-6). Not long after the Lord healed him of a serious disease, the heir to the throne of Babylon, Merodach-baladan, sent envoys to Judah to take Hezekiah his best wishes and a gift.

Suddenly, Hezekiah forgot to be a good steward of what God had given him.

A proud Hezekiah showed the envoys everything in his treasure houses and his armory. Before the visit came to an end, Hezekiah had shown off his kingdom's every possession (see 2 Kings 20:13).

In years to come, Hezekiah's pride would continue to prove troublesome for the kingdom of Judah. God warned him that the same Babylonian nation that had sent the envoys would one day destroy his kingdom (see 2 Kings 20:14-18).

God gave Hezekiah an additional fifteen years that he could have used to continue faithfully serving the Lord. When he allowed his pride to get the best of him, he contributed to major trouble in his kingdom.

God has generously given you everything you have—your talents and abilities, money, family, and your time on earth. You'll find further blessing when you use these resources to glorify God and bless others.

September 19

When Right Is Risky
BARZILLAI OF GILEAD

Barzillai of Gilead had come down from Rogelim to escort the king across the Jordan. He was very old, about eighty, and very wealthy. He was the one who had provided food for the king during his stay in Mahanaim.   2 Samuel 19:31-32

John Witherspoon, a clergyman and the president of Princeton University, championed high principles and often took risks for the causes he believed in. He even risked his own safety when he signed the Declaration of Independence.

How did Witherspoon approach the risks he took in signing the document? In his own words, "If your cause is just, if your principles are pure, and if your conduct is prudent, you need not fear the multitude of opposing hosts."

Barzillai, a wealthy resident of Gilead, was a fine biblical example of courage in the face of risk and contrary public opinion.

David's popularity had waned by the time he met Barzillai. The king's son, Absalom, had staged a coup and assumed the throne, sending David and his loyal men running for their lives. When David stopped in a town called Mahanaim, a hospitable contingent, including Barzillai, gave David and his men food, water, and lodging (see 2 Samuel 17:27-29).

Barzillai knew the risks involved in aiding David, but he still stood up and did what he knew was right.

Barzillai revealed the iron in his soul when he risked his own well-being by caring for a man of God in his most dire hour of need. Many years later, David had regained his throne, quelled the rebellion, and lay on his deathbed. Even then, he remembered Barzillai's kindness and courage and commended the man's children to his son Solomon (see 1 Kings 2:7).

Godly character means doing and saying what you know is right, even when no one seems to be watching. It also means doing what is right when others are watching—even those who despise God and his Word. God sees your good character, and he will bless you for it.

September 20

Feeling Alone?
JEREMIAH

Then the LORD told me about the plots my enemies were making against me. I was like a lamb being led to the slaughter. I had no idea that they were planning to kill me! "Let's destroy this man and all his words," they said. "Let's cut him down, so his name will be forgotten forever."   Jeremiah 11:18-19

At spawning time, salmon make incredible efforts to return to their birth-place. Sometimes the salmon come up against a seemingly impassable water-fall. At that point, each fish is completely alone. There is no teamwork, no well-hatched plan to make sure that all the fish make it over the waterfall. Each individual salmon relies on its own instincts and strength to clear the obstacles—or dies trying.

Have you ever felt completely alone, as if you were the only one even *trying* to live a godly life? The prophet Jeremiah felt that way long before you did.

Jeremiah had an unpleasant message for Judah's people—a shocking prophecy of God's judgment upon their stubborn unfaithfulness. The people didn't receive his message well; they plotted to kill him rather than listen to any more of it.

At times, Jeremiah must have felt completely alone in faithfully trusting and serving God. Although he was grieved by his people's plans to kill him, it grieved him more that no one listened to his message.

Humanly speaking, Jeremiah had plenty to fear and plenty to discourage him. He clearly had days when he wanted to give up on the whole enterprise (see Jeremiah 20:8-9). Every time, he placed his eyes firmly on the One who promised never to abandon him (see Jeremiah 1:8).

Like Jeremiah, you may have times when you think, *What's the use? It's just too hard. I don't think I can do this anymore.* Yet you never have to feel aban-doned or alone, even when you think, *I'm the only one.*

In those times when you feel alone in your life of faith, you can find strength and encour-agement by turning to the One who has promised never to leave you. He will always give you just what you need to endure and even thrive.

September 21

Ready to Follow
JESUS AT CANA

This miraculous sign at Cana in Galilee was the first time Jesus revealed his glory. And his disciples believed in him. John 2:11

When the well-known evolutionist Thomas Henry Huxley spent a weekend with a group of men at a house party, he awoke Sunday morning to find most of them preparing to go to church.

Wanting to hear some evidence for Christianity, Huxley approached one man well-known for his faith and asked him to stay with him and explain why he was a Christian.

This Christian man agreed to sit and talk to Huxley, and when he finished, a tearful Huxley said, "I would give my right hand if only I could believe that."

Though Christianity is a matter of faith, the Bible cites several examples of people who became convinced only after seeing God move in a miraculous way. One day at a wedding party in a small town called Cana, Jesus performed his very first miracle when he changed water into wine.

By that time, Jesus probably had called six of his twelve apostles: Andrew, Simon Peter, Philip, Nathanael, and the brothers James and John. These men followed Jesus because they believed that he was their long-awaited Messiah.

That day, they learned that their Messiah was much more than they had ever expected.

In those days, running out of wine at a wedding was a major social *faux pas*. That is why Mary, Jesus' mother, asked him to fix the problem. Jesus commanded the servants at the party to fill six stone pots with water. After they obeyed, the wine began to flow once again, and in fact, it was the best they had ever tasted.

The perplexed headwaiter didn't know where the wine had come from and wondered *why they had saved the best for last*. The servants knew, however, and so did Jesus' disciples. They would never see Jesus in the same way again.

Jesus met his mother's request. More importantly, he glorified his Father in heaven and established in his disciples' minds just Who had called them to follow.

When you identify yourself as a follower of Jesus, people will watch you closely to see what kind of difference your faith makes. Your life may be just what it takes to convince someone to believe and follow Jesus.

September 22

Full Obedience
AN UNNAMED PROPHET FROM JUDAH

The old prophet answered, "I am a prophet, too, just as you are. And an angel gave me this command from the LORD: 'Bring him home with you so he can have something to eat and drink.'" But the old man was lying to him.   1 Kings 13:18

You probably have a drawer full of instruction manuals somewhere in your house for your computer, your television, your DVD player. Most of those instructions include this warning: "Please read manual completely before operating."

Manufacturers know that failure to fully follow instructions can mean improper operation and even damage to some items.

First Kings 13 tells the story of a prophet whose failure to fully obey God's instructions led to personal disaster. God had given this unnamed prophet from Judah very specific instructions. He was to travel to Bethel in Israel and confront King Jeroboam, who had desecrated this once-honored town by erecting a calf idol and a pagan altar there. God also told the prophet not to eat or drink anything while in Bethel.

The prophet executed the first part of his mission perfectly. He personally rebuked Jeroboam, pronounced destruction on his altar, and taught the king a thing or two about keeping his hands off of a true prophet of God.

From there, things went downhill fast.

As the prophet made his way out of town, an elderly prophet from Bethel sent for him and invited him home for dinner. When the prophet from Judah explained that God had commanded him not to eat or drink anything while in Bethel, the old man lied. He told him that God had sent an angel to command him to bring the man from Judah into his home and give him food and water.

Sadly, the prophet listened to these lies, ignored God's previous command, and lost everything (see 1 Kings 13:18-26). He is a sobering reminder to us that partial obedience is really disobedience.

When you know you have heard a word from the Lord—especially when that word comes from the pages of the Bible—don't let anyone tell you that God has changed his mind. God sometimes allows such tests to see whether you will believe what he says and trust in his direction. Ensure yourself of all God's blessings by obeying his instructions fully, even if others encourage you to do otherwise.

September 23

A Change in Plans
JONAH

When God saw what they had done and how they had put a stop to their evil ways, he changed his mind and did not carry out the destruction he had threatened. This change of plans greatly upset Jonah, and he became very angry.
JONAH 3:10–4:1

Some men have an innate need to plan out everything ahead of time. They need to map out every moment of their workdays, their weekends, and even their vacations to the very last detail. Any deviation from their plans throws their world into chaos.

The Bible recognizes the value of planning; it also includes blessings for those who learn a little flexibility as they follow and serve God.

Jonah disliked God's command to warn Nineveh of its coming destruction, and he became downright angry when God spared the city after the Ninevites heard Jonah's preaching and repented. That wasn't part of Jonah's plan!

"Didn't I say before I left home that you would do this, LORD?" Jonah complained. "That is why I ran away to Tarshish! I knew that you are a merciful and compassionate God, slow to get angry and filled with unfailing love. You are eager to turn back from destroying people" (Jonah 4:2).

Jonah hated the Ninevites and really wanted God to kill them all, thereby snuffing out a very real threat to Jonah's own people, the Israelites. When God spared the city, he deviated from what Jonah saw as the perfect plan.

In the end, God posed this question to his unhappy prophet: "Nineveh has more than 120,000 people living in spiritual darkness, not to mention all the animals. Shouldn't I feel sorry for such a great city?" (Jonah 4:11).

The question bears a clear message: Jonah was God's servant, not his advisor. God had instructed Jonah to obey, preach, and leave the results up to the Lord of perfect knowledge, love, and compassion.

Though you can choose to faithfully obey God, you don't often get to choose what he'll do with your acts of obedience. You will be more happy and peaceful when you simply do what God tells you to do and leave the results to him.

September 24

Harmonious Service
ANDREW

Andrew, Simon Peter's brother, spoke up. "There's a young boy here with five barley loaves and two fish. But what good is that with this huge crowd?"
JOHN 6:8-9

When someone asked the great conductor Leonard Bernstein which instrument was most difficult to play, he replied, "The second fiddle. I can get plenty of first violinists, but to find someone who can play the second fiddle with enthusiasm, that's a problem. And if we have no second fiddle, we have no harmony."

The apostle Andrew had plenty of practice at playing second fiddle. After all, he played that role with his brother Peter for his entire time with Jesus.

Only once does the New Testament mention Andrew's name without connecting him with Peter (see John 12:22). Andrew is last mentioned in Acts 1:13, which lists the names of the eleven remaining apostles following Jesus' return to heaven. After that, he disappears from view.

Other than being Peter's brother, Andrew established his reputation by bringing people to Jesus. First, he brought Peter (see John 1:42), then a boy with some food (see John 6:8-9), and finally, some Greeks who wanted to meet the Master (see John 12:20-22).

Andrew understood the need for harmony! He recognized his role, and he understood and accepted that Jesus had called Peter to a special position of leadership among the apostles. You would have found no sibling rivalry there!

Though the Bible says nothing about Andrew's ministry following Pentecost, tradition suggests that he continued to bring people to Jesus by preaching in Asia Minor and Scythia.

As Jesus' servant, Andrew played second fiddle even within his own family. He set an example by willingly keeping the harmony so necessary for an effective church.

God probably hasn't called you to have the same widespread impact as Peter. You can still play an important supporting role in his Kingdom as you bring people to him one by one. Whom do you know that you can bring? What stops you from bringing them?

September 25

Encouragement
SILAS AND JUDAS

Judas and Silas, both being prophets, spoke at length to the believers, encouraging and strengthening their faith. They stayed for a while, and then the believers sent them back to the church in Jerusalem with a blessing of peace. Acts 15:32-33

Phil worked hard as a Christian businessman. His daily schedule was so filled with important tasks that he rarely had time to talk to his clients or coworkers. One day, he began wracking his brain to think of ways he could spread God's love and encouragement.

Then Phil had an idea. Every time he talked to someone on the phone or corresponded through e-mail, he would end the conversation or message with these words: *God bless and make it a great day!*

Before long, Phil's words of encouragement made a difference in several people's lives, including one particularly needy man who called and asked him about his faith in Jesus.

The Bible often highlights the need for encouragement in the body of Christ. Silas and Judas were two devout believers from Jerusalem who set a good example.

Silas and Judas first appear in Scripture after they were chosen to travel with Paul and Barnabas to Antioch. They helped to deliver a letter that communicated what the apostles had decided about what Jewish laws the Gentile Christians needed to observe.

Silas and Judas had a specific task to complete in Antioch, but they didn't just finish it and head back home. They took time to speak words of encouragement and strength to the believers.

Silas and Judas went out of their way to strengthen and bless those they didn't even know personally through their encouragement. Who in your world needs that kind of strength and blessing today?

Your daily schedule may be filled to the brim with important tasks, but you can bless others as you go out of your way to encourage them. What can you say today to encourage a fellow believer, or anyone else who needs encouragement and a quick glimpse of God's love?

September 26

In It Together!
MOSES, AARON, AND HUR

Moses' arms soon became so tired he could no longer hold them up. So Aaron and Hur found a stone for him to sit on. Then they stood on each side of Moses, holding up his hands. So his hands held steady until sunset. Exodus 17:12

Ornithologists (scientists who study birds) have observed a great example of cooperation in common gulls. Like other birds, gulls need to preen themselves regularly to remove parasitic ticks. However, gulls have trouble reaching the parasites on their own heads. The birds solve that difficulty through cooperation. After they preen their own bodies, they take turns grooming one another's heads.

Moses, Aaron, and Hur experienced the importance of cooperation during the Israelites' battle against the armies of Amalek. Moses ordered Joshua, his top military man, to gather some men and go to battle. Moses' important part in the battle plan was to provide spiritual support for his army.

Moses stood on a hill overlooking the battlefield, raised his hands, and held up the staff of the Lord, which represented Israel's dependence on God. When he held up the staff, the Israelite soldiers had the advantage. When he became tired and dropped it, the Amalekites gained the upper hand.

Israel ran into problems when Moses became too tired to hold the staff up any longer. Israel's army was in big trouble unless Moses, Aaron, and Hur could come up with a solution.

Thinking quickly, Aaron and Hur found a stone for Moses to sit on, then stood on either side of him and held up his hands. From that moment on, what had been a fierce battle became a decisive victory for the Israelites.

The problem was solved through cooperation!

Time and time again, God taught the people of Israel that they must utterly depend on him. That day, they learned another lesson on the importance of cooperation.

Are you a cooperative person? God never intended for you to live or operate independently of others. He has placed other believers in your life—including your own family and close friends—to give you encouragement, support, and assistance when you need it.

September 27

Blessed, Not Honored
BARAK

Barak told her, "I will go, but only if you go with me." Judges 4:8

Chicago crime commissioner Frank Loesch became legendary for his courage in putting an end to mobster Al Capone's domination over the Windy City. Though even the FBI feared Capone, Loesch courageously endured threats to his own life—and the lives of his family and friends—and continued working to bring Capone to justice and make Chicago a safer place to live and do business.

Frank Loesch earned respect and honor for his courage.

An Old Testament military leader named Barak had an opportunity to earn honor among his people. He took part in Israel's great military victory over the Canaanites, but his reluctance to lead courageously was costly.

At God's direction, the judge Deborah ordered Barak to raise an army to fight the Canaanites, who had held the Israelites in subjection for two decades. God promised Barak victory, but Barak told Deborah he would go only if she promised to go with him.

On the positive side of the ledger, Barak demonstrated a measure of respect and honor for Deborah and for the position to which God had called her. His refusal to go to war if she stayed home also demonstrated a certain lack of courage and faith on his part.

As a prophet and judge, Deborah served God and her nation well. She never claimed to be a military leader—that was Barak's job. So Deborah chided Barak in a way that must have stung him deeply: "Very well," she replied, "I will go with you. But you will receive no honor in this venture, for the LORD's victory over Sisera will be at the hands of a woman" (Judges 4:9).

For his faithful military service, Barak is listed in the Bible as a man of faith (see Hebrews 11:32-35). Because he didn't step out when God called him, he missed an opportunity to establish an even greater name among his countrymen.

How do you respond when God calls you to do something great? To what great thing might he be calling you right now? When God calls you to accomplish something, set yourself up for blessing and honor by relying on him and stepping out in trust and obedience.

September 28

The Right Prophets
JEREMIAH

The LORD said, "These prophets are telling lies in my name. I did not send them or tell them to speak. I did not give them any messages. They prophesy of visions and revelations they have never seen or heard. They speak foolishness made up in their own lying hearts." Jeremiah 14:14

If you thought you might have a serious medical condition, would you choose a doctor that you knew would give you an accurate diagnosis so you could begin treatment, or some quack who spoke soothing words in an attempt to convince you that nothing was wrong?

If you wanted a chance to regain your health, then obviously you would go to the first doctor. You would want to know the truth about your condition and find out what was needed for a full recovery.

It also works that way in the spiritual realm.

It is always important to hear God's true word, and it's especially important when you face a difficult situation. During the prophet Jeremiah's ministry, self-professed "prophets of God" contradicted Jeremiah's warnings about coming divine judgment. They insisted that everything was all right and that God hadn't *really* given Jeremiah any messages about his coming wrath.

Their false messages made a dire time in Judah even worse. Even after repeated warnings to turn back to the Lord, the people continued to rebel. Speaking through the true prophet Jeremiah, God pronounced certain judgment, but the people did not want to hear the truth. They wanted comfort rather than conviction, so they listened to the false prophets and continued marching toward their doom.

We have plenty of false prophets today, too; even people with good intentions might try to steer you away from God's revealed will for your life. They often use pretty words and comforting thoughts, but the real question is whether or not their words match up with God's words.

You can never go wrong by listening closely for God's voice in the midst of your life's challenges. Always ask yourself, *Does this message line up with what I know God teaches in the Bible?* Comfort, convenience, and getting along are not the issue. The real treasure is found where truth is told.

September 29

Childlike Believers
JESUS

One day some parents brought their children to Jesus so he could touch and bless them. But the disciples scolded the parents for bothering him. When Jesus saw what was happening, he was angry with his disciples. He said to them, "Let the children come to me. Don't stop them! For the Kingdom of God belongs to those who are like these children." Mark 10:13-14

Something about a baby or small child touches the hearts of most adults. They love the innocence and the inborn knowledge that nothing good comes unless Mom or Dad brings it.

Jesus had a heart for children. He showed his compassion and tenderness to anyone who knew they needed it, and he treated children with special kindness.

Jesus often used day-to-day events as object lessons. Though it angered him to see his disciples keeping parents from bringing their children to him, he used their ignorance and missteps to teach them that "anyone who doesn't receive the Kingdom of God like a child will never enter it" (Mark 10:15). Then Jesus took the children in his arms and blessed them.

What did Jesus mean when he said to "receive the Kingdom of God like a child"? Jesus spoke of a childlike sense of utter dependence on God's goodness and generosity. We can also have an unshakable faith that God is the source of everything good—in this life and in the life to come.

Do you have that kind of dependent faith in your loving heavenly Father? Would you call your faith *childlike* or *childish*?

How do you approach God—as your Creator, Provider, and loving heavenly Father? God desires to bless you, care for you, and guide you when you approach him with an attitude of childlike dependence and faith.

September 30

Good Things Ahead
PAUL

I have fought the good fight, I have finished the race, and I have remained faithful. And now the prize awaits me—the crown of righteousness, which the Lord, the righteous Judge, will give me on the day of his return. And the prize is not just for me but for all who eagerly look forward to his appearing.
2 TIMOTHY 4:7-8

Prior to his death in 1975, Aristotle Onassis, the famous shipping tycoon and one of the wealthiest men of the twentieth century, began giving enormous amounts of money to various charities. Was this an act of benevolence? Was Onassis trying to bring something good out of his impending death? Not quite. It appears that Onassis gave away his money because he wanted to *earn* a place in heaven.

As the apostle Paul contemplated his own end, a very different sort of resolve filled his soul. He had spent most of his adult life faithfully serving God, and he knew the futility of trying to earn God's favor. He also knew that faithful service would prepare him for God's staggering blessings.

Paul clearly felt at peace with his imminent death. That was natural because he didn't see his life as his own. He believed that everything about his life—what he did and whatever happened to him—belonged completely to Jesus (see 2 Timothy 4:6).

Paul was also at peace because he knew that he had remained faithful to his calling and would enjoy the eternal benefits of that career choice. "And now the prize awaits me—the crown of righteousness, which the Lord, the righteous Judge, will give me on the day of his return." Paul found great comfort in realizing what lay ahead for him beyond the executioner's sword.

Although you're not an apostle, you can enjoy the same comfort today. As Paul wrote, "The prize is not just for me but for all who eagerly look forward to his appearing."

Nothing in this life—enjoyable or painful—can compare with what awaits you in heaven as a follower of Jesus Christ. In the meantime, your job is to faithfully serve Jesus so that you can more fully enjoy his blessings in this life and encourage others to work toward their own eternal reward.

October 1

You'll See
ABRAM

The LORD had said to Abram, "Leave your native country, your relatives, and your father's family, and go to the land that I will show you."   Genesis 12:1

Anyone who has taken a son or daughter to a surprise destination—maybe to a fun place for dinner or to the newest, most exciting amusement park—has dealt with the inevitable question: Where are we going, Dad? Most parents want to keep the destination a secret for as long as possible and give a non-answer such as, "You'll see!"

God didn't give Abram (later renamed Abraham) a lot of details when he called him to leave his lifelong home in Haran and head out for "the land that I will show you." He had promised Abram that he would father a great nation and that the entire earth would be blessed through him (see Genesis 12:2-3).

Still, there had to be questions.

Where exactly is this place?

What will we do once we get there?

How are you going to make me a great nation when my wife can't bear children?

How can I be a blessing to all the families on earth?

Yet Abram went. He didn't ask questions or request signs; he simply went.

Abram had never been to Canaan and had no idea how God would fulfill his promises, but he trusted God completely. He confidently and obediently took his family and headed out.

Since Abram believed God enough to step out in obedience, God used Abram to help bring the salvation we enjoy into the world.

Obedience always comes with an added blessing. We might like it more if God filled in the details for us ahead of time, but that isn't what a life of faith entails. When he instructs us to go, we go. He knows what he's doing even when he doesn't give us a complete itinerary at the front end.

October 2

Take a Shot
ELIJAH AND ELISHA

When they came to the other side, Elijah said to Elisha, "Tell me what I can do for you before I am taken away." And Elisha replied, "Please let me inherit a double share of your spirit and become your successor." 2 Kings 2:9

By the time his illustrious twenty-one-year National Hockey League career ended in 1999, Wayne Gretzky, "The Great One," owned nearly every offensive record in the books, in both the regular season and in the playoffs.

Gretzky wasn't the biggest, strongest, or fastest to ever lace up skates, but he was arguably the smartest. One time, he shared part of what made him the greatest offensive player in the game. "You miss 100 percent of the shots you never take," he said.

Success in life means being willing to take your own shots when they are there for the taking.

The prophet-in-training Elisha achieved greatness because he had the faith to ask for a blessing when he had the opportunity. Three times Elisha's predecessor and mentor, Elijah, told him to stay behind and not follow him any further, and all three times Elisha answered, "As surely as the LORD lives and you yourself live, I will never leave you!" (2 Kings 2:2-6).

Elisha wanted something, and when Elijah gave him the opportunity to ask for it, he didn't shy away. After the two men crossed the Jordan River together for the last time, Elijah asked his young protégé what he wanted. Elisha didn't hesitate: "Please let me inherit a double share of your spirit and become your successor" (2 Kings 2:9).

Elijah had worked tirelessly to bring Israel back to God, and he knew better than anyone what Elisha was asking for—and why he would need a double portion of his spirit to accomplish it. As God took Elijah up into heaven, Elisha received exactly what he had requested.

When you feel the need for God's empowerment, take your shot and ask for it in faith. That's a shot you'll never miss because God promises to give you what you need 100 percent of the time when you ask.

October 3

When a Brother Sins
SAMUEL

"As for me, I will certainly not sin against the LORD by ending my prayers for you. And I will continue to teach you what is good and right." 1 Samuel 12:23

In 1975, an unemployed schoolteacher rushed into the Rijksmuseum in Amsterdam, approached Rembrandt's famous painting *The Night Watch*, and cut several zigzag slashes in the canvas.

Although the man had badly damaged the painting, the museum could not simply write off the masterpiece and throw it out. Museum officials called in the most qualified experts to painstakingly restore it. The painting still displays some visual evidence of the damage, but *The Night Watch* has reclaimed its place on display.

We may sometimes feel tempted to write off a brother in Christ who has made a mess of his faith and has hurt himself and those close to him in the process. The Bible teaches us to pray for such a man and do everything we can to restore him. The prophet and judge Samuel gives an excellent example of how to do this.

Samuel knew that the people of Israel had made a foolish and ungodly choice. Against his stern warnings, they had insisted on a flesh-and-blood king to rule them, so God acceded to their wishes and gave them Saul.

Samuel felt grieved and disappointed, but he didn't just write off the people God had called him to lead. Instead, he took the following steps:

> He spoke the truth about the people's sin.
> He encouraged them to continue growing in their relationship with God.
> He warned them not to sink further into sin.
> He reaffirmed God's love and commitment toward them.
> He pledged to continue praying for and encouraging them (see
>   1 Samuel 12:20-23).

Samuel refused to give up on his people even though they had made some wrong choices. How can you follow his example when someone close to you—even a member of your own family—stumbles and falls?

When someone close to you gives in to temptation, don't give up on him or her. Instead, follow Samuel's example and take the necessary steps to restore that person.

October 4

The Reward
THE FAITHFUL SERVANT

A faithful, sensible servant is one to whom the master can give the responsibility of managing his other household servants and feeding them. If the master returns and finds that the servant has done a good job, there will be a reward.
MATTHEW 24:45-46

Two kinds of people normally work in every office setting. There are those whom the boss must watch like a hawk because their attitude about work reflects the old saying "When the cat's away, the mouse will play." They may get their jobs done, but their hearts aren't in it. Come time for their annual reviews, they're lucky if they get even the smallest raise.

Then there are those who demonstrate faithfulness and enthusiasm in their work. These are the people the boss doesn't need to watch because they make the best use of their time. They do their jobs well because they approach their work with enthusiasm.

Jesus once told a story about the second kind of employee. He was a faithful servant whom the master knew he could count on to manage the other servants. The master would reward this man for his faithful, conscientious service.

This particular servant had earned his master's trust because he had already demonstrated his faithfulness in the big issues his job presented as well as in the smaller details. His master knew that he could leave this servant with important responsibilities. He would treat his fellow servants kindly and wouldn't waste the master's time by partying and drinking (see Matthew 24:45-49).

Are you faithful in serving God, your family, and your employer? If so, you're the kind of servant who earns God's confidence. He will reward you for your faithfulness and give you more privileges and responsibilities in the Master's house.

God gives you many opportunities to serve him, your family, and your employer. God richly rewards you when you approach all opportunities with an attitude of faithfulness.

October 5

Not for Human Consumption
ZIBA AND MEPHIBOSHETH

"And where is Mephibosheth, Saul's grandson?" the king asked him. "He stayed in Jerusalem," Ziba replied. "He said, 'Today I will get back the kingdom of my grandfather Saul.'" 2 Samuel 16:3

On October 30, 1938, thousands of calls flooded East Coast newspaper offices and police stations. Scores of people required medical treatment for shock and hysteria while countless others cowered in their homes, too terrified to go out. They had all heard the radio reports: The Martians had arrived with destruction on their minds.

It was all a hoax—a well-intended hoax but a hoax all the same.

That night, thousands of people misinterpreted a convincing radio adaptation of H. G. Wells's *The War of the Worlds* as an actual news report of an alien invasion. Panic-stricken listeners who heard only part of the story were convinced that the world was coming to an end.

Gossip often works that way. When you spread gossip or listen to it, you probably tell or hear only part of a story and in turn damage another person. When Ziba, a servant in Saul's house (see 2 Samuel 9:2), gave King David some juicy gossip about Mephibosheth committing treason, he did very real damage.

Ziba's gossip damaged Mephibosheth's reputation and his standing in David's kingdom. When David listened to Ziba's hearsay, he stripped Mephibosheth of what rightfully belonged to Saul's heir and gave it to Ziba instead (see 2 Samuel 16:4).

Mephibosheth eventually met with David and cleared his name. He restored his relationship with the king, but only after enduring the pain and humiliation that Ziba's false reports inflicted on him.

Ziba's slander stands as a reminder of the damage that gossip—even with some factual basis—can cause you, your family, your friends, and your brothers and sisters in faith.

Are you often tempted to gossip about someone? One way to combat the temptation is to remind yourself that what you say can significantly damage another person. Blunt the temptation by choosing to speak of (and listen to) only things that build up your brother and not what might tear him down.

October 6

Trust God
AHIMELECH

David went to the town of Nob to see Ahimelech the priest. Ahimelech trembled when he saw him. "Why are you alone?" he asked. "Why is no one with you?" "The king has sent me on a private matter," David said.   1 Samuel 21:1-2

Confederate general Stonewall Jackson was known for his extraordinary courage under fire. After one particularly fierce battle, one of his officers asked him how he remained so calm amid the horrors of war. Jackson replied, "Captain, my religious belief teaches me to feel as safe in battle as in bed. God has fixed the time for my death. I do not concern myself about that, but to be always ready, no matter when it may overtake me."

The Bible teaches that we can overcome our fear of what men can do to us by clinging to our faith and remembering that God superintends everything that comes our way.

Sadly, even David, one of the Bible's true heroes of the faith, once forgot that. David was on the run from King Saul when he met Ahimelech, a high priest in a place called Nob. When the priest asked him why he was alone, David told him, "The king has sent me on a private matter."

The Bible describes David as a man of great courage, conviction, and faith. Though he did something positive in his time of need by approaching the house of God, he did grievous wrong in lying to the high priest. It's not hard to figure out why David lied to Ahimelech. Simply put, at that point in his life, David feared Saul, who wanted him dead, more than he trusted God, who had already anointed him as the future king of Israel.

When you find yourself in a situation where you fear men, do you focus on the fear or trust in the God who already has your future mapped out?

When you focus on God's absolute ability and willingness to bring about his plans for your life, your fear of other people will melt away.

October 7

The Pressure Is On
DANIEL

"I thank and praise you, God of my ancestors, for you have given me wisdom and strength. You have told me what we asked of you and revealed to us what the king demanded." Daniel 2:23

Pressure. Everyone has it and has to deal with it, but not everyone handles it in the same way.

Someone once used a saturated sponge to illustrate a man's response to pressure. When you squeeze it, you know immediately what it holds on the inside. The prophet Daniel once got "squeezed," and what came out of him under pressure saved his life.

One night Nebuchadnezzar, the king of Babylon, had a strange dream. Naturally, he wanted to know what it meant, so he called in his advisors and demanded that they first describe his dream and then tell him what it meant—or else. When they couldn't do either, he flew into a rage and ordered that they all be executed.

Since Daniel and his friends were among the king's advisors, that decree included them.

Using some God-given wisdom and discretion, Daniel calmly talked Arioch, the commander of Nebuchadnezzar's guard, into delaying the executions. Then he asked the king directly if he could take a crack at interpreting the royal dream.

The pressure was on. Daniel needed answers—and soon!

Daniel went home and asked his friends to pray for divine revelation. That very night, Daniel received a vision that clearly explained the king's dream. The next day, he appeared before Nebuchadnezzar—perhaps hours before he and his friends were to die—and told him his dream and its meaning.

The Lord gave Daniel exactly what he needed to save his life, his friends' lives, and the lives of other wise men in Babylon . . . and not a minute too soon! When Daniel was squeezed, out came his faith in the God who does his best work under pressure.

When the pressure is on, you have a place to go for comfort, wisdom, answers, and directions: directly to your heavenly Father's throne room. There you receive from his hand everything you need to deal with any life situations that have you in a squeeze.

October 8

Brag on God
ASAPH

As for me, how good it is to be near God! I have made the Sovereign LORD my shelter, and I will tell everyone about the wonderful things you do.
PSALM 73:28

The Grand Rapids Press reported the story of a new car owner whose incessant boasting about his automobile's gas mileage began to irritate his friends. Wanting to put a stop to his constant bragging, they played a prank on him. Each day, one of them sneaked into the lot where he parked his car and poured a few gallons of gas into his tank. Before long this braggart felt the frustration of trying to convince people that he was getting as much as ninety miles per gallon.

Then came phase two.

Instead of adding fuel to his tank, his friends siphoned some off every day. Within a week, he stopped talking about gas mileage. His car's fuel economy had dipped to fifteen miles per gallon!

It's never a good idea to establish a reputation as a braggart, but it's always good to count your blessings and boast of God's goodness.

Asaph, a leader in King David's choir, loved to boast in that way. Asaph saw the value of openly and consistently telling others of God's goodness and of the many wonderful things he did for him every day. Asaph felt grateful for God's protection and provision and for the fellowship he enjoyed with the Lord.

This isn't just "glass half full" talk, either. In Psalm 73, Asaph expressed his frustration and anger to God at the rampant injustice, oppression, and godlessness in the world around him. But though those things displeased him, he still remembered to thank God for his blessings and to tell those around him just how good God is.

How often do you brag on God and his goodness? Count your blessings regularly, whether they are physical, emotional, or spiritual. Then tell those around you of the many wonderful things God does for you each day.

October 9

Use Common Sense
KING SAUL

The men of Israel were pressed to exhaustion that day, because Saul had placed them under an oath, saying, "Let a curse fall on anyone who eats before evening— before I have full revenge on my enemies." So no one ate anything all day, even though they had all found honeycomb on the ground in the forest.
1 SAMUEL 14:24-25

Admiral Hyman G. Rickover, who spearheaded the development of the nuclear submarine, interviewed thousands of business-school graduates over a period of years. What he saw did not impress him.

"What it takes to do the job will not be learned from management courses," he said. "It is principally a matter of experience, the proper attitude, and common sense, none of which can be taught in a classroom."

King Saul had many gifts and talents, but he often lacked common sense, such as when he took the men of Israel into battle against their archenemies, the Philistines. As his soldiers prepared for battle, Saul gave them the curious order that anyone who ate anything during the daylight hours would be cursed. I guess he reasoned that daylight was for fighting, so the men could eat at night.

Saul's oath defied common sense. God could have commanded them not to eat anything during the battle, but God did no such thing. Saul made the order simply to save time; he was so focused on taking revenge on his enemies that he forgot that his men needed nourishment to fight well.

King Saul's rashness and impatience led to poor decisions and outright disobedience, which helped to scuttle his once-promising reign. Though the Israelites defeated the Philistines that day, the victory might have been far more decisive had Saul not placed such a foolish burden on his men.

At times, God may call you to do something unusual. But use common sense and make sure that you don't move out ahead of God and make impulsive decisions or vows. That could cause big problems in your life and the lives of those close to you.

October 10

Humility and Gentleness
JESUS

"Take my yoke upon you. Let me teach you, because I am humble and gentle at heart, and you will find rest for your souls."   Matthew 11:29

Most people who met him found him a man of genuine humility and gentleness. They were awed by his demeanor and delighted with his disposition. They also noticed the deep affection in his children's eyes for their father, and so they knew that he acted in private just as he did in public.

Who would have expected such a thing from one of the world's most celebrated politicians? Yet that is what visitors experienced when they spent time at the home of antislavery crusader William Wilberforce.

Though Jesus never married or fathered children, he spent enough time with his apostles that they could see how genuinely humble and gentle he was. Jesus is the ultimate example of humility because he freely left heaven to take on human flesh so that he might save all who come to him in faith. In his absolute kindness, he never failed to reach out to those in need. He never struck back at those who did him harm but called on his Father to forgive them.

Never once did Jesus tell his disciples to do anything that he refused to do himself. He could expect them to be humble and gentle because that is what he was like.

Do people use the term *humble* to describe you? Do people look to you when they need a gentle word or action? Some men do not consider these to be strong qualities, so they do not try to embody them. To that degree, they fail to follow the example of Jesus Christ, the strongest man who ever lived.

In what area of life do you most struggle with humility? In what ways is it an effort to embody gentleness? What could you do this week to more closely follow Jesus in these areas?

October 11

A Strong Foundation
NEHEMIAH

When I heard this, I sat down and wept. In fact, for days I mourned, fasted, and prayed to the God of heaven.   Nehemiah 1:4

Scientists who monitor the Leaning Tower of Pisa say that it's only a matter of time before the famous structure falls over. The 179-foot tower moves about one-twentieth of an inch a year, and it is now more than seventeen feet out of plumb.

In truth, the tower began falling over before it was even completed, partly because it was erected on soft ground (the word *pisa* means "marshy land") and partly because its foundation is only ten feet deep.

Nothing good comes of building on a faulty foundation—in construction or in our faith. Nehemiah understood both aspects of this principle.

Nehemiah had taken on a huge task. While he faithfully served a pagan king hundreds of miles from his ancestral homeland, he learned that the dilapidated walls around Jerusalem had left its Jewish residents vulnerable to attack. The news alarmed him, and he knew that something had to be done about the situation.

But what could *he* do?

Absolutely nothing—until he talked to God about the crisis. Nehemiah didn't utter a quick "help me, Lord" kind of prayer, either! He offered the kind of prayer that God delights in answering.

He praised and worshiped God. It was Nehemiah's personal habit to address God relationally through meaningful praise and worship.

He confessed his sins and the sins of his people. Nehemiah recognized that his people's sin had put them in their present situation. He also knew that God wanted to restore what had been lost.

He thanked God for all things. Nehemiah knew that God would finish what he had started, and he thanked him for all that he had already done.

He made his requests known. Nehemiah had a sense of mission and of his need for God's empowerment. He didn't rush into the task before first pleading for God's favor (see Nehemiah 1:5-11).

God has given you the privilege of building an unshakable foundation for everything you do. When you go to him in prayer, praise him, confess your sins, thank him, and tell him exactly what you need. He will richly reward your attention to these details.

October 12

Coming Attractions
MOSES, ELIJAH, AND PETER

As Moses and Elijah were starting to leave, Peter, not even knowing what he was saying, blurted out, "Master, it's wonderful for us to be here! Let's make three shelters as memorials—one for you, one for Moses, and one for Elijah." But even as he was saying this, a cloud overshadowed them, and terror gripped them as the cloud covered them.   Luke 9:33-34

Get to your movie at the advertised hour, and you're still a good fifteen minutes from show time. If you're lucky, however, you may see something worthwhile in the previews of coming attractions.

An effective movie preview doesn't just give you time to warm up your seat; it leaves you wanting more. It plants pictures in your head and sometimes brings you back to the theater the following weekend.

Peter, James, and John once saw a spectacular preview of a coming attraction, and it changed them forever. After hiking with Jesus to the top of a mountain, the tired disciples dozed off as Jesus prayed. As they awoke from their slumber, they saw Jesus in an unexpected light. His entire appearance had changed. His face looked *different,* and his clothes glowed a dazzling white. To top it off, Moses and Elijah appeared and began talking with Jesus.

What a way to wake up!

None of the disciples knew what to say, but that never stopped Peter. He suggested that they build temporary shelters for Jesus, Moses, and Elijah. Of course, the heavenly visitors ignored Peter's suggestion. As God's messengers, Moses and Elijah had certainly earned a place of honor, but not on the same plane as Jesus. Only God's chosen One deserved their worship.

About four decades later, Peter wrote, "We saw his majestic splendor with our own eyes when he received honor and glory from God the Father" (2 Peter 1:16-17). Peter eventually understood that they had seen some of the *divinity of* Jesus that day.

He couldn't wait to see more.

Nothing affirms your faith and wakes you up like a glimpse of the loving, comforting Jesus who is also Lord and King of all. When did you last have that kind of encounter with Jesus? Did it leave you longing for more?

October 13

Set Yourself Apart
PAUL AND TIMOTHY

I have no one else like Timothy, who genuinely cares about your welfare. All the others care only for themselves and not for what matters to Jesus Christ. But you know how Timothy has proved himself.   Philippians 2:20-22

In his memoir *Death Be Not Proud,* American author John Gunther recounted his son Johnny's courage and selflessness when his doctors told him about the brain tumors that would take his life.

When doctors first informed Johnny Gunther of his prognosis, he didn't think of himself, but of his mother and father. He looked his surgeon in the eye and asked, "How shall we break it to my parents?"

That rare kind of selflessness puts others' needs ahead of its own—and Timothy provides us with a great example of it.

The apostle Paul instructed the Philippians to selflessly look out for each others' needs (see Philippians 2:3-4) and then put a face on his instruction by pointing to Timothy, the best example he knew of such selflessness.

Paul knew Timothy well. The young man had accompanied the apostle on his second missionary journey (see Acts 16) and had visited the Philippians several times over the following years. During those visits, Timothy stood out to Paul and the Philippian Christians as a selfless servant (see Philippians 2:22).

Timothy regularly put his character and faith on display in meaningful, tangible ways. He didn't just *possess* God's love; he poured it out on others as he served with little concern for himself.

Timothy didn't set himself apart through loud bragging or self-promotion but by serving others from a sincere and compassionate heart. Isn't that something you could do?

You set yourself apart from the crowd when you focus your attention on meeting others' needs. Of course, to do that, you first have to know what they are. What are your wife's greatest needs? What does your family need from you? Your work associates? Your friends? If you don't already know, spend some time this week finding out.

October 14

A Higher Example
KING AMAZIAH

Amaziah did what was pleasing in the LORD's sight, but not like his ancestor David. Instead, he followed the example of his father, Joash. Amaziah did not destroy the pagan shrines, and the people still offered sacrifices and burned incense there. 2 Kings 14:3-4

Most baseball players can only dream of doing what Mickey Mantle did as a center fielder for the New York Yankees. In Mantle's mind, however, his notorious abuse of alcohol kept him from fulfilling his enormous potential. Shortly before he died in 1995, Mantle said, "God gave me the ability to play baseball. God gave me everything, and I blew it. For the kids out there, don't be like me."

Mantle reportedly came to faith in Christ before he died, and he understood how following the right example—or the wrong one—can affect a man's life.

Amaziah, the eighth king of Judah, blew it when he failed to follow a higher example. Amaziah rejected King David's godly example and instead followed in the footsteps of his father, Joash.

Joash started out strongly but fell flat on his face later in life. Joash faithfully served God early in his reign, but then he defaulted on his spiritual responsibilities. Like his people, he abandoned the worship of God to worship man-made idols.

In short, Amaziah led *reactively* instead of *proactively,* just like his father.

In his early life, Amaziah did some great things for his kingdom, such as defeating the Edomites (see 2 Chronicles 25:11-12). After claiming this victory, Amaziah had an opportunity to make a lasting impact on his people. Instead, he allowed them to continue offering sacrifices and burning incense at pagan shrines. He even worshiped idols that he took from the Edomites.

As a Christian man, you have the opportunity to follow many different examples. Your challenge is to follow godly ones rather than ones like Amaziah, who started out well but finished poorly. Finish strong!

What good examples have you seen that encourage you to develop a strong walk of faith? How can you follow them? What negative examples have made an impact on you? How can you avoid their sad track records?

October 15

Humble Response
KING ZEDEKIAH

Zedekiah was twenty-one years old when he became king, and he reigned in Jerusalem eleven years. He did what was evil in the sight of the LORD his God, and he refused to humble himself when the prophet Jeremiah spoke to him directly from the LORD. 2 Chronicles 36:11-12

An investigation that followed a deadly collision in 1986 between two ships in the Black Sea ruled out technological malfunctions or inclement weather as causes of the accident. They learned that the collision occurred when the ships' captains—each knowing that the other was there—refused to yield the right-of-way. That terrible day, hundreds of people died off the coast of Russia because of human stubbornness.

In order to receive the good things God has promised, listen to what he has to say and respond in humble obedience.

Those who prefer to receive nothing from God should pave their way with stubborn defiance.

Judah's King Zedekiah could testify to all of this. Zedekiah ascended the throne at age twenty-one and from the outset conducted himself like a doomed ruler. He steadfastly refused to listen to the Lord's word as spoken by the prophet Jeremiah. How much better Judah's future might have been had Zedekiah humbly listened to God instead of stubbornly closing his ears!

How might you change *your* future for the better by humbly listening to God? In what areas of life are you stubbornly closing your ears right now? *No man* who maintains a stubborn attitude has ever done anything great for the Lord or received anything great from him.

Will you willingly receive God's instructions and position yourself to receive God's very best?

If you want to receive all that God has for you, your heart must remain pliable toward him. With such a heart, there's no limit to God's blessing on you, your wife, your children, and your work.

October 16

The Courage to Act
GIDEON

"Bring out your son," the men of the town demanded of Joash. "He must die for destroying the altar of Baal and for cutting down the Asherah pole."
JUDGES 6:30

Paul Rusesabagina made quite a name for himself in the hotel business. This courageous man didn't earn that fame for his business work in the hotel but by heroically risking his life to save the lives of over one thousand people. As his home city of Kigali crumbled around him during the Rwandan genocide of 1994, he gave refuge to frightened members of the Tutsi tribe in the *Hôtel des Diplomates,* which he managed.

Have you ever considered what you would do if standing up for what you knew to be right meant taking a big risk to your health and safety, or even your life? Would you have the courage to do this?

The Old Testament hero Gideon had the courage needed to champion his principles and God's name, even when doing so meant risking his skin.

Tearing down the altar of the idol Baal was no small offense to the locals in Gideon's hometown. When Gideon did that, they were more than ready to exact revenge in the name of their god. Only the intervention of Gideon's father, Joash, kept the mob from killing Gideon.

What made Gideon's behavior so radical? He saw beyond the surface of things and recognized that accommodating Baal amounted to treason against God. By destroying the altar of Baal and replacing it with an altar to the Lord, Gideon showed that he had the courage needed to stand against what is wrong and champion what is right, even in the face of extreme danger.

Take a look at your own world. Think of your home, workplace, church, and neighborhood. Do you see any "altars of Baal" there? Is there any place that you believe a courageous man of God should take a radical stand? If so, what keeps you from being that man? Put your faith in God's power, and ask him to help you to speak and act as a godly man of courage.

October 17

Take the Bible Seriously
NADAB AND ABIHU

Aaron's sons Nadab and Abihu put coals of fire in their incense burners and sprinkled incense over them. In this way, they disobeyed the LORD by burning before him the wrong kind of fire, different than he had commanded. So fire blazed forth from the LORD's presence and burned them up, and they died there before the LORD. Leviticus 10:1-2

With tears in his eyes and a trembling voice, the elderly pastor of a small urban church asked his congregants, "When are you people going to get it through your thick heads that God wants to bless you?" He knew that many in his flock had adopted a carefree approach to their walk with Christ, and he longed for them to know God's best.

This dear man understood something that many of us miss today: God didn't give us the Bible in order to control us or hold us back; he gave us the laws and guidelines that will help us to achieve God's best in our lives. It's a lesson that Aaron's sons Nadab and Abihu never understood.

God had called these young men to be priests for the ancient Hebrew nation. As priests, they were given many significant and solemn responsibilities. There was very little wiggle room in the regulations governing the Tabernacle and the sacrifices. Sadly, Nadab and Abihu wiggled too much. They treated God's commands casually and carelessly, and it cost them everything.

Why did the two brothers act in this way? The Bible doesn't say. It does make it clear that their failure to take God's Word seriously cost them the blessings that God wants to generously give to everyone who will listen to him and obey his Word. Nadab and Abihu couldn't get it through their thick heads that God wanted more than anything to bless them.

How do you regard the Word of God? Is it a code of conduct? A book of restrictive rules? Or is it a road map to blessing, honor, and joy?

God has given you his written Word as an instruction manual to help you become the man of God, husband, father, worker, and friend he calls you to be. When you take his Word seriously, you will receive the blessings that God reserves for those who humbly hear and obey him.

October 18

The Consequences of Greed
JOEL AND ABIJAH

As Samuel grew old, he appointed his sons to be judges over Israel. Joel and Abijah, his oldest sons, held court in Beersheba. But they were not like their father, for they were greedy for money. They accepted bribes and perverted justice. 1 SAMUEL 8:1-3

The classic movie *The Treasure of the Sierra Madre* is a great adventure story about three men on a gold-mining expedition in Mexico. Like so many classics, it is also a great study in human nature—in this case, about how greed can destroy friendships, ruin lives, and lead to senseless death.

The Bible repeatedly warns believers not to fall into the trap of greed and its evil twin, the love of money. Yet greed remains among the top sins most likely to tempt followers of Jesus Christ.

Samuel's sons Joel and Abijah show the far-reaching consequences of loving money more than God. The prophet Samuel had appointed his boys as judges over the nation of Israel, but these corrupt and greedy men "accepted bribes and perverted justice." By choosing such a path, they brought dishonor on themselves, their father, and God, and they disqualified themselves from further service.

Joel's and Abijah's evil behavior also hastened the end of the era of the judges and prompted Israel to take another step of national rebellion. In their outrage over the sinful acts of these men, the Hebrew people demanded that Samuel appoint a king to rule over them instead of relying on their heavenly King, the Lord of hosts.

God placed Joel and Abijah in a position where they could have served God well. When they rejected contentment in favor of greed, they failed God and his people. God has also placed you in a position where you can serve him well. As you look at your life, does contentment or greed dominate?

You can defeat greed by being content with what God has given you and by freely choosing to serve God and others. Ask yourself, *Do I think I'd be happier if only I had more stuff? How much time do I spend praising God for what he has already given me?*

October 19

Discipline Begins at Home
HOPHNI AND PHINEHAS

Now the sons of Eli were scoundrels who had no respect for the LORD or for their duties as priests. 1 Samuel 2:12-13

Have you ever sat at a restaurant next to a family whose children have atrocious, loud manners? Have you tried to relax on a long cross-country flight in front of a little boy who continually kicks the back of your seat while Mom and Dad seem not to notice? Have you tried to enjoy a movie with your wife while two rug rats behind you keep chattering?

If you answered yes to any of the above, you know that few things are more annoying than having to endure the behavior of children who lack proper training and discipline. What are their parents *doing* when they should be teaching and disciplining their kids?

That question comes to mind regarding two young men named Hophni and Phinehas. Their father was a good man, an elderly high priest named Eli, who raised and mentored Israel's first prophet, Samuel. However, he failed to teach his own sons the basics of godly living.

Hophni and Phinehas became the talk of the town in Shiloh, and not for good reasons. They brazenly disrespected the Lord, the priesthood, and the people of Israel. They behaved in disgusting ways, even forcing themselves sexually upon young women who came to the Tabernacle to worship God.

Eventually, Eli reprimanded his sons for their wretched behavior, but they had long since stopped listening to anything he had to say. The day of reckoning arrived when God told Eli that his sons would die and that his family would forever lose the privilege of serving in the priesthood.

This was a harsh punishment, but this tragic episode should remind all believing fathers of the crucial importance of their role as leader and mentor at home. Eli was a good man but not a strong man, and children need their fathers to be both.

When you became a husband and then a father, God called you to lead your wife and children along a path that honors him and blesses those around you. Whether you serve God in the church or in the wider Christian community, remember Eli's sad story and remind yourself that your most important ministry begins at home.

October 20

"Mr. Dependability"
ELIEZER

The servant took an oath by putting his hand under the thigh of his master, Abraham. He swore to follow Abraham's instructions.   Genesis 24:9

Let's face it—you just can't depend on some guys.

"I'll be at your house around nine Wednesday morning," Roscoe the computer geek promises. *Great,* you tell yourself, *I'll be back online by noon.*

But Roscoe doesn't show up at the appointed time. By Thursday afternoon, you have left ten unanswered messages on his answering machine, your blood pressure has risen to 180/90, and your patience has grown thinner than a ninety-nine-cent hamburger at Burger Bits.

Eliezer, Abraham's household manager, didn't repair computers, but if he had, he would have kept his boss's machines up and running. His track record of utter dependability impressed Abraham so much that he trusted Eliezer to travel to a distant land to bring home a suitable wife for his son Isaac.

How would you have liked *that* kind of responsibility? Most of us find it hard enough to locate the right gal for ourselves. Imagine the enormous difficulty of such a task in an age before eHarmony or church singles' groups came on the scene.

Eliezer accepted his assigned task. He "he loaded ten of Abraham's camels with all kinds of expensive gifts from his master, and he traveled to distant Aram-naharaim. There he went to the town where Abraham's brother Nahor had settled." (Genesis 24:10). Eliezer wisely enlisted the Lord's help. "O Lord, God of my master, Abraham" he prayed. "Please give me success today, and show unfailing love to my master, Abraham." (Genesis 24:12).

He had scarcely finished his prayer when along came Rebekah, the future Mrs. Isaac. Mission accomplished!

Do people know they can rely on you when you accept a task? Or do they hesitate to ask because they doubt that you will come through? Do you see a little of Eliezer when you look in the mirror?

What has God given you to do? Are you doing it faithfully? Think of the people who know you the best, on the job or at home. Can they honestly call you "Mr. Dependability"? Can others count on you?

October 21

Grappling with God
JACOB

This left Jacob all alone in the camp, and a man came and wrestled with him until the dawn began to break. When the man saw that he would not win the match, he touched Jacob's hip and wrenched it out of its socket. Then the man said, "Let me go, for the dawn is breaking!" But Jacob said, "I will not let you go unless you bless me." Genesis 32:24-26

When did you last wrestle with God? Maybe it was when a relationship with a friend was damaged and you didn't know how to fix it. Perhaps a loved one died, and you thought that God was unjust for taking that person from you. Maybe someone mistreated or misjudged you, and you wondered why God didn't step in to correct the situation. You may have carefully applied biblical principles to your family life, only to watch a child sink into serious rebellion.

For most men, the idea of wrestling with God seems a little "out there." Maybe it did to Jacob, too, just before he found himself in the ring with God.

With *God*? It certainly seems that way, for immediately after this incident, Jacob exclaimed, "I have seen God face to face, yet my life has been spared" (Genesis 32:30). Jacob grappled with God and lived to tell about it; he also received the blessing that he so desperately wanted.

God could have ended this struggle with a single word. In fact, this account tells us that with a simple touch, he dislocated Jacob's hip. God allowed the wrestling match to go on for one reason: He wanted something from Jacob—and *for* Jacob!

When you wrestle with God over the important issues of your life, he has you right where he wants you. Sometimes, that is when you are most ready to receive a blessing.

Are you seeking answers or blessings from God? Are you willing to struggle persistently for them? Maybe God wants you to ask the tough questions so that you can find out more about yourself, about God, and about his plans and purposes for you. How will you know unless you willingly go to the mat?

October 22

A Glimpse of Jesus
ZACCHAEUS

He [Zacchaeus] tried to get a look at Jesus, but he was too short to see over the crowd. So he ran ahead and climbed a sycamore-fig tree beside the road, for Jesus was going to pass that way. Luke 19:3-4

In the classic holiday movie *A Christmas Story,* little Ralphie Parker, a kid living in 1940s Indiana, is a perfect picture of desperation. More than anything, he wants a Red Ryder BB gun for Christmas, and he'll stop at nothing to make sure that his parents know what he wants. Eventually, Ralphie reaches out to his last option: a surly department store Santa Claus.

Desperation can cause a man to go far out of his way to get what he wants or needs!

Zacchaeus, a shady tax collector, is a first-century illustration of this principle. Zacchaeus understood his wretched condition well. He knew better than anyone how desperately he needed forgiveness. He sensed that he could obtain that forgiveness by making contact with an itinerant preacher named Jesus.

Zacchaeus had another problem: We might call him "stature challenged." The crowds mobbing Jesus made it all but impossible for him to get close enough to see the Master. Many of us would have given up and gone home, but not Zacchaeus. This little man used his head and found a good vantage point from which to get Jesus' attention. He went up a tree that was next to the road where Jesus would pass by.

Zacchaeus's willingness to do whatever it took to see Jesus paid off. Jesus recognized the man's desperation and gave him what he wanted—and a whole lot more. Jesus called him down from the tree, invited himself to a home-cooked dinner, and changed Zacchaeus into a new man.

Are you desperate to see and hear from Jesus? To what lengths would you go if you knew the Master had scheduled a trip to your city, but his route would take him into a neighborhood where no one would welcome you? How uncomfortable are you willing to be to spend some time with Jesus?

Jesus will never disappoint you when you go out of your way for a glimpse of him. Of course, you don't have to climb a tree to see him; you have only to open your Bible and read. How desperate are you for a fresh touch of the Master's hand?

October 23

Eager and Ready
JAMES AND JOHN

A little farther up the shore [Jesus] saw two other brothers, James and John, sitting in a boat with their father, Zebedee, repairing their nets. And he called them to come, too. They immediately followed him, leaving the boat and their father behind. Matthew 4:21-22

Revolutionary War buffs know that certain members of the Massachusetts militia formed what we call the minutemen—so named because they were ready to drop everything and head out to battle at a moment's notice. The minutemen made up about a fourth of the entire militia. These younger, more mobile men could respond to any threat, and thus they played a huge role in the colony's victory over British forces.

The readiness of the minutemen recalls the eagerness of two young fishermen who dropped everything to follow Jesus. The brothers James and John didn't waste so much as a minute when Jesus called them to his side.

James and John worked for their father, Zebedee, who owned his own fishing business. When they heard Jesus call them, these first-century minutemen responded immediately. They left their father and his hired hands to follow the Teacher's lead.

As far as the biblical record is concerned, James and John didn't even ask about their destination or agenda. They simply dropped their nets and followed.

Suppose that Jesus came by your place of business today and said to you, as he did to James and John, "Follow me." Could you be called a minuteman for Christ? Could you immediately follow and serve him, wherever he went and whatever he asked you to do?

Though Jesus doesn't call you to walk away from the life responsibilities he has given you, he still calls you to follow him in every area of life. Where do you think that call might take you? What do you believe that call will entail? What obstacles will you have to overcome to accept and follow? What changes must you make to become a minuteman for Christ?

October 24

A Sure Way Down

JONAH

Jonah got up and went in the opposite direction to get away from the LORD.
JONAH 1:3

Recall a time when your parents or some other authority told you to do something that simply didn't make sense to you. Did you grumble and complain about having to do something so dumb, only to realize later that, just maybe, they knew something you didn't?

Jonah, a stubborn prophet of God, found himself in that kind of situation. God had given Jonah specific instructions to go to the Assyrian capital of Nineveh and warn its wicked residents that God was about to bring judgment on them.

So what did Jonah do? He spun on his heel and headed in the opposite direction.

Jonah wasn't stupid; he knew what he was doing. He didn't get lost on his way to Assyria; he simply didn't like his assignment. As a prophet, perhaps he foresaw that in just a few decades, the Assyrians would attack and destroy the nation of Israel and wondered why would God send him to warn them. Jonah *wanted* them dead! Corpses could not devastate his homeland.

Go ahead and judge them, he apparently thought, *because I'm not going!*

Have you ever felt like running from God? If so, take careful note of Jonah, for we have no better biblical example of the consequences of such a foolish choice. When Jonah ran, his life went nowhere but down—*down* to the seaport at Joppa, where he caught a ship for Tarshish; *down* to the hold of the ship; *down* to the depths of the sea; and *down* to the belly of the fish (see Jonah 1:5, 15-17).

After Jonah spent a few excruciating days on the ocean floor, he finally came to his senses and obeyed God's instructions. The chastised prophet preached, the people of Nineveh repented, and God spared the city for a time.

What marching orders has God given you that seem to make little sense? Are you struggling with a decision that keeps you up at night—not because you don't know what God wants you to do but because you do? If you could have a long conversation with Jonah at this moment, what do you think he would tell you?

When God tells you to do something out of the ordinary, put your doubts behind, listen, and act because he might just be planning something extraordinary.

October 25

Whose Voice Is It?
AARON

"Come on," they said, "make us some gods who can lead us. We don't know what happened to this fellow Moses, who brought us here from the land of Egypt." So Aaron said, "Take the gold rings from the ears of your wives and sons and daughters, and bring them to me."   Exodus 32:1-2

Every father has heard those persistent childish voices clamoring for things that are not good for them. Maybe it's the third slice of birthday cake, that extra cookie before bed, or an extra hour of sleep on Sunday morning instead of getting ready for church.

We are all tempted to surrender to those voices if only to buy a few moments' peace. Every father knows the importance of remaining loving, yet firm, even when the voices grow louder.

Sometimes it is hard to ignore voices that insist you do something unhealthy, unhelpful, or wrong. Aaron, Moses' brother and second in command, certainly knew such a temptation. With Moses away, Aaron heard many insistent voices clamoring for him to do wrong, in this case, by making a god to worship.

What did Aaron do?

Aaron knew the commandment, "You must not make for yourself an idol of any kind or an image of anything in the heavens or on the earth or in the sea" (Exodus 20:4). Yet at the moment of truth, he caved. Rather than put his foot down and remind the people that their worship belonged to God alone, he agreed to give them what they demanded.

Aaron had a golden chance that day to make a bold statement for the Lord. Instead, he made a golden idol. He listened to the screeching voices of the rebellious people God had called him to lead and meekly bowed to their depraved will.

Who has God called you to lead? When that leadership gets difficult and you feel tempted to cave in to popular decisions that will lead people away from God's best, can you stand strong?

Whether they come from your home, your office, or your friends, you will hear raucous voices clamoring for you to give your best to some little god. That's your moment to stay strong and continue to be the man and leader God has called you to be. Will you stand alone? You might have to. But having a big crowd backing you up can have a huge downside—just ask Aaron.

October 26

The Message Makes the Man
PAUL

When I first came to you, dear brothers and sisters, I didn't use lofty words and impressive wisdom to tell you God's secret plan. For I decided that while I was with you I would forget everything except Jesus Christ, the one who was crucified.
1 CORINTHIANS 2:1-2

Twentieth-century Swiss theologian Karl Barth is still considered one of the most brilliant and influential Christian thinkers of his time. When someone asked him to summarize his many books, he set aside his vast understanding of Scripture and theology and simply sang an old children's Sunday school song: "Jesus loves me, this I know, for the Bible tells me so."

This simple yet profound message from a brilliant man was very much like the one that the apostle Paul consistently preached.

People who encountered Paul knew for certain what he considered most important: Christ's sin-defeating death and grave-defeating resurrection. As a former Pharisee, Paul knew the Law. He had spent much of his former life making sure that people observed Jewish laws, rules, and traditions. Now, however, Paul embraced a new mission, a new focus, and a new message: salvation through faith in Jesus Christ.

Paul made it a point to forget everything else—his impressive education, his impeccable religious pedigree, and his personal wisdom—and instead preach Jesus, the One who was crucified but rose from the grave so that Jews and Gentiles alike could enjoy restored fellowship with God.

Paul had the education and life experience to preach any number of messages, but he stuck to the one he knew the Corinthians needed to hear: a simple message of faith and love.

You are Christ's ambassador to the people around you. Does your life convey the simple message that Jesus loves them?

October 27

A Life of Separation
MOSES

It was by faith that Moses, when he grew up, refused to be called the son of Pharaoh's daughter. He chose to share the oppression of God's people instead of enjoying the fleeting pleasures of sin. Hebrews 11:24-25

As a man stands at the altar, his friends, family, and God listen as the preacher reads a series of questions. "Will you have this woman to be your wife; to live together in the covenant of marriage? Will you love her, comfort her, honor and keep her, in sickness and in health; and . . . forsaking all others, be faithful to her as long as you both shall live?"

That final portion of the "question of intent" means that the groom promises to leave his single life, in which he had the freedom to spend his time as and with whom he wanted. It means he has separated himself from his old life and joined himself to his bride for life.

The writer of Hebrews tells us that Moses made a choice very much like that. He left his life of ease under Pharaoh and identified himself with the suffering of his own people, the Hebrews.

Moses was born to a poor Hebrew mother, but he was raised in a world of privilege. Still, he chose to separate himself from the systems, beliefs, and practices of the world he knew best and cling to those of his people and his God. Moses disowned himself as an adopted member of Pharaoh's family and reclaimed his inheritance as a flesh-and-blood descendant of Abraham, Isaac, and Jacob.

When Moses made that choice, he began a journey that would make him one of the great heroes of the faith. He is an excellent example of what it means to separate oneself for God's use.

When you identify yourself with Jesus Christ, you leave behind your old ways of thinking and join yourself to the ways and thoughts of God. Such radical separation puts you squarely in the middle of God's will. It also positions you to receive his unlimited blessings.

October 28

Deceptive Feelings
JOB

I long for the years gone by when God took care of me, when he lit up the way before me and I walked safely through the darkness.   Job 29:2-3

Think of the last time one of your loved ones was going through a difficult time. Did your feelings toward that person change during that time?

Most men focus their attention more intensely on loved ones in pain; they know the hurting ones need them more than ever even if they can't feel their special love and concern.

During his worst time of misery, Job began wondering if *God* still cared about him. He had suffered so much that he fell into a pit of depression and hopelessness.

Job had experienced God's presence in the past. He knew that God had taken care of him and kept him from harm. Now, after he had lost everything— including his children, his wealth, and his health—Job felt abandoned and longed for the good old days.

Job's feelings deceived him. In truth, God knew exactly how much Job had suffered, and he focused his attention on his faithful servant more than ever, even if Job couldn't *feel* it.

Job was so focused on his suffering and loss that he had lost sight of the unchangeable fact that God *would never* abandon him.

Intense emotional or physical pain can make any man feel isolated or abandoned. Even then, you can look through eyes of faith and *know* that God is still caring for you, perhaps more than ever, even when you can't *feel* it.

You can always count on God to be there for you, especially during times of difficulty. When your feelings tell you that he's distant and uninterested, stop listening to those feelings. They speak truthfully of your pain, but they lie about God's response to your pain. God has never abandoned anyone he loves, and that means that he will never abandon you, his faithful follower.

October 29

Personal Integrity
KING JOSIAH

"Don't require the construction supervisors to keep account of the money they receive, for they are honest and trustworthy men." 2 Kings 22:7

PGA golfer Mark Wilson won the praise and admiration of fellow pros and golf enthusiasts around the world when he assessed himself a two-stroke penalty in the second round of the 2007 Honda Classic.

Why the penalty? When competitor Camilo Villegas asked Wilson's caddy what club he thought Wilson used, the caddie innocently gave his opinion—and that, according to the sometimes perplexing rules of golf, brings a penalty for offering advice to a competitor. Wilson called the penalty on himself, told his caddy not to give it another thought, and went on to dramatically win the tournament in a four-man playoff. Mark Wilson thus embodied what someone once defined as integrity: doing the right thing when no one is watching.

The Bible has much to say about integrity, including some great examples of men who consistently conducted themselves well. Consider, for example, the unnamed men who supervised the restoration of the Temple during King Josiah's reign.

These trustworthy men were so honest that Josiah ordered the high priest to stop keeping accounts of the money they spent to repair God's holy Temple. Think about that for a minute. This money came from the Temple of God, and Judah's king, a godly man, wrote what amounted to a blank check to get the work done.

Why did Josiah place these construction supervisors in a position of trust? Simple—they had already proved themselves faithful. They received the pay due them and also the high honor of repairing and renovating God's holy Temple.

How do you conduct yourself when no one is watching? Does consistent integrity govern the way you do business at work and everywhere else?

When you demonstrate integrity in everything you say and do, you earn the trust of those in authority over you. You don't have to advertise integrity or try to get people to notice it. They notice its presence as well as its absence.

October 30

Understand Authority
JESUS AND THE ROMAN OFFICER

The officer said, "Lord, I am not worthy to have you come into my home. Just say the word from where you are, and my servant will be healed." Matthew 8:8

As Christian Archibald Herter ran hard for a second term as governor of Massachusetts in the 1950s, he arrived late one afternoon to a church barbecue. Herter hadn't eaten since breakfast and had worked up quite an appetite chasing votes. As he moved through the serving line, he held out his plate to the woman serving chicken. She put a single piece on his plate and turned to the next person in line.

"Excuse me," the governor said, "do you mind if I have another piece of chicken?"

"Sorry," the woman told him. "I'm supposed to give one piece of chicken to each person."

Herter had a reputation as an unassuming man, but after another unsatisfying verbal exchange with this woman, he decided to use the power of his office.

"Do you know who I am?" Herter asked. "I am the governor of this state."

"Do you know who I am?" the woman retorted. "I'm the lady in charge of the chicken. Move along, mister."

Understanding authority and knowing who has it have important implications for many areas of life, including the spiritual. When you understand the authority of Christ over all things, you open yourself to receive his very best.

Jesus had an encounter with a Roman military officer. As a man *under* the authority of his superiors and with authority over his subordinates, he expected that when he gave an order, it was as good as done. This Roman understood some things about Jesus Christ that even the Lord's own people didn't get. He recognized that Jesus, as the Son of God, had absolute authority to carry out whatever he agreed to do.

What amazing things would Jesus do for *us* if we only asked him to do them and believed that he could! What sort of confidence do you have in Jesus' authority? Would your life change if you had the confidence of this Roman officer?

Jesus Christ has absolute authority and power over everything in your life and the lives of your loved ones. How could you glorify him by asking him to use that authority and power on your behalf according to his will?

October 31

A Happy Marriage
PETER

In the same way, you husbands must give honor to your wives. Treat your wife with understanding as you live together. She may be weaker than you are, but she is your equal partner in God's gift of new life. Treat her as you should so your prayers will not be hindered. 1 Peter 3:7

Several years ago, ABC newsmagazine *20/20* host John Stossel aired a program citing several studies that made a shocking claim: *Men and women are different!*

Imagine that! Men and women, who have been living together in marriage for several millennia, are different from one another. They aren't better or worse, just different in how they think, talk, relate to others, and process their emotions.

The apostle Peter never met John Stossel or watched *20/20,* but he probably understood the differences between the genders. Peter was a married man (see Matthew 8:14) who understood how God expected him to treat his wife.

Peter instructed his married male readers to honor their wives and treat them with understanding as equal partners in the Christian faith.

What did Peter mean by that?

Simply that you should remain humble in your marriage and avoid exalting yourself over your wife in any way. Your wife may be physically weaker than you are, but you must respect her as your equal in God's eyes.

Peter warned that husbands should treat their wives appropriately so that their "prayers will not be hindered." Peter knew that only sin hinders our prayers, so Peter obviously wanted his readers to understand how seriously God takes the way they treat their wives.

If God takes how you treat your wife seriously, so should you!

Do you want a happy, peaceful home life? Follow Peter's instructions and treat your wife with understanding, compassion, and respect. When you do so, you're sure to please the God who gave her to you.

November 1

Secure in God's Love
PAUL

I am convinced that nothing can ever separate us from God's love.   Romans 8:38

A man greeted a good friend on the street outside his favorite coffee shop one day with the obligatory, "How're you doing, Phil?" Before his visit with this friend had ended, he probably wished he had never asked.

"Well," Phil began, "my wife and I aren't getting along, my kids have been getting in trouble, I lost my job last week, and the mortgage is due tomorrow. I have a toothache that's killing me, and this being summer and all, I've got a heat rash about the size of Rhode Island on my behind. But you know me! I can't complain!"

When a man goes through difficult times, he may be tempted to think, *Somebody up there must really hate me!*

Some have a misguided idea of the relationship between difficulties and God's love. They believe, perhaps unconsciously, that when times get tough, it's because God is angry with them or just doesn't care anymore.

The apostle Paul opposed such thinking. He had endured suffering that most believers in the early twenty-first century can't begin to imagine, yet he never saw his suffering as an occasion to doubt God's love for him.

Paul posed this question to the believers in Rome: "Can anything ever separate us from Christ's love? Does it mean he no longer loves us if we have trouble or calamity, or are persecuted, or hungry, or destitute, or in danger, or threatened with death?" (Romans 8:35).

The answer is a resounding *no!* "Despite all these things," Paul wrote, "overwhelming victory is ours through Christ, who loved us" (Romans 8:37).

Paul learned the truth of God's love firsthand. He came to understand that whatever we may have to endure, we can rest in the realization that Jesus still loves us.

Everyone goes through difficulties, sometimes serious ones. As a child of God, you never have to see your problems as evidence that God loves you any less. You can always rest secure in God's love, knowing that he promises to be with you through anything you have to endure.

November 2

Perfect Patience
JESUS

God had mercy on me so that Christ Jesus could use me as a prime example of his great patience with even the worst sinners. Then others will realize that they, too, can believe in him and receive eternal life. 1 Timothy 1:16

A friend of Phillips Brooks, a nineteenth-century American preacher, once saw him feverishly pacing the floor in obvious frustration. "What's the trouble, Mr. Brooks?" he asked. Brooks shot back, "The trouble is that I'm in a hurry, but God isn't!"

Some of history's great men of God have struggled with impatience. Yet the Bible tells us that patience is one of the fruits we'll exhibit when we are filled with the Holy Spirit (see Galatians 5:22).

Jesus was filled with the Spirit of God, and he was the most patient man who ever lived.

Jesus lovingly ministered to the worst of sinners, dealt with the cynicism of corrupt religious leaders, and shepherded twelve often-clueless apostles through three years of traveling around Palestine, preaching God's salvation.

He did all that with patience beyond human understanding.

When you read through the Gospels, you can see that the Twelve often acted like little kids who couldn't hear a word Jesus said and who certainly couldn't apply much of what he taught them.

At times, Jesus chided his apostles for their lack of understanding, but he always patiently prepared them to take the reins after he returned to heaven. That way, the world could continue to hear the Good News.

The good news for you today is that you serve the very same Jesus who always extends incredible patience to those he loves.

Are you a patient man? You can best learn patience by understanding that God daily extends his patience to you, even when you make unwise choices.

November 3

He Couldn't Help It
ELISHA

Elisha returned to his oxen and slaughtered them. He used the wood from the plow to build a fire to roast their flesh. He passed around the meat to the townspeople, and they all ate. Then he went with Elijah as his assistant. 1 KINGS 19:21

A young Bible college student was in conflict over what God had called him to do with his life. He sat down in his wise, elderly counselor's office and told him that he was trying to decide if his calling was to be a pastor or a full-time missionary.

"Young man," the counselor said, "my advice to you is to be neither a pastor nor a missionary if you can help it."

The stunned student wondered if his counselor was playing some kind of joke on him. "Why would you discourage me from being a pastor or a missionary?" he asked.

"I'm not trying to discourage you," the counselor explained. "I have learned that it's not a good idea to become a full-time minister unless you are truly called to do that. And if God has truly called you to serve in that capacity, you won't be able to help it."

Elisha, a young man of means who lived near the wilderness of Damascus, couldn't help becoming a prophet of the Lord. As Elisha tended his family farm one day, the prophet Elijah approached him and silently threw his cloak over Elisha's shoulder. Elisha knew what this meant. The Holy Spirit had touched his heart, and he felt ready to leave everything, follow Elijah, and serve God as a prophet.

"First let me go and kiss my father and mother good-bye, and then I will go with you!" Elisha said. "Go on back, but think about what I have done to you," Elijah answered (1 Kings 19:20).

How could Elisha forget? He had no choice in the matter, for it was God, not Elijah, who had called him to leave everything and follow him.

When you allow the Holy Spirit free reign in your life, you can do nothing but say yes when God calls you to serve him. How has he called you to serve him? In what sphere of life do you believe he wants to use you to make a difference? How are you cooperating with him to make that difference?

November 4

Failure Isn't Final
JESUS AND PETER

After breakfast Jesus asked Simon Peter, "Simon son of John, do you love me more than these?" "Yes, Lord," Peter replied, "you know I love you." "Then feed my lambs," Jesus told him.   John 21:15

In 1902, the *Atlantic Monthly*'s poetry editor returned a stack of poems he had received with this curt rejection note: "Our magazine has no room for your vigorous verse." The rejection note's recipient was the great American poet Robert Frost, a four-time Pulitzer Prize winner.

Frost's experience shows that one failure doesn't mean the end for someone who approaches his work with passion.

Peter promised Jesus that he would never leave him nor deny him, so he must have felt like an utter failure after doing both. In a moment of cowardice, he denied even knowing Jesus Christ, not just once or twice, but *three times*.

We can imagine the sorrow Peter must have felt. Even after Jesus had risen from the grave as he'd promised, Peter knew that this little incident had to be resolved. He couldn't forget his three passionate denials.

Peter didn't realize it, but Jesus had big plans for him. He wasn't about to let the man's temporary failure get in the way of the incredible future he had mapped out for him. So he sought out his wayward apostle to restore him and ready him for things to come.

Three times Jesus asked Peter if he loved him, and all three times Peter reiterated his love for his Master and his awareness that Jesus *knew* he loved him. Then Jesus instructed Peter to put his love into action: "Feed my sheep."

That morning, Jesus fully restored Peter's relationship with him, and Peter became a new man with a new mission. He would no longer make promises he had no way of keeping. Under the power of the Spirit, Peter would speak, teach, and perform miracles with the kind of courage he only *thought* he had before.

Everyone takes a few tumbles now and then, and you won't be an exception. Your failures don't have to be final. God won't give up on you when you fail, but he will use that failure to move you closer to enjoying everything he has planned for you.

November 5

Exciting Marriage
SOLOMON

You are as exciting, my darling, as a mare among Pharaoh's stallions. How lovely are your cheeks; your earrings set them afire! How lovely is your neck, enhanced by a string of jewels. Song of Solomon 1:9-10

Joe Namath of the New York Jets and Roger Staubach of the Dallas Cowboys were two of the best quarterbacks in the National Football League. Both made names for themselves on the football field, but off the field they were as different as night and day.

Namath was the world's most eligible bachelor in the early 1970s, known for his promiscuous lifestyle. Staubach was a Christian family man whose life appeared boring to some people next to that of Namath.

In one interview, Staubach compared his sex life with "Broadway Joe's," saying, "I like sex just as much as Joe Namath. Only I like it with one person—my wife, Marianne."

One of the devil's biggest lies is that godly men aren't allowed to enjoy sex. The Bible teaches that married men can enjoy a mutually exciting and passionate sexual relationship with the wife God has given them. The excitement in *that* bedroom can far eclipse anything Broadway Joe ever knew.

The young Solomon enjoyed his beloved on a physical level and found her exciting in the way she looked, dressed, smelled, and talked. Just nine verses into his poem, Solomon tells his beloved Shulamite that she excites him in every way.

Solomon doesn't provide us with a great example of monogamous love—he had hundreds of wives by the end of his life—but he does illustrate the kind of excitement you can find with your wife, most definitely including the marriage bed you share with her.

Love your wife as God intended. He designed sex as a means of procreation and as an exciting, enjoyable expression of love between you and your wife.

November 6

Thriving *Because* of Adversity
PHILIP

Philip . . . went to the city of Samaria and told the people there about the Messiah.
Crowds listened intently to Philip because they were eager to hear his message and
see the miraculous signs he did. Many evil spirits were cast out, screaming as they left
their victims. And many who had been paralyzed or lame were healed. So there was
great joy in that city. ACTS 8:5-8

The church in Vietnam has grown, not just in spite of the adversity it faces daily, but in many ways because of it. From World Serve Ministries, an organization that serves suffering and persecuted Christians around the world, comes a report of amazing spiritual renewal in Communist Vietnam. Despite decades of repression and persecution, the church there is growing exponentially, from fewer than fifty-five thousand believers in 1975 to more than one million today.

A New Testament evangelist named Philip would have appreciated how that works. Philip was among the first-generation believers in Jerusalem who fled for their lives from the persecution in the city to the relative safety of the outlying areas. Like so many of those believers, Philip didn't hide out but preached the gospel everywhere he went.

Philip created quite a stir in a city called Samaria, where people eagerly listened to his message and watched in amazement as he healed people and cast out demons in Jesus' name. Philip learned to thrive in the midst of adversity. He didn't focus on his own situation but on other people's needs.

God can use any situation in life to move, mold, and shake you so that you become all that he wants you to be. No one enjoys persecution, hardship, tribulation, or heartache, but neither are we to let them quash our spirits or ruin our outlooks. We serve a God who enables us to thrive even in adversity.

God uses all kinds of means to move people from place to place. Wherever he places you—and however he chooses to place you there—never forget that he has called you to bear his message of salvation through Jesus Christ.

November 7

The Problem with "Right Now"
ABSALOM

When people tried to bow before him, Absalom wouldn't let them. Instead, he took them by the hand and kissed them. Absalom did this with everyone who came to the king for judgment, and so he stole the hearts of all the people of Israel.
2 SAMUEL 15:5-6

Children can be living pictures of impatience. They want what they want *right now.* Sometimes a simple promise of going to the movies, going out to eat at their favorite hamburger joint, or going on a family vacation brings out this insistence. They want to go, and they want to go *now!*

The Bible speaks often of God's blessing on those who are willing to wait. We may want it *right now,* but that is frequently not in heaven's game plan.

As King David's eldest surviving son, Absalom was in a likely position to ascend the throne of Israel one day. He had to flee Jerusalem when he murdered his brother Amnon for assaulting his sister. A few years later, David forgave him and reinstated him.

Absalom could have received a huge blessing in this new place, but in his desire to have what he wanted *right now,* he lost everything.

Almost immediately after David welcomed Absalom back to the family, the handsome young man began plotting to kill his father so he could take the throne of Israel. He began his treason by first winning the people's hearts and minds.

Though Absalom temporarily succeeded in taking David's rightful place, in the end, David's troops defeated him, and he died a painful, humiliating death.

Despite Absalom's talents, good looks, leadership skills, and potential, his impatience scuttled his chance at greatness. He left behind no son and no legacy of godly leadership, just a stone memorial that he had built for himself (see 2 Samuel 18:18).

God gives you all the talents, abilities, and gifts you need to succeed in whatever he has called you to do. When you remain patient and allow him to exalt you in his way and time, you will receive the very best he has to offer.

November 8

Blessed, Scolded, Humbled
JESUS AND PETER

As he talked about this openly with his disciples, Peter took him aside and began to reprimand him for saying such things. Jesus turned around and looked at his disciples, then reprimanded Peter. "Get away from me, Satan!" he said. "You are seeing things merely from a human point of view, not from God's."
MARK 8:32-33

Any good football coach knows the importance of balancing words of praise with words of criticism. He knows that if he doesn't regularly build up his players, they will lose confidence. He also knows that if he doesn't humble them once in a while, they will become overconfident and start accepting their errors.

In a matter of just a few moments, Peter experienced both ends of the continuum.

Peter must have felt great when Jesus publicly blessed him for his God-given insight into the Master's true identity. In the next second, Peter showed that he needed to be knocked down a peg.

Jesus stunned the disciples when he told them that he was going to Jerusalem to suffer and die and then be raised from the dead three days later. None of them expected to hear such a thing, especially Peter. He took Jesus aside and privately scolded him for suggesting it.

Jesus could not let Peter stray so far out of line. He wouldn't allow him or any of the disciples to act as roadblocks in the path God had set before him. So he gave Peter a strong and stinging reprimand: "Get away from me, Satan!"

He didn't mean it as a compliment.

Jesus knew that Peter had failed to see things from an eternal perspective. He hadn't yet grasped the idea that though Jesus was the conquering King, he was also the suffering Servant. To fulfill Scripture, he had to endure the awful things he had just described.

Jesus had called Peter to play a big part of his mission, but before the burly fisherman could play that part, he needed to humbly trust and obey his Lord. That meant remembering that the Master knew better than anyone what he was doing.

When God has to reprimand you for some misstep, his words of discipline aren't meant to tear you down but to remind you why you're here. You are his representative on earth; he is not your servant in heaven.

November 9

Clear the Air
MEPHIBOSHETH

"You've said enough," David replied. "I've decided that you and Ziba will divide your land equally between you." "Give him all of it," Mephibosheth said. "I am content just to have you safely back again, my lord the king!"
2 SAMUEL 19:29-30

What is more painful than having an important relationship with a friend, family member, or coworker go sour because of a misunderstanding? So far as you know, you have done nothing to hurt that person, but for some reason, communication is severed and the fellowship you once enjoyed evaporates.

Sometimes all it takes to restore the lost relationship is to go out of your way to clear the air, much as a man named Mephibosheth once did with King David.

Mephibosheth, Jonathan's son and the grandson of the late King Saul, had outlived all other heirs to Saul's dynasty. At one time, David had offered Mephibosheth great kindness, but the relationship between the two soured when Ziba, Mephibosheth's servant, told David that his master had abandoned the king when David's son Absalom attempted to take the throne (see 2 Samuel 16:1-4).

Mephibosheth knew about Ziba's deception, and after David regained the throne, he traveled to Jerusalem to reconcile with his old friend. Mephibosheth probably trembled with fear as he approached David, but he was determined to risk everything in order to heal the rift between them.

When David heard Mephibosheth's account, he restored to him half of what he had previously given to Ziba. Mephibosheth cared little about that. He was satisfied with knowing that David had returned to his rightful place on the throne of Israel, and that a once-severed relationship had come back to life.

Has a relationship you once enjoyed gone sour through miscommunication or misunderstanding? If so, what can you do to clear the air? Take a risk by taking the first step, and do what you can to restore the relationship. When you do that, you handle conflict in a godly way.

November 10

Stressed Out?
DAVID

David heard these comments and was very afraid of what King Achish of Gath might do to him. So he pretended to be insane, scratching on doors and drooling down his beard. Finally, King Achish said to his men, "Must you bring me a madman? We already have enough of them around here! Why should I let someone like this be my guest?" 1 Samuel 21:12-15

In his 1981 book *Stress/Unstress,* author Keith W. Wehnert lists some personal symptoms of being a little stressed out. Among those symptoms is difficulty in making large or small decisions; the use of tobacco, alcohol, or tranquilizers; trouble concentrating; outbursts of anger; and changes in your usual behavior.

Nothing reveals what's inside you quite like a stressful situation. When you feel afraid, worried, surprised, or grieved, your levels of courage, faith, and commitment to God are put on display for all to see.

David, who would one day be Israel's greatest king, faced an extremely stressful situation when he fled from the murderous King Saul. When David arrived in a pagan city called Gath, he wanted to remain incognito. When he realized that King Achish's officers knew his true identity, he allowed stress to get the best of him.

David feared for his life, so he acted insane, scratching on doors and drooling on himself like a mad dog. That's hardly the kind of behavior you would expect from Israel's next king!

David failed for a time to keep his focus on the God who had already called him to bigger and better things and who promised to protect and guide him. He allowed stress rather than his God-inspired courage to rule the day.

Stress is unavoidable in this fallen world. You may not be able to avoid stressful situations, but you can decide for yourself how you'll respond to them.

Everyone feels stressed out at times. Few things test your courage and faith like a stressful situation. You can defeat the effects of stress when you remember that God has promised to give you the strength and courage to victoriously confront anything that comes your way.

November 11

Visionary Prayer
JABEZ

There was a man named Jabez who was more honorable than any of his brothers. His mother named him Jabez because his birth had been so painful.
1 CHRONICLES 4:9

Have you ever been absolutely convinced that God has given you a vision for something specific, but you don't know exactly how to pray for it? You may have a vision for ministry, for your family, or for a career move.

When God gives us a vision, it's easy to just freeze and wait to see what happens, but the Bible teaches that when we receive a vision for something specific, we are to pray equally specifically.

Jabez understood the importance of praying with that kind of vision.

The Bible doesn't tell us much about Jabez except that he was an honorable man whose name meant "pain." His only recorded words are this well-known prayer: "Oh, that you would bless me and expand my territory! Please be with me in all that I do, and keep me from all trouble and pain!" (1 Chronicles 4:10).

God said yes to everything Jabez asked for because Jabez had the faith and courage to ask for these things:

That God would bless him. Jabez began his prayer with the premise that God desired to bless him. Jabez went to the Source of all good things for what he needed.

That God would expand his territory. Jabez understood the importance of praying specifically. He knew that God wanted to bless him on many levels, and he wasn't afraid to ask for that!

That God would be with him in all that he did. Jabez understood that he was headed nowhere without God's hand of guidance, protection, and strength on him. He knew that his sufficiency was not in his possessions, family, or personal prestige but in the God who promises to be with his people.

That God would keep him from all trouble and pain. Another version of this same request reads, "Keep me from evil, that I may not cause pain." Jabez asked God for a humble heart and for an ability to do right by other people.

When you know Who to pray to, what to ask for, and how to pray for it, you are well on your way to receiving the blessings reserved for those who earnestly and consistently pray the way Jabez did.

November 12

Thanks "In Spite Of"
JONAH

"I will offer sacrifices to you with songs of praise, and I will fulfill all my vows. For my salvation comes from the LORD alone." Jonah 2:9

Pete stunned more than a few of his fellow believers when he stood up one Sunday morning and *thanked* God for the difficulties he had endured. In the space of one week, his mother had passed away, and he had lost his job just as his wife prepared to deliver their first child.

"No matter what happens to me," Pete said, "I know that God is good and is looking out for me. I praise God for everything that comes my way because I know that something good will come of it."

It's easy to sing God's praises from a mountaintop, but what about during those times in the valley? Can you praise God for your times of difficulty, your weaknesses, or your burdens?

The runaway prophet Jonah knew the value of praising God from a place of difficulty.

You remember the story. Jonah defied God's command to preach to the people of Nineveh and fled in the opposite direction from where he had been told to go. As a result, he did some time in the belly of a sea creature.

Jonah was in a place so dark and foul that it defies human imagination. As he lay there struggling even to move, he found it within himself to speak thankfully to God.

Jonah didn't have to ask, "Why me?" He already knew why. He had made a mess of his life, but now he prayed in repentance and thanked God in the very midst of his mess.

God knew that Jonah had come full circle.

Almost immediately after Jonah spoke these words of praise, God arranged for his freedom (see Jonah 2:10). God knew that Jonah's words of thanksgiving and his promise to fulfill his vows as a prophet meant that he was ready and willing to obey God.

God wants you to speak words of thanksgiving and praise to him even when you are in a bad place in your life. Can you do as the apostle Paul instructs and "be thankful in all circumstances" (1 Thessalonians 5:18)?

November 13

First Things First
HAGGAI

Zerubbabel son of Shealtiel, and Jeshua son of Jehozadak, the high priest, and the whole remnant of God's people began to obey the message from the LORD their God. When they heard the words of the prophet Haggai, whom the LORD their God had sent, the people feared the LORD. Haggai 1:12

In an art gallery in Berlin, Germany hangs German painter Adolf von Menzel's partially finished image of Prussian king Fredrick II the Great speaking with some of his generals. Menzel painted the generals and the background, leaving Frederick until last. Unfortunately, Menzel died before finishing it.

Setting priorities is a key to doing anything well. That is true in your life as a believer, husband, and father.

The Old Testament prophet Haggai believed strongly in setting the right priorities and in encouraging others to do the same.

The people of Jerusalem had a problem with priorities after they returned from the Babylonian captivity. They were settling nicely into their homes, but they forgot the vital importance of the holy Temple. They had begun the project of restoring it, but after sixteen years, it remained unfinished.

That's where the prophet Haggai stepped into the picture.

Haggai was probably born in Babylon. He returned to Jerusalem with Zerubbabel and scolded the people for their misplaced priorities: "Why are you living in luxurious houses while [God's] house lies in ruins?" (Haggai 1:4).

Haggai knew that the people of Jerusalem were missing out on God's richest blessings because they hadn't finished the Temple, and he knew that they hadn't finished the Temple because it wasn't at the top of their to-do list.

He also knew that God would be with them as they made God's Temple a priority (see Haggai 1:13).

Haggai preached the right message at just the right time. The people listened to him, and with their sense of priorities straightened out, they got busy!

Think about the priorities in your life and ask yourself if they are pleasing to the Lord. Do you make daily prayer and Bible reading a priority? Do you give to a ministry that God has put on your heart? If not, it may be time to rearrange your priorities.

November 14

No Middle Man
KING HEZEKIAH

When Hezekiah heard this, he turned his face to the wall and prayed to the LORD, "Remember, O LORD, how I have always been faithful to you and have served you single-mindedly, always doing what pleases you." Then he broke down and wept bitterly. 2 Kings 20:2-3

Faced with an important, potentially life-altering decision, a man stood up at his weekly couples' Bible study, told his friends what was going on, and asked them to pray for him. When one particularly forward woman in the group asked him how *he* was praying, he had no answer.

He had spent hours thinking his situation through and had sought the advice of several friends, but he had forgotten to go directly to his heavenly Father, who has all the answers.

Hezekiah was a godly man who knew how to cut out the middle man and go directly to the Source of all good things, even when he received terrible news.

Hezekiah had been deathly ill for some time, and the prophet Isaiah's prognosis wasn't encouraging. The king was to set all his affairs in order because his illness was terminal (see 2 Kings 20:1).

Hezekiah knew that Isaiah the prophet had a special connection to God, so it may have been tempting for him to plead his case directly with Isaiah to see if he would ask the Lord to change his mind.

That's not what Hezekiah did.

When Isaiah told him he was about to die, Hezekiah went to his private place of prayer and talked directly to the Lord. Hezekiah didn't plead with God to extend his life, but he reminded God that he had been a good and faithful servant who always did what pleased the Lord.

God decided to extend Hezekiah's life. Before Isaiah had even left the palace courtyard, the Lord sent him back to Hezekiah to announce that he had heard Hezekiah's prayer and would heal him.

Hezekiah's willingness to go straight to God saved him time, and it saved his life.

You save time and energy when you take your needs, concerns, thanksgivings, and praises straight to your heavenly Father. He will freely give you everything you truly need.

November 15

Seek Jesus
THE WISE MEN

About that time some wise men from eastern lands arrived in Jerusalem, asking,
"Where is the newborn king of the Jews?" MATTHEW 2:1-2

The famous violinist Fritz Kreisler once said of the effort and personal sacrifices required to become a master of his craft, "Narrow is the road that leads to the life of a violinist. Hour after hour, day after day, and week after week, for years, I lived with my violin. There were so many things that I wanted to do that I had to leave undone; there were so many places I wanted to go that I had to miss if I was to master the violin. The road that I traveled was a narrow road and the way was hard."

Effort is a key to success in any area of life, including the spiritual. The wise men who visited Jesus in Bethlehem exemplify that truth.

The Bible says little about who these wise men were or where they had come from. What is really important is what they did.

These men watched for signs that the ancient prophets of God had written about centuries before. Then they traveled several hundred miles by camel to see the newborn King Jesus.

In a time and culture where it's often a struggle to make it to church by 10:30 AM, there is something inspiring about men who would travel such a great distance to worship the Son of God.

These men went to incredible lengths to find Jesus Christ. When they finally found him in Bethlehem, they bowed before him in worship, then presented him with precious gifts.

Like the wise men who traveled so far to see Jesus in Bethlehem, you should make it a priority to worship him passionately and give him your best each day. You don't have to travel hundreds of miles to find Jesus because he lives in your heart when you put your faith in him.

November 16

Self-Discipline
AMNON

These are the sons of David who were born in Hebron: The oldest was Amnon, whose mother was Ahinoam from Jezreel.   1 Chronicles 3:1

You might not like hearing this if you're trying to lose a few pounds, but the consensus among experts in the field of weight loss and fitness is that the key to losing weight is self-discipline. As one specialist put it, "Show me an individual who lost weight and is successfully keeping it off and I guarantee that individual is practicing self-discipline."

Self-discipline is vital to success in any area of your life—family, business, or the spiritual.

Sadly, many gifted people fail to achieve all they could because they lack self-discipline. There are few better biblical examples of this than Amnon, King David's first son.

Talk about a pedigree! As the first son of Israel's greatest king and heir apparent to the throne, Amnon could have accomplished great things for God and his people.

Sadly, Amnon is relegated to the "Where did they end up?" file of Bible characters because he lacked self-discipline.

Amnon sealed his fate when he looked lustfully at his beautiful half-sister Tamar. The Law of God specifically forbade such behavior and laid out harsh penalties for those who did such things. Amnon forced himself on Tamar, then had her removed from his home (see 2 Samuel 13:1-19). That led to Amnon's murder by his outraged and vengeful brother Absalom.

All of this happened within the family of Israel's greatest king!

Self-discipline and a deep, abiding love of God are prominent qualities of any true man of God. Amnon had neither, so his life was cut tragically short before he could do anything of note for God or his people.

God has given you the talents and gifts you need to do great things for him in every area of our life. You can accomplish those things through a combination of personal faith, obedience, and self-discipline. That's a recipe the devil can't beat!

November 17

God Sees Us
SHAMGAR

After Ehud, Shamgar son of Anath rescued Israel. He once killed 600 Philistines with an ox goad.   Judges 3:31

One day, the great Renaissance artist Michelangelo joyfully overheard a group of people praising his *Pietà* a statue depicting Jesus on his mother's knees after his death on the cross. His joy turned to chagrin when a man in the group attributed the work to another sculptor.

That night, Michelangelo returned to his sculpture and carved his name on it so that everyone would know whose work it was.

Most people like recognition for doing something of note, but the Bible teaches that we are to do our acts of kindness and obedience in a quiet, anonymous manner so that God can reward us when we enter his eternal Kingdom.

That will be the case for an Old Testament judge named Shamgar.

Shamgar was one of thirteen people who were judges in Israel. These men and women were responsible for maintaining law and order during some very dark times following Joshua's death.

The exploits of some judges, such as Deborah, Gideon, Samson, Eli, and Samuel, rate extensive coverage in the Scriptures, whereas only two Bible verses mention Shamgar (see Judges 3:31; 5:6). Nothing is said about his spiritual convictions, family background, friends, or contemporary context. He is simply listed as "the son of Anath."

The Bible says that Shamgar rescued Israel. He did this in a most heroic, unlikely fashion. He killed six hundred dreaded Philistines, using nothing but an ox goad, a wooden farm implement used to prod oxen.

Yet Shamgar earned only a passing mention in the Bible.

God had a purpose and a mission for Shamgar that left him in relative obscurity. Though his name isn't prominent in Scripture, God is well aware of everything that Shamgar did for his nation and for the Lord.

Shamgar's reward was waiting for him in heaven.

Though people may give you little recognition for your acts of obedience and faith, you can be sure that God sees, acknowledges, and records those things so that you can one day enjoy your reward.

November 18

Rise to the Occasion
JOSEPH OF ARIMATHEA

Now there was a good and righteous man named Joseph. He was a member of the Jewish high council, but he had not agreed with the decision and actions of the other religious leaders.... He went to Pilate and asked for Jesus' body.
LUKE 23:50-52

"Think about your heart!" Denise Cammarata called out to her husband as he headed out their front door in New York one freezing morning in December 2004.

John Cammarata had recently undergone angioplasty, but when he heard the screams coming from the burning house across the street, he had to do something, heart condition notwithstanding.

Cammarata called 911, pulled on his sweats, and ran over to the burning house. He charged into the house three times to pull everyone to safety, then ran door to door waking his neighbors and warning them to get out of their homes.

John Cammarata was an ordinary man who, in his neighbors' moment of need, rose to the occasion and did the extraordinary.

Joseph of Arimathea also rose to the occasion.

Luke's Gospel says that Joseph was a member of the Jewish high council. He was a "good and righteous man" who followed Jesus, but he kept his discipleship a secret out of fear of his fellow council members, according to John's Gospel.

Joseph's fellow high council members had condemned Jesus to die, but somehow he had the courage to approach Pilate, Judea's Roman governor, and get permission to remove Jesus' body from the cross so that he could be buried.

Joseph then assumed family responsibilities in caring for the body and providing a tomb. He and Nicodemus, a fellow high council member, made final preparations for the burial. Then Joseph rolled a large stone against the tomb to protect Jesus' body from vandals and grave robbers.

A fearful Joseph had failed to stand up for Jesus in his life, but a newly emboldened Joseph extended to Christ the honor due to him in death.

You may never be the kind of hero John Cammarata was, but there may be times in your life of faith when God will call on you to rise to the occasion. Are you ready and willing?

November 19

Your Legacy of Faith
JONATHAN

"Let's go across to the outpost of those pagans," Jonathan said to his armor bearer. "Perhaps the LORD will help us, for nothing can hinder the LORD. He can win a battle whether he has many warriors or only a few!" 1 Samuel 14:6

Pete was a bona fide, on-fire Christian whose commitment to God, his Word, and his church was beyond question. Everything he did and said reflected his reliance on the Holy Spirit and his life's goal of bringing others to a more mature faith in Christ. This included his own wife and children.

You might think that a man like Pete had been raised in a home where his spiritual growth and sense of faith were encouraged and nurtured, but you would be wrong. As a boy, Pete had a terrible home life. His father was an abusive alcoholic; his mother suffered from manic depression and often escaped her misery through drug abuse.

Pete knew from the moment he committed his life to Christ that he had a lot of work to do if he wanted to begin a legacy of faith in his family. He approached that goal with the kind of passion God honors.

Jonathan, the son of King Saul, was in the same situation as Pete. His father had shown flashes of faith, but his overall lack of spiritual focus led to his ouster as king and a strained relationship with Jonathan.

Jonathan took a much different approach in his relationship with the Lord. Once, he took his armor bearer and daringly left his father and six hundred men at their encampment at Gibeah to launch an overwhelmingly successful attack on Israel's archenemy, the Philistines.

Jonathan's dependence on God won the confidence of his assistant: "Do what you think is best," the armor bearer replied. "I'm with you completely, whatever you decide" (1 Samuel 14:7).

That's how it works when you make a legacy of faith and commitment to the Lord.

You may not have the spiritual roots that a Christian upbringing has given to some men of faith. You can still begin a family legacy of faith and obedience to God. What are you doing to get started?

November 20

Seek Confirmation
GIDEON

Gideon said to God, "If you are truly going to use me to rescue Israel as you promised, prove it to me in this way. I will put a wool fleece on the threshing floor tonight. If the fleece is wet with dew in the morning but the ground is dry, then I will know that you are going to help me rescue Israel as you promised."
JUDGES 6:36-37

Are you a person who takes things at face value? Do you know when you have heard God clearly and step out without need of further confirmation? Or do you take a more measured approach to life and want to be absolutely sure you've heard him correctly before you take a step forward?

God has wired each one of us differently as believers. Some move out courageously and say, "Let's get started!" while others need to test the waters before taking their steps of faith.

Gideon was a man of God who needed to be sure.

Some believers think that when Gideon twice asked God for confirmation by using a sheepskin and the morning dew, he was demonstrating lack of faith and a reluctance to obey.

Let's not jump to conclusions!

Gideon apparently wasn't sure that he had heard correctly when the word of the Lord commanded him to lead the Israelites in battle against the Midianites. Instead of moving out immediately, he "tested the spirits" by twice asking God to give him signs of confirmation, first a soggy sheepskin on dry ground, then a dry fleece on dewy ground.

He got both.

A different man might have moved out immediately, but Gideon wanted to be sure. When he asked God for these signs, it wasn't because he doubted God. He wanted to know without a doubt that he understood God's calling, which he then accepted and executed brilliantly.

At times in your life of faith when you're not sure what God has called you to do, it's not a bad idea to ask for confirmation. God wasn't angry when Gideon asked him to confirm his commands, and he won't be angry with you, either.

November 21

Choose Partnerships Carefully
KING JEHOSHAPHAT

[Ahab] turned to Jehoshaphat and asked, "Will you join me in battle to recover Ramoth-gilead?" Jehoshaphat replied to the king of Israel, "Why, of course! You and I are as one. My troops are your troops, and my horses are your horses."
1 KINGS 22:4

History is filled with examples of foolish alliances. Among the worst was the Munich Pact, a 1938 peace treaty between British prime minister Neville Chamberlain and German chancellor Adolf Hitler. Following this agreement, which historians agree was just an attempt at appeasement, Chamberlain famously declared, "I believe it is peace for our time."

The "peace" that Chamberlain brokered with one of history's most notorious leaders didn't last. Germany occupied Prague and invaded Poland the following year, forcing Chamberlain to declare war on Germany in September of 1939.

The Munich Pact and its aftermath were a reminder of the danger of entering into alliances with evil men who have no intent to keep the peace.

You can see the same lesson in the story of Jehoshaphat, the godly king of Judah. Like many other kings in that era, he began his reign by doing great things for his kingdom.

Jehoshaphat marred his legacy when he entered into an ill-advised—and eventually disastrous—military alliance with Ahab, the godless king of Israel (see 1 Kings 22:43-44). This alliance led to a stinging defeat for Israel and Jehoshaphat as well as a strong rebuke from the prophet Jehu (see 2 Chronicles 19:1-3).

Though Jehoshaphat erred when he entered into partnership with such an evil man, God spared him because he had otherwise served him faithfully as king of Israel.

Jehoshaphat made what could have been a great reign into a good one because of his compromise and lack of wisdom in dealing with Ahab.

Life will present you with opportunities to enter into all sorts of agreements or relationships in business, friendship, and even marriage. It's important that you carefully consider which agreements, friendships, and alliances you will form, and with whom you will form them.

November 22

Eyes of Faith
ELISHA

Elisha prayed, "O LORD, open his eyes and let him see!" The LORD opened the young man's eyes, and when he looked up, he saw that the hillside around Elisha was filled with horses and chariots of fire. 2 Kings 6:17

Nearly every war movie ever made has two contrasting characters. There's the new guy who is unsure of what to do, badly frightened, and prone to cowering in a corner when things get rough. And there's the grizzled combat veteran who is wired to stand up courageously in the fiercest battle.

By the end of the movie, the new guy has fought side by side with the veteran in several close scrapes and usually becomes a competent soldier.

A man who has been through a lot in life and has seen how God responds to a faithful heart has a great resource. He can walk in faith and courage and encourage others to do the same.

The prophet Elisha and his unnamed servant did this.

The king of Syria had sent his army to the city of Dothan and surrounded it during the night. When Elisha's servant woke up the next morning, the first thing he saw was that the enemy's chariots, horses, and soldiers had surrounded them.

It isn't hard to understand that a sense of panic might set in under such circumstances. Naturally, this fearful young man ran directly to his master, who was a man of faith.

Elisha knew that prayer was just what was needed. He asked God to open the servant's eyes to see his power at work in their situation so that he could know that the battle was already won.

The servant lacked the experience to realize something that Elisha already understood. The situations he faced—even a potentially overwhelming enemy attack—were just a chance for God to demonstrate his glorious power.

You may know a fellow believer who is going through a crisis of faith right now. If so, do as Elisha did and pray that his eyes of faith would be opened so he could focus on God's power at work in his life.

November 23

Forgiveness
JESUS

When they came to a place called The Skull, they nailed him to the cross. And the criminals were also crucified—one on his right and one on his left. Jesus said, "Father, forgive them, for they don't know what they are doing." And the soldiers gambled for his clothes by throwing dice. Luke 23:33-34

Sister Leonella Sgorbati, a Catholic nun who devoted her life to serving the sick and desperately poor in the most volatile regions of war-torn Somalia, knew that her work was dangerous. People who knew her say that she often joked that a bullet somewhere in Somalia had her name on it.

On September 17, 2006, that bullet found her.

Two gunmen shot and mortally wounded Sister Leonella as she made her way to a pediatric hospital in the Somalian capital of Mogadishu. As she lay dying, she used her final few breaths to forgive the men responsible for her death. "I forgive! I forgive!" she gasped in her native Italian just before she passed away.

That's an astonishing demonstration of forgiveness—the same kind that Jesus extended to those responsible for his death.

During his earthly ministry, Jesus always did something before commanding his disciples to do it. That included loving those who hated and persecuted him (see Luke 6:27-36).

Jesus could have called on thousands of angels to destroy the world and set him free. Instead, he went to the cross willingly and obediently. He took this act of love and forgiveness to even more unthinkable lengths when he asked his heavenly Father to forgive his executioners.

Jesus freely forgave and prayed for those who harmed him. Who in your life seems eager to do you harm? Are you willing to forgive them as Jesus did?

In this life, there's little chance that you can completely avoid feeling hurt or damaged over other people's words and actions. When you choose to forgive and pray for those who hurt you, you have loved and forgiven as Jesus did.

November 24

God's Approval
MOSES

May the Lord our God show us his approval and make our efforts successful. Yes, make our efforts successful!   Psalm 90:17

Have you ever known or worked with a "yes man" who stops at nothing to gain approval from everyone he knows, and especially those in authority? In the end, the "yes man" usually doesn't succeed in any area of life because others' opinions and desires so easily sway him.

Someone once said, "I can't give you the formula for success, but I can give you the formula for failure: Try to please everyone."

The Bible teaches that lasting blessings come when you make pleasing God and seeking his approval your focus, which Moses understood well.

Moses wrote Psalm 90, the oldest of the psalms, apparently during the Israelites' forty years of wilderness wandering. He spoke plainly about the consequences of their stubbornness and disobedience.

Even though Moses knew that most of those who had left Egypt would never see the Promised Land, he still found hope in understanding the connection between willing obedience and divine blessing. Moses wanted his people to receive God's very best. Though Moses forfeited the privilege of entering the Promised Land because of disobedience on one occasion, God faithfully answered his prayers and allowed the Israelites to claim and enter the land he had promised them centuries before.

Life is far too short and God's blessings far too wonderful to miss anything he wants to give you. Spend every minute of every day living for God's approval, for a life of obedience will never disappoint you.

Most men want to do things in their own way and time. You will find yourself greatly blessed when you first seek God's approval and blessing on whatever you do.

November 25

Eastern Hospitality
LABAN

"Come and stay with us, you who are blessed by the LORD! Why are you standing here outside the town when I have a room all ready for you and a place prepared for the camels?" So the man went home with Laban, and Laban unloaded the camels, gave him straw for their bedding, fed them, and provided water for the man and the camel drivers to wash their feet. Genesis 24:31-32

Hospitality is big business these days. What is referred to as the "hospitality industry" includes hotels, food service, casinos, and various types of tourism. Hospitality is now an estimated $3.5 trillion sector in the worldwide economy.

Hospitality isn't just good business; it's also a lifestyle that God commands his people to adopt. The apostle Paul wrote, "When God's people are in need, be ready to help them. Always be eager to practice hospitality" (Romans 12:13).

Laban, the brother-in-law of the Jewish patriarch Isaac, understood the blessings of those who practice hospitality because he had received them himself.

When Eliezer, Abraham's Canaanite servant, traveled to Aram-naharaim to find a wife for Abraham's son Isaac, Laban welcomed him into his home and cared for his camels.

Laban understood that being hospitable to Abraham's servant held a blessing. When he extended that kindness, he received a blessing beyond the dowry that Eliezer gave him in exchange for allowing him to take Rebekah back to Isaac. Rebekah, Laban's sister, would become Isaac's wife and would thus be in the lineage of Jesus Christ.

Someone once said that a man who practices hospitality "entertains God." That was true in Laban's case, and it can be true for you, too!

When you extend to others the hospitality God has shown you, you put yourself in a position to receive extra blessings from the Lord. You will also be doing the Kingdom work he has assigned to you.

November 26

Do Ends Justify Means?
JACOB

Jacob took the food to his father. "My father?" he said. "Yes, my son," Isaac answered. "Who are you—Esau or Jacob?" Jacob replied, "It's Esau, your firstborn son. I've done as you told me. Here is the wild game. Now sit up and eat it so you can give me your blessing." Genesis 27:18-19

If you're a football fan, you know that deception is one of the most important weapons in the game. Teams line up in special formations, send men into motion, run fake handoffs and passes, and use other forms of trickery in an attempt to fool the opposing defenses.

Though deception is an accepted part of competitive sports, it is never an acceptable part of a godly man's life.

The book of Genesis tells the story of a man who engaged in deceit even as he tried to accomplish something that God had already said was his will.

Jacob and his mother, Rebekah, had a noble goal in mind—Jacob should receive the birthright from his father. Where they went terribly wrong was in scheming, conniving, and lying to make that goal a reality.

The plan of deception was simple: While Jacob's brother Esau was out hunting wild game for Isaac's supper, Jacob would disguise himself as Esau and take his father his favorite stew for dinner.

The plan worked perfectly. Jacob received his father's blessing but only after lying to him at least four times. He told Isaac that he was Esau, said that he had done as he had been told, assured his father that what he was about to eat was wild game (it was a family goat), and that God had provided some wild game for his father's dinner.

Working together, Jacob and Rebekah deceived his father, thus accomplishing through sinful means what God had wanted to do through righteous means.

Jacob received the blessing all right, but he would also face many consequences for his sin, most notably Laban's deception before giving him Laban's daughter Rachel as Jacob's wife (see Genesis 29:16-30).

Though deception can be tempting, God blesses you far more richly when you make it your life's goal to speak and act honestly every day.

November 27

He *Looks* like Peter
PETER

Peter's words pierced their hearts, and they said to him and to the other apostles, "Brothers, what should we do?" Peter replied, "Each of you must repent of your sins and turn to God, and be baptized in the name of Jesus Christ for the forgiveness of your sins. Then you will receive the gift of the Holy Spirit."
ACTS 2:37-38

Remember the old sci-fi movie *Invasion of the Body Snatchers*? It's about a small Northern California town whose population is replaced by alien look-alikes. Sure, they *looked* like the same people they had always been, but somehow they were different.

Some of the people who knew the apostle Peter and heard him preach following Jesus' return to heaven had to wonder if he was the same person they had seen flat on his face so many times.

Peter lost his nerve and sank like a rock in the Sea of Galilee after *asking* Jesus to let him walk on the water (see Matthew 14:22-33). Three times, he denied even knowing Jesus (see Luke 22:54-62), and he was nowhere to be found as his Master was nailed by his hands and feet to a wooden cross.

Humanly speaking, it didn't look as if Peter had the right stuff to be the kind of ambassador that Jesus had called him to be.

Peter was also the man who later preached with power and courage without regard to what could be some very painful consequences for speaking the name of Jesus Christ in the city of Jerusalem. He knew that his preaching would get him in deep trouble with the Jewish religious authorities in Jerusalem, but he preached anyway, so powerfully that thousands of people turned to Jesus in one day (see Acts 2:41).

Talk about a turnaround of biblical proportions!

Peter was a living example of what can happen in the life of a man who knows Jesus Christ and learns to live by the Holy Spirit's empowerment.

When you combine your commitment to serving Jesus Christ with the Holy Spirit's empowerment, you receive the kind of faith, courage, and power it takes to do things you would never have thought possible.

November 28

More Than Changed
SAUL OF TARSUS

When Saul arrived in Jerusalem, he tried to meet with the believers, but they were all afraid of him. They did not believe he had truly become a believer!
ACTS 9:26

Walid Shoebat has quite a testimony. Shoebat was a Palestinian terrorist who hated everything that didn't fit with his radical Muslim agenda, including the nation of Israel, the West, and Christianity.

Shoebat was transformed when he came to faith in Jesus Christ. Although he once acted out a message of hatred and anger, he now lives in love and forgiveness.

Not surprisingly, many people, including some Christians, have viewed Shoebat's conversion and the message he speaks today with a jaundiced eye, wondering if he is for real or if he has some hidden agenda.

The apostle Paul would understand how Shoebat must feel.

After his conversion experience, Saul endured that same kind of skepticism. His incredible encounter with Jesus changed the direction of his life forever, but some believers who heard his new message couldn't quite believe their ears.

Wasn't this the same Saul that violently persecuted Christians in Jerusalem and was on his way to do the same in Damascus?

Yes and no!

Saul was transformed into someone quite different than when he had left on this trip. He was now Paul, the man who wrote, "Anyone who belongs to Christ has become a new person. The old life is gone; a new life has begun!" (2 Corinthians 5:17).

Paul knew a little something about becoming a new creature. In an instant, he was transformed from a hateful, threat-making enemy of Jesus Christ into his most vocal follower.

When Jesus saved you and welcomed you into his eternal family, he also changed you into a living testimony of God's power to transform a man into someone new.

November 29

Stop Doubting
THOMAS

One of the twelve disciples, Thomas (nicknamed the Twin), was not with the others when Jesus came. They told him, "We have seen the Lord!" But he replied, "I won't believe it unless I see the nail wounds in his hands, put my fingers into them, and place my hand into the wound in his side."   John 20:24-25

Most people think of Mother Teresa as a faith-filled servant of God who devoted her life to caring for the poorest of the poor in Calcutta, India. But in *Mother Teresa: Come Be My Light,* a collection of her letters to some of her brothers and sisters in the faith, she revealed that she sometimes endured nagging personal doubts.

Mother Teresa had a lot of company. The Bible includes accounts of men who struggled with doubt, the best known being the man we know as "Doubting Thomas."

The eleventh chapter of John's Gospel shows us a faith-filled, courageous Thomas who rallied his fellow disciples to follow Jesus into Judea, where his life had already been threatened. "Let's go, too—and die with Jesus," Thomas exclaimed (John 11:16).

That looks like a man of unshakeable faith, doesn't it?

Skip ahead to the days following Jesus' death. There you see an emotionally and spiritually drained Thomas who flatly refused to believe that Jesus was alive even though the other disciples had already *seen* him.

Fortunately, that wasn't the end of Thomas's story.

After eight of the most miserable, discouraging days Thomas would ever endure, his Master appeared to him. "Put your finger here, and look at my hands," he encouraged Thomas. "Put your hand into the wound in my side. Don't be faithless any longer. Believe!" (John 20:27).

In his joy at finally seeing the resurrected Jesus, Thomas exclaimed, "My Lord and my God!" (John 20:28).

Where do you go when your faith has weakened and given way to doubt? When you go through times like those, continue in your life of faith by humbly asking Jesus to reveal himself to you in a way that replaces doubts with faith.

November 30

Rejected but Undaunted
JESUS IN NAZARETH

[Jesus] said, "You will undoubtedly quote me this proverb: 'Physician, heal yourself'—meaning, 'Do miracles here in your hometown like those you did in Capernaum.' But I tell you the truth, no prophet is accepted in his own hometown."
LUKE 4:23-24

It's hard to imagine someone who has seen the classic movie *The Wizard of Oz* not remembering the defining line in the movie: "There's no place like home."

For most men, that is very true. Home is where your family and old friends live. It's where you go to reminisce and visit places that hold special memories. It's where you visit the old fishing holes, movie theaters, and burger joints that meant so much to you as a youngster.

Soon after Jesus began his earthly ministry, he took the time to visit his hometown of Nazareth. There he had worked with his earthly father, Joseph, in the carpentry shop, studied the Scriptures in the local synagogue, and played with other Nazarene children.

The people of Nazareth welcomed Jesus home and allowed him to speak at their Sabbath service at the synagogue. At first, the things Jesus said amazed them, but it wasn't long before he ruffled some feathers.

What had been a peaceful Sabbath-day congregation turned into an irate mob intent on throwing Jesus off a nearby cliff.

These were Jesus' friends and family!

Jesus miraculously escaped the angry crowd in Nazareth that day. Although it's difficult to imagine his feeling anything but grieved at what had happened, he didn't allow his hometown's rejection to discourage or sidetrack him from completing his mission.

It never feels good when you're rejected, and it's especially difficult when rejection comes from your own friends and family. Don't take the rejection of your life of faith personally, but see it as another way that you can follow in Jesus' footsteps.

December 1

Willing to Confront
PETER AND PAUL

When Peter came to Antioch, I had to oppose him to his face, for what he did was very wrong. Galatians 2:11

Former Miami Dolphins coach Don Shula once talked to reporters about the importance of confronting his players' mistakes in practice.

"What is a small flaw?" he asked. "I see that with my children. I've let a lot of things slide by because I was too tired. I didn't want another confrontation. But uncorrected errors do multiply. You've got to face them some day. . . . If I could do it over again with my children, I'd face the errors on the spot. It's easier on them and on you. That works in relationships with anyone."

Few of us enjoy confrontation. We don't like pointing out another person's flaws, and we certainly don't like having our own exposed, even when they need to be. Spiritual health sometimes calls for loving confrontation, which the apostle Paul demonstrated in an uncomfortable situation with the apostle Peter.

Peter had erred in refusing to dine with uncircumcised Gentile Christians after some Jewish Christians—who believed that salvation required circumcision—arrived in Antioch. Instead of standing for the true gospel of Christ that had ended the need for adherence to ceremonial law, Peter snubbed the Gentile believers.

Peter was clearly in the wrong, and Paul confronted him directly, man-to-man.

In so doing, Paul modeled the importance of loving confrontation with regard to crucial issues of faith. Paul knew that if he let this error slide, bigger errors would soon bury the young church. It had to stop right there.

Do you confront a person every time you believe he or she is wrong on some issue? Of course not. None of us is always right, and not all issues call for direct confrontation. But as a husband, father, friend, and brother in the faith, there will be times when God will ask you to confront and correct in love.

Confrontation is rarely easy, and it's often not even appropriate. For serious issues that threaten the health or well-being of your family, church, or other significant group, you must find the courage to confront and correct someone in error regardless of the perceived risks.

December 2

Best Supporting Actor
JOHN THE BAPTIST

"I am the one who needs to be baptized by you," [John] said, "so why are you coming to me?" MATTHEW 3:14

Do you like watching the Academy Awards? If so, how much attention do you pay to the performer who wins for Best Supporting Actor? This guy plays second banana to the leading man, adding something important to a film while never imagining that the story revolves around him. He knows his place and happily takes it.

As in showbiz, a healthy relationship with Jesus Christ means knowing where you fit in with the cast of characters playing their various roles to fulfill God's purposes. Perhaps the most famous best supporting actor in the New Testament is John the Baptist, the man who the Old Testament prophets said would prepare the way for the Messiah's coming.

John had the confidence and the conviction to preach the message God had given him, and he also welcomed the real star of the show, Jesus Christ. John ministered at a time when the people of Israel had grown more than ready for their Messiah to arrive. John repeatedly had to set the record straight about his own identity, for only then could he continue to play the part in which God had cast him.

John demonstrated the humility of knowing his place in God's plan. When Jesus approached him on the banks of the Jordan River asking to be baptized, John protested that *he,* not Jesus, needed to be baptized. But he continued to obey, which meant playing the part God had given him.

Though it may seem easy to play a supporting role to a star as bright as Jesus, what if God asked you to play a similar role to a colleague at work or a care-group leader at church? What if you honestly think you'd make a better leading man?

What can you learn from John the Baptist about the part you have to play in God's plan of redemption? In what places in your life has he asked you to be a best supporting actor rather than a leading man? How can you win God's Academy Award for your performance?

December 3

Faithfulness *in* Misfortune
JOSEPH

The LORD was with Joseph in the prison and showed him his faithful love.
GENESIS 39:21

Have you ever wondered why God allows unpleasantness to come your way when you are serving him faithfully? Most of us find it easy to think that *if God really loved us, he wouldn't allow [fill in the blank] in our lives.*

The next time you are tempted to connect the dots between God's love and the peace and tranquility you would like to enjoy, try putting yourself in Joseph's shoes for a moment. Though he lived an upright life, Joseph endured more than his share of injustice at a young age. His jealous brothers sold him into slavery, and though he thrived in Egypt in Potiphar's house, he eventually found himself in prison, falsely accused of rape.

That sounds like more than a bad break, doesn't it? But if you think that Joseph spent his time grumbling or complaining about the injustice of it all, think again! Through everything, Joseph continued to serve God and those in authority over him. His stellar conduct earned him the respect and admiration of everyone who knew him.

How did Joseph do it? How did he maintain a faithful heart when at times it must have seemed that God had abandoned him? The Bible has a five-word answer to that question: "The LORD was with Joseph."

Though Joseph had to endure some incredibly difficult times, he appears to have maintained a constant sense of God's presence in his life. Since Joseph *knew* that God was with him, he prospered in every situation he faced, including his false imprisonment. He didn't know how or when things would improve, but he remained steadfast in his commitment to God, sure that God would reveal his hand in due time.

God doesn't promise you or any believer an easy, trouble-free life. What he does promise is his continued presence through everything you have to endure, however difficult or agonizing the challenge may seem.

December 4

Jesus Needed the Holy Spirit
JESUS

Jesus returned to Galilee, filled with the Holy Spirit's power. Reports about him spread quickly through the whole region. He taught regularly in their synagogues and was praised by everyone.   Luke 4:14-15

Prior to Dwight L. Moody's historic evangelistic campaign in Great Britain, a local pastor protested, "Why do we need this Mr. Moody? He's uneducated, inexperienced. . . . Who does he think he is, anyway? Does he think he has a monopoly on the Holy Spirit?"

Another pastor who knew Moody well responded, "No, but the Holy Spirit has a monopoly on Mr. Moody."

Any man who has accomplished something for the Lord owes his success to the empowerment of the Holy Spirit. Jesus promised to send the Spirit to us after he returned to his Father in heaven (see John 16:13), and he left us an example of how to depend on the Spirit for power, guidance, and encouragement.

Jesus lived his whole life on earth relying on the Spirit's power. Every wise word he spoke and every miraculous deed he performed grew out of the Spirit's prompting. The Bible teaches that Jesus didn't even begin his public ministry until "the Holy Spirit, in bodily form, descended on him like a dove" at his baptism (Luke 3:22). Following that step, Jesus rose from the waters of the Jordan River and shook his world to its foundations.

By submitting to the empowering of the Holy Spirit, Jesus received his heavenly Father's approval to do his work on earth and the heavenly resources he would need to obediently and humbly complete his mission.

So here's the question of the day: If Jesus, as the perfect Son of God and Son of Man, needed the empowerment of God's Spirit, how much more do *you* need his power today?

Do you want to make a godly impact in every corner of your world for Jesus Christ? If so, recognize that you will need more than knowledge of God's Word, desire, or natural ability. You need to walk every day in the power of the Holy Spirit, the same power that Jesus counted on to complete his earthly ministry.

December 5

The High Road
JOB

When Job prayed for his friends, the LORD restored his fortunes. In fact, the LORD gave him twice as much as before!   Job 42:10

The American humorist and cartoonist Kin Hubbard once very accurately observed, "Nobody ever forgets where he buried the hatchet." Indeed, part of our fallen human nature is to hold grudges against those who have done us wrong or spoken wrongly to or about us.

The Bible is about the forgiveness that God offers sinful mankind and the forgiveness he commands each of us to extend to those who have hurt or offended us.

As Job's painful but enlightening story draws to a close, he faces a choice: How will he handle Eliphaz, Bildad, and Zohar, friends who have sat with him in his suffering and offered nothing but accusations, recriminations, and condemnation? *If you're suffering like this,* they told this man that God called "blameless," *it must be because your sin has angered God!*

Most of us shrink from those who attack our character. *Why should I sit and listen to this?* we might wonder, feeling completely justified in giving our accusers the cold shoulder.

Job did no such thing.

Rather than hold a grudge and complain to God about the things they had said about him, Job prayed for them so genuinely and fervently that God heard his prayer on their behalf. Job blessed those who had accused him, and God blessed him in return (see Job 42:10).

Job took the high road by refusing to hold grudges against his friends. He took an even higher one when he prayed for them. He chose the same understanding and forgiveness that God had extended to him after he had spoken wrongly against the Lord.

How do you respond when you're unfairly criticized or falsely accused? Do you cut off the other person, all the while feeling justified because of the rotten things he or she has said about you? Or do you take the highest road and sincerely pray that God will bless the person who has hurt you? Job says, "Take the high road!"

December 6

Approach the Impossible
ELISHA

When Elisha arrived, the child was indeed dead, lying there on the prophet's bed. He went in alone and shut the door behind him and prayed to the LORD.
2 KINGS 4:32-33

When the great American inventor Charles Kettering headed up research at General Motors and wanted a problem solved, he would call a meeting of his engineers. When they arrived at the meeting room, they were greeted with this sign: "Leave slide rules here."

"If I didn't do that," Kettering explained, "I'd find someone reaching for his slide rule. Then he'd be on his feet saying, 'Boss, you can't do it.'"

In raising the dead son of a woman from Shunem back to life, the Old Testament prophet Elisha demonstrated that it is essential to do the impossible, also known as what *we* can't do.

Elisha had sent his assistant Gehazi ahead to try to raise the boy, but he had failed. After Elisha took over, the boy's mother was soon carrying her living son out of his bedroom.

What made the difference? Elisha was a prophet and Gehazi wasn't, but that wasn't the difference maker. Nor was it the fact that Gehazi was Elisha's humble servant.

It all came down to their different approaches.

When Elisha arrived at the woman's home, he walked into the bedroom where the dead boy lay and shut the door behind him. Then he did what any man of God should do when he needs a miracle: He prayed.

After Elisha had thanked God and sought his direction and strength, he acted. He stretched out twice over the boy's lifeless body so that he came face-to-face with him. On the second attempt, the boy opened his eyes, sneezed seven times, and came to life! Part of what made Elisha a great man of God—and an example for us today—was that he consistently communicated with God before he acted.

What difficult challenges lie before you today? Have you remembered to commit them to God in prayer, asking for his guidance, help, and blessing? Whose approach are you most likely to follow, that of Elisha or of Gehazi?

December 7

The Groundwork of Prayer
DANIEL

I, Daniel, learned from reading the word of the LORD, as revealed to Jeremiah the prophet, that Jerusalem must lie desolate for seventy years. So I turned to the LORD God and pleaded with him in prayer and fasting. I also wore rough burlap and sprinkled myself with ashes. Daniel 9:2-3

When God is about to bring big changes into your life—marriage, fatherhood, a major career change—how do you prepare for what's coming? Do you just wait to see what happens, or do you become proactive and begin to prepare yourself?

The prophet Daniel, who lived with his exiled Hebrew countrymen in Babylon, once found himself in such a situation. He set a perfect example for us of what to do when big changes are afoot.

As Daniel read Jeremiah's prophecies about the Babylonian exile, he realized that the seventy predicted years of captivity had nearly run their course. Daniel knew that God would shortly be up to something, and sooner rather than later.

Daniel didn't know exactly what God had in mind, so he did the one thing he knew to do in such a situation: seek God in prayer. He fasted, confessed his sins, praised, and pleaded with God to give him some answers. In response, God sent the angel Gabriel to explain to him the exact meaning of the visions he had seen and the prophecies he had read (see Daniel 9:21-27).

Since Daniel wanted to be ready for what God planned to do with him and his people, he prayed. What do *you* do when you sense that God is about to do something big in your life or in the lives of those you love?

God promises to reward and bless you when you sincerely seek him (see Hebrews 11:6). All he asks is that you have the faith to believe that he exists and that he keeps his promises. So pray fervently and persistently, and God will allow you to see him at work within you and on your behalf.

December 8

This Is a Test
JESUS AND PHILIP

Turning to Philip, he [Jesus] asked, "Where can we buy bread to feed all these people?" He was testing Philip, for he already knew what he was going to do. Philip replied, "Even if we worked for months, we wouldn't have enough money to feed them!" John 6:5-7

Psychologists tell us that one of the most common recurrent dreams is a flashback nightmare in which people find themselves back in college. They realize that finals are the next day, and they haven't studied or attended class all semester.

Who could pass a test under such circumstances? That's why the dreamer feels such relief when he or she wakes up and gets ready to head to work.

Jesus had a little test for the apostle Philip for which he obviously hadn't studied. With thousands of hungry people gathered and nothing to feed them, how could Philip come up with enough bread and fish to satisfy everyone? Would he look at the task before him through the lens of faith or the lens of his own lack of resources?

Jesus fully intended to perform a miracle that day. When he asked Philip how they might feed all these thousands of people, the apostle could only look out over the throng and focus on his personal lack of resources. Had Philip answered along the lines of, "I don't know how you're going to do it, but I know you're going to show me," he would have passed the test.

He didn't, and he failed, but his instructor kept teaching.

Philip obviously had a long way to go before he understood who Jesus was. He failed his test of faith because he focused on the lack of visible provision instead of on the Provider who stood before him.

What seems impossible in human thinking becomes entirely doable when you remember that God specializes in doing what you could never do on your own. That's a test that God always wants you to pass!

How do you respond when God directs you to do what seems impossible? Do you answer, "It can't be done!" or "What do I do next to make it happen?" God always blesses faith that leads to action.

December 9

Don't Miss Your Chance
KING ASA

At that time Hanani the seer came to King Asa and told him, "Because you have put your trust in the king of Aram instead of in the LORD your God, you missed your chance to destroy the army of the king of Aram." 2 Chronicles 16:7

George Parker, one of the most daring and creative con men in American history, made a living by selling famous New York City landmarks to gullible tourists.

One of Parker's favorite sale items was the Brooklyn Bridge, which he sold twice a week over a period of several years, convincing his marks that they could make a killing if they controlled access to the roadway. More than once, police had to remove conned buyers as they attempted to erect toll barriers on the bridge.

Some people will always put their trust in the wrong people. Asa, Judah's third king, made that mistake.

Like so many kings of ancient Judah, Asa started out doing good things for his kingdom. The prophet Azariah had told him, "The LORD will stay with you as long as you stay with him! Whenever you seek him, you will find him. But if you abandon him, he will abandon you" (2 Chronicles 15:2).

For a time, Asa trusted and obeyed God, but later in his reign, he failed by relying on humans and human institutions instead of on God. The results spoke for themselves.

Asa showed his true colors when he entered into an agreement with Syria to stand against Israel, whose army he could and should have destroyed. Asa's solution worked for a time, but it had grave consequences in the long run.

Asa's refusal to rely solely on God contributed to his death. When he developed a life-threatening foot disease, he went to his doctors rather than first seek God's help (see 2 Chronicles 16:12). He thus missed another chance, and no one gets an unlimited supply.

Where do you turn in your times of need? Do you consider prayer a "first resort" or a "second resort"? You can never go wrong by fully trusting God to care and provide for you and for those you love. He will never let you down.

December 10

Guard Your Heart
KING DAVID

Late one afternoon, after his midday rest, David got out of bed and was walking on the roof of the palace. As he looked out over the city, he noticed a woman of unusual beauty taking a bath. He sent someone to find out who she was, and he was told, "She is Bathsheba, the daughter of Eliam and the wife of Uriah the Hittite."
2 SAMUEL 11:2-3

In the aftermath of an illicit sexual affair, we've all heard someone say, "We didn't plan it. It just happened."

Though no man in his right mind would *plan* an indiscretion that could ruin his marriage, his children's lives, his reputation, and his relationship with God, it's inaccurate to say that such affairs just happen. Far from it! In every case of infidelity or sexual immorality, someone takes steps that lead to trouble.

Let's be honest. Since the dawn of creation, our enemy the devil has worked overtime to trip up godly men. He knows our weaknesses, and he knows how readily we respond to visual stimuli. That's how God has wired us, and that's why sexual temptation so often comes to us through what we see.

The tragic story of King David's sin with Bathsheba graphically demonstrates how the enemy uses our eyes to trip us up. David fell because he allowed himself to stare lustfully at the beautiful Bathsheba. Once he began mentally entertaining illicit possibilities, a sinful thought quickly turned into a sinful action.

David apparently learned from his blunder because he later wrote, "I will refuse to look at anything vile and vulgar" (Psalm 101:3). Consider it hard-earned wisdom that doubles as great advice.

Have you learned to safeguard your heart by safeguarding your eyes? When you train yourself to go on the offensive and keep guard over where your eyes linger, you hold the key that prevents sexual immorality from just happening.

For just a moment, imagine that you are David. You see a lovely young thing bathing in the next apartment. What do you do? You could continue looking, or you could quote some pointed counsel from God's Word to yourself: "Can [a man] walk on hot coals and not blister his feet? So it is with the man who sleeps with another man's wife. He who embraces her will not go unpunished." (Proverbs 6:28-29).

December 11

A Consistent Life
JOSHUA

Serve the LORD alone. But if you refuse to serve the LORD, then choose today whom you will serve. Would you prefer the gods your ancestors served beyond the Euphrates? Or will it be the gods of the Amorites in whose land you now live? But as for me and my family, we will serve the LORD. Joshua 24:14-15

What do the following men have in common?

    —The man who reads his Bible and prays every day
    —The man who always shows up for work on time and puts in his best
      effort until he goes home on time
    —The man who takes his family to church every Sunday and
      Wednesday and leads family prayer and Bible study

You can count on each of these men because they demonstrate consistency in some of life's most important areas.

One of the greatest character qualities of any leader—spiritual, family, business, or military—is the willingness to consistently "walk the walk" and not just "talk the talk."

Joshua was that kind of leader.

Like every flesh-and-blood man, Joshua had his flaws, but he consistently exercised his faith and obeyed the God who called him to lead. That's why he could confidently challenge his people to "choose today whom you will serve."

Joshua spoke those words as part of a speech of rededication and recommitment to the covenant God had made with his people at Sinai. He dared the Israelites to rid their lives of any remnants of idol worship and choose instead to consistently and wholeheartedly serve and obey God.

Joshua established himself as a hero of the faith partly because he bravely led his people into the Promised Land through what could have been some serious military and spiritual potholes. More than that, we consider him a hero because he consistently served and obeyed God.

God blesses you when you choose to follow, trust, and serve him with everything you have. "Steady as she goes" tends to be a lot more effective in the long run than "Full speed ahead! Ramming speed! No, full reverse! No, . . ." Strive for consistency.

December 12

Courage and Faith
EHUD

*"Follow me," he said, "for the LORD has given you victory over Moab your enemy."
So they followed him.*   Judges 3:28

Near the end of his book *Five Days in London,* historian John Lukacs quotes a letter from Harold Nicolson, one of Winston Churchill's associates during World War II. In it, Nicolson tells his wife, Vita Sackville-West, how the British prime minister's courage in standing up to Nazi Germany had affected him: "My darling, how infectious courage is. I am rendered far stronger in heart and confidence by such bravery."

Courage and faith have an infectious quality. They inspire others to bravery and reliance on God. That certainly was the story of an Old Testament character named Ehud.

God raised up Ehud, the second of the twelve judges who ruled over Israel, at a time when Moab's King Eglon held the upper hand. Moab had dominated Israel for eighteen years, and Ehud knew that it was time for a change.

He was just the man to set that change in motion.

Ehud confronted Eglon in his own palace after convincing the king that he had a secret message for him. When Eglon ordered his servants to leave the room, Ehud drew out his dagger and killed the obese king where he sat.

Ehud escaped and fled to the hill country of Ephraim, then led a band of men down from the hills into Moab. "Follow me," Ehud ordered his men. Ehud's courage inspired his men, who earned back their freedom with a rousing victory over the Moabites.

Ehud's men followed him into battle because he had demonstrated his fitness to lead by courageously facing Eglon on the king's own turf. He demonstrated his faith by his actions and with his words: *The Lord has given you victory.*

Ehud had the courage and faith to step up when no one else could, and his people reaped the benefits with eighty years of peace.

How do you inspire those you love to follow you? If you want to do great things for God's Kingdom, for your family, and for others, you'll need the two overwhelming weapons of courage and faith—courage to step up when you're needed, and faith to believe that God will give you victory.

December 13

Baby Steps of Faith
PETER

Peter called to him, "Lord, if it's really you, tell me to come to you, walking on the water." "Yes, come," Jesus said. So Peter went over the side of the boat and walked on the water toward Jesus. Matthew 14:28-29

All parents love to see small children take their first steps. The experience can also be nerve-wracking as they worry that those wobbly little legs will give way and result in a nasty bump or fall.

Learning to walk can be a time of smiles and pride for everyone involved, but it's also frequently a time of stumbling and falling, with perhaps a few tears. It can feel both wonderful and stressful to watch a toddler learn to coordinate his or her legs and feet and try something completely new.

Believers in Christ who are taking their first steps of faith go through a similar experience, with similar emotions. As we dare to take those steps, we often have moments of success followed by incidents of failure when we fall flat on our faces.

The apostle Peter is a famous biblical example.

Peter was easily the most impulsive of Jesus' twelve apostles. He said things that the others only thought about and did things they didn't dare to try. In the Gospels, Peter is the baby in faith who tries new things to discover what he is able to do.

Peter has gained a lot of notoriety for his impulsiveness in getting out of the boat and walking to Jesus on the surface of the Sea of Galilee, only to panic and begin sinking like a rock when he took his eyes off his Master. He allowed the howling wind and crashing waves around him to overwhelm his faith.

Many think of Peter as the disciple who couldn't keep his eyes on Jesus. But though he failed to do what Jesus had plainly said he could do, he succeeded in doing what no one else even had the nerve to try. He took a few baby steps of faith toward the mature believer in Christ he would one day become.

Sometimes you may step out and follow Jesus more closely, only to stumble and fall. Don't be afraid to get out of the boat and try something new. Your faith grows as you exercise it, so risk the unknown and the unfamiliar. Jesus will always be there to catch you when you fall.

December 14

Finish What You Start
PAUL AND TITUS

If anyone asks about Titus, say that he is my partner who works with me to help you. And the brothers with him have been sent by the churches, and they bring honor to Christ.   2 Corinthians 8:23

Read the following list and ask yourself what these items have in common:

—Plans to lose weight and get in better shape
—Plans to finish reading the book that sits on your nightstand with a bookmark at the halfway point
—Plans to finish the kitchen remodeling you started that your wife keeps reminding you about

If you answered, "Things that require diligence to get finished," then you're on the right track, and perhaps well on your way to becoming a man that people can count on to finish what you start.

Diligence motivates you to complete what you begin, even when it entails personal sacrifice or hardship. It's a character quality that a man named Titus demonstrated in just about everything he did.

Paul knew that he could count on Titus to finish what he started and to do it with enthusiasm motivated by love for his fellow believers. That is why Paul referred to Titus, whom he had sent to Corinth as a personal delegate, as "my partner who works with me to help you."

A great bond of affection cemented Paul to Titus, a Greek convert. They built this bond on brotherhood in the faith and on trust because Paul knew that he could count on Titus to finish what he started.

The Bible repeatedly promises that those who diligently seek, obey, listen to, and serve God will never be disappointed. When you demonstrate your diligence toward him, it is sure to spill over into all areas of your life.

Do others see you as a man who can be counted on to finish what you start even if it means personal sacrifice? Dependability and diligence don't often characterize people today, but they are crucial to your making a difference in your own home and in the world around you.

December 15

Temper, Temper
KING SAUL

Saul boiled with rage at Jonathan. "You stupid son of a whore!" he swore at him. "Do you think I don't know that you want him to be king in your place, shaming yourself and your mother? As long as that son of Jesse is alive, you'll never be king. Now go and get him so I can kill him!" 1 Samuel 20:30-31

Someone once tried to rationalize outbursts of anger to the American evangelist Billy Sunday by telling him, "There's nothing wrong with losing my temper. I blow up, and then it's all over."

"So does a shotgun," Sunday replied, "and look at the damage it leaves behind!"

Few emotions have the potential to harm our hearts and relationships like uncontrolled anger. In the Bible, anger led to Cain's slaying Abel, to Samson's downfall, and to King Saul's attempts to kill a young and faithful servant named David.

Saul's anger erupted out of his jealousy. David had made quite a name for himself as a warrior and leader, and Saul knew that he was a threat to his position as king. His anger was so fierce and overwhelming that at least three times he tried to murder the future king of Israel who had faithfully served him.

That wasn't all.

Anger has a sneaky way of spreading and infecting relationships with those closest to us even when they aren't the objects of our anger. Saul was so consumed with anger at David that he lashed out at his son Jonathan because Jonathan was a close friend of David and had attempted to protect him from harm.

Saul had already proven himself unworthy to lead the people of Israel. He showed his true colors when he allowed anger to control his every motivation, decision, and action.

At times, it may be appropriate or even righteous to become angry, but you should always stop before you pop and make sure that you feel angry for the right reasons. Then be sure to express it in a fitting way.

December 16

Pray, Plan, Act
NEHEMIAH

"The God of heaven will help us succeed. We, his servants, will start rebuilding this wall." Nehemiah 2:20

Surely you have met the man named "I'm Gonna." He's the one who has the vision and the ability to accomplish something but somehow fails to put action behind his intentions.

He's the man who dreams but never gets anything done.

The Bible teaches that God gives men the vision, the faith, and the ability to get things done, but we must still act on what we know.

When Nehemiah first realized that the walls around Jerusalem needed rebuilding, he didn't just sit back and pray, "Thy will be done!" Yes, he bathed his vision in prayer, but he also planned and then *acted* on his plans.

Nehemiah knew how long the project would be and what it would take to finish it. He even knew where to get the materials and the labor he needed.

He knew that the hand of God was upon his plans.

Nehemiah knew that he and his people faced a daunting task. He knew that rebuilding the wall around Jerusalem would require long hours of hard work in the face of his neighbors' outspoken opposition. He approached the work with absolute confidence that he would succeed simply because God had called him to it and had promised to be with him as he oversaw the work.

Knowing all those things, Nehemiah didn't wait—he *acted*!

Has God given you a vision of something he wants you to accomplish? If so, pray, plan, and act!

You demonstrate your faith best when you hear and believe God, then act on what you believe. Faith isn't just giving mental assent to God's promises; it's taking the initiative to do the work it takes to receive what he has already given you.

December 17

A Godly Legacy
SAMUEL

Now Samuel died, and all Israel gathered for his funeral. They buried him at his house in Ramah. 1 Samuel 25:1

One of the most important questions you will ever have to ask yourself is, *How do I want to be remembered? What kind of legacy do I want to leave behind?*

Dictionaries define the word *legacy* as something passed down from one generation to the next. In the spiritual context, your legacy refers to the things you do and say to influence those around you, beginning with your wife, children, and other family members, and extending out to the rest of your world.

Think of your spiritual legacy as the eternal inheritance you will leave behind.

The prophet Samuel made a big impression on everyone who knew him. The Bible tells us that when he died, the entire nation mourned his passing. Though the people didn't always listen to him or heed his warnings, everyone in Israel gathered to pay their respects when he passed away.

Samuel left behind a legacy of faith, obedience, and courage because he faithfully and consistently took God at his word, acted on what he knew God wanted, and refused to worry about personal consequences.

The Israelites didn't remember Samuel as a man of great means or as a great entertainer. They mourned him as a man who faithfully loved and served God and his people.

Samuel teaches us that our primary goal in life should always be to make a positive mark for the Kingdom of God. When our time on earth draws to a close, it won't matter how much money we made or what we accomplished in the business world. What will matter are the souls we touched because we followed in Samuel's footsteps by living with faith, obedience, and courage.

The things you do and say on earth, through faith, will determine the legacy you leave behind. What you leave behind for your children will have a great effect, for either good or evil, on them, your children's children, and the people in their lives. Make the positive choice.

December 18

Sidekick
JONATHAN AND DAVID

Jonathan made a solemn pact with David, because he loved him as he loved himself. Jonathan sealed the pact by taking off his robe and giving it to David, together with his tunic, sword, bow, and belt.   1 Samuel 18:3-4

The Lone Ranger had Tonto. Marshal Matt Dillon had Festus Hagan. Batman had Robin, and Andy Taylor had Barney Fife. All classic television characters, it seems, must have their sidekicks.

The sidekick is the character who provides support, encouragement, and comic relief when needed. Though the sidekick plays a lesser role in the story, the hero couldn't be the hero without him.

Often in life it's good to be the sidekick. Sometimes God wants you to step back and allow someone else to take the lead and the credit. David's friend Jonathan was content to play the role of sidekick in David's rise to power in ancient Israel.

Jonathan's dad was King Saul, Israel's first monarch, but God hadn't called Jonathan to succeed his father on the throne. A different man might have felt angry and indignant at this apparent slight, but Jonathan remained David's close friend and ally.

In Jonathan, David had everything he could possibly want in a comrade and coworker. Jonathan was a selfless friend and ally (see 1 Samuel 19:1-2), a courageous warrior (see 1 Samuel 14:7-14), and a man of unshakable faith (see 1 Samuel 14:6). He humbly stood back and rejoiced as his friend rose to the prominent place God had planned for him.

How willing are you to stand back and let others shine as they take their places in God's plans? If you were Jonathan, who would your David be?

God has put you in the place where you can best suit his purposes at this time. Do you believe that? How can you lend your love, support, and loyalty to those he has called to what may seem like a higher place—even a place you might not mind occupying yourself?

December 19

The Enemy of Self
SAMSON

When her son was born, she named him Samson. And the LORD blessed him as he grew up. And the Spirit of the LORD began to stir him while he lived in Mahaneh-dan, which is located between the towns of Zorah and Eshtaol.
JUDGES 13:24-25

When asked what traits set actors apart from other people, British actor Michael Wilding answered, "Without a doubt, you can pick out actors by the glazed look that comes into their eyes when the conversation wanders away from themselves."

People tend to look up to those with big egos—fame-seeking pop stars, chest-thumping athletes, power-hungry politicians—but it's the man who learns to put self aside who makes a difference for God's Kingdom.

If anyone had the chance to leave a legacy of greatness, it was Samson. The Bible says that God blessed this strong man from the time he was a boy and that his Spirit began to stir within him in his youth.

That's when self got in the way.

Something went terribly wrong between God's Spirit and Samson that prevented his establishing himself with other giants of the faith such as Abraham, Joseph, and David.

The problem, simply put, was that Samson didn't use the gifts God had given him as the leader and deliverer God called him to be. Instead, he used them for his own agenda. Samson was a consistently proud and often immoral man who arrogantly disregarded the counsel of others. He used his incredible strength to exact revenge and settle scores.

Samson didn't care about being obedient to God or serving his people.

God gave Samson all the strength he needed to succeed in anything he set out to do. Samson squandered an opportunity for greatness and left a legacy of pride because he was only looking out for himself.

God has given you all the gifts you need to be a difference maker in your home, at your workplace, and in your church. Will you use those gifts for his benefit, or will you use them just for yourself?

December 20

Speak Up
ABSALOM AND AMNON

Though Absalom never spoke to Amnon about this, he hated Amnon deeply because of what he had done to his sister. 2 Samuel 13:22

It is horrible to find yourself at the business end of the silent treatment. Maybe you've unknowingly done something that hurt or offended someone, and instead of talking to you about it, they have become sullen and withdrawn.

It can be hard to speak up when you are offended by someone's hurtful actions, even unintentional ones, but you need to do so if you want to keep your important relationships healthy and growing.

Absalom, King David's second-eldest son and the half-brother of Amnon, shows what can happen when the lines of communication between two people break down.

The whole royal family knew what had happened. Amnon had raped Absalom's sister, Tamar, and when David failed to discipline Amnon, Absalom's anger and frustration grew into a deadly plot to murder Amnon.

Though Absalom had every right to feel angry toward Amnon, he went terribly wrong in refusing to talk about it. Absalom had no way of knowing if Amnon felt sorry for what he'd done, and he made no effort to try to resolve the situation.

His anger grew, deep inside, until it became implacable hatred.

Absalom waited for the right opportunity to order his servants to kill Amnon (see 2 Samuel 13:28). Though he probably felt some temporary satisfaction at taking vengeance, he paid a heavy price for his failure to resolve his conflict openly and peacefully.

Absalom demonstrates how anger and animosity can grow when you choose silence over talking after someone hurts or offends you. That's why it's always best to open up and talk when you feel wronged. Don't let it fester!

Keeping lines of communication open helps you to keep any relationship healthy and growing. Remember that God never gives you the silent treatment when you blow it. Instead, he reaches out and lets you know where you've messed up. Determine now to follow his example. When someone does something to hurt or offend you, don't hesitate to talk about it.

December 21

Show Respect
SHEM AND JAPHETH

Shem and Japheth took a robe, held it over their shoulders, and backed into the tent to cover their father. As they did this, they looked the other way so they would not see him naked. Genesis 9:23

Clark Clifford, an influential American lawyer who worked for several presidential administrations, once told how President Truman reacted to a letter from Saudi king Ibn Saud, which began, "Your Magnificence."

"Your *Magnificence*!" Truman laughed. "I like that. I don't know what you guys call me when I'm not here, but it's okay if you refer to me from now on as 'His Magnificence.'"

Certain offices command respect—government authorities, your mother and father, your wife, your boss, your church's leaders. The Bible teaches that God blesses you when you pay respect to those he has placed in your life.

Shem and Japheth, Noah's two eldest sons, respected their father and what he stood for. In a moment of indiscretion, Noah drank too much wine and passed out in his tent. Though their brother Ham sinned against Noah and God when he "saw that his father was naked" (Genesis 9:22—the original language implies staring), Shem and Japheth went out of their way to cover their father by taking a garment and walking into his tent backward so they wouldn't see him naked.

Ham dishonored Noah and himself, but Shem and Japheth respected their father so deeply that they did everything they could to protect his honor.

Shem and Japheth demonstrated respect and submissive faith that day. As a result, they and their descendants enjoyed a blessing from which their brother, Ham, had disqualified himself (see Genesis 9:24-27).

How much value do you place on respect? God expects you to honor and respect certain people in your life. Though some people see respect as a sign of weakness, that doesn't reflect God's opinion. Showing respect puts you in a great position to receive God's blessings and strength.

December 22

A New Frame of Reference
JESUS

As Jesus was walking along, he saw a man who had been blind from birth. "Rabbi," his disciples asked him, "why was this man born blind? Was it because of his own sins or his parents' sins?" "It was not because of his sins or his parents' sins," Jesus answered. "This happened so the power of God could be seen in him."
JOHN 9:1-3

Nothing shapes the way you think about God, life, love, or suffering quite like your own background and upbringing. Sometimes God changes your personal frame of reference so he can teach you more about himself and how he works through your circumstances.

Jesus' disciples had all grown up in a culture where people believed that bad things happened to sinners. One day, when they saw a blind man in Jerusalem, they naturally assumed that either he or his parents had sinned and that his blindness was God's punishment.

Jesus quickly corrected the disciples' faulty thinking. He denied that this man's blindness had come about because of anyone's sin. Instead, this man came into the world blind so that he could one day bring the people's attention to Jesus' divine power and authority.

The disciples had never thought of *that*.

With the disciples looking on, Jesus spat on the ground, smeared some mud on the man's eyes, and told him to wash his face in the pool of Siloam. When he obeyed, he was able to see for the first time in his life.

Before long, the news of his healing shook up the residents of Jerusalem, including the religious authorities. Some wondered if this could really be the man that they had seen begging near the Temple. The man kept insisting that it really *was* him and that someone named Jesus had healed him.

Jesus' miracle glorified God that day, and it changed the disciples' notions about God and how he works through human circumstances.

Sometimes your difficulties come as a result of your own sin and errors. At other times, God may use the troubles you face—sickness, family problems, financial difficulties—to demonstrate his power, goodness, mercy, and love. Are you willing to be used in that way, even if it costs you something?

December 23

What's Your Motivation?
PAUL

"I [Paul] am ready not only to be jailed at Jerusalem but even to die for the sake of the Lord Jesus." Acts 21:13

In an interview in *Forbes* magazine, American industrialist Charles M. Schwab said that money was never his motivation for work. He said, "I work just for the pleasure I find in work, the satisfaction there is in developing things, in creating. Also, the associations business begets. The person who does not work for the love of work, but only for money, is not likely to make money or find much fun in life."

Proper motivation goes a long way in determining whether or not your life will become everything God wants it to be. The apostle Paul understood that truth.

Paul changed the world for Jesus despite enduring incredible suffering and persecution on account of his preaching. He had been beaten, imprisoned, falsely accused, and according to tradition, executed because of his witness, yet he never considered quitting.

What would motivate a man to go through what Paul endured? Why didn't he just settle into an easier life? The answer, very simply, had to do with love.

Paul served out of his love for Christ. After receiving a prophecy declaring that he would be bound and persecuted in Jerusalem for his declaration of faith, the apostle Paul said to a group of Christians in Caesarea, "Why all this weeping? You are breaking my heart! I am ready not only to be jailed at Jerusalem but even to die for the sake of the Lord Jesus" (Acts 21:13).

Paul served out of his love for people. Paul wrote to the church in Thessalonica, "May the Lord make your love for one another and for all people grow and overflow, just as our love for you overflows" (1 Thessalonians 3:12). Paul's life was a fountain of love for other believers. Whether he was encouraging, rebuking, or praising believers in his letters, Paul did and said everything out of a spirit of love.

What is your motivation?

You find more joy and satisfaction in life when you serve God and others out of love and not from a sense of duty or obligation.

December 24

Greed Is *Not* Good
GEHAZI

Gehazi, the servant of Elisha the man of God, said to himself, "My master should not have let this Aramean get away without accepting any of his gifts. As surely as the LORD lives, I will chase after him and get something from him."
2 KINGS 5:20

In the 1987 movie *Wall Street,* Gordon Gekko, a ruthless brokerage-house owner played by Michael Douglas, delivered his infamous "Greed Is Good" speech to his employees. Greed, he claimed, would propel them toward success in their chosen field.

Although the movie portrayed Gekko as the villain, many in the investment community saw him as an inspiring role model. They saw greed as a good thing, just as Gordon Gekko taught.

Though the Bible encourages hard work, it repeatedly warns against greed. Gehazi, a servant of the prophet Elisha, is a sad example of a man who failed to heed those warnings and paid a steep price for it.

Through Elisha's ministry, God had miraculously healed the Syrian general Naaman, who gratefully offered the prophet a gift in gratitude. Elisha refused the gift and sent Naaman on his way, but Gehazi chased after him without consulting his master, hoping to collect for himself what Elisha had turned down.

Gehazi's greed ruined his life. He took for himself what he had no right or authority to have, he lied to Naaman to obtain it (see 2 Kings 5:22), and he lied when Elisha confronted him (see 2 Kings 5:25).

Though Gehazi did not die for his sin, his greed cost him his health from that day on. The leprosy that Elisha had healed in Naaman permanently attached itself to Gehazi. Ever after, Gehazi only had to look at his hands and feet to see the serious consequences of greed.

God delights in your desire to achieve and work hard to make a good life for yourself and your family. The sinful desire to acquire more, also known as greed, displeases him. How can you balance your desire to earn more with a commitment toward contentedness with what God has already given you?

December 25

Terrified but Overjoyed
JESUS

That night there were shepherds staying in the fields nearby, guarding their flocks of sheep. Suddenly, an angel of the Lord appeared among them, and the radiance of the Lord's glory surrounded them. They were terrified.   Luke 2:8-9

In the classic C. S. Lewis novel *The Lion, the Witch, and the Wardrobe*, Mr. and Mrs. Beaver prepare the young girl Lucy to meet Aslan the lion, who represents Jesus Christ. When Lucy learns that Aslan is a lion, she tells Mrs. Beaver that she feels nervous about meeting a lion. She wonders if he is safe.

"Safe?" replied Mr. Beaver. "Who said anything about safe? Of course he isn't safe. But he's good. He's the king, I tell you!"

Nothing will seem more frightening—and at the same time joyful and comforting—than coming face-to-face with the living God. Though he is anything but safe, he is good in every way.

A group of shepherds who were guarding their flocks the night of Jesus' birth saw God's frightening side and his comforting side. As they watched their flocks, an angel suddenly appeared, interrupting the night's silence and darkness with his radiant glory.

The sight terrified them.

The angel quickly replaced their fears with unspeakable joy as he made the staggering announcement that their long-awaited Messiah had come!

Today we tend to represent angels as cuddly, cute, harmless little fluffs of niceness, like the cherub you place on top of your Christmas tree every December. The angels brought the best news the world had ever heard, but these shepherds felt awe and terror at seeing them, followed by joy at what they had to say.

That is the only fitting reaction when a man of faith has a real encounter with the living God.

How do you reconcile biblical commands to fear God and love him at the same time? You have the privilege of serving and loving a God who elicits fear and joy whenever he appears. God is anything but safe—but he's the very definition of goodness.

December 26

God's Curveballs
JOSEPH AND JESUS

After the wise men were gone, an angel of the Lord appeared to Joseph in a dream. "Get up! Flee to Egypt with the child and his mother," the angel said. "Stay there until I tell you to return, because Herod is going to search for the child to kill him."
MATTHEW 2:13

Has life ever thrown you a curveball? You're happily and peacefully enjoying your family, your work, your friendships, and out of nowhere something happens. This may be something from God's own hand that will change your plans and alter your existence.

The Bible teaches the importance of being able to adjust our course when God wants to take us in another direction. Joseph, the man God called to the role of Jesus' earthly father, was able to adjust to what God wanted him to do, and God blessed him for it.

After Jesus' birth, Joseph probably thought that he and Mary would be typical parents, raising their son through an ordinary childhood in their hometown of Nazareth. Joseph would return to his work as a carpenter, and everything would go on as it had before.

The wise men from the East had just left Joseph and Mary when, as they all slept, an angel appeared to Joseph in a dream and told him to get up immediately and take Mary and Jesus to Egypt because Herod intended to kill Jesus.

Though questions swirled in Joseph's mind, he didn't hesitate. He roused Mary from her sleep, and they packed up their meager belongings and took Jesus to Egypt, where they stayed until the coast was clear.

Joseph played a huge part in Jesus' birth and childhood because he listened when God spoke and was ready to get up and move as God directed him.

You will probably never have an angel appear to you in a dream and ask you to change your life's course, but that doesn't mean that God won't throw a curveball or two into your life. God doesn't always allow your life to go according to your plans. God knows what he's doing, and he will bless you in unexpected ways.

December 27

Sin Leads to Loss
MOSES

When they came near the camp, Moses saw the calf and the dancing, and he burned with anger. He threw the stone tablets to the ground, smashing them at the foot of the mountain. Exodus 32:19

What makes you angry? Make a list if you want to. Now look at the things you just listed and ask yourself:

> Which are my personal pet peeves?
> Which have the potential, through sin and disobedience, to make me forfeit God's blessings?

Moses knew a little something about both kinds of anger. When he returned from his mountaintop experience with God to find his people—with the help of his brother and right-hand man, Aaron—worshiping a golden calf, he lost it. The people had violated the first of the Ten Commandments (see Exodus 20:3) and thus had broken their covenant with God. In his anger over what the people had done, Moses threw the holy tablets containing the Ten Commandments to the ground and smashed them to bits.

Moses may partly have felt angry because the people had wasted his time and effort. He could have felt angry because his own brother had sold him out. More than that, Moses' anger burned because the people that God wanted to richly bless had so quickly and easily turned away from him.

God miraculously rescued the Israelites from Egyptian slavery, lovingly provided for them, and had promised them a fabulous new home in Canaan. Yet they turned their backs on him and on the blessings they would have enjoyed had they remained faithful.

God wants more than anything to bless you and your family. That happens when you faithfully obey, trust, and worship him. You have everything to gain through obedience and everything to lose through disobedience. Make the easy choice.

December 28

Passionate Obedience
JESUS

Jesus explained: "My nourishment comes from doing the will of God, who sent me, and from finishing his work."   John 4:34

Once there was a dog so obedient to his master that rather than disobey a command to stay in his doghouse, he died as a grass fire swept through the backyard, burning the doghouse down around him.

Willingness to obey God is one thing, but you enter a new level of walking with God when you develop a *passion* for obedience. That kind of passion makes a life of faith exciting, for God loves to reward and bless it.

Jesus demonstrated that kind of passion every day of his life on earth. He told his disciples, "My nourishment comes from doing the will of God." In other words, Jesus lived to obey his heavenly Father.

Though Jesus left paradise to take the form of a man and walk the earth, he remained passionately and single-mindedly devoted to accomplishing his Father's will. Although he knew that such uncompromising obedience would take him to an excruciating death on the cross, nothing could stand in the way of his accomplishing that goal.

Jesus knew that the smallest deviation from what God had planned would defeat his program for saving humankind. That plan was never in jeopardy, for Jesus had a *passion* to obey everything his Father directed.

Jesus set you the perfect example of passionate obedience to the Father's will. What do you feel most passionate about today? Are you willing to obey God, or do you feel eager to do so? When you eagerly give your full obedience to God, you put yourself in a position to receive his very best—for yourself and your family.

December 29

A Strong Finish
SOLOMON

In Solomon's old age, [his wives and concubines] turned his heart to worship other gods instead of being completely faithful to the LORD his God, as his father, David, had been. 1 Kings 11:4

Most professional football scouts saw Terry Bradshaw, a senior quarterback at Louisiana Tech, as a "can't miss" prospect. The Pittsburgh Steelers agreed and selected him with the first pick of the 1970 NFL draft.

Before Bradshaw finished his rookie season, Steelers fans must have wondered if their team had made a huge mistake. He threw six touchdown passes and twenty-four interceptions while completing less than 40 percent of his passes—all terrible numbers even for a first-year player.

After a two-year adjustment, Bradshaw came into his own and led the Steelers to four Super Bowl championships in six years, earning two MVP awards along the way. Terry Bradshaw began slowly, but he finished strongly enough to earn a spot in the pro-football Hall of Fame.

The Bible teaches the importance of finishing strong in the life of faith. It also includes the story of Solomon, who did great things for God and Israel before finishing his life with a thud.

Solomon was the proverbial riddle wrapped up in an enigma. The Bible refers to him as the wisest man who ever lived, but he turned away from God and toward pagan idols, which led to the loss of everything he had accomplished (see 1 Kings 11:11-13).

All of this happened although God had appeared to him twice and blessed him in every conceivable way.

God had continually urged, warned, encouraged, and prodded Solomon to follow and obey him. He even promised him a long, prosperous life and greater blessings if he did so. In the end, Solomon's poor choices tainted his service and led to big problems for the kingdom of Israel.

It's great to get off to a good start in your life of faith. It is far more important that you persevere and focus on the eternal prize God has for those who finish strong (see 1 Corinthians 9:24-25).

December 30

It's Not about Me!
PAUL

Because I preach this Good News, I am suffering and have been chained like a criminal. But the word of God cannot be chained. So I am willing to endure anything if it will bring salvation and eternal glory in Christ Jesus to those God has chosen. 2 Timothy 2:9-10

In July 2006, Chinese police arrested four Christian missionaries in China's Yunnan province, charging them with "superstitious activity." They tortured these believers for more than six hours. One female missionary had much of her hair torn out, and police threatened to turn two others over to a local tribe to be raped.

Despite all that, the police couldn't prove *any* wrongdoing on the part of the missionaries and released them after confiscating their Bibles, computer disks containing hymns, and the U.S. equivalent of four hundred dollars.

Though most American believers don't suffer this kind of persecution, such events remind us that taking the message of Christ to a needy and sometimes hostile world can involve suffering.

The apostle Paul freely chose to suffer for Christ. Despite being arrested, chained, imprisoned, and beaten, he refused to stop preaching. He faced opponents, many of them violent, wherever he went, yet he gladly continued to speak the name of Jesus Christ.

Paul actually considered it an honor to suffer for Christ's name. Was he a masochist? Hardly. He didn't enjoy his chains, beatings, or jail cells, and he actively tried to win his release from incarceration whenever possible (see Acts 26:29). Yet he wrote that he would endure *anything* if that would help to get the gospel message preached to those who needed to hear it.

Paul's life revealed the driving force behind his incessant missionary activity: "So I am willing to endure anything if it will bring salvation and eternal glory in Christ Jesus to those God has chosen." Paul gladly suffered because he had the humility to know that *everything* is about "Jesus Christ, the one who was crucified" (1 Corinthians 2:2).

Living and speaking for Christ are bound to attract opposition. "Yes," Paul wrote, "everyone who wants to live a godly life in Christ Jesus will suffer persecution" (2 Timothy 3:12). Remember that nothing you endure is really about you. Rather, it's about making sure that people hear the name of Jesus.

December 31

Your Ultimate Resource
GIDEON

The LORD said to Gideon, "You have too many warriors with you. If I let all of you fight the Midianites, the Israelites will boast to me that they saved themselves by their own strength." Judges 7:2

Tim owned a small framing business that employed six full-time laborers. One year, as things became very busy for Tim and his business, he ran into a huge problem. Two of his men left to take other jobs, and another was hurt and couldn't work. With three jobs needing attention in the next few weeks, Tim was in deep weeds!

Have you ever felt that you have important work to do, but lack the talent, manpower, or resources to get it done?

Gideon once faced that situation, but in the end, his faith in God's provision saved the day.

God called Gideon to lead his army of about thirty-two thousand men out to meet their Midianite enemies. There was one caveat: The vast majority of those men wouldn't be going. God wanted to keep Gideon and the rest of the Israelites humble, and he wanted them to know their Source of victory.

He directed Gideon to send most of his men home.

The first cut wasn't difficult. Gideon told the men who were afraid to fight to go home, which cut his manpower by twenty-two thousand. He then reduced his forces to only three hundred men, based on how they drank water from a nearby stream.

Gideon knew that God was with him and had called him to lead, but he had to wonder if he was being set up for failure. The Bible doesn't tell us specifically how many men were in the enemy camp, but it does tell us that they "had settled in the valley like a swarm of locusts. Their camels were like grains of sand on the seashore—too many to count!" (Judges 7:12).

God humbled Gideon's forces before they headed out to battle, and then he sent them out to claim an overwhelming victory.

God wants to do great things in your life, and he wants you to know that he is your Source for every victory you claim. When you feel that you don't have what it takes to complete the tasks he has put before you, he may be about to perform a miracle on your behalf.

Do-able. Daily. Devotions.

START ANY DAY THE ONE YEAR WAY.

For Women

The One Year®
Devotions for
Women on
the Go

The One Year®
Devotions for
Women

The One Year®
Devotions for
Moms

The One Year®
Women of the
Bible

The One Year®
Coffee with God

The One Year®
Devotional of Joy
and Laughter

The One Year®
Women's
Friendship
Devotional

The One Year®
Wisdom
for Women
Devotional

The One Year®
Book of Amish
Peace

The One Year®
Women in
Christian History
Devotional

For Men

*The One Year®
Devotions for
Men on the Go*

*The One Year®
Devotions for Men*

*The One Year®
Father-Daughter
Devotions*

For Families

*The One Year®
Family
Devotions, Vol. 1*

*The One Year®
Dinner Table
Devotions*

For Couples

*The One Year®
Devotions for
Couples*

*The One Year® Love
Language Minute
Devotional*

*The One Year® Love
Talk Devotional*

For Teens

*The One Year®
Devos for Teens*

*The One Year®
Be-Tween You
and God*

For Personal Growth

*The One Year®
at His Feet
Devotional*

*The One Year®
Uncommon Life
Daily Challenge*

*The One Year®
Recovery Prayer
Devotional*

*The One Year®
Christian History*

*The One Year®
Experiencing God's
Presence Devotional*

For Bible Study

*The One Year®
Praying through
the Bible*

*The One Year®
Praying the
Promises of God*

*The One Year®
Through the
Bible Devotional*

*The One Year®
Book of Bible
Promises*

*The One Year®
Unlocking the
Bible Devotional*

TheOneYear.com

CP0145